The Indonesia Reader

THE WORLD READERS

A series edited by Robin Kirk and Orin Starn

Also in this series:

THE ALASKA NATIVE READER

Edited by Maria Williams

THE
INDONESIA
READER

HISTORY, CULTURE, POLITICS

Edited by Tineke Hellwig and Eric Tagliacozzo

DUKE UNIVERSITY PRESS *Durham and London* 2009

© 2009 Duke University Press
All rights reserved
Printed in the United States of America on acid-free paper ∞
Typeset in Monotype Dante by Achorn International
Library of Congress Cataloging-in-Publication Data appear
on the last printed page of this book.

Contents

VI *The Last Decades of the Indies* *245*

VII *From Nationalism to Independence* *291*

VIII *The Old Order, the New Order—Political Climate* *329*

Acknowledgments

The preparations for this book took a good amount of time and energy over a number of years. We conceptualized the project and had to make difficult decisions over what to include. We singled out the approximately one hundred selections of sources from the many thousands that exist. The most arduous part of compiling *The Indonesia Reader* was to make choices knowing that we had to omit a great many interesting texts and topics. Once our selections were complete, we needed to begin translating the Indonesian and Dutch materials. The next step was researching and annotating the selections; writing the section introductions took more time, as did that of the introduction for the entire book. In addition we had to wrap our heads around the unfamiliar tasks of dealing with images, copyrights, orthographies, and other details.

We are very glad that this book is finished, the more so because it gives us the opportunity to share our passion for Indonesia and its people with others. There are a number of people we wish to thank for their continuous support and encouragement. At Duke University Press, we are first and foremost indebted to Valerie Millholland, who as the editor of the book patiently guided us through this whole process over a long time. We also need to thank Miriam Angress, Alexis Pauline Gumbs, and Neal McTighe at Duke University Press who generously helped us in a number of ways with their technical and administrative skills and insights. Our research assistants, Manneke Budiman and Heather McLoughlan, chased down copyrights and images, wrote to publishers, and performed a number of other time-consuming tasks. Without them the preparation of the manuscript would have taken much longer. We are grateful to Manneke Budiman, Oiyan Liu, and A. van de Rijt for their assistance with the translations. We also thank Jaap Anten, Marieke Bloembergen, Karel van der Hucht, Korrie Korevaart, Betty Litamahuputty, Mieneke Mees, Willem van der Molen, Dolores Puigantell, Ling Xiang Quek, Henk Saaltink, Dirk Verbeek, and Wil van Yperen for all the help they provided to us in a variety of ways.

Our respective partners, Hubert Vrolyk and Katherine Peipu Lee, probably never thought that this project would go on as long as it did. They are as pleased as we are to see it appearing in print.

A Note on Style and Spelling

This anthology contains works from many different periods, authors, and points of view. Some of the language may sound awkward or inappropriate to contemporary readers. However, except for some careful abridgement and editing where necessary for clarity, we have chosen to retain the original wording in the interest of preserving tone and of reflecting the historical context in which each work was written. Those familiar with the history of Malay and Indonesian (*bahasa Indonesia*) will notice the variations in the spelling of names and commonly used words, among others *oe/u* (Soematra/Sumatra), *dj/j* (Djakarta/Jakarta), *tj/c* (Atjeh/Aceh), *j/y* (Surabaja/Surabaya).

For the sake of readability we use the term Indonesia (and the adjective Indonesian) to refer to the geographical region that is present-day Indonesia, even though for some periods under discussion Indonesia as a political entity did not yet exist.

Introduction

In 1883 at the Amsterdam Colonial Fair the Dutch erected a pavilion to show-case the wonders of their flourishing, sprawling colony, the Netherlands East Indies, now better known as Indonesia. A number of exhibits displayed the different cultures, societies, and artifacts of the Indies' varied peoples. An entire transplanted Javanese village formed the centerpiece of the exhibition. It was replete with Javanese peasants, but Sundanese and Sumatran people were also on view, revealing a variety of their cultures and lifeways. In precolonial times these widely divergent ethnic groups would never have considered themselves as part of any discrete political construct; in the postcolonial era many of these peoples' descendents might question the same assumption. But at that moment, at the turn of the twentieth century, the Dutch trumpeted the existence, and indeed the creation, of a unified Dutch East Indies as a victory and as an achievement: a triumph over disorder and a feat of coerced unity in the face of centuries of supposed anomie and unrest in a very remote corner of the world.

More than one century later Indonesia is the largest archipelago nation-state in the world, and its almost eighteen thousand islands both separate and link the Indian and Pacific Oceans. Only six thousand of these islands are inhabited, but the word Indonesians use to refer to their "homeland" or "fatherland" is *tanah air*, meaning "land and water," indicating the significance of both elements to national identity. Indonesia's population of 230 million is rich in cultural diversity, and since earliest times the island dwellers have sailed across the seas to build networks among the various societies. The waterways divide but also bind communities.

Indonesia's western part is located on the Sunda Shelf that is geologically part of Southeast Asia's mainland. The Sahul Shelf in the east (West New Guinea) was once part of Australia. A fault line in the Indian Ocean runs west of Sumatra, where the India Plate dives beneath the Burma Plate. Tectonic activity causes frequent seismic tremors: the December 26, 2004, earthquake with a 9.15 magnitude on the Richter scale and the subsequent tsunami of gigantic proportions resulted in the loss of lives of thousands, not only in Indonesia.

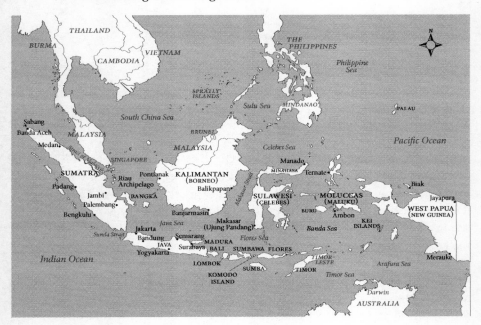

Map of Indonesia.

The islands are shaped in two arcs of active volcanoes with deep troughs be-tween them. They are part of the so-called Ring of Fire that runs along the Pacific Rim flowing onto the west coasts of North and South America. The catastrophic 1883 eruption of Krakatoa was destructive to humans, the natu-ral environment, and weather patterns around the globe. Yet volcanic ash pro-vides fertile soil that guarantees sufficient food crops for the populace. On Java, where two-thirds of today's population are concentrated, people say that if one plants a broomstick, a lush tree will soon flourish. The Javanese worship Mount Merapi in central Java with reverence and awe, as it is always spewing smoke or ash, rumbling at times as if to convey a message to the surround-ing residents. They usually respond promptly with offerings to the volcano's spirits.

The archipelago straddles the equator over three thousand miles. The trop-ical climate brings high humidity throughout the year with two seasons, a dry one and the monsoon. The islands' mountain ranges were originally covered by dense and inaccessible jungle. Differences in altitude correspond to cul-tural variation and distinct power relations between *hulu* and *hilir* (upstream and downstream) societies, as well as between coastal, lowland areas in which trade and commerce prospered versus mountainous inland communities

Vendor with chili peppers. Photo by Dolores Puigantell. Indonesian food can be very spicy depending on the region. Chili peppers (*cabai* or *lombok*) are the main ingredient in hot pepper sauces known as *sambal* for which an enormous variety of recipes exist. *Cabai rawit*, a small green pepper, is exceptionally spicy. Chili peppers are widely believed to stimulate the appetite, and it is not uncommon to see an Indonesian eat just a plate of white rice with *sambal*.

with more "tribal" peoples. In this tropical region one only finds eternal snow on Puncak Jaya, the highest peak of 5,039 meters in West New Guinea.

Many visitors to Indonesia are overwhelmed by the natural beauty of its environment. The lush rain forests, the tremendous diversity in flora and fauna, the dazzling colors and aromatic smells captivate newcomers. This is the land of the stunning bird of paradise, the monstrous Komodo dragon, of pungent durian fruit and exotic spices much sought after by people in Antiquity: nutmeg, mace, cloves, and pepper. In the past indigenes could rely on an abundance of timber and forest products such as resin, sandalwood, and medicinal plants. From the mid-nineteenth century onward, however, a rapid depletion of the forests as a result of increased population and logging, some of it illegal, has occurred. Virgin forests were turned over for agricultural use to produce rice, grown in terraced *sawahs* (wet rice fields) on the mountain slopes, and subsistence crops, but also trade commodities such as coffee, tea, cocoa, sugar cane, tobacco, indigo, and a range of palm products. Deep in the ground Indonesia is rich in natural resources such as oil, gas, tin, copper, gold, and bauxite. Beneath the ocean's surface one encounters a mosaic of colorful marine life: Indonesians have for centuries harvested the plentiful bounty of the sea to sustain their diet.

Indonesia's strategic location along the main sea routes between East and West made it a crossroads for travelers, material, and ideas. Foreign ships passed across the waters for hundreds of years, and some seafarers stayed a while after reaching the safety of the islands' shores. Europeans were among those who settled with no intention to leave. They gained positions of power, and in the end colonial rule defined Indonesia's boundaries. Negotiations with the Netherlands after the Second World War determined how the borders of the nation-state were to be drawn. As children learn in a nationalist song, the country stretches "dari Sabang sampai Merauke"—from Sabang, on the tiny island We, at its most northwestern tip, to Merauke on the south coast of West New Guinea. Sabang and Merauke represent two geographical extremes: one is located in the devout Muslim province of Aceh, the "Verandah of Mecca," while the other forms part of the Melanesian world of Papuans. They also signify political trouble spots: regions in the periphery that long resisted—and continue to resist—European colonialism and integration into a Java-centric sovereign state. Their respective independence movements have led to violence and civil war, causing endless human suffering.

Using *Bhinneka Tunggal Ika* (Unity in Diversity) as the nation's motto, the nationalist agendas of postcolonial politicians have aimed to respect cultural diversity and to balance out wide regional heterogeneity. A myriad of ethnic groups, speaking more than four hundred languages and dialects, adheres to a range of values and beliefs. Yet almost all of these people can now converse with one another in *bahasa Indonesia*, the national language constructed out of Malay, which was used for market interactions over centuries. *Bahasa Indonesia* now perhaps serves as the best index of the achievement of a modern nation, where before there was only allegiance to village and to town, or in some cases to the notion of people on a particular island having some sort of connection with each other. Ethnic and racial stereotyping persists, however, particularly among the Javanese with their often strong sense of superiority. Bataks and Madurese are considered *kasar* (rude), while Moluccans, Dayaks, or Papuans on the so-called Outer Islands are often looked down on as "uncivilized." Immigrants are easy targets of othering too, and at times they fall victim to racism and violence. Chinese immigration is the most prominent besides that from India and the Arab world. Chinese scholars, mostly Buddhist, moved to the archipelago during the first millennium of the Common Era. Some centuries later Chinese men settled down and married local women. Their offspring, referred to as *peranakan* (Chinese-Malay), remains a

Logo of *Luwak* Coffee (*Kopi Luwak*). Copyright and trademark by Raven's Brew Coffee. Anyone who orders "a cup of Java" in North America will get a cup of filtered or espresso coffee. Indonesians, however, do not at all associate Java with coffee. They consider Toraja coffee from the island of Sulawesi to be exclusive. Moreover, in Indonesia most people do not drink filtered coffee but *kopi tubruk*, strong coffee made by pouring boiling water over coffee grounds in a glass. However, one of the most exquisite types of coffee with prices up to $600 per pound is *kopi luwak*. A *luwak* is a nocturnal animal that resembles a civet cat. It has a special taste for the ripe fruits of the coffee bushes and knows how to pick the sweetest coffee berries. The animal digests these and then excretes the hard beans. For centuries villagers have collected coffee beans from *luwak* dung, processed, roasted, and consumed them. *Luwak* coffee is rare and known to be delicious.

visible minority. *Peranakan* families who have lived in Indonesia for generations deconstruct any notion of racial and cultural essentialism. Their very existence raises not only the question of Chineseness but also asks: Who is, or can claim to be, Indonesian?

Outside the archipelago certain cliché images of what Indonesia stands for also persevere. The shadow puppet theatre, or *wayang*, is an acclaimed Indonesian art form, even when its best-known characters such as Arjuna, Kresna, and Duryudana originate in Indian mythology. Many Westerners recognize the gamelan music that accompanies a *wayang* performance as typically

Indonesian. Another stereotype, particularly in North America, is the famous "cup of Java," which holds the promise of a taste of fine coffee. But generally Indonesia is known as the fourth most populous nation after China, India, and the United States of America. It is also the largest Muslim country, a fact particularly emphasized in the Western world since the September 11, 2001, attacks on the twin towers in New York. Bali scores high in the perception of the West as a "tourist paradise" and the "island of the gods." The Balinese adhere to their version of Hinduism, their everyday lives filled with ceremonial customs. The Dutch colonial administration came to Bali only in the early 1900s, but once it was established, Europeans and Americans flocked to the island east of Java, exoticizing its culture, traditions, and art forms. It became an artist's heaven and a dream holiday destination. Tourism boomed, and some foreign travelers to Bali would return home not even realizing they had been in Indonesia. However, the stream of visitors came to a halt when Islamist terrorists carried out deadly bomb attacks in October 2002. Bali's economy has since plummeted, experiencing the severe effects of the post–9/11 world.

One of Bali's attractions is its aesthetic ritual, expressed through music, dance, the visual arts, and daily offerings of colorful flowers and incense. Religious practices leave a considerable mark on society. Lifestyles and values, morality and normative behavior are primarily guided by prescriptions of the faith. Before the major world religions arrived, belief systems on the islands included animism and the worship of ancestors, spirits, and supernatural forces. The islanders lived in close harmony with nature, and women played a prominent role in social and kinship relations. Married couples often resided with the bride's parents or relatives; in a bilateral system children belonged to both their mother's and their father's families, and some societies were explicitly matrilineal. Women were visibly present in the village's public life and had decision-making power in the (household) economy.

Shifts in indigenous socioreligious patterns first occurred when Hinduism and Buddhism found their way southeastward from India. These religions amalgamated with one another and with existing beliefs into new local versions. Islam trailed behind the Indian religions. It, too, was adopted, adapted, and culturally transformed. Islam in Indonesia differs from that in the Middle East in the way it has incorporated pre-Muslim thought and practice and devotees have adjusted the doctrine to their needs, at times creating their own folk version of the religion. Islam arrived in the archipelago peacefully, traveling with merchants and reaching Aceh first. Marco Polo noticed Muslims in this region in 1292. Over the centuries it gradually spread further east when increasing numbers of local rulers converted to the new religion. Those in the coastal areas embraced Islam first, as they had the most contact with foreign-

Minangkabau family in front of their traditional house, West Sumatra, 1910. Photo no. 2423, courtesy of KITLV, Leiden.

ers. By the late seventeenth century sultanates could be found from Sumatra to as far east as Sumbawa, northern Sulawesi, and the Moluccas.

Europeans brought Christian missionaries who were mostly successful in more isolated, upland areas that had not yet converted to Islam. Churches were able to proselytize the local population only if they left room for native spirituality or traditional rituals. All in all one finds in Indonesia's multilayered syncretism many complexities in terms of religion, culture, and social relations. It shows in the matrilineal and matrifocal kinship system of the Islamized Minangkabau of western Sumatra or in the popularity of Hindu tales as performed in the *wayang* among Muslims on Sumatra and Java. In general Islam as practiced in Indonesia has been remarkably tolerant of other religious elements still found in daily life, though this has begun to change in some communities, often to the alarm of many local peoples themselves.

When a few small ships from Portugal docked in the Moluccas in the sixteenth century, they had found what they were looking for: the famed Spice Islands. These ships had traversed the entirety of the Atlantic, crossed the vast Indian Ocean, passed through the Muslim-dominated seas of the Indies, and had finally dropped anchor in several tiny bays. They had been in search of spices that grew nowhere else on earth but here. The Portuguese were followed by the Spanish, and the Spanish by the English and the Dutch until the latter managed to evict all the others and erect an imperfect monopoly on the trade in these items to the other side of the world. Control over the tiny islands of eastern Indonesia became a matter of financial and political life and death. At one point the Dutch exchanged one of the small remaining English islands in the Moluccas for an island of their own in the distant New World—New Amsterdam, now better known as Manhattan. It is difficult to think of a more apt example of Indonesia's centrality to the processes of history. Yet visits to modern Manhattan and to Pulau Run, the Moluccan island in question, would likely fill one with a sense of the unpaid debts of the past because of the latter island's poverty.

The first two centuries of Dutch presence, from 1600 to 1800, marked the age of mercantilism dominated by the voc (Vereenigde Oost-Indische Compagnie, the United East Indies Company). The founder of Batavia (in 1619) and the voc governor general, Jan Pieterszoon Coen, once remarked "ende dispereert niet, . . . daer can in Indiën wat groots verricht worden" (and do not despair, . . . something magnificent can be achieved in the Indies). The voc administered its trading posts in the Far East from Batavia. It allowed, even encouraged, Dutch bachelor men to engage in sexual liaisons with local women. Similar to *peranakans*, their mixed race progeny, a significant "class" of so-called *Indos*, would confound any concept of racial purity or sense of "true" Indonesian—or for that matter, Dutch—identity.

The Dutch began to unify some of the islands under their coercive control, forging alliances with indigenous rulers. In 1800 a phase of state colonialism set in after the bankruptcy of the voc. Travel took on a different importance, because voyages were rarely neutral in intent—something was usually there to be "won," whether this was commerce, knowledge, or actual territory for the expanding colonial state. The intensified administration and exploitation of natural resources and the labor force meant huge profits for the Netherlands and a pauperization of the indigenous peoples. The latter were ethnically divided and therefore in no position to oppose colonialism. No inhabitants of this huge archipelago would have thought of themselves as forming part of a large political project. The Dutch, on the other hand, were determined to impose their will even on remote areas. To maintain race and class privileges they made hierarchical divisions between Europeans, *Indos*, so-called foreign Orientals (i.e., Chinese, Arabs, and Japanese), and *inlanders* ("natives"). The unhappy legacy of these race relations can still be felt today, particularly in the tensions between Indonesians and Chinese. The Dutch also added another layer to Indonesia's mosaic, namely, one of Dutch-European bourgeois values and modernity.

Rice drying in Kampung Naga, West Java. Photo by Dirk Verbeek. Rice is Indonesia's staple food, except for on some eastern islands and in West Papua, where sago porridge (*papeda*) is traditionally the primary food item. Rice is grown in wet rice fields called *sawahs* with their intricate irrigation systems, as well as in dry fields. Women plant the seedlings one by one by hand, spending days on end with their hands and feet in the mud. At harvest time men and women work side by side under the glaring sun. On Java and Bali people believe that Dewi Sri, the goddess of fertile soil, guarantees food for the population.

The Japanese occupation in 1942 marked the abrupt end to the Dutch East Indies. The Japanese interned Europeans and Australians in prisoner of war camps, while they rallied for support among the Indonesians using "Greater East Asia Co-prosperity Sphere" propaganda. The new occupiers trained the younger generation in military organizations. Japan desperately needed Indonesia for food supplies (especially rice), its natural resources, and labor. Two days after Japan capitulated, on August 17, 1945, Sukarno and Hatta proclaimed Indonesia's independence. Since then the postcolonial nation has lived through three distinct periods: 1945–65 under President Sukarno, 1967–98 under President Suharto, and *Reformasi*, from 1998 onward. For many Indonesians Sukarno (1901–70) lives on as the nationalist leader who successfully discarded the yoke of colonialism. He was an effective orator and populist who used his captivating charisma to sculpt his own personality cult. Different political factions challenged Sukarno's authority, especially when he tried to balance nationalism, communism, and Islam during the last years of his presidency. The film *The Year of Living Dangerously* (1982, by Peter Weir) represents this turbulent time in great detail, showing the intricate networks behind the political drama about to unfold. Suharto succeeded Sukarno after a failed coup attempt that triggered months of violence and mass killings targeting alleged communists. He steered the country toward development and a capitalist economy under increasingly tight military control. Suharto (1921–2008) projected himself as the benevolent father (*Bapak*) of the nation. Yet by the end of his thirty-one years in office he and his family members were accused of large-scale corruption, collusion, and nepotism.

With a state ideology called *Panca Sila* (the Five Pillars) Indonesia circumvented becoming a Muslim state. Indonesia has faced serious challenges to establishing political stability, democratic order, and a sound economy in the past sixty years. Presently a great many residents still live below the poverty line, and glaring inequalities segregate the rich from the poor, the educated from the illiterate, urbanites from rural villagers. During Suharto's presidency multinational investors were invited in, yet blatant corruption meant that only a select few benefited. The woeful lack of infrastructure time and again indicates that Indonesia still has to go a long way to secure higher standards of living for all its citizens. Yet the political turning point of 1998 has proven that transformations can take place, even in a relatively short period. There is more freedom of speech, a more democratic system, and more openness to debate political issues or critique authorities than ever before. Human rights find more protection than in the past. Yet a fair society in which everyone has equal access to quality education and health care and in which the less fortunate can count on social and financial support through government programs remains a goal to be realized. It is unfortunate that Indonesia usually makes headlines in the international media because of natural or other disasters: earthquakes, flooding, volcanic eruptions, forest fires, plane crashes, or sinking ferries. While the country's sheer size and geographical constitution can prove a hindrance to good governance and prosperity for all, Indonesia seems to be evolving in the right direction.

At the turn of the twenty-first century most Indonesians feel part of something larger than themselves. This shift in cadence and attitude demands some kind of explanation of how Indonesia came about, where it now stands, and where it may be heading in the future. *The Indonesia Reader* attempts to answer some of these questions. The *Reader* is made up of some one hundred selections encompassing literary texts, paleographic inscriptions, sailing instructions, newspaper clippings, personal documents, photographic images, and more. A good number of them have been translated into English for the very first time to make them accessible to a nonspecialized audience. The editors—a historian and a scholar of literature teaching at universities on either side of North America—have brought these selections together over the course of several years of searching in Indonesia, the Netherlands, and other places where repositories of relevant information are particularly rich. Inevitably, we had to make subjective choices, and the sources in this book present a small fragment of available materials. They can thus only tell an imperfect and incomplete story. Yet taken together they show some of the arc of Indonesia's histories and societies over the centuries, from geographic, cultural, political, economic, and religious points of view. The *Reader* is a primer for anyone who wants to know why Indonesia looks the way it does today.

The book is split up into ten sections of more or less equal size, largely ordered chronologically, though sometimes set up more thematically. Part 1 looks at the earliest incarnations of Indonesia's past—what we know, what we do not, and how we have come to these determinations as an intellectual community studying the thousands of dispersed islands over a long period of time. Part 2 dwells on the early modern period of Indonesia, a time when trade, travel, and contact with the outside world began to pick up in terms of pace and frequency. The following section, part 3, focuses on indigenous voices in this transitional period, as the various cultures of the world ultimately collided with each other in the warm waters of the archipelago. Part 4 specifically puts travel under the lens: the opening of the vast new spaces of the archipelago to the searching eyes of the West, particularly in the nineteenth century. This was a time when Europe was still testing the possibilities of colonialism, as it was unclear how fast and how far the imperial project might reach, especially in outstretched places like the Indies. Part 5 treats the high colonial period of Indonesian history through a series of documents chosen to highlight the complexity and totality of establishing Dutch control. Parts 6 and 7 take the reader into the twentieth century, into the final decades of colonial administration and the Second World War, which signified a major turning point in Indonesia's history. The last three parts then present selections from the postindependent period. Politics and the sociocultural climate during the presidencies of Sukarno and Suharto are examined in separate chapters. The book ends with a section on contemporary developments and on the most recent changes that have taken place since 1998.

It is our hope that *The Indonesia Reader* provides historical, political, and cultural insights, as well as a critical understanding of Indonesia's complexities. We have included a broad range of points of view, the voices of common people, those of men and of women, but also those of rulers, politicians, scholars, activists, and public figures—Indonesian as well as non-Indonesian. Indonesia is a fascinating part of the earth, and it deserves much broader attention. The *Reader* aims to help those who are interested in this unique country to discover more about its culture and history in a rapidly changing world.

I

Early Histories

The earliest history of Indonesia is shrouded in myth, legend, and doubt; we have very little idea what Indonesians two thousand years ago thought, and only a slightly better idea of what they did in their daily lives. Texts from this period are almost nonexistent; a few inscriptions, carved in stone, are all that remain until about fifteen hundred years ago. The archaeological record complements this scriptural paucity, but even here the clues are few, and often difficult to untangle. It is clear that there were small Indonesian societies in the first five hundred years of the Common Era (CE), but they were scattered throughout several of the archipelago's islands, and it remains unclear how much they had in common. Certainly there was some degree of contact among them, and even between these communities and the outside world. The presence of high-fire beads, ceramics, and iron-slag heaps attest to this outward-cadence for trade even from the earliest times.

In the second half of the first millennium CE some of the polities began to grow and to become more complex as state or protostate organizations. In remote eastern Borneo, the first written inscriptions that still survive today appeared; they were written in South Asian Pallava script, though the language spoken through the stones was actually ancient Sanskrit. Inscriptions appeared after this in several places in Java and in Sumatra, always linking this burgeoning world of archipelago statecraft with India, where complex civilizations had appeared centuries earlier. Chinese travelers, wandering the long trade routes between their homeland and India, where many of them voyaged to read the great Buddhist books of learning, also began to leave records of complex societies in the "lands beneath the winds," as they later came to be known. Seafaring Persians and Arabs eventually completed their accounts, leaving tantalizing glimpses of a succession of polities spaced out among equatorial islands like a string of pearls.

The ambitions that began to take shape during this era unmistakably owed much to Indian societies half an ocean and many months of travel away. Some of the first Indonesian kingdoms were Hindu, while some were Buddhist, but the majority seems to have taken on a syncretic character with attributes of both these religions. Rulers held absolute power in their small domains: they took whichever daughters of their populations inspired their fancy, and they extracted taxes in rice, produce, and labor for the greater glory of themselves and their kingdoms. Stone buildings began to be built for religious and state purposes, first on a rather small (yet beautifully intricate) scale, like the temples of the lush Dieng plateau in central Java, later on a massive scale, such as the Buddhist Borobudur and the Hindu Prambanan, also in central Java. These two temple structures and their adjacent complexes range among the finest examples of early religious architecture in the world. That both these structures can be found in Indonesia shows how far the archipelago's native genius had come in a very short time.

The Borobudur and Prambanan, though clearly influenced by Indian religious thinking, are unmistakably Indonesian buildings. In their architectural symbolism and in their narrative sculptural friezes they espouse worldviews that are Indian, yet their conception and execution as local religious monuments also clearly marks them as Indonesian. In this they represent a process of borrowing and adaptation occurring throughout parts of the archipelago at this time, as local peoples imported foreign ideas yet constantly recast them into local idioms. Several of the early kingdoms in Java grew larger and larger and were gradually able to hold sway over more peasants and the rice they produced, in turn feeding the construction of more religious buildings. Medieval Java, particularly eastern and central Java, became fairly littered with ornate stone temples. The remains of these structures still survive today, surrounded by the rice fields of farmers whose ancestors' labor contributed to their building.

In the seventh century, with the growth of Srivijaya—a maritime kingdom probably centered on southern Sumatra, though with radials of authority in other places as well, including the Malay Peninsula—Indonesian kingdoms started to become more ambitious in their suzerainty. Srivijaya traded with many places, including a number of polities far from Southeast Asian shores such as India, Arabia, and even distant China. The rulers of Srivijaya demanded stringent taxes for the right to pass through the choke point of the Straits of Malacca, which they controlled, and this stranglehold on economic geography brought these men many riches. It also brought them many enemies. In the early decades of the second millennium CE, Chola navies from southern India sacked Srivijaya, and though the kingdom survived for another two centuries, the apex of its power had passed. Majapahit, a land-based power in eastern Java, became the most vigorous kingdom in this island world for most of the fourteenth and fifteenth centuries. Though its rise to power was based on its control of a largely fertile landscape, Majapahit also quickly became a maritime power, trading for spices, slaves, and gold all the way to New Guinea.

It is tempting to see in these early centuries of rule a story with two main themes: cultural transmission and adaptation from the outside world, particularly from India, and the political expansion of local, rice-based states that ended up as regional maritime empires. These processes happened, and they do constitute the main story lines of parts of the archipelago, but the realities of this thousand-plus-year period were infinitely more complex. Many "Indonesians" scattered in the hills and swamps, or living their lives quietly in remote, untrafficked islands, had little to do with these phenomena or with the changes they brought. They continued to eat local products, sew their own clothing, and worship their own local gods, which they called by their local names. Yet a sea change was undeniably sweeping the archipelago, eventually incorporating increasing numbers of its people.

The Kutei Inscriptions in Borneo

Anonymous

The earliest writing preserved in the entire Indonesian archipelago occurs on seven stone pillars found in the region of Kutei, eastern Borneo, dating from the fifth century CE. The inscriptions were written in Sanskrit, the language of high culture in India at the time, and the script was derived from Pallava, a writing format from southern India in contemporaneous use with the Kutei inscriptions. The inscriptions tell the story of King Mûlavarman and his community in eastern Borneo, replete with descriptions of merit-making activities, gifts of objects ("tawny cows and sesame seeds"), and itinerant Brahmins. Though spare in what they describe of Borneo society as whole, these stone-pillar etchings offer fascinating windows into what this ancient society thought was worth recording, namely, the virtuous activities of the (locally) all-powerful king. The language and script of the inscriptions link this isolated outpost of Indonesia with India of the same epoch; the names and concerns expressed show that a diasporic Indian orbit already existed in monsoon Asia at a very early date. There is every chance that these seven inscriptions constitute only a fraction of many others produced at the time, but that have long since perished.

Anonymous, Inscribed Stones from Borneo, ca. 400 AD

All seven of these inscriptions (five of which are reproduced here) come from the region of Kutei, in the eastern portion of the island of Borneo. They are undated, but on the basis of their writing style have to be associated with a date not later than ca. 400 AD.

A

The illustrious lord-of-men, the mighty Kundunga, had a famous son, Asvavarman by name, who like unto Amshumang, was the founder of a noble race. His were three eminent sons resembling three sacrificial fires. Foremost among these three and distinguished by austerity, strength, and self-restraint was the illustrious Mûlavarman, the lord-of-kings, who had a Bahusuvarnaka

Kutei inscription. Photo no. 1625, courtesy of KITLV, Leiden.

sacrifice performed. For that sacrifice this sacrificial post has been established by the eminent Brahmans.

B

When the illustrious and eminent prince King Mûlavarman had given a gift of twenty thousand cattle to the Brahmans who resemble the sacrificial fire, at the most sacred place, namely Vaprakeshvara, for that deed of merit this sacrificial post has been made by the priests who had come hither.

C

Let the foremost priests and whosoever other pious men [there be] hear of the meritorious deed of Mûlavarman, king of illustrious and resplendent fame [let them hear] of his great gifts: Bahudâna, Jîvadâna, Kalpavṛkshadâna, and Bhûmidâna. For these multitudes of pious deeds this sacrificial post has been set up by the priests.

E

Hail to the mighty king, the illustrious Mûlavarman of exalted rank, whose gifts have been recorded at this holy spot after he, the most excellent king, has bestowed on Brahmans the gifts of water, ghee, tawny cows, and sesame seeds, as well as eleven bulls.

F

The illustrious king Mûlavarman gave away in charity a heap of sesame seeds together with a multitude of lamps. This sacrificial pillar has been engraved upon [and set up in commemoration of] those two [gifts].

The Shadow of India

Upendra Thakur

It was clear to anyone studying the roots of Indonesian civilization that the archipelago owed much to classical India, a place that exported culture in the form of religion, epics, and architecture to large parts of Southeast Asia. Indonesia's moniker "Insulindië" and parts of the Southeast Asian mainland's designation as "Indochina" in Dutch times point to this identification of Southeast Asia with India. Many interpreters of these ties, which involved shipping, trade, and the movement of itinerant priests (known as Brahmins) overstated the importance of India for Indonesia, however. Upendra Thakur's text leans in this direction, though much pertinent information on how Indian inscriptions and institutions traveled from one place to the other is also presented. Thakur's writing is representative of a debate on so-called Indianization, which has been waged for more than a century. In it some scholars attribute less (and some more) to India as a cultural influence on distant Indonesia. The text is useful for getting a sense of the debate, and also for its disentangling of the many strands of Hinduism and Buddhism that came to the archipelago—in different forms—over a long period of time.

1

Unlike their modern counterparts the ancient Indians were a people of great enterprise. Since the time of the Indus civilization they made great strides in various walks of life. Zealous seekers of truth and love, they speculated upon the various problems of life in this world and beyond, and in the process they developed great religions of India–Brāhmaṇism and Jainism and Buddhism— to give direction to the Indian way of life. And, all this stock of knowledge, in the course of time got transmitted to other parts of Asia through trade and missionary activities of the preachers.

In spite of the efforts of a section of scholars to minimise, from time to time, the extent of Indian influence on South-East Asia, "the evidence for their importance is there for all to see and cannot the controverted." The countries of South-East Asia and Central Asia were so politically and culturally influenced by the Indians in early times that most historians in the beginning described those regions as "the extended part of India," "Greater India," "Further India," etc. Though it is difficult to endorse such extreme claims of the so-called "Greater India School," there is no doubt that such influences did occur and play a significant part in the development of the various cultures of this region. Sylvain Levi feels that some of the true Indian masterpieces were produced in foreign lands such as Cambodia and Java (Malay Archipelago) under foreign inspiration, reflecting the marvelous Indian genius.

Thus, the story of the Brāhmaṇa and Buddhist missionaries who went to various countries of South-East Asia to propagate their religion and culture is a fact of human history which eloquently speaks of the realization by races of their affinity of minds, their mutual obligation of a common humanity. Such a rare event did happen and the path was built up between the Indians and the people of South-East Asia and East Asia in an age where physical obstruction needed heroic personality to overcome it and the mental barrier a moral power of uncommon magnitude. It reminds us of the great pilgrimage of those noble heroes who, for the sake of their faith, their ideal of the liberation of Self, accepted banishment from home and all that was familiar to them. Many perished and left no trace behind. A few were spared to tell their story: a story not of adventures and trespassers whose heroism has proved a mere romantic excuse for careers of unchecked brigandage, but a story of pilgrims who came to offer their gifts of love and wisdom, a story indelibly recorded in the cultural memory of their hosts.

Against this background it may be interesting to note that the two Indian religions—Brāhmaṇism and Buddhism—with their many sects and sub-sects played a very significant role in South-East Asia in early times. The numerous inscriptions and art objects that have been found in different parts of this region throw considerable light on the various aspects of these religions. Unfortunately these inscriptions have not been studied from a religious point of view: they have been chiefly utilised as a source of political history. On close scrutiny one finds that most of the inscriptions, particularly those in Cambodia and Java, are religious in character, and their chief object is to describe some religious *foundations*. For instance, of all the countries of South-East Asia, the philosophical activities were most pronounced in Java from where religious texts of great importance have come down to us which form an invaluable treasure of Indo-Javanese literature. These records, as a whole, present a clear picture of the general tendencies of these religions in those countries, some of which patronized Śaivism, some Vaiṣṇavism, some both and yet others Buddhism.

2

As we know, after the commercial intercourse of the first century and the traces of a somewhat deeper penetrating Indian influence from the beginning of the second century, the settlement appears to have become an accomplished fact in the fourth century A.D., and by the beginning of the fifth century A.D, Brāhmaṇism had already firmly planted itself in the Malay Archipelago (Java, Sumātrā, Bali, and Borneo: modern Indonesia).

We have a very interesting eye-witness (contemporary) account of a small state in the Malay Peninsula which throws light on a colony in the making, named *Tuen-suin* by the Chinese. It says: "Its market was a meeting-ground between the east and the west, frequented every day by more than ten thousand men, including merchants from India, Parthia and more distant kingdoms who come in large numbers to carry on trade and commerce in rare objects and precious merchandise. It contains five hundred merchants' families, two hundred Buddhist and more than a thousand Brāhmaṇas of India. The people of *Tuen-suin* follow their religion and give them their daughters in marriage, as most of these Brāhmaṇas settle in the country and do not go away. Day and night they read scriptures and make offerings of white vases, perfumes and flowers to the gods." In the Malay Peninsula, the Brāhmaṇas formed an important element of the population and the Brāhmaṇical rites and ceremonies were in great favour at their courts. And, of these islands, the island of Bali was the most important centre of Brāhmaṇism which still retains its old Brāhmaṇical culture to a considerable extent. It was here that the onrushing wave of Islam met with a dismal failure and could not penetrate into the soil of this island. Bali still affords a unique opportunity to study Brāhmaṇism as it was "modified by coming into contact with the aborigines of the archipelago."

3

Thus we find that the two religious systems of India took deep roots in its soil during the early period of Indian settlements. So far as faith, beliefs, and religious practices are concerned, the colonies in the far East were almost a replica of the motherland. But the indigenous faiths and beliefs did not vanish altogether, they were partly eliminated by, and partly absorbed into, the higher and developed system. But, in some respects the latter was also affected and moulded by the former.

As we know, in Java, Buddhism—particularly Mahāyāna—led to the erection of the famous Borobudur *stūpa* and several other magnificent temples. In Eastern Java the religion has left a prominent trace in Candi Jago and other

Statue of Ganesha,
Prambanan temple. Photo
by Dolores Puigantell.

small temples scattered all over the island. The same thing may also be said of
Sumātrā. In fact, the international character of Buddhism gave Suvarṇadvīpa
a status and importance that brought it into intimate contact with India and
other Buddhist countries. As a result, the Śailendra kings had cultural exchange with the political powers and the Buddhist preachers from Bengal
such as Atīśa Dīpamkara of Bengal (eleventh century) and Dharmapāla of
Kānchī, an eminent *ācārya* of the Nālandā University (seventh Unt.), went to
Suvarṇadvīpa which was an important seat of Buddhist learning and culture.
The study of Buddhist literature in Java is proved not only by the discovery of
important Buddhist texts but also by the sculptures of Borobudur and other
religious monuments which pre-suppose a wide range of knowledge in its
various branches.

A study of the Buddhist iconography in Java explains the absence of any
material modification of its principal tenets and beliefs, which is best illustrated by the appearance of the entire hierarchy of the Mahāyānist deities
in almost identical forms and names, e.g., Ādi-Buddha and Prajñāpāramitā,

Dhyānī Buddhas and Mānusī Buddhas, the Bodhisattvas and the Tārās, with the familiar postures, called *mudrā*, of the images. It also shows that besides the image of Gautama Buddha, the images of Bodhisattva Avalokiteśvara were most popular in Java and Sumātrā, though Maitreya and Mañjuśrī were also very familiar. In other words, with minor modifications here and there, their entire Mahāyānist pantheon seems to be well represented in Java. Besides this, as in India, so in Java also, we come across the later phases of Mahāyāna Buddhism, such as the adoption of Hindu gods in the Buddhist pantheon, introduction of minor deities of terrible appearance and the development of Tantrika cult and mode of worship and gradual rapproachment between Mahāyāna and Brāhmaṇical religions.

Thus it can be safely concluded that Tantricism which flourished later in Eastern Java had already its beginnings in the early tenth century A.D., while the Palas were ruling in Bengal. The Tantrika teachers played a very prominent part during the reign-period of Airlangga and Jayabhaya (eleventh to twelfth centuries A.D.) in Java, and in the thirteenth century this cult found its two great devotees in king Kṛtanagara and Ādityavarman of Java and Sumātrā respectively. The accounts of these two kings, the images of Bhairava, Heruka, and other Tantrika gods and goddesses, as well as the Tantrika texts provide an unmistakable proof of the nature and extent of this degraded form of Buddhism in Java and Sumātrā of which the Dutch scholar Moens has given a very scintillating account.

According to Moens, king Ādityavarman was a great follower of the Bhairava cult and he is said to have indulged in *Kapalika* practices. He assumed the title of *Viśaṣdharanī* after performing the highest consecration ceremony (according to the Bhairava cult) which included a human sacrifice in the cremation ground. Whatever the real nature of his *sadhana*, his inscriptions leave us in no doubt that he was a follower of *Tantrayāna* and indulged in its obnoxious practices. He looked upon himself as an incarnation of Bhairava and his queen that of Mātanginī, one of the ten Mahāvidyās.

The last phase of Mahāyāna marked a syncretism of the different gods of the Hindu and Buddhist pantheon. In India, while on one hand there was a growing tendency of rapproachment between Śaivism and Vaiṣṇavism (e.g., the joint representation of Śiva and Viṣṇu: Hari-Hara), on the other hand, there was also an attempt at synthesis between Vaiṣṇavism and Buddhism by regarding the Buddha as an incarnation of Viṣṇu. With the development of *Tantrayāna*, however, these identities assumed a more definite form.

Similarly, the close association between Śiva and the Buddha was a characteristic feature of the Javanese religion as is evident from the Tāntrika texts such as the *Kuñjarakarṇa* and the *Sutasoma*. According to Kern, in modern

Balinese theology, the Buddha is regarded as the younger brother of Śiva, and there is a close rapproachment between the two doctrines. A similar Śiva-Buddha cult also existed in Java. Latest researches in this field have shown that Śiva, Viṣṇu, and the Buddha were all regarded as identical and so were their *Śaktis*. Here, again the point is well illustrated by the case of Kṛtanagara who called himself *Narasimhamūrti*, an image of Viṣṇu in the incarnation of *Narasimha*. He was also known as Śiva-Buddha and was represented after his death by an image of Śiva-Buddha. His father king Viṣṇuvardhana was also represented after his death by the images of both Śiva and Buddha, while the cousin of the latter who also shared the royal honours with him was called Narasimhamūrti, but was represented by an image of Śiva. All these evidences point to the popular belief that all these gods were identical. This is further supported by the growing popularity of the image of Hari-Hara during this period. It may be noted here that king Kṛtarajasa, the son-in-law and successor of Kṛtanagara, is represented by a fine composite image of Hari-Hara.

A more popular but degraded form of the Mahāyāna doctrine in Java is preserved in the *Kamahayanan Mantranaya* which contains a short preamble followed by forty-one Sanskrit verses with Javanese commentaries elaborating the Mahayanist conceptions of the various Buddhas, particularly *Bajrasattva*, the chief of all the Buddhas. The esoteric character of the teaching is clearly indicated by a verse which forbids the devotee to communicate the secrets of *bajra*, *ghanta*, and *mudrā* to those who do not belong to the *Mandala*. On the whole, the text is throughout devoted to the exposition of the *Tantrayana* or *Vajrayana*, both in its theoretical and practical aspects.

Besides Java, the island of Sumātrā has also preserved some very interesting remains of Buddhism. We have already noted above some of the characteristic traits of this religion in this area which has yielded important archaeological finds having direct bearing on this religion. The ruins of brick temples, called *biaro*, are found in large numbers in the Highlands of Padang and Tapanuli. Some of them are fairly large, for instance, *Biara si Pamutung* at the mouth of the Panai river, containing Buddhist images. Ruins of stone-temples exist in the residency of Palembang. Besides the temples, we have a fairly large number of Buddhist *stūpas*, such as those of Tanjung Medan and Muara Takus in which golden plates with mystic syllables in Nāgarī script were discovered. We have also numerous *Dagabas*. The images from the Highlands of Padang, Tapanuli, Palembang, and Jambi contain stone images of the Buddha, Bodhisattvas, and minor deities like Haruka, etc.; a silver image of *Bajrasattva* (from Buo); stone images of Śiva, Gaṇeśa, Nandī, Brahmā or *Trimūrti*; and bronze images of Gaṇeśa and Kubera. Moreover, we have a large number of Buddhist inscriptions, especially of Ādityavarman in the district of Fort Van de Capellen, the very centre of Minangkabau. The existence of Buddhism in Borneo is indicated by the ruins of temples and detached images, but it is very difficult to assign any approximate date to them. Thus, we have evidences to show that besides Java and Sumātrā, Buddhism was preached and spread by Indian missionaries in some other islands of Malay Archipelago, particularly Bali and Borneo. But as Brāhamaṇism was a more vigorous and widely popular religion in those areas, Buddhism could not make much headway and disappeared from the scene very soon.

The Genesis of Indonesian Archaeology

R. P. Soejono

Only a few countries are as rich from an archaeological point of view as Indonesia, which is littered with remains from a long and fascinating past. Early European visitors to the archipelago marveled at structures they came upon, which seemed to indicate that there had been complex civilizations in the region with the capacity to build monumental architecture. R. P. Soejono was one of the first indigenous chroniclers of the archaeological tradition in Indonesia, and he held a strong interest in the history and evolution of the science, questioning its development and directions over the decades. He outlines here a framework for studying the history of archaeology in the archipelago, which links the earliest Dutch efforts at preservation and classification with postcolonial developments as Indonesians began to sort out their own archaeological patrimony. The writing here explores the state of archaeological knowledge in the Dutch colonial period and shows how early Western attempts at understanding gradually gave way to a more complex, multifaceted project of knowledge carved out by later colonial overlords of the region.

Characteristics of the Phases of the Development

Since its inception as an amateurist activity until its present status as a branch of science demanding special instruction and the execution of tasks in an institutional framework, archaeology in Indonesia has gone through a definite evolution. This development up till now can be divided into a number of phases, each with its distinct characteristics.

The first was that of registration (description) of early remains, without any coordination by an organization authorized to carry out archaeological activities (up to and including the nineteenth century). The second phase was that of the beginning of the institutionalization of archaeological activities, so that archaeological tasks could be defined and their implementation supervised (beginning of the twentieth century).

The consolidation of archaeological activities, both through the stimulation of the compilation of archaeological data and the formulation of hypotheses relative to all kinds of archaeological fields, is the mark of the third phase of the development (which lasted until the outbreak of World War II).

The fourth phase is characterized by the continuation of archaeological activities with the aim of filling in "gaps," as well as the perfection and/or creation of all kinds of theories and methods (from Independence until the present).

Developments before the Twentieth Century

In its earliest stages, before attaining the status of a science, archaeology in Indonesia showed several facets in its development. The first acquaintance of ancient objects was made through the localization and descriptive explanation of these artifacts, sometimes accompanied by an explanation of their historical background. This background was partly mythological, based on the beliefs of the local people. This kind of descriptive activity can be said to have already been carried out by Prapanca, as witness several cantos of the *Nāgara kertāgama* (Krom 1923: 1, 2, 47; Pigeaud 1960: iii).

With the arrival of Western power in Indonesia, there was an increase in the descriptions of ancient objects and remains. These descriptions were made by Westerners intrigued by the curiosities (*curiositeiten*) which they found on their wanderings through the Indonesian Archipelago and by their predisposition to write about whatever appeared important to them (cf., inter alia, Rumphius 1705). Such facts which they considered strange and worthy of description were first and foremost those in connection with local traditions, history, and the economic situation, and also several kinds of prehistorical remains. The category of people writing about their experiences and the "curiosities" of Indonesia comprised persons from different professions, such as merchants, scholars, soldiers, civil servants, nature lovers, travellers, etc. (cf. Koentjaraningrat 1958: 15–48).

The observations on prehistoric remains by people from these different walks of life are generally of a descriptive nature, being concerned with what they came across on their travels (Krom 1923: 1–43). These descriptions, which were initially in the form of reports (eighteenth century), were later supplemented with more accurate observations of prehistoric remains, such as, for instance, the measurements in respect of Prambanan by F. van Boeckholtz in 1790. The foundation of the *Bataviaasch Genootschap van Kunsten en Weten-schappen* (Batavian Society of Arts and Sciences) in 1778 exercised a great influence on research into the history, traditions, and prehistoric remains of Indonesia.

The nineteenth century showed an increase in activities in several archaeological domains. Apart from the more extensive observations with regard to ancient remains, especially temples, the methods of dealing with the problems posed by these ancient remains were also more advanced. The archaeological activities were of a documentary nature with particular emphasis on temples, taking the form of drawings (H. Cornelius, H. N. Sieburgh, C. J. van der Vlis, F. C. Wilsen), photographs (J. van Kinsbergen), inventories (F. Junghuhn), restoration (e.g., Mendut), and excavations (the temples on the Dieng Plateau). Surveys began to be carried out systematically by people who produced descriptions which have remained important sources on these antiquities until the present day (J. F. G Brumund, C. Leemans, W. P. Groeneveldt, R. D. M. Verbeek, J. Crawfurd, T. S. Raffles, etc.).

The methods evolved in Europe were also tried out in Indonesia, viz. the technique of making glass negatives of the Borobudur monument by A. Shaefer in 1845, which was clearly unsuccessful.

In the prehistoric field (Soejono 1969) several activities stand out which were considered important in the nineteenth century, such as the grouping (classification) of rectangular axes (C. N. Pleyte and others) and the concentration of interest on megalithic remains (H. E. Steinmetz, etc.) and bronze kettledrums (J. J. A. Worsaae, A. B. Meyer, and others). One most significant achievement of prehistoric surveys/research was the discovery of Pithecanthropus Erectus by E. Dubois a Trinil in 1891.

There was as yet no interest manifest in the Islamic past in the nineteenth century. Activities in this field took the form of reports of discoveries of ancient gravestones in Aceh (1884) and a plan for the documentation (drawings, photographs, rubbings) and restoration of these remains (Tjandrasasmita 1977).

As regards the historical background of these ancient remains, either temples or megalithic remains and bronze objects, there was a tendency to consider them as Hindu works. This was a consequence of the archaeological activities by the British in India, the results of which were widely disseminated, and the presence of similarities between the design of temple complexes and the images of gods here and those found in India.

The increase in systematic interest in relics from the past in the nineteenth century also involved attempts at establishing special organizations in the field of prehistory, such as the foundation of the *Commissie tot het Opsporen, Verzamelen en Bewaren van Oudheidkundige Voorwerpen* (Commission for the Discovery, Collection, and Conservation of Ancient Objects) in 1822, which was apparently unsuccessful in performing its task. An attempt by the private sector to assist with prehistorical research was the foundation of the *Archaeologische Vereeniging* (Archaeological Society) in 1885, chaired by the engineer J. W. IJzerman. The latter succeeded in exposing the foot (sou-basement) of the Borobudur temple, which was obviously decorated with Karmawibangga reliefs, and at present is covered by the lower terrace.

In summary, the nineteenth century witnessed the development of archae-ology in Indonesia in the direction of a systematic discipline. The basis for the work had been laid by the Dutch in the fields of documentation, restora-tion, excavation, and interpretation. These activities were parallel with the developments in Europe in that century (Daniel 1950), where the advances in prehistoric research took place step by step, to be applied subsequently to regions outside Europe, such as Western Asia, Egypt, India, Southeast Asia, and Indonesia itself. In fact, by about the middle of the nineteenth century the principles of archaeology had been formulated in Europe, which repre-sented the centre of the development of this science. These principles were: the application of the Three Age System to ancient objects, diffusion and ho-motaxis, typology, the comparative method, synchronization techniques, and the technique of stratigraphic excavation. Only a few of these principles were successfully applied in Indonesia (inter alia, diffusion, typology, and homo-taxis). The reason for this was that practitioners of archaeology in Indonesia were by and large amateurs who were not able by themselves to fully grasp the development of the methods of prehistoric research in Europe which had turned archaeology into a profession (C. J. Thomsen, Mariette, A. H. Layard, H. Schliemann, and others).

The Developments until the Middle of the Twentieth Century

The main focus of nineteenth-century archaeology was the classical field, and this situation was continued in the twentieth century until the fall of Dutch power in World War II. In the meantime, the need for an organization to tackle the prehistoric domain had become pressing, and in 1901 the *Commissie in Nederlandsch Indië voor Oudheidkundig Onderzoek op Java en Madura* or O.C. (Commission in the Dutch East Indies for Archaeological Research in Java and Madura) was instituted. The name of this commission already points to its limited powers and research scope, so that it was unable to function in a satisfactory way as a research body. Underlying the establishment of this commission was the unfinished state of the antiquities in Java, which had not been subjected to careful and systematic examination, and the realization of the necessity of a special organization similar to those already in existence in Indochina and India. The improvement of this commission was only effected in 1913. Because the commission was hardly functioning any longer after the death of J. L. A. Brandes (chairman of its board), an official organization was created and confirmed by the Government of the Dutch East Indies, which was named *Oudheidkundige Dienst* or o.d. (Archaeological Service), with N. J. Krom at its head. The o.d.'s tasks, authority, and staff were extended in order that its prehistorical activities might have the proper results.

The establishment of the o.c., later consolidated as o.d., which was able to undertake prehistorical investigations in an effective manner, is certainly an important step in the development of archaeology in Indonesia. Considering the extent and many-sidedness of archaeological activities, a centre for the planning and direction of these activities is an absolute must.

Since the existence of an institutional centre for the development of archaeology in Indonesia, there have been obvious improvements in prehistorical research in various respects. What became an important precondition for archaeological activities was the publication of research results, which from the earliest period of the foundation of research organizations was systematically directed in the form of the *Rapporten van de Oudheidkundige Commissie* or r.o.c. (Reports of the Archaeological Commission), later continued as *Oudheidkundig Verslag van Oudheidkundige Dienst in Nederlandsch Indië* (Archaeological Report of the Dutch East Indies Archaeological Service) or r.o.d. Important results of archaeological work are contained in these journals, including personal notes and administrative affairs, as well as research findings and scientific articles, so that progress in archaeological work can be traced in a continuous way. Thus, there is a basis for continuing and improving activities considered incomplete or unsatisfactory.

The creation of the Archaeological Service in 1913 as an official board for carrying out archaeological activities has opened new perspectives in the development of archaeology in Indonesia (cf. Soekmono 1977). First of all schedules had to be drawn up which when completed would cover archaeological fields in every part of Indonesia (and not only Java and Madura), and the technical manpower for the implementation of these plans brought up to strength. This manpower (H. Leydie Melville, P. J. Perquin, J. J. de Vink) was employed in the domains of inventorization and documentation (photographs, drawing), which have been stimulated since the early days of the o.c. The field which received the o.d.'s special attention was the restoration of Javanese temples. There were obviously differences of view regarding the execution of these restorations. On the one hand there was the desire to restore on a limited scale as far as remains of such monuments were still present, and the important point here was a reconstruction on paper only (Krom). On the other hand there was a tendency to conduct restorations as far as possible in accordance with what could be justified on the basis of a reconstruction plan

(Brandes, Bosch). Especially when F. D. K. Bosch was in charge of the o.d. in 1916 there was conspicuous progress in temple restoration in Java. The restoration activities resulted in the formation of a permanent technical staff especially for the restoration work, and this staff was to reside at Prambanan.

As the archaeological organization reached maturity, there was an extension in interest to other fields of archaeology, apart from improvement in the activities in classical archaeology. Thereupon the o.d. directed its special energies to tackling Islamic remains (P. J. Moquette), prehistoric remains (P. V. van Stein Callenfels), and the remains of the Portuguese and the Dutch East India Company (V. I. van de Wall). The investigation of the inscriptions which was pioneered in the previous century by R. M. Th. Friederich, Cohen Stuart, Kern, and others was stimulated more and more. The scope of the investigations was also extended and archaeological activities were carried out in Sumatra, Kalimantan, Sulawesi, Bali, the Lesser Sunda Islands, and the Moluccas.

Archaeological activities were also supported financially by prominent people outside the o.d., namely by civil servants and experts from other government institutions and from private circles. The position of archaeology in Indonesia became more stable still after the Dutch East Indies Government promulgated the *Monumenten Ordonnantie* (Ancient Monuments Conservation Act) (1931), which offered ancient remains protection against various general acts aimed at causing damage to, removing, or destroying ancient remains and their sites.

The improvement in research and other activities in the different fields of archaeology also gave rise to theories/hypotheses regarding the elements surrounding antiquities which were connected with the history of their creators, the period of their development, their distribution, the style of their art, their social and religious function, and so on. Especially Bosch's hypothesis concerning the role of the Indonesian people itself in the construction of the temples (Bosch 1919) overthrew the views whereby the Indians were the architects of these buildings and the Indonesians were only their labourers. These Indonesia-centric theories were supplemented more and more by the views of other scholars (Krom, Stutterheim, etc.). Other landmarks of the development of archaeology here were the publications of basic books on the Jago, Singasari, and Panataran monuments by Brandes (1904, 1909), the Borobudur by Krom (1920) and Van Erp (1931), together with Krom's work on Hindu-Javanese history (1929, 1931) and Hindu-Javanese architecture (1919, 1923). A period of growth in archaeological activities from the scientific point of view occurred when the o.d. was headed by W. F. Stutterheim (1936). But at the same time a decline in fieldwork occurred, caused by a shortage of staff and the economic crisis which struck in those years.

It may be said that archaeological activities of an institutional and scientific character were very productive in the twentieth century until the outbreak of World War II in East Asia, although only a Dutch professional cadre was active in this field. The organization which supervised the archaeological programme was not large, but was made up of a core of Dutch workers capable of directing their activities to various areas and fairly extensive regions.

Archaeological work in Indonesia stagnated during the Japanese occupation and the Revolution. During the Japanese occupation only the technical staff at Prambanan was still able to carry out its tasks of restoration and excavation, in particular at the Prambanan and neighbouring temples, until the Revolution.

In the meantime the Dutch army occupying Jakarta re-organized the O.D. again in 1947. It should be noted that in 1945, at the time of rising against the Dutch army, many documents which had been collected in Jakarta since the beginning of archaeological activities in Indonesia (archives, photographs, glass negatives, drawings and books, as well as a collection of research objects) were destroyed or disappeared.

Javanese Inscriptions

Himansu Bhusan Sarkar

By the mid-eighth century in Java, inscriptions were starting to look different from earlier prototypes found in Borneo and Sumatra. Language began to get more complicated, and the clear early reliance on Indian forms began to be replaced by a more hybrid style that elevated Javanese concerns. The Sañjaya inscriptions from Canggal, dated very precisely to October 6, 732 CE, show the beginnings of these changes. Though still clearly influenced by Indian forms, the actual diction of the Sañjaya inscription differs from its almost purely Indian antecedents. Descriptions of a "body [that] dazzles like gold and whose matted locks are comparable to the flames of the fire" are more sensuous and fuller than earlier writings; "he, who lies on the surface of the watery bed, the petal of whose eye-lotuses are red though meditating," evokes a very different image than the more prosaic writings of earlier inscriptions. It is clear that the Javanese of this period were beginning to experiment with their own styles, not abandoning Indian templates, but rather increasingly bending them to their own purposes. When we are told that the local Javanese king named Sanna has "the splendor of the bright color of gold that has been smolten in the flaming fire" and that he has "great arms, big thighs, and (a) head upraised like the mountain peaks," we believe it. These are the boasts of a vigorous new civilization flexing its muscles.

The Inscription of Sañjaya from Canggal, Central Java,
Dated October 6, AD 732

(1) When the year of the Saka king that is brought to numbers with four, five, and six [654] was passed, on Monday, the thirteenth day of the bright half of the month, which follows [the tithi] Bhadra, in [the month of] Karttika, while the lagna stood under Kumbha in the part called "fixed," the king [who is] the illustrious Sañjaya, for obtaining tranquility, established on the hill, a linga [i.e., phallus] with [all] auspicious marks.

(2) He who is a Sun in the darkness of the world; who had for his crest jewel the Moon on his matted locks which are beautiful by the surging waves of the Ganges; on whose body dazzling with the brilliance of ashes,

scatters its brilliance the necklace of snakes; who is praised by the gods with graceful and soft palms [of their hands] folded in the form of a vessel; he, Siva, may bestow on you the most perfect bliss!

(3) May that irreproachably beautiful pair of feet-lotuses of the three-eyed one [Siva] which are constantly praised by the greatest of gods and demons and other with their bent crowns which are [comparable to] the bees [that kiss the lotus]; whereof the slightly copper-coloured petals are the toes and whereof the end is decorated by bright filaments or rays [issuing] from the nails, may [that pair of feet] grant you perpetual bliss!

(4) May the three-eyed one [Siva] whose matted locks are adorned with the crescent moon, who, by reason of excess of His divine attributes, is a receptacle of great, and even wonderful, things; who, given to solitude, by his renunciation [of all things] always creates the wonder of yogins [i.e., ascetics]; who, by his eight-fold bodies and through compassion but not selfishness, sustains the universe; may he, the lord of [all] beings, protect you!

(5) May the self-created Lord [Brahma], the object of worship of the world, whose pair of feet-lotuses are revered by the gods; who has fixed the regulations of the world to the post of the Vedas; who is the source of religion, worldly prosperity, and desire; whose body dazzles like gold and whose matted locks are comparable to the flames of the fire of his own body; may he, the lord of Yogins, the venerable one, reward you with success!

(6) May he, who lies on the surface of the watery bed, the petals of whose eye-lotuses are red through mediation; who is behymned by the gods for protection; who is always frowningly viewed by the goddess Sri on seeing the beauty of her own image reflected on the side levels of the jewels on the upturned crown of the king of serpents; may he, the lord of Sri, grant you prosperity!

(7) There is a great island called Yava, abundantly supplied with rice grains and other seeds and rich in goldmines; that [island] is acquired by immortals [by mantras] and other means; where there is a wonderful place dedicated to Sambhu, a heaven of heavens, surrounded by the Ganges and other holy resorts and laid in a beautiful woodland habited by elephants, existing for the good of the world.

(8) In that excellent island called Yava which is the great mark of footprints of Purusha, there was a king of very noble lineage of the name of Sanna who was of established reputation and who, by means of conciliation and gift, ruled the subjects in a proper way, out of attachment, just like a father [taking care of] the child from his very birth and who with

his enemies subdued, protected the world for a long time with justice like Manu.

(9) He [the king] named Sanna, the [very] Moon of the family, while thus ruling over the goddess of royalty, having, in the fullness of time, gone to enjoy happiness in the heaven which is the accumulated results [of his meritorious deeds]. [Then] the earth, separated [from him] roamed in grief for being bereft of her lord.

(10) The one who sprang from him was like the [Mount] Meru and possessed a wealth of manifold qualities: he has the splendor of the bright color of the gold that has been smolten in the flaming fire; he has great arms, big thighs, and head upraised like the mountain peaks, and has the shelter of his high-raised feet on the kings of stable dynasties obtaining on the earth.

(11) The illustrious king called Sañjaya, who is beautiful and respected by the assembly of the learned as an adept in the subtle meanings of Sastric lore; who, excelling in bravery and other virtues, has, like Raghu, overthrown many circles of feudal lords; who is like the sun in fame and whose splendor spreads in all regions; he, the son of Sannaha, the very life of his sister, is [now] ruling the kingdom justly.

(12) While he is ruling the earth which has for her girdle the waves of the seas and for her breasts the mountains, people can sleep on the roadside without being startled by thieves or by other fears. And men rich in fame, always earned in plenty [the three aims of life, namely,] religion, worldly prosperity, and the objects of desire. Certainly Kali is crying much in despair as no sign of [Kali's] limbs is shining [i.e., is in existence].

What Was Srivijaya?

George Coedès

George Coedès is perhaps the most important of the early scholars of the twentieth century who really started to put the study of classical Indonesia on a firm, scientific basis. Coedès was a paleographer and a critic of old texts, yet he also kept track of advances in the archaeological record, and on the basis of these two branches of knowledge he put forth the first coherent descriptions of Srivijaya. Srivijaya was the first sizeable kingdom in the archipelago; it existed between the seventh and twelfth centuries and was probably centered around southern Sumatra, in the area of what is today Palembang. Unlike concomitant kingdoms in Java, Srivijaya left almost nothing by way of architecture: a few scattered sites and some well-worn stele are all that survive of it. Yet there was textual evidence, and Coedès was the first to piece together divergent texts from India, China, and Southeast Asia to form an integrated account of what this vast polity may have looked like. Coedès's contemporary H. G. Quaritch Wales was trying to interpret the scattered evidence about Indonesia's first great maritime kingdom at the same time. In the selection that follows, Coedès replies to Quaritch Wales's assertion that Srivijaya may in fact have been centered on the Malay Peninsula, rather than in southern Sumatra where Coedès had done most of his own work.

In recent years, the history of Sriwijaya has undergone many ups and downs. Following my article published in 1918, the equation *Śrīwijaya* = (*Che-li*)*-fo-che* = *San-fo-t'si* = *Zābag* = kingdom of the *Śailendra* = kingdom of Palembang, upheld by the authority of Vogel (1919) and Krom (1919, 1926) and by Ferrand (1922), was uncontested for a decade. The first attack was launched in 1929 by Stutterheim, in the booklet where he showed that the Sailendras were a Javanese dynasty. More recently, in 1933–1934, R. C. Majumdar attacked this equation from a different angle, by trying to prove that the Sumatran kingdom of Sriwijaya had extended its domination as far as Nakhon Si Thammarat at the end of the eighth century, as that shortly afterwards it was absorbed by the *Jāwaka* kingdom, the Chinese *San-fo-t'si*, whose capital was in Nakhon Si Thammarat, and which was governed by the Sailendras of Indian origin.

The name of *Jāwaka*, in the form of *Zābag*, was applied by Arab sailors to all possessions of the Sailendras, which from the end of the eighth century onwards included Java, and extended in the eleventh century throughout Sumatra and the entire Malay Peninsula.

Wales takes up this theory, modifying it on certain points, and completing it. He accepts the Chinese accounts placing a state named *Śrīwijaya* in the seventh century (I suppose he is thinking of *Fo-che*), but he doubts that the suzerainty of this kingdom could have extended throughout the Malay Peninsula and that the Wat Sema Muang inscription of 775 implies this suzerainty. To explain the presence on the Peninsula of this inscription in the name of a king of Sriwijaya, he proposes one of the following alternatives: either the Peninsular kingdom of *Jāwaka* had already absorbed the Sumatran kingdom of Sriwijaya by 775 and taken its name, or the country of *Jāwaka* also bore, independently, the same name, *Śrīwijaya*. Whatever may be the origin of the name Sriwijaya, insomuch as it designates the region of Chaiya, Wales bases this new geographical location of Sriwijaya firstly on the archaeological richness of the site, secondly on its toponymy (Chaiya = *Jaya*; Sivivha i = *Śrīwijaya*, the name of the hill situated south of the village), and lastly on some rather unclear phonetic considerations: "A difference in the native pronunciation of the word Sriwijaya in the region from its pronunciation in Sumatra might well account for the Chinese form *San-fo-t'si* being applied to the empire from the tenth century onwards, while in the seventh and eighth centuries the Sumatran state of Sriwijaya had been referred to by the Chinese as *Fo-che* = *Che-li-fo-che*." While admitting that the existence of an independent kingdom named Sriwijaya in Sumatra in the seventh century was likely, Wales considers that Majumdar's research and his own has clearly demonstrated that this Sumatran kingdom did not in following centuries attain the importance that I myself and other authors have attributed to it.

It can be seen that the problem is becoming more and more complicated, and the situation is in no way simplified by Stutterheim's latest theory (1935), which would tend to locate Sriwijaya (*Che-li-fo-che*) at Indragiri in Sumatra. I think the time has come to separate the undoubted improvements which have been brought to the initial equation since 1918 from the untenable hypotheses whose absurdity must be demonstrated. I shall take the terms of the equation one by one, and will indicate for each of them the certain facts concerning them.

> *Śrīwijaya*. In 683–686 this name appears in three inscriptions in Old Malay, one from Kedukan Bukit in Palembang, the second from Karang Brahi in the Jambi hinterland, and the third from Kota Kapur in Bangka: in

the latter two texts, *Śrīwijaya* appears as a state exerting its authority over the territories where the inscriptions were found (Coedès 1930). In 775, the Wat Sema Muang stone from Nakhon Si Thammarat, which Wales gratuitously supposes to originate from Chaiya, bears on its first side, an inscription in the name of a king of Sriwijaya. In 1006, the great charter of Leyden names *Mārawijayottunngawarman*, son of *Cūḍāmaṇiwarman*, from the *Śailendra* family, king of *Katāha* (in Tamil: *Kiḍāra*) and of *Śrīwiṣaya*. These two kings are mentioned in Chinese texts as kings of *San-fo-t'si*. In 1030, an inscription from Tanjore relates the campaigns of *Rājendracola I* against the king of *Kaḍāram* and *Śrīwijayam*, who appears to be the suzerain of a series of states located in Sumatra and the Malay Peninsula.

Che-li-fo-che or *Fo-che* is mentioned in Chinese texts from 670 to 742. It is a neighbouring state of Malayu (Jambi), which it conquers at the end of the seventh century. Phonetically, this term corresponds very closely to *Śrīwijaya*.

San-fo-t'si appears in Chinese texts after the end of the T'ang dynasty (beginning of the tenth century) and is mentioned regularly until the Ming dynasty. Phonetically, *fo-t'si* may represent *vijaya*, but *san* remains puzzling. Historically, *San-fo-t'si* may be identified with the *Śrīwiṣaya/Katāha* of the greater charter of Leyden, since *Cūḍāmaṇivarman* and his son *Māravijayottuṇgavarman* are named in the Song Annals as kings of *San-fo-t'si*. Geographically, *San-fo-t'si* is located by the Chinese in Palembang. In 1225, Tchao Jou-koua said that the country was situated in the Ocean, and was in possession of the straits via which all foreign traffic had to pass from the west to China, and vice versa. Among the dependencies of *San-fo-t'si* enumerated by this author there are several states mentioned in the Tanjore inscriptions as *Rājendracola's* conquests during his campaigns against the king of *Śrīwiṣayam/Kaḍāram*.

Zābag. This is the empire of the *Mahārāja*, "king of the Islands," often cited by the Arabs from the ninth to the sixteenth century. Phonetically, this term corresponds to *Jāwaka*, the name of a kingdom which has some contentions with Ceylon in the thirteenth century, and which an inscription dating from 1230 found in Chaiya enables us to locate in the region between Chaiya and Nakhon Si Thammarat (Coedès 1927). Geographically, the information supplied by the Arab authors, who too often tend to repeat each other, does not enable any precise location to be given. According to them, the two main "dependencies" of *Zābag* are *Sribuza* and *Kalah*: *Sribuza*, which certain authors such as Abūlfidā, present as "the Maharajah's island," corresponds phonetically to *Śrīwijaya*,

and *Kalah* either to Kra or Kedah—in any case, part of the Malay Peninsula. The pair formed by *Sribuza/Kalah* is the equivalent of *Śrīwijayam*
(*Śrīwiṣaya*)/*Kaḍāram (Kiḍāram, Katāha)* of the Indian inscriptions.

Śailendra. This name appears for the first time in 775 on the second side
of the Wat Sema Muang inscription which is absolutely independent of
the first in the name of a king of *Śrīwijaya*. Almost at the same date—in
778 in Kalasan and in 782 in Kelurak—king Panangkaran, apparently belonging to a purely Javanese dynasty, presents himself as a member of
the *Śailendra* family. In 850, the Nalanda charter connects this family to
a king of Java (*Yavabhūmipāla*), who was the grandfather of *Bālaputra*,
the king of *Suwarṇadwipa* and the founder of a monastery in Nalanda.
In 1006, the great charter of Leyden names two kings of *Śrīwiṣaya/
Katāha*, known by Chinese historians as sovereigns of *San-fo-t'si*, as
members of the *Śailendra* family.

By combining these various elements, we reach the following conclusions:
Śrīwijaya, corresponding phonetically to the Chinese (*Che-li*)-*fo-che* and to the
Arabic *Sribuza*, designates a state which extended its domination over Palembang, Bangka, and the Jambi hinterland at the end of the seventh century,
conquered Malayu (Jambi) at about the same time, and in 775 left evidence
of its domination on the east coast of the Malay Peninsula. At the beginning
of the eleventh century, it was governed by rulers belonging to the Sailendra
dynasty, who were also kings of *Katāha (Kaḍāra)* and extended their authority
to part of Sumatra and of the Malay Peninsula. Two of these kings, named
in the great charter of Leyden, were known to the Chinese as kings of *San-
fo-t'si*. I think it is very difficult to cast doubt upon the equation *Śrīwijaya*
(*Che-li-fo-che*) = *San-fo-t'si* = Palembang. The chronology of the documents
shows fairly clearly the expansion of this kingdom's power, first confined to
the south of Sumatra (end of the seventh century), then extending to the
east coast of the Peninsula (end of the eighth century), and finally securing it
almost in its entirety (eleventh to thirteenth centuries).

The Sailendras entered Javanese history at the end of the eighth century
(778–782), appeared in Nakhon Si Thammarat certainly later than 775, and in
1006 were the rulers of *Śrīwiṣaya/Katāha*, i.e., according to the Chinese, of
the kingdom of *San-fo-t'si*.

Zābag is an expression of little geographical accuracy, but its two main dependencies, *Sribuza* and *Kalah*, are the very ones mentioned in Indian epigra-
phy in the eleventh century as components of the Sailendra empire, in which,
I repeat once more, the Chinese have enabled us to recognize the kings of
San-fo-t'si. If the name of *Zābag* is really borrowed from that of the kingdom

of *Jāwaka* attested in the Peninsula in the middle of the thirteenth century, its use by Arabs to designate all the possessions of the Maharajah, king of the Islands, is only one more example of the habit consisting in naming a country after the first province of ethnic group that is met on arrival.

From the impartial observation of these facts, it seems difficult not to conclude that the geographical terms of *Śrīwijaya*, (*Che-li*)-*fo-che*, *San-fo-t'si*, *Zābag*, kingdom of the *Śailendra*, kingdom of *Palembang*, simultaneously or successively designated as a state whose cradle was in Palembang, and which, as it expanded northwards to Kedah (*Kaṭāha, Kaḍāram*) or the isthmus of Kra (*Kalah*) succeeded in dominating the Straits. The equation between these terms therefore remains correct, subject to the following remarks, which represent definite improvements on the theory I myself presented in 1918, and which Ferrand developed in 1922.

1. (*Che-li*)-*fo-che* and *San-fo-t'si* were attested at different dates; the first name designates the Sumatran kingdom at the beginning, the second applies to the empire at the height of its power. I have recently written in this regard that the identification of *Che-li-fo-che* with *San-fo-t'si* is neither historically nor phonetically certain. I shall give further detail here: historically, these two terms succeed one another; phonetically, they cannot be entirely superimposed (Coedès 1934).

2. *Zābag* corresponds phonetically to *Jāwaka* in the Peninsula, and its identification would be almost certain if the name of *Jāwaka* had been attested in the ninth century, where the name of *Zābag* appeared in the Arab texts. Whatever the case may be, *Zābag* nevertheless designates the empire as a whole, including *Sribuza* = *Śrīwijaya*.

3. The Sailendra were probably a Javanese dynasty, a branch of which became rulers of Sriwijaya, either by conquest or inheritance, either at the end of the eighth century or the beginning of the ninth (second side of the Wat Sema Muang stone), in any case before 1006 (great charter of Leyden).

4. The centre of the kingdom of Sriwijaya, which was in Palembang at the end of the seventh century, may, at some time, have been duplicated or rivaled by another centre situated in the Peninsula: this is the duality we find in the pairs of names *Śrīwijaya/Kaḍāram* = *Sribuza/Kalah*. It is in this sense that I have been able to "recognize the strength of Majumdar's arguments, taken from my own work, which tend to place the centre of *Zābag* in the Malay Peninsula" (Coedès 1934).

But the error of Majumdar and Wales is to look for the single, permanent centre of the empire in this place, and it is for this reason that I wish to voice my opinion here. One of their main arguments is the archaeological poverty of the Palembang site compared with the riches of the Malay Peninsula. It is true that there are not yet many archaeological remains in Palembang, although recent research, unknown to Wales, has greatly enriched these. However, Wales is making a mistake in saying that the few sculptures from this site are almost of late Javanese style: the great stone Buddha unearthed by Westenenk, the head of which has recently been found by Schnitger in the Batavia Museum, is a remarkable work of the Amarawati school. Also, Krom emphasizes the non-Javanese nature of the sculptures found near Bukit Seguntang. Finally, the bronze statuettes found at the mouth of the Komering, although works of Javanese art, are by no means "late." The apparent riches of Chaiya, which, however, makes rather a poor showing compared with certain sites in Campa, Cambodia, or even central Siam, may be due to the fact that this locality has been extensively excavated, following Prince Damrong's discovery of the fine bronze Boddhisattwas in the Bangkok Museum.

To support his hypothesis, Wales takes his argument from place names, compares the names of Chaiya and of the Sivichai hill with that of Sriwijaya, and wonders whether the name of the river *Girirāṣtra* ("kingdom of the mountains") is not similar to that of the Sailendras ("king of the mountains"). In Siam, it is unwise to take Sanskrit geographical names into account, especially when their form is as correct and as well-preserved as that of *Girirāṣtra*, for it is more than likely that they were coined by one of the three scholarly kings who succeeded to the throne of Siam between 1851 and 1925. This is indeed the case of Pracuop Kirikhan (*Girikhaṇḍa*), a recent, official name for the most southerly district of Ratburi province, where the word *giri*, "mountain," can be found. The names of Chaiya and the Sivichai hill are more likely to be old, but when Wales uses this basis for his argument that there may have been two Sriwijayas, one in Palembang and the other in Chaiya, we are tempted to remind him that Siamese historical tradition places Sivichai in Phra Pathom, that there is a place in central Siam called Phichai (*Wijaya*), and that one of the capitals of Campa was in *Wijaya* in the twelfth century (in present Binh-dinh province in Viêt-nam).

The toponymic argument therefore seems of little value to me, since (*Śrī*)*wijaya* is not attested only in Palembang and Chaiya, but in many other places. To choose between Chaiya and Palembang, which are the only places concerned for the minute, there is a geographical fact that Wales has ignored, yet which appears decisive.

Chaiya lies at the far end of the bay of Ban Don, itself situated in the Gulf of Siam. I admit that Chaiya's position at the end of a transit route crossing the Peninsula must have given it a certain importance in trade. But how could this place, several days' sea journey from Singapore, have been able to control Straits traffic? It was his privileged position in the archipelago, at the entry to the Straits which, according to the Arabs and Tchao Jou-kuoa, made the fortune of the *Mahārāja* of *Zābag*, the "king of the Islands," and of the rulers of *San-fo-t'si*. Supposing that future research is able to show that Palembang was not always the capital of the empire—which is possible—, or even that it was never the capital—which seems much more difficult to reconcile with the texts—concordant historical accounts would necessarily lead us to search for the capital in the archipelago, within reach of the Straits.

I am perfectly willing to admit that Chaiya played an important commercial role in the northern provinces, corresponding roughly to *Kaṭāha (Kaḍāram)/ Kalah* in the texts. But that this place, in an outlying position, at the end of a cul de sac, could have been the capital of a marine power, from which the *Mahārāja* supervised and exploited sea-going trade through the Straits, is a geographical impossibility which alone would be sufficient to invalidate Wales' hypothesis.

Hanoi, December 1935

Srivijaya Revisited

Michel Jacq-Hergoualc'h

If Coedès can be considered the father of studies on the history of Srivijaya, then in Michel Jacq-Hergoualc'h he has found a worthy successor in our own age. The latter scholar has only very recently published his opus The Malay Peninsula, *but it is already destined to be a classic about the nature of this early Indonesian polity. In the decades since Coedès first wrote, much archaeological data has been compiled and many new texts found that describe the late centuries of the first millennium* CE *and the early centuries of the second millennium. Jacq-Hergoualc'h has exhaustively mined these sources, as well as many new archaeological studies, to reinterpret Srivijaya's place at the great maritime crossroads of the Straits of Malacca. At issue is whether Srivijaya was bicephalous, with power centers on both the peninsula and Sumatra, or whether it operated out of Palembang, but with a vast array of tendrils (both political and economic) spinning in different directions. Jacq-Hergoualc'h is also concerned with the nature of power exercised by Srivijaya, as the kingdom has usually been described as autocratic in nature, demanding high payments from anyone passing through its waters and desiring trade.*

Śrīvijaya: Myth or Reality?

The existence of Śrīvijaya as the dominant thalassocracy of the Southern Seas during an incredibly long period, from the seventh to the thirteenth century, that is, for more than six centuries, has practically never been questioned up to the present time. On the contrary, new epigraphic discoveries in Palembang itself and in the south of Sumatra confirmed researchers in the idea that this maritime empire, emerging from the oblivion to which history had unjustly relegated it, had enjoyed considerable fortune, and had proved quite willing to be bellicose towards its neighbours, which did not prevent it from being—as we learn from certain passages in the books of the Chinese pilgrim Yijing, dated to the end of the seventh century (Chavannes 1894, Takakusu 1896)—an important centre of Buddhist scholarship.

In the absence of any real challenge to the idea of the existence and power of this new imperialist entity on the already congested political chessboard of Southeast Asia, different researchers still expressed doubts about the location of its centre of operations in the southeast of Sumatra, Palembang. A case was made concerning the topographical difficulties of the site, which are undeniable. The present city of Palembang which covers the site of the former city (a circumstance that greatly complicates contemporary archaeological research), is established on the edge of the northern bank of the Musi River, on low and swampy land where submerged forest and mangroves hold sway all the way to the sea. This zone, writes P.-Y. Manguin (1987: 344), is "very flat," and allows the tide to engulf right into the interior, which makes it possible for large ships to go up the Musi as far as the city. Certain geologists, basing their opinions on poorly-interpreted cartographic documents, believed that this formation was very recent, and that at the latitude of Palembang, the coast had advanced by eighty kilometers [roughly the distance separating the site from the Straits] in the space of a thousand years: in so doing, they transformed Śrīvijaya-Palembang into a coastal port. The re-examination of the Chinese sources from the fifteenth century, and of various sixteenth-century Portuguese sources, proved that the coastline had in fact not budged for half a millennium, and therefore that there was no chance that it could have moved these eighty kilometres in less than five centuries. Clearly what we must think of when we consider Palembang in the Śrīvijaya period is of a site built at the edge of a river.

Nevertheless, the efforts of the archaeologists during the eighties and to the present day have borne fruit, and P.-Y. Manguin (1987) showed convincingly that the analysis of the Chinese ceramic shards on the Palembang sites by B. Bronson and J. Wisseman had been a little too rapid, and that in the collection of samples that had been used to argue for an absence of early material, "numerous pieces that must be dated with certainty to the Tang dynasty, between the eighth and ninth centuries, were found in Palembang" (Manguin 1987: 341). Once the fact that the site had been occupied in the early period had been confirmed in this way, the claim that the inscriptions and ancient statues discovered locally had been brought there during later periods no longer held water. Recent digs have established this fact, at the same time revealing traces of ancient religious structures (Manguin 1992, 1993), and even if many questions remain to be answered, it now seems irrefutable that the early capital of Śrīvijaya was at Palembang. Ceramic evidence [. . .] clearly indicates a densely populated and commercially active harbour city as early as the eighth to tenth centuries, i.e., soon after the formative stages of Śrīvijaya state in the seventh century [. . .].

The settlement pattern revealed so far in Palembang confirms the evidence provided by written sources. A riparian pattern, as expected, is by now clearly discernible: the multiple hubs of activity (some of them seemingly short-lived) have been found scattered along some twelve kilometres on the northern bank of the Musi river and its smaller tributaries—there is so far no solid evidence for early sites on the southern bank (Manguin 1992: 71–72).

Śrīvijaya, then, during the first centuries of its existence (from the seventh to ninth centuries at least) would indeed have been the active and expansionist entrepôt port that has been described since the work of G. Coedès. This is not the place to go into detail about the history of Śrīvijaya, except when it intersects with that of the chiefdoms and city-states of the Malay Peninsula. Let us remember briefly a number of facts extracted long ago from the Chinese texts or from inscriptions found locally.

The first of these, which are reliably dated, take us back to the beginning of Śrīvijaya's rise in power; once again these details are drawn from the writings of Yijing, whose works we have cited frequently. At the time of his first trip to the holy places of Buddhism in 671, the pilgrim stopped in Śrīvijaya for six months to study Sanskrit grammar (Chavannes 1894: 119). "In the city of Foshi," he wrote,

> there are more than a thousand Buddhist priests whose minds are turned to study and good works. They examine and study every possible subject, just as Madhyades´a [India]; the rules and ceremonies are identical. If a Chinese priest wishes to go to the West to hear and read [the original Buddhist texts], he would do better to stay in Foshi for a year or two and practice the appropriate rules, then could go on to central India.

It is this passage from the writings of Yijing that gave rise to the thought that the capital of Śrīvijaya, far from being merely an important entrepôt port, was also a key centre of Buddhist scholarship, on a par with the greatest Indian universities.

On his return from India, where he had spent ten years at the University of Nālandā, Yijing again stayed in Śrīvijaya, this time for four years, from 685 to 689, during which time he copied and translated Sanskrit Buddhist texts into Chinese. In 689, after a brief trip to Canton, where he had gone to fetch four assistants, he returned to set himself up in Śrīvijaya, writing his two memoirs there (Chavannes 1894, Takakusu 1896). In 692, he sent his manuscripts to China, returning there himself in 695. This was also the year in which Śrīvijaya sent its first ambassadorial mission to China (Pelliot 1904: 334). During his second stay in Palembang, Yijing noted, in his second work, that Malāyu, where he had made a stopover for two months in 671, "is now the

country of Srîbhoga [Śrīvijaya]" (Takakusu 1896: 10), a brief sentence that
has caused much ink to flow in the effort to interpret it, but which undeniably marks the imperialist advance of Śrīvijaya among the rival principalities
still sharing the southern part of the island of Sumatra at the end of the seventh century. The seven inscriptions discovered locally, some of them dated,
appear to fall into two classes: commemorative stones inscribed to record
certain royal gifts or victories, and oath stones designed for use in ceremonies performed to ensure political loyalty. Both classes provide information
concerning the polity. The commemorative stones (all of which have been
found in Palembang, with the exception of the single line added to the Kota
Kapur oath stone) tell us not only that the polity bore the Sanskrit name of
Śrīvijaya, but also that the ruler had taken the Sanskrit name and epithet
Śrī Jayanāśa. The ruler's title, however, was a local one: *punta hiyang*. This
was, moreover, a religious title rather than a political one. Jayanāśa's activities for which he commissioned commemorative inscriptions included: his
performance (in AD 683) [Kedukan Bukit inscription (Palembang)] of a ritual to ensure success before leading a military expedition upstream to an-
nex part of the interior; two other military campaigns against internal rivals;
the dedication (in AD 684) [Talang Tuwo (Palembang)] of a garden for public
use as part of a programme of Buddhist good works; a visit to a Buddhist
monastery; and (in AD 686) [Kota Kapur inscription (Bangka)] the dispatch
of a military expedition against "Bhūmi Jāwa" (apparently referring to Java),
which was not submissive to Śrīvijaya (Wisseman-Christie 1995: 265–66).

The result of all this is that the period of time covered by the historical
and dated documents we have been speaking of does not extend beyond the
last quarter of the seventh century, and that after this, historically speaking,
we possess only brief allusions in the Chinese annals to some diplomatic missions from Śrīvijaya to China in 702, 716, 724, 728, and 742.

In these, Śrīvijaya emerges more as a place of Buddhist scholarship than
as a centre of international trade; nevertheless, some observations of an imperialist nature give reason to believe that the practice of Buddhism did not
preclude the basely materialistic concerns of a young state wishing to secure
revenues without commercial competition.

Arab Navigation in the Archipelago

G. R. Tibbetts

Though Chinese travelers such as Fa Hsien and I-Ching traveled through Southeast Asian waters in the first millennium, sailors from further West—India, Persia, and especially the Islamizing lands of the Arab Middle East—also passed through this watery domain. Arab geographers, navigators, and historians have left an important documentary record about Southeast Asia in the early period. It is clear that the Arabs knew about Sumatra, Java, and even islands farther east than these, and they associated precious commodities with all of these places, sometimes erroneously but also often correctly. The Indonesian archipelago was seen as the site of "Ophir," or "land of gold," but it was also a strange, distant place where horns, bezoar stones, and rare spices could be procured, albeit at great cost. Indonesia was also important to these geographers because they knew it lay athwart the oceanic routes to China, a place for which Arab worldviews held almost as much esteem as did the burgeoning consciousness of Europe. Knowledge of Indonesia's islands was passed down generationally among Arab geographers, with some of the information transmitted rather uncritically from one writer to the next. Other fragments of knowledge about toponyms, geographies, and the availability of commercial products—such as the ones translated here by the historical geographer G. R. Tibbetts—were slowly amended over time.

The island of Sumatra was not known in great detail to the Arab sailors except for a portion of the north coast and the route down the west coast to Fansūr. The rest of the islands is given by the texts as a series of places at certain latitudes often with a large number of variations. The islands off the west coast are a little confused, because of the different uses of the term Mārūs and Manqāmārūs.

The route from the northern point of Sumatra to Fansūr is not terribly clear, but as there was only one practicable passage for sailing vessels down this coast, it is possible to follow Sulaimān's directions from the *Minhaj*. Throughout the route his bearings are too near the south point and he him-

self says elsewhere that the general direction of this coast is south-east. Because of the high mountains on the mainland in this part of Sumatra, the
ship could remain in sight of land all the way to the port of Susu. The most
tricky part to navigate in this area is the channel between the Banyak Islands
and the mainland and the usual passage is between the island of Jawi Jawi
and the mainland but keeping fairly close to the former. The rock with the
trees on it mentioned by Sulaimān may be one of the rocks north of Pulau
Banyak, perhaps one of the group Pulau Delapan. It may, on the other hand,
be the island of Jawi Jawi itself as this forms the landmark for all attempts to
pass through this passage. There are no trees in Jawi Jawi at the present time,
but many of the islands have one or two conspicuous coconut trees on them.
The cape which juts out to the sea soon after these islands must be Ujong
Singkel or Ujong Raja. As in the previous part of the route, the directions for
the second part are too near the south point. A course SE by S from Ujong
Singkel does not pass near any islands, there are one or two further out to the
sea and many close to the coast; in fact far more than seven. The seven most
prominent are perhaps Pulau Kasi, Sikandang, Birakan, two called Mankir,
Panjang, and Karang or instead of this perhaps Ujong Silabi. The island of
Bangā or Bangāla is presumably Pulau Karang outside the harbour of Baroes
(Fansūr).

Among the other places mentioned by the texts on this part of the west
coast of Sumatra, Fansūr is obviously the camphor port of Baroes. The
Minhaj says that it is famous for *Riyāhī* camphor. The latitude usually given
to Fansūr is 6° L.B., but Sulaimān in the '*Umda* gives 6½° as an alternative,
and Ibn Mājid in one place in the *Fawā'id* gives 5°. South of Fansūr appears
Bāsalār. The form of the name is the same as that used for Pulau Parcelar on
the Malay Peninsula and the two are probably confused. The island meant
here is Pulau Masalar or Musala, opposite the town of Sibolga and a little to
the south of Barus.

Sinkel (6½° L.B.) and *Shūshū* (7° L.B.) are two ports bearing the same names
at the present time, although the modern form for the latter is Susu.

Mākūpāng at 7½° L.B. (alternative form in the *Fawā'id*) is the kingdom of
Mancopa given by Tomé Pires, which he equates with Daya. Cortesão in editing Pires's work shows that Barros makes these separate places. He therefore
equates Mancopa with Laboh. Our text, however, makes it fairly clear that
Mākūpāng must have been in the vicinity of Daya; Laboh is too far to the
south.

On the lower part of the west coast of Sumatra are found the places
Pariāman (5° L.B.) and *Indrapūrā* (4° L.B.) still existing today. The former, to

the north of the modern port of Padang was the port for the Minangkabau kingdom in the interior and the Arab texts also called it *Manaqābūh*, a reading which is probably correct.

The islands off the west coast of Sumatra are mentioned in detail although the terms Manqāmārūs and Mārūs which are applied to them lead to a certain amount of confusion. Manqāmārūs (practically always in the texts) at 7° L.B. is the same as Tomé Pires's Maruz or Maruz Minhac. There are a number of early references to the term *marus* in this part of Sumatra, both as an island and as a race. Marsden in his *History of Sumatra* states that a people called Marus or Maruwi lived on the islands of Nako-nako (Hinaku) west of Nias and in Hog Island or Simalu and in the Banyak Islands. Schroeder, in his book on Nias, says that the present-day name of Maruwe is Hulo Siitu, and that it is a small island off the west coast of Nias. There are other references on seventeenth- and eighteenth-century maps to this name applied to one or other of the islands of this group and it is possible that the whole group were at one time called Marus. Hence the Arab reference to "many islands." Cortesão, when editing the text of Tomé Pires says that Minhac Marus is Nias, but the Arab texts makes it clear that Manqāmārūs must be the large island to the north known as Si Malu or Simeuleu (Horsburgh's Hog Island).

The term *Mārūs* may be an alternative form for Manqāmārūs or may be a general name for all these islands north of Nias, whereas Manqāmārūs is the name of the largest of them (Simalu). In one place, Sulaimān equates Mārūs with Banyak. Ibn Mājid makes Manqāmārūs an island and Mārūs a mountain on the Sumatran mainland. Sulaimān also states that the *Batak* people who inhabit the highlands of Sumatra originally came from Manqāmārūs.

The east coast of Sumatra has two practical routes according to the texts, one fairly close to the coast calling at the ports of Sumatra, 'Arūh and Rokan, and the other out to sea, from Sumatra to Pulau Berhala and then to Pulau Jumar. The latter is the one Ibn Mājid uses to reach Malacca. *Jāmis Fūla* at 1° P.S. is the starting point for all the routes round the island of Sumatra. This is the Gauenispola of Marco Polo, Gomespola of Linschoten, and Pulo Gomez of later European authors. Thomas Bowrey makes it a large island twenty miles west of Pulau Way, which is called Pulau Bröeh or Lampuyang today (Horsburgh's Pulo Brasse). The highest mountain on this island bears the name Gunong Chömö and this may be a remnant of the old name. The large island is obviously that meant by the Arabs, although Horsburgh called a small island to the south Pulo Gomez. This is called Pulau Kelapa in the map in Hurgronje's *The Achehnese* (English ed., 1906), but Pulau Bunta by the *Malacca Strait Pilot* (1934). Ferrand sees the name as compounded of the Malay "Pulau" and the Perso-Arab "buffalo." Close by is *Mās Fula* which probably stands for Pulau Mas "the island of gold." It must be, from the directions given, the same as Pulau Way but the latter does not occur as Pulau Mas on any European map.

On the coast here the texts first place Lāmurī which is the port in the neighbourhood of Acheh mentioned by the early geographers. Jebel Lāmurī would be the range of mountains behind, this name applying to the range as far east as Pedir. *Mandara* mentioned in the '*Umda* is a new port which had arisen probably in place of Lāmurī, which disappears about this time. The actual position of Mandara is as much a puzzle as that of its predecessor, for this is the only reference to it and the town of Acheh arose at the beginning of the sixteenth century and presumably replaced Mandara as a port. Further south come *Pēdir* at 7¾° L.B. and *Shumutra* at 7½° L.B. The former was a well-known port and minor kingdom in Sumatra before the rise of Acheh, on the site of the present day village of Pidië, and the latter represents that port of Samudra-Pasé, one of the earlier Muslim kingdoms of South-East Asia and visited by Ibn Battuta. There is still a small village of Samoedra on the Pasé river which enters the sea a little to the east of Lho' Seumawe.

In this neighbourhood, the *Minhaj* also mentions *Jibāl Jā'iza*. The word in the text is and could be an adjective after *Jibāl* (mountains) but there is no word in classical Arabic which would make good sense, although there is a South-Arabian colloquial word which may mean "isolated" or "elongated." On the other hand, it could be the name of a place in Sumatra, or the name of a place elsewhere whose mountains are compared to those in Sumatra. If it is read Jā'iza, it could represent the Malay Gajah "elephant." No Gunong Gajah exists in this part of Sumatra, but Gle Goh, the hills immediately behind Diamond Point, and hence the first hills seen when sailing from the direction of Penang, were called by early European sailors, Elephant Mountains (Oliphantsberg). Varthema uses the term Gaza for the Straits of Malacca, and Winter Jones says that the Arabic for this strait is Boghāz. Perhaps Jebel Jā'iza means the mountains of the Malacca Strait.

Perlak, *Ra's Pērak* may be Diamond Point, but is more likely to be Ujong Peureula further to the south. It was here that the state of Perlak existed, which was mentioned by Marco Polo. The name is mentioned by the Arabs once more.

'Ārūh is Aru, a large bay on the east coast of Sumatra, but to the north of Medan. In Sulaimān's text 'Ārūh appears to the south of Medan at 6° L.B. It is possible that the Arabs confused this place with the Aroe Islands (Pulau Jumar). Both are marked on early European maps as Aruh and the mainland of Sumatra opposite the Aroe Islands sometimes bears the name of Aruh on these maps. The port called Ārūh by the Arabs therefore seems to have been

at the mouth of the Pannai river. The latitude given to Ārūh by the Arabs varies between 7° and 6° L.B. but is always less than that of Medan (7°) where the
two are mentioned together. It is never far enough north for a position on the
modern Aru Bay. Medan occurs as *Madyanā* and this must represent Deli, an
early kingdom and the port of Medan at the present day.

The Islands in the South-East

The Arab authors have only a very vague idea of these islands, and only a few
indications of latitude are given, these with many alternatives. The islands
are divided roughly into two groups; large islands comprising those north of
the Java and Banda Seas, and small islands, known as the Timor islands. The
first group includes what is probably Formosa, but the only mention of the
Philippines is extremely doubtful.

Jilolo was the largest island in the south-east according to Sulaimān: hence
it is obvious that Borneo was not recognised as one complete island. It is actually the largest of the Molucca Group, also called Halmahera. The island
of Borneo is shown as *Barnī* or *Burnai*, and in one case *Barānī*. The latitude
range (5° P.S.–6° L.B.) shows that the whole of the island must be meant; this
range is therefore approximately correct but the whole is placed too far to
the north with regard to the Malay Peninsula. It was thought probably to
consist of several smaller islands. Sulaimān and in most cases Ibn Mājid calls
the South China Sea, the Sea of Barnī from Cape Kanbūsā. *Maqāsar* presumably stands for the whole of Celebes. The range of latitude allowed this island
(in one case 3½° and in another 5°, i.e., 6° L.B.–1° L.B.) shows that the Arabs
must have regarded this as a large island too but unlike Borneo it appears too
far to the south in relation to the Malay Peninsula. *Malūkū* or the Moluccas,
and the latitude given varies between 6° L.B. and 2° L.B. *Bāndan* (7° G.B.) is the
Banda Islands. All of these islands appear a long way from Java, because of the
latter's inclination to the south-east.

Of the other islands mentioned outside the Timor Group *Kīramu* and
Karīmu is mentioned by Ibn Mājid and used by him as a centre for a complete
set of bearings round the compass. Its position shows that it is probably Kari-
moendjawa. *Bayān* is possibly the island of Bawean. *La'ūdī* is probably Pulau
Laut, the large island in the south-east of Borneo. Tomé Pires mentions a port
of Laue on the coast of Borneo, east of Tanjongpura, although Portuguese
maps have it to the west near Sukadana (as Lao, Lave, Laoe). This place is
another possible equivalent. *Sūluk* must be the Sulu islands, north-east of
Borneo and finally *Karīmātā* actually would be the Karimata Islands to the
west of Borneo.

The term *Timor* according to the texts includes the whole of the islands to the south-east of Jāwa but what is actually meant is all the islands south and east of Sumbawa and Sumba. Whether or not Flores is included it is impossible to tell. Sulaimān divides the islands of Timor into two groups which he calls *Tīmor Lor* and *Tīmor Kīdul*, that is North and South Timor. Ferrand imagines Timor Lor to be a mistake for Timor Laut which is an island to the east of Timor also called Tanimbar, but there is no need for this as the point of the Kidul is then lost. Just which islands belong to each group is very difficult to ascertain. Perhaps the Timor Laut group are the Northern group and Timor proper and the islands round it, Timor Kidul. In this case Timor Laut would be the same as Timor Lor. (Is this possible that the Javanese Lor has been misunderstood by the Malay sailors of the Archipelago and the name corrupted to Timor Laut?) Another division of the islands would be to call Timor proper, Timor Kidul and to make the Zuidwester Eilanden, Timor Lor. Ibn Mājid also has the North-South division of Timor, but he gives them the Arabic forms *Jāhī Tīmor* and *Suhailī Tīimor*.

Viewing the Borobudur

Jan Poortenaar

*Built in the eighth century CE in central Java, the Borobudur is one of the most famous
religious monuments in the world and the largest Buddhist structure on the planet.
With thousands of stone Buddhas and miles of friezes, sculptures, and adornments,
it is the supreme manifestation of the Buddhist tradition still left in Indonesia. As
the archipelago started to become more and more Islamicized from the sixteenth century onward, the Borobudur fell into disrepair, as it was considered a place built by
unbelievers. Life went on around the Borobudur as parts of it crumbled in the tropical climate. When Europeans "found" the structure in the mid-eighteenth century, it
took on a very different meaning as a place of pilgrimage and connection with Java's
vaunted classical past. A string of Western travelers, artists, writers, and aesthetes
trekked great distances to see the huge temple/mountain and to wax poetic about its
meanings and legacies in a quickly changing world. Jan Poortenaar, a Dutch artist
who visited the Borobudur during the colonial period, thought that the structure was
a man-made, stone-clad gateway to the possibilities of eternity and nirvana in a different world.*

Of the Borobudur itself what can be said? In its manifold beauty, architecture
and all that architecture can express reaches its apotheosis, so that one feels
that faithfulness to any single one of its elements would add immeasurable
value to the best in our contemporary buildings. Rich beyond power or description in ornament, yet highly monumental; baroque and classical; exu-
berant and restrained; fragile and massive; severe yet full of mystery; it is the
incarnation of the inevitable and eternal, beyond earthly understanding. It is
the universe itself symbolized in carved stone.

Obscure is its origin, like the ages which brought it forth. The Javanese
regime which fell in the eighth century of our era is lost in the mists of antiquity; forgotten too is the great maritime power which at that time conquered
Mid-Java; but here in this phantasmagoria of breathing stone, the spiritual
life of those dark powers lives on, and bears its inscrutable witness to their

Buddha statue at Borobudur temple. Photo by Tineke Hellwig.

passing. Since the eighth century, when it was built, the temple has borne the witness.

Like jewels in some exquisitely modeled medieval tiara the Buddhas are set, hundred beyond hundred. Many are damaged, but many more remain seemingly untouched of time. The tempests and earthquakes of a thousand years have left their beauty unimpaired.

Soft, like blossoms, are the mosses which fleck the stones with green and silver-pale loveliness. Far above on the highest terraces glows the symbolled life of eternity. Urging toward it the earthly existence of Buddha its sculptured Banaspatis guard each gateway to the remoter beyond. Shiva they are, the Devourer of Time, through whom everything passes away into Nirvana reigning above.

In Praise of Prambanan

Though the Buddhist Borobudur temple is undeniably more famous, many scholars find the Hindu Prambanan temple complex, constructed at about the same time (eighth to ninth centuries), to be an even more beautiful marvel of historical Javanese architecture. Prambanan was built by the Sanjaya dynasty in devotion to the pantheon of Hindu gods. The stories of the classical Ramayana, inherited from India but given their own life and form in classical Indonesia, adorn the walls of the structure, telling the tales of Prince Rama, his wife Sita, and the abduction of the latter to Sri Lanka by the demon Ravana. Sita was eventually saved by the monkey Hanuman, and the narrative of this great epic is woven into the very architecture as a story in stone. Prambanan is the single greatest relic of Hinduism in Java, where the religion once had extreme importance before receding to a few isolated polities and to the nearby island of Bali. Though Prambanan was crumbling and in a state of disrepair for many centuries, the Dutch archaeological service eventually restored the temple, so that it appears today largely how it must have looked more than a millennium ago (sadly, an earthquake in 2006 again damaged the structure). It is still one of the most beautiful artifacts of Indian influence in Indonesia today.

Prambanan temple. Photo by Tineke Hellwig.

The *Nāgarakṛtāgama*

Mpu Prapañca

During the fourteenth and fifteenth centuries, the Majapahit kingdom of eastern Java was the strongest polity on that island, and indeed in eastern Indonesia generally. It was ruled by a succession of powerful Hindu/Buddhist kings, though the most famous single personage of the entire kingdom was undoubtedly a man named Gajah Mada, a minister rather than a king. The Nāgarakṛtāgama is one of the most important texts of this classical period. It was written in Old Javanese in epic ballad form by Mpu Prapañca in 1365, and it describes the pomp and circumstance of the Majapahit court at the height of its power. Ceremony was important in Majapahit, and as this selection makes clear, everyone had their place in the grand processionals of the court and was treated according to their station. The offerings on display were sumptuous, and each prince or courtier tried to outdo the next by presenting a display of conspicuous consumption that would awe the court and the assembled retinue of elites. On the sixth day of the ceremony the prime minister Gajah Mada himself made his offering, and as was the custom in classical Java, the largess of this most important of the ruler's servants ultimately outshone all the rest.

Canto 65

1 The morning of the day of the full moon was the time when it came
   forth to receive homage in the midst of the court,
Loud trumpets, conches and *gañjaran* drums in front escorting it in
   countless numbers.
On the splendid throne, high and mysterious, that was the place where it
   was paid homage,
And when all the Buddhists, young and old, had gathered they uttered
   praises in due order.
2 Then the princes came together into the presence to offer flower-
   worship, humbly with wives and children,
Joined by the Prime Minister Gajah Mada as the most eminent of those
   who came forward with their wives to pay their respects.

As well as the officials stationed in the Outer Regions and kings of all the
   other countries;
When they had finished devotedly paying their respects, their seats were
   arranged according to rank.
3 The Prince of Paguhan was the first to present his perfect food,
And Śrī Handiwa-handiwa was the form of his float which bore *dakūla*
   cloth and betel-leaf.
As for the Prince of Matahun, his float was a white bull and also resembled
   Nandinī;
This produced money and food from its mouth in a remarkable way
   without ceasing.
4 As for the Prince of Wĕngkĕr, his excellent food was neatly arranged and
   carried in a single-pillared pavilion;
Its arrangement was amazing in every respect and of great value,
   accompanied by the bestowal of money equally among the court.
The Prince of Tumapĕl's float was also unusual and charming, with the
   bodies of loving women;
Each one had a day of his own for expressing a variety of ideas.
5 The main one was His Majesty's: an extraordinary Mount Mandara was
   his carrier for the wonderful food,
At the time when it was being turned, models of the host of gods and
   demons circling around it—those who saw it were awed.
Carp of an exceedingly large size filled a fish-pond, swimming around
   together,
As if ill and drunken because of the sea-water, increasing the bustle of
   the court.
6 Thus every day all kinds of floats, whatever was superior and excellent,
   were intended as offerings to the deity;
The wives of officials, assessors and priests received a share of what was
   left of them, just the right amount each one;
Also the nobles, the leading relatives of the King, were bestowed with
   gifts as appropriate,
Not to mention the choice foods that were passed around among all the
   Kings troops in the court.

Canto 66

1 On the morning, then, of the sixth day, Bhatāra Narapati duly came
   into the presence with food,

As well as the most eminent of the nobles: their pavilions and
   processional shrines filled the place, carried in row on row.
The two Superintendents had as carriers ships, each depicting a scene
   from the ballads,
And as big as real ships; gongs large and small resounded back and forth
   to escort them, deeply impressing onlookers.
2 The Prime Minister, Gajah Mada, on the same day made an offering in
   the presence:
His fine float was of grieving women in the shade of a *nāgasari* tree,
   rājasa blooms vying to entwine it.
The officials and Āryas in charge of the districts followed on with the
   village heads and joined them in making offerings;
Many were the shapes of their carriers for food: some were boats,
   mountains, pavilions or fish—they kept on coming.
3 The good taste of the princes' celebration was most wonderful, the very
   ultimate in excellence,
For on the seventh day the money, clothing with limitless food did not
   stop.
They were distributed to the Four Estates, primarily the priests followed
   by the countless officials, who were pleased,
And in their enthusiasm the *juru* and *sāmya* started clapping their hands
   because the drinks were flowing like a torrent (?).
4 Crowds of onlookers from all directions milled noisily without a gap;
The appearance of the court and those offering food, these they watched,
   pushing for a place.
The Queen danced in the hall, and it was only ladies who looked on in
   her Presence,
All seated in serried rows, tightly packed—some forgot themselves as
   they looked on in speechless wonder.
5 Every performance that might please the people the King held:
See the story tellers and masked dancers taking turns with all kinds of
   singers every day!
Not to mention the warriors shouting challenges—naturally the ones as
   loud as thunderclaps gave people a fright and made them laugh,
And in particular the constant donations to every kind of person begging
   alms caused everyone to be joyful.

Images Arjuna and Kresna

In the early centuries of the Common Era the great Indian epics, the Ramayana and Mahabharata, found their way to the islands of Southeast Asia. During the period of the Hindu kingdoms their narratives were absorbed, narrated, translated, adjusted, and transformed. They laid the foundation for the story cycles in the wayang (theatre) performances, a tradition that continues today. While the Ramayana is particularly popular on Bali, scenes from the Mahabharata are more commonly performed on Java. Wayang kulit is the shadow-puppet theatre in which a single puppeteer (dalang) manipulates two-dimensional figures made of perforated leather (kulit means "leather" or "hide") behind an illuminated screen. In a nightlong performance that lasts some nine hours, the dalang narrates, chants, and brings the puppets to life accompanied by a gamelan orchestra. The undisputed male hero of the wayang is Arjuna, the third of the Pandawa brothers. He is emblematic for what the Javanese consider refined (alus) because he is insightful, skilled as a warrior, and charming toward women. Kresna, his loyal charioteer and advisor, is Vishnu's avatar.

The shadow puppet figure of
Arjuna. J. Kats. *Het Javaansche
Tooneel*, vol. 1, *Wajang Poerwa*.
(Weltevreden: Commissie voor
de Volkslectuur, 1923).

The shadow puppet figure of
Kresna. J. Kats. *Het Javaansche
Tooneel*, vol. 1, *Wajang Poerwa*.
(Weltevreden: Commissie voor
de Volkslectuur, 1923).

II

Early Modern Histories

If Indonesia was crowded with a range of foreign visitors by the end of the medieval period, then the early modern age in the archipelago was positively a festival of diversity. Many scholars of Indonesia use the term *early modern* to roughly correlate the fourteenth to eighteenth centuries of Indonesian history with similar patterns occurring in the wider world, though this may be an imperfect comparison. In Indonesia, in addition to the Persians, Indians, Arabs, and Chinese who had been passing through the region in the first millennium CE, Portuguese, Spaniards, Englishmen, Dutchmen, Frenchmen, and a range of other Europeans also came during this time. Contrary to the normative narrative of immediate European impact on this part of the world, for the most part Europeans fit themselves into the motley throng of actors who had come to Indonesia to trade and travel as chance allowed. Only in a few places, namely, in Batavia (modern Jakarta) and in certain outposts of the Moluccas, or Spice Islands, did the initial European presence prove transformative or hugely consequential.

This was so because at first Europeans came in very small numbers. Indonesians were used to travelers passing through: men like Ibn Battuta, who had voyaged all the way from Morocco by way of Mecca, India, and the Maldives and who had attached himself to regional courts as an honored guest. Marco Polo had also come through alone, but it was the ships of another unexpected visitor—the Chinese admiral Zheng He and his enormous fleet—that made by far the greatest impression on early modern Indonesians. Of these voyages (there were seven in total between 1405 and 1433) only a few touched down in the archipelago, but there were enough to convince the local population that China had much more to offer—and fear—than anything Europeans might bring. Zheng He's legacy included some immigrants and possibly a helping hand in the transmission of Islam (he was a Muslim), but the arrival of the first European ships would have a far greater impact. No one knew this at the time, however; most Europeans mixed in local markets and were probably considered more or less like everyone else.

This particular moment, however—the middle centuries of the second millennium CE—did not entirely resemble earlier times. Though itinerant travelers such as the Chinese monk Fa Hsien in the fourth and fifth centuries and Marco Polo in the late thirteenth century had been transiting through Asia for a very long period, in early modern times the traffic grew denser. More people were on the move, and they were traveling in better ships and carrying more cargo with them over longer distances. Indonesia, blessed with a number of valuable natural products but particularly nutmeg, mace, and cloves—the "big three" of the international spice trade—was becoming an ever more popular destination for adventurous ships. Though the earliest Europeans fit into existing networks and traded in these products along with everyone else both locally and translocally, by the early seventeenth century the Dutch attempted to put an end to these well-worn patterns. Concentrating their will (and their firepower) on the spice-producing islands of the Moluccas, they killed and destroyed rivals to secure the islands for themselves. This was accomplished within only a few decades. By the mid-seventeenth century, the Dutch had garrisoned the Moluccas, which had served as a crossroads of interethnic trade for a long time.

Through the vehicle of the voc, the *Vereenigde Oost-Indische Compagnie* (United East India Company), the Dutch thus waged constant war on anyone who tried to defy their hugely profitable monopoly on Indonesian spices. Spices were marked up many times as they changed hands across Eurasia, finally reaching European consumers back in Europe; the Dutch would eventually control this trade from producer to consumer across the length of the entire Old World. A tiny country's control of much of the world's largest archipelago became one of the most important facts of the early modern age and significantly conditioned the processes of history over the course of several centuries. The Dutch monopoly was never complete and underwent constant challenges from a range of interested parties, European and Asian, but it brought Indonesia into the center of world events and of global geopolitics for much of the early modern period.

The documents reproduced here show some of the outline of this evolving story. Far from being solely a narrative about Europeans, an account of the early modern age in Indonesia must take into account Ibn Battuta and Zheng He, Iberian forts and Dutch settlement, all in one interwoven story. In an attempt to regulate the unwieldy process of commerce that stretched across this huge array of islands, and across nearly as large a panoply of interested parties, the Dutch closed contracts for protectorates. But although the contracts were concluded and signed, the Dutch did not have the wherewithal to always enforce them, which led to cracks in their monopolies, as well as in their façade as rulers of a conquered archipelago. That particular story line would come true later, but in early modern Indonesia power was multipolar, and trade was carried out by a wide range of commercial actors. Accounts such as Willem Lodewijcksz's and Edmund Scott's show how diverse Indonesia's ports remained, even after the European presence in the islands was nearly a century old. Everyone who wished to trade still had a place, yet those freedoms would eventually come to an end.

It remains to be asked what legacies the early modern age left in Indonesia—what is still with us, how did it change the islands, and were Indonesians better off for the opening of their world to the global economy, and its concomitant pressures and opportunities? It seems clear that Indonesia became a far more important place than it had previously been in the global economy, and the textiles, manufactures, and people that washed onto its shores bore testament to this newfound centrality and importance, not just as a thoroughfare but as a final destination for many ships. Yet this period might also, in hindsight, be seen as the beginning of Indonesia's subjugation to outside forces, some of which were content to take what they could from the islands and give little back in return. In the early seventeenth century, one island in the Moluccas was bartered between the English and the Dutch for another in the New World: the island in the Moluccas is Pulau Run, the one in the Americas was called New Amsterdam, now better known as Manhattan. It is in this dissonance that some of the irony of the legacies of the early modern age still makes itself felt, both to Indonesians and to Americans through their unlikely, entwined pasts.

Ibn Battuta at Pasai

Ibn Battuta

Ibn Battuta traveled in the mid-fourteenth century to Pasai, a small coastal sultanate in northern Sumatra and the first place in Indonesia to accept Islam. Muslim traders (and perhaps missionaries) had traveled there from India several decades prior to this, but this part of Sumatra had clearly been engaged through trade, envoys, and occasional war with the wider world of the Indian Ocean for a very long time. Ibn Battuta was a Moroccan jurist, and much historiography compares his vast travels to those of Marco Polo; he traveled farther than the Venetian did, however, and his perspectives on life along the maritime routes have a distinctly Muslim flavor. Because of Ibn Battuta's high status as a man of learning, he was accepted in many places including India, Sri Lanka, the Maldives, and perhaps even China. In Pasai, he was a fellow Muslim, so his stories of the wider world were eagerly devoured by the sultan of that place and the ruling classes, who desired to know more about happenings in the rest of the Daral-Islam (the abode of Muslim lands). Yet Ibn Battuta was also keen to report on what he saw in Islamic northern Sumatra—a frontier outpost of his religion that fascinated both him and his readers.

Twenty-five days after leaving these people we reached the island of Jawa [Sumatra], from which the incense called *jawi* takes its name. We saw the island when we were still half a day's journey from it. It is verdant and fertile; the commonest trees there are the coco-palm, areca, clove, Indian aloe, jack-tree, mango, jamun [jambu], sweet orange, and camphor cane. The commerce of its inhabitants is carried on with pieces of tin and native Chinese gold, unsmelted. The majority of the aromatic plants which grow there are found only in the districts occupied by the infidels; in the Muslim districts they are less plentiful. When we reached the harbour its people came out to us in small boats with coconuts, bananas, mangoes, and fish. Their custom is to present these to the merchants, who recompense them, each according to his means. The admiral's representative also came on board, and after interviewing the merchants who were with us gave us permission to land. So we went ashore to the port, a large village on the coast with a number of houses, called Sarha.

It is four miles distant from the town. The admiral's representative having written to the sultan to inform him of my arrival, the latter ordered the amir Dawlasa to meet me, along with the qadi [kadi] and other doctors of the law. They came out for that purpose, bringing one of the sultan's horses and some other horses as well. I and my companions mounted, and we rode in to the sultan's capital, the town of Sumatra, a large and beautiful city encompassed by a wooden wall with wooden towers.

The sultan of Jawa, al-Malik az-Zahir, is a most illustrious and open-handed ruler, and a lover of theologians. He is constantly engaged in warring for the Faith [against the infidels] and in raiding expeditions, but is withal a humble-hearted man, who walks on foot to the Friday prayers. His subjects also take a pleasure in warring for the Faith and voluntarily accompany him on his ex-peditions. They have the upper hand over all the infidels in their vicinity, who pay them a poll tax to secure peace.

As we went towards the palace we found near by it some spears stuck in the ground on both sides of the road. These are to indicate to the people to dis-mount; no one who is riding may go beyond them, so we dismounted there. On entering the audience-hall we found the sultan's lieutenant, who rose and greeted us with a handshake. We sat down with him and he wrote a note to the sultan informing him of our arrival, sealed it and gave it to a page, who brought the reply written on the back. After this a page brought a *buqsha*, that is, a linen bag. The lieutenant taking this led me by the hand into a small house, where he spends his hours of leisure during the day. He then brought out of the *buqsha* three aprons, one of pure silk, one of silk and cotton, and the third of silk and linen, three garments like aprons which they called un-derclothing, three garments of different kinds called middleclothing, three woollen mantles, one of them being white, and three turbans. I put one of the aprons in place of trousers, according to their custom, and one garment of each kind, and my companions took the rest of them. After food had been served we left the palace and rode in company with the lieutenant to a garden surrounded by a wooden wall. In the midst of the garden there was a house built of wood and carpeted with strips of cotton velvet, some dyed and others undyed. We sat down here along with the lieutenant. The amir Dawlasa came bringing two slave girls and two men servants, and said to me "The sultan says to you that this present is in proportion to his means, not to those of Sultan of Muhammad [of India]." The lieutenant left after this, and the amir Dawlasa remained with me.

The amir and I were acquainted with one another, as he had come as an envoy to the sultan at Delhi. I said to him "When can I see the sultan?" and he replied "It is the custom of our country that a newcomer waits three nights before saluting the sultan, that he may recover from the fatigue of his journey." We stayed for three days, food being sent to us thrice a day and fruits and sweetmeats every evening and morning. On the fourth day, which was a Friday, the amir Dawlasa came to me and said "You will salute the sultan [today] in the royal enclosure of the cathedral mosque after the service." After the prayer I went in to the sultan; he shook me by the hand and I saluted him, whereupon he bade me sit down on his left and asked me about Sultan Muhammad and about my travels. He remained in the mosque until the afternoon prayers had been recited, after which he went into a chamber there, put off the garments he was wearing (these were the robes of the kind worn by theologians, which he puts on when he comes to the mosque on Fridays), and dressed in his royal robes, which are mantles of silk and cotton. On leaving the mosque he found elephants and horses at the gate. Their custom is that if the sultan rides on an elephant his suite ride on horses, and vice versa. On this occasion he mounted an elephant, so we rode on horses, and went with him to the audience hall. We dismounted at the usual place [where the lances were] and the sultan rode on into the palace, where a ceremonial audience was held, the sultan remaining on his elephant opposite the pavilion where he sits [at receptions]. Male musicians came in and sang before him, after which they led in horses with silk caparisons, golden anklets, and halters of embroidered silk. These horses danced before him, a thing which astonished me, though I had seen the same performance at the court of the king of India.

My stay at his court in Sumatra lasted fifteen days, after which I asked his permission to continue my journey, since it was now the sailing season, and because it is not possible to travel to China at all times of the year. He fitted out a junk for us, provisioned us, and made us rich presents—may God reward him!—sending one of his courtiers with us to bring his hospitality gift to us on the junk.

Chinese Muslims in Java

H. J. de Graaf and Th. F. Pigeaud

H. J. de Graaf and Th. F. Pigeaud, two Dutch scholars working in the middle decades of the twentieth century, translated and annotated the so-called Malay Annals of Semarang. *The* Annals *make for a problematic text that describes, among other things, the history of Chinese Muslim communities on the north Java coast. The text is significant because it gives details about the beginnings of this community at a very important time—the decades after the great voyages of Zheng He, the Chinese admiral who arrived on Java in the early fifteenth century, en route to other destinations in the Indian Ocean. The Chinese Muslim connection with Java in this period is interesting to scholars because Islamization of the archipelago has traditionally been assumed to have come via Indian, Arab, and Persian traders from farther West. There is now considerable evidence that Chinese Muslims may have had more to do with the process than thought earlier, with the* Annals *comprising only a part of a corpus of texts, archaeological data, and linguistic vestiges mined for this particular history. Regardless of the complete veracity of the Semarang annals, the translation by de Graaf and Pigeaud helps to shine further light on the notion that Islam came to Indonesia from many sources—not just from the Middle East, but from other way stations along the Islamizing world of Asia that had already begun to convert.*

Malay Annals of Semarang: Text with Translation

[I. INTRODUCTION]

1368–1645
The Ming dynasty, which employed a very great number of Hanafite Muslim Chinese officials, reigned in China.

1403–1424
The reign of the emperor Ceng Tsu, called the Yung Lo period. This was the heyday of China in maritime matters.

1405–1425

The fleet of the Ming emperor of China, commanded by Admiral Haji Sam Po Bo, dominated the seas and shores of Nan Yang (South-East Asia).

[2. BEGINNING OF THE CHINESE EXPANSION]

1407

The fleet of the Ming emperor of China seized Kukang (= Palembang) which from ancient times had been a nest of Chinese pirates, non-Muslims, from Hokkien. Cen Tsu Yi, the chief of the pirates of Kukang, was taken prisoner and brought in chains to Peking. There he was publicly decapitated as a warning for the Hokkien Chinese all over Nan Yang countries. In Kukang the first Hanafite Muslim Chinese community in the Indonesian Archipelago was established. In the same year another was settled in Sambas, Kalimantan.

1411–1416

Hanafite Muslim Chinese communities were also established in the Malay Peninsula, in Java, and the Philippines. Java mosques were built in Ancol/ Jakatra, Sěmbung/Cěrbon, Lasěm, Tuban, Tse Tsun/Grěsik, Jiaotung/Jo-ratan, Cangkil/Majakěrta, and in other places.

[3. SETTLEMENTS OF CHINESE MUSLIMS IN JAVA]

1413

The fleet of the Ming emperor of China put in for a month at Sěmarang for ship repairs. Admiral Sam Po Bo, Haji Mah Hwang, and Haji Feh Tsin came very often to the Hanafite Chinese mosque in Sěmarang for divine service.

1419

Admiral Haji Sam Po Bo appointed Haji Bong Tak Keng in Campa to control the flourishing Hanafite Muslim Chinese communities which were spreading along the coasts all over the Nan Yang countries. *(Note this was again done by the Japanese Army which appointed Marshal Terauchi in Saigon, 1942–1945, to control all Japanese generals/Saikosikikans all over the Nanyo countries.)* Haji Bong Tak Keng appointed Haji Gan Eng Cu in Manila/Philippines to control the Hanafite Muslim Chinese communities there in Matan/Philippines.

1423

Haji Bong Tak Keng transferred Haji Gan Eng Cu from Manila/Philippines to Tuban/Java to control the flourishing Hanafite Muslim Chinese communities in Java, Kukang, and Sambas. At that time, Tuban was Java's main port, with the kingdom of Majapahit as hinterland.

Haji Gan Eng Cu became a kind of consul-general of the Chinese government, the Ming emperor, having control of all Muslim Chinese communities in the southern Nan Yang countries including Java, Kukang, and Sambas. In respect of the still existing but degenerated Majapahit kingdom Haji Gan Eng Cu became a kind of Muslim "Kapten Cina" [Head of the Chinese community] in Tuban. But then, since the Chinese fleet of the Ming Emperor dominated all navigation in the seas of the Nan Yang countries, Haji Gan Eng Cu became also de facto harbour-master in Tuban. As a reward for his services as a provider to the court of Majapahit [of foreign supplies] from the harbour of Tuban he was given the title A Lu Ya by the Majapahit Government. It was given to him by Raja Su King Ta, Ruler [Queen] of Majapahit, 1427–1447 *(Supposition: Haji Gan Eng Cu is Aria Teja, and he is the father of Nyi Agĕng Manila who was born in Manila, Philippines.)*

1424–1449

His Excellency Haji Ma Hong Fu was appointed ambassador of the Ming emperor of China at the court of Majapahit. Haji Ma Hong Fu was a son of the War Lord of Yunnan, and a son-in-law of Haji Bong Tak Keng. On the way to the court of Majapahit Haji Ma Hong Fu and his family were escorted by Haji Feh Tsin who had already visited the court of Majapahit three times as a roving ambassador. *(Supposition: Putri Campa was the wife of Haji Ma Hong Fu.)*

[4. SAM PO BO IN JAVA]

1425–1431

Admiral Haji Sam Po Bo became the Governor of Nangking and de facto viceroy of South China including the Nan Yang countries. In the Hanafite Chinese mosque of Sĕmarang a special divine service was celebrated with congratulatory prayers on behalf of Admiral Haji Sam Po Bo.

1430

Admiral Haji Sam Po Bo himself occupied the district of Tu Ma Pan in East Java and presented this district to Raja Su King Ta. Gan Eng Wan, Haji Gan Eng Cu's brother, became Governor of Tu Ma Pan, under the suzerainty of the Majapahit ruler. He was the first Regent in the Majapahit kingdom who professed Islam.

1431

Admiral Haji Sam Po Bo passed away. The Hanafite Muslim community of Sĕmarang celebrated a "Ghaib" divine service.

[5. GAN ENG CU IN TUBAN]

1436

Haji Gan Eng Cu went to China to pay respects to emperor Yang Yu. Tuban, which controlled Kukang, Tse Tsun, and Sambas, was emancipated from Campa and became a Chinese Crown Colony under the immediate authority of the Governor of Nangking. Emperor Yang Yu conferred upon Haji Gan Eng Cu the rank and robes of a Supreme Mandarin, complete with the token of his rank in the shape of a golden girdle.

[6. BEGINNING OF BONG SWI HOO'S CAREER]

1443

Swan Liong (= Diamond Dragon), the head of a gunpowder factory in Sĕmarang, was appointed by Haji Gan Eng Cu to be a Muslim Kapten Cina in Kukang, which was often attacked by non-Muslim Chinese pirates. Swan Liong was a very efficient artillery officer. He was a half-blood Chinese born in Cangki/Majakĕrta from a Chinese damsel. Swan Liong was said to be in fact a son of Yang Wi Si Sa/Raja Majapahit.

(Note: Half-blood Chinese whose fathers were non-Chinese were usually given names consisting of only two syllables without the hereditary first names which for the Chinese are family names. Half-blood Chinese whose fathers were Chinese were given complete names consisting of three syllables. Supposition: Swan Liong is Aria Damar. Yang Wi Si Sa is Prabu Wisesa, the last Raja of Majapahit but one.)

1445

Bong Swi Hoo was made assistant to Swan Liong in Kukang, to have on-the-job training. Bong Swi Hoo was a grandson of Haji Bong Tak Keng in Campa. In the same year Bong Swi Hoo was entrusted by Swan Liong with a mission to pay his respects to Haji Gan Eng Cu in order to get an appointment as Muslim Kapten Cina somewhere.

1446

Bong Swi Hoo called at the Hanafite Muslim Chinese community in Sĕmarang.

1447

In Tuban Bong Swi Hoo married a daughter of Haji Gan Eng Cu. *(Supposition: Bong Swi Hoo is raden Rahmat, called Sunan Ngampel. Bong Swi Hoo's wife is Nyi Agĕng Manila.)*

1447–1451

Bong Swi Hoo was appointed by Haji Gan Eng Cu to be Muslim Kapten Cina in Jiaotung/Bangil which is situated at the mouth of the Brantas Kiri (= River Porong).

[7. DECLINE OF CHINESE IMPERIAL AUTHORITY IN JAVA]

1448

The Regent Gan Eng Wan (alias Aria Suganda) was murdered. The district Tu Ma Pan freed itself from Majapahit suzerainty. In the following fifty years, many Hanafite Muslim Chinese were killed by the Tu Ma Pan people who had retained their Hindu-Javanese religion.

1449

His Excellency Haji Ma Hong Fu called at Sĕmarang on his return travel to China. Haji Ma Hong Fu's wife passed away and was buried in Majapahit according to Islamic rites.

[8. ACTIVITIES OF BONG SWI HOO IN SURABAYA]

1450–1475

As a consequence of the decline of power of the Ming dynasty the fleet of the Chinese Ming Dynasty did not come any more to visit the Hanafite Muslim Chinese communities in the Nan Yang countries. These Hanafite Muslim Chinese communities degenerated. A very great number of Hanafite Chinese mosques were changed into Sam Po Kong temples complete with a status of the demi-god Sam Po Kong in the place of the pulpit. This was the case for the instance in Sĕmarang, Ancol, Lasĕm, and other places.

After the death of Admiral Haji Sam Po Bo, Haji Bong Tak Keng, and Haji Gan Eng Cu, Bong Swi Hoo out of necessity took the initiative to rule the deteriorating Hanafite Muslim Chinese communities of Java, Kukang, and Sambas, without any connection to China.

Editors' Note

Bong Swi Hoo took also the initiative to switch over to the Javanese language and to reinforce his deteriorating Hanafite Muslim Chinese communities with Javanese people. The result was decisive for the history of Java.

Portuguese Sources on Products and the Monsoons

Robert Nicholl

Portuguese documents on the arrival of Iberians in the Indonesian archipelago con-stitute a little used source for writing the larger history of these islands, which has been penned almost entirely in English and in Dutch. The Portuguese and Spanish both arrived in the sixteenth century, though the Portuguese presence proved the more durable of the two Iberian projects. The Portuguese took Malacca by force in 1511, and from this port on the Malay Peninsula they sent ships to reconnoiter the Spice Islands in particular, hoping to gain control of the transit of nutmeg, mace, and cloves to European markets. This endeavor proved beyond the means that the Portuguese possessed in Southeast Asia, but they did manage to act as impor-tant traders in these and many other goods—notably gold dust, camphor, and other valuable animal and plant products—throughout a wide section of the archipelago. Portuguese ships touched down in Ternate, Tidore, Borneo, and a number of other Indonesian islands; they left a lasting legacy, some of it genetic, in Flores and Timor. The letters below, written between 1524 and 1574 and compiled by the historian Rob-ert Nicholl, show the increasing Portuguese cognizance of the "lands beneath the winds."

18. *The Capture of the* Trinidad *by the Portuguese—1522*

Letter from Jorge de Albuquerque, Captain-General of Malacca to King João III, dated Malacca, 1 January 1524. Insulindia. *Vol. I, page 184.* Translation by R. P. Manuel Teixeira.

The Castilians came to the Maluco, as I have written to your Highness, (I say to your Highness, for it was addressed to your father, whom God has called to himself). Regarding the ship, which I had said had left the island of galleons, as I was informed, I have had no more news of her. The junks in this year five hundred and three (*sic*) did not bring much news from there, and it is not known what has happened to her. It is my opinion, and I believe it, that she may be completely lost, because she leaked badly, and if she was saved, it would be better known in Portugal than in these parts.

The other ship, that remained in the Maluco for repairs because she leaked so badly, completed her repairs, took her cargo on board again, and left for Castile. She wished to return the way she had come, but when she had gone 1,300 or 1,400 leagues, she encountered head-winds from the east, either north-east or south-east. When they ran out of provisions and water, they saw that it was useless to go on, so they returned again by way of the Maluco, and when they were in the Maluco on their way to Burneo, where there are many islands, Dom Gracia Henriques, who had sailed to the Maluco with Antonio de Brito, as I have already written, and wanted to explore Borneo and from Borneo to go to Malacca, met the ship on the way and captured her. The Castilians surrendered to him, and he took her again to the Maluco, and the ship remained in the Maluco, where she last was. He took the Castilians in his ship and brought them here to Malacca, whence he sent them to Cochin to the Captain-General, as the late King has commanded me in his letter, which I shall show to your Highness when you care to see it. The other ship left for Castile, but these Castilians are in the hands of your Highness.

19. *The Route from the Moluccas to Malacca by Brunei—1523*

Letter of Antonio de Brito to King João III, dated Ternate, 11 February 1523. Insulin-dia. *Vol. I, page 137.* Translation by R. P. Manuel Teixeira.

I, Sire, took with me Dom Garcia from Banda, whom I met in the ship that I left Malacca for Jorge de Albuquerque, because he had nobody to navigate it, as I have already said to your Highness, on account of the news that I found there about the Castilians.

I sent him by way of Borneo, because by that way there are four hundred leagues to Malacca, and by the way I came there are six hundred leagues, and as from Banda to the Moluccas there are five (*sic*) leagues, it is necessary to wait for another monsoon, for it seemed to me to render a great service to Your Highness in sending him to explore (that route), and also to send him this way with news of what was happening here in the year 1522. By this route they can come from Malacca to the Moluccas in a month. It (the route) had been discovered in the time of the King of Malacca, and they navigated from Borneo to the Moluccas. I hope in Our Lord that this May 1523, towards the end (of the month) I shall finally explore it for Your Highness, for Dom Garcia did not explore it as the pilot was incompetent, and he returned to the Moluccas.

20. *Simon De Breu's Exploration of Borneo Waters—1523*

Discoveries of the New World. By Antonio Galvão. Hakluyt Society, *Vol. xxx, 1862, page 152.*

In the same year, 1523, in the month of May, Antonio de Britto, being Captain of the Isles of Maluco, sent his cousin Simon de Breu to learn the way by the isle of Borneo to Malacca. They came in sight of the islands of Manada and Panguensove, they went through the Straits of Treminao and Taquy and to the Islands of St. Michael, standing in seven degrees, and from thence discovered the islands of Borneo and had sight of Pedra Branca, or the White Stone, and passed through the Straits of Cicapura, and the citie of Malacca, acquiring knowledge of many islands, sea and land.

21. *The Importance of Borneo—1524*

Letter from Jorge de Albuquerque, Captain General of Malacca, to King João III, dated Malacca, 1 January 1524, and attached to the previous letter. Insulindia. *Vol. I, page 152.* Translation by R. P. Manuel Teixeira.

I have not sent them (the prisoners from the *Trinidad*) in this caravel of Dom Garcia, because there would be more Castilians than Portuguese; and also (in order) to discover the route from the Moluccas to Malacca by way of Burneo, whence they (the prisoners) came, because from Burneo to the Moluccas is one hundred leagues, and there will be found pilots to take us thence, because there are always many junks sailing from Burneo to Malacca. And by this route one may sail from Malacca and arrive at the Moluccas in a month, as I have already related above to Your Highness, and because Burneo is one of the richest islands that exists in these parts, where is much gold, camphor, and very great trade to many places, where Your Highness may get great profit.

27. *Voyaging by the Monsoons—1529*

A Summary Description of the Moluccas and Banda, dated 1528. Insulindia. *Vol. IV, page 17.* Translation by R. P. Manuel Teixeira.

From Cochin to Malacca they set sail from the 15th April to the 8th May, and from Malacca to the Moluccas by way of Burneo they leave from the 10th August to the 20th of the same month. They have to remain in Moluccas for five months in order to return by way of Burneo; they have to return in March or April of the following year. From Malacca for Cochin they will set sail in August and September and will arrive at Queda. Seventy leagues from Malacca, where they wait one and a half months for the monsoon. They will arrive in Cochin in November. Thus a junk setting sail for the Moluccas will go there and return in eighteen months going and returning by way of Burneo. The said junks setting sail from Cochin on the 1st May, voyaging safely and arriving in Malacca, loading cargo and going by the way of Borneo, can go and return in fourteen or fifteen months to Malacca. Coming by the way of Banda will take the same time or one month more, because in this time it can go and come to Cochin, but those of Burneo will arrive first at Malacca and will be refitted there, while those coming from Banda cannot do so.

28. *The Extent of the Brunei Dominions ca. 1530*

Asia Portuguesa. Vol. ii, page 349. Translation by R. P. Manuel Teixeira.

Chapter V. Of the isles of the Moluccas, of which João de Barros treated in his Decada iii, Book V, Chapter V and in other parts.

The fourth part is the archipelago of the Celebes to the east [*sic*] of the Moluccas. Here are many famous islands, the chief of which are Mindanau, the Celebes with many rivers, Bisaia with much iron. Maszaga and Masbate with much gold, Sologo with many pearls. But they are not collected by the natives. Some obey the King of Borneu, others those of Ternate and Tidore.

76. *Voyaging by the Monsoons ca. 1579*

Summary of Matters Appertaining to the Province of the East Indies. By Padre Alexander Valignano s.j. 1579. *Insulindia. Vol. iv, page 151.* Translation by R. P. Manuel Teixeira.

The Moluccas lie more than four hundred leagues from Malacca, wither one can come and go in two monsoons, that is, two certain times of the year, which are the 1st August by way of Borneo, and the 2nd December by way of Jaoa and Amboino.

77. *Instructions to Don Juan De Arce for the Second Expedition to Brunei—28 February 1579*

Blair & Robertson. Vol. iv, pages 186 sq.

Instructions as to what Captain Don Juan Arce de Sadornil is to observe in this present expedition to the island and city of Borney, which belongs to his Majesty:

The route and navigation, both going and coming, are known, and you have a pilot. Therefore I shall say nothing more than to warn you not to disembark on any of the islands, unless forced to by necessity, and then with a force of men, so that the natives may commit no treason.

When you reached the island of Borney in the district of (*illegible words in* M.S.)—the place to which Captain Esteban Rodriquez went for *contrayerva*, and the people engaged in trade and gave information as to the condition of Borney—where, they tell me, is the *panguilan* Maraxa de Raxa, you shall halt at the coast to see if he is there, which you will ascertain from such Moro vessels as you will meet before reaching that place. And finding him there, you will give him my letter. You will ascertain from him the condition of affairs in Borney; the whereabouts of Soltan Lijar, and what he intends to do; whether Portuguese have gone thither, and if they are still there; and other things which may seem proper to you.

You are already aware that I left as commander in Borney the *panguilan* Maraxa de Raxa, and that I gave him a letter of assurance and friendship, and another to the *panguilan* Salalila; you must observe all friendship toward them.

As soon as you have arrived, you must confer with the *panguinals* (sic: *panguilans*); you shall ascertain from some Indians whether the king of Borney has returned, and his condition, and that of the settlement. If these *panguilans* tell your Grace that you should not go to (the port of Borney), but should remain where you are, and that they are going to talk to the king—or whatever other reasons they may adduce, your Grace will tell them that you are ordered to anchor at the island of Mohala, where the battle occurred, and that your Grace will await them there for conference; and your Grace will tell them that they should read my letters to the king. And, if it seems advisable to your Grace, you shall write to the king, briefly, telling him of the firm friendship that he will receive from me, and the great advantage that will undoubtedly accrue to him in becoming a vassal of his Majesty, the king, our sovereign.

The First Dutch Voyage to the Indies, 1596

Willem Lodewijcksz

*Cornelis de Houtman's voyage to the Indies established the first Dutch presence there
at the end of the sixteenth century. Iberians had been coming to the area for many
decades already, though they had left only a very small footprint. It was by no means
clear that the Dutch would be able to come all the way to the Indonesian archipelago
in large numbers either, as the distance from Europe was exceedingly far, and the dangers that ships and their crews had to face along the journey made even the thought of
such voyages extremely harrowing. Mortality ratios on many of these voyages reached
50 percent. It was evident when de Houtman arrived in Java that other "foreigners"
had reached these waters first—including the aforementioned Portuguese, but also
Chinese, Indians, and Persians. De Houtman's journey set the stage for more Dutch
ships to arrive, with this system of isolated voyages giving way by the early seventeenth century to a united effort at trade, contact, and exploration initiated under
the aegis of the VOC. De Houtman's voyage marked the beginning of centuries of
commerce, occupation, and eventual accommodation.*

How We Came to Sunda Harbor and What Happened There on Arrival

Sailing slowly then (because of the unfavourable currents and also the change
of wind: for after midnight the wind is from the east until 10 a.m. and then
from the west until evening, which makes it difficult to pass through the
Straits) we came, on June 22nd, to Bantam Harbor and the Coast of Sunda,
seeing before us an uninhabited, green, beautiful island which is called Pulo
Panjan [Pulau Pandjang, or Long Island] by the Javanese; it is said to be a long
island. To the north of it we saw about seventy small sails, which looked like
a forest from afar; these were (as we were told) all fishing boats, which made
it evident that Banten must be a very large, populous town. In a bay of the
Java country we saw a *iunco* [junk], which is a Javanese ship . . . and a canoe
came to us from this ship, but we could not understand what was said, so they
went back to the *iunco* and brought someone who spoke Portuguese, who
asked us where we came from. And when we asked him to come aboard,

First voyage of Dutchmen to the East Indies. Drawing no. 37A-106, courtesy of KITLV, Leiden.

he went back to the *iunco*, which immediately hoisted sail and disappeared around a corner, where we lost it (from sight). In the afternoon we measured thirty-four fathoms, after that twenty-four, and after two hours ten, so that the bottom seemed to become drier very suddenly; for shortly afterwards we measured only eight fathoms and our shallowest depth was seven fathoms, but then it became deeper again. We had the high Java mainland to starboard, and Pulo Panjan to port, the former to the east, the latter to the west; we measured a depth of ten fathoms. To the east we saw some more, uninhabited islands, also straight ahead the town of Bantam, whither the small sailboats were heading; the wind was northeast from the sea and we sailed a course (at the wish of our sounding-man) of southeast to south. Towards evening a *Parao* [prow] came from the town, carrying six Portuguese with their slaves; they came aboard and told us they had been sent by the Governor, who, together with all the inhabitants, was greatly afraid of us; they asked us from whence we came, to which we replied: from Holland, in order to trade with them, in all friendship, their spices against our merchandise; to this they answered that we certainly had come to the right place but at an unsuitable time: because five days ago they had sent five *somas* (which are Chinese ships) to China and that one we had seen lying in the bay that morning was looking for cargo along the coast; they showed us great friendship. And since we inquired urgently about the King they told us that he had succumbed before Palimban [Palembang] (a town situated on Sumatra, which had rebelled) with many of his people, at the time they occupied most of the town but then, because of the death of their King, they had left town again. . . .

Through the Portuguese we offered the Governor all friendship and service. The Portuguese upon leaving our ship feigned pleasure and so sailed to the town, where they told the Governor of their experiences.

On the 24th we came somewhat closer to the island, and cast anchor at seven fathoms close to the Island of Pulo Panjan; to the southwest of us we had another uninhabited green island, from which a tiny river flowed; here we stayed and our sounding-man went to the town of Bantam which we saw from afar lying two miles away. The naval admiral, called Tomogon Angabaya, came to our ship(s?) and talked to us through an interpreter, offering us friendship and refreshment in the name of the Governor, and all that was in the Governor's power; (asking us) to come to the town as well as to him personally; we thanked him very much for this, telling that if he should like to come over he would be welcome. He wanted some (ship's) biscuit, which was given him, after which we excused him, since he had some business on the long island, so he said; (but) then we saw him go back to the town without having gone to the island. . . . Shortly afterwards the Judge of the King's Tolls, called Sabander [*shahbandar*, collector of the harbor dues or harbormaster] came, and with him the Portuguese, who offered us all friendship in the name of the King and the Council, as a proof of which they brought us many chickens, goats, and other fruits. . . .

The next day Tomogon Angabaya came with the Sabandar, offering us on behalf of the Governor and themselves all that we might need, and expressing the wish that we should not trust the Portuguese because they were seeking to play us tricks and were so double(-faced) that one could never know their hearts and their manner, and we need not be afraid: for the harbor was free for all merchants: promising also that we should receive all spices in preference to others. They wished to see some merchandise and we showed them some, presenting them with eight (lengths) of green *Caffa* [gauze cloth used for Moslem turbans]. After this a black man came to us on behalf of the Governor; he was a *Quillin* [a Klingalese, from the Coromandel coast of India] commonly called Quillin Panjan, or the tall Quillin, acquainting us with the fact that the whole kingdom desired a service from us, that is, that we should sail to Palimban [Palembang] situated on Sumatra and take it under fire from the sea; that they would march by land in order to capture the town; they would give us all that would be found in the town; this we refused since we had come to trade and not to wage war, he then left our ship, just before . . . two . . . men had come on board, who wished to see our nautical maps, on which we showed them how far we had come in order to obtain their friendship and their trade, with which they showed themselves very satisfied, the more so when they heard that we could come thence and go back in six months; also that we had been underway fourteen months looking for the way. . . .

The next day, being the 26th of that month, (people of) several nationalities came on board, with whom we traded in all friendship and who wished that we would not trust the Portuguese. We showed them some merchandise which pleased them exceedingly. We sent a manned boat to the western corner of Java, three miles farther west than Pulo Panjan, where there was a small village, in order to buy some cattle, but since the people were slaves they were not allowed to sell any; so we bought a large pot of wet indigo for three little Nuremberg mirrors. In the meantime a high courtier (or so it seemed) came to the ship *Mauritius*; we showed him our maps and then he left our ship again; later we understood that he was a bad character sent by the Portuguese to spy upon us. The Chinese brought several kinds of merchandise on board, as porcelain, silk goods, silk, and others. . . .

The 27th of the month many *Paraos* came alongside in the morning . . . (and) the Sabandar came aboard, very urgently requesting that we should come and greet the Governor on land and present him, according to the old customs, with some gem on behalf of our King, in token of peace and confederation; four midshipmen were sent for this purpose with a gift of beautiful crystal glasses, a gilded mirror, and some scarlet cloth; they went with this Quillin Panjan. When they came to the harbor they found the water very low, the harbor was even dry, but from the marks on the palisade it was clear that at high tide the depth must be as much as eight feet. On arrival, they were met by the Portuguese and after a feigned *Beso las manos* [I kiss your hands] they [the midshipmen] were separated from the others and met by the Sabandar who led them to the Governor's palace; the latter was still at table and therefore they waited in the front courtyard. . . . The Governor appeared here within a short time . . . (and) they immediately presented (him) with their gifts, asking him if it might please him to come and visit their masters in order to negotiate a firm alliance and covenant; through his interpreter he answered that he would take this into consideration. From there they went to the Sabandar's courtyard, who then served them some preserves, and from here they went back on board that same evening. The next day we brought all our guns on deck since we heard the news that the Governor would come and visit us the next day; we prepared everything in order to receive him well. Several gentlemen came aboard, also merchants from Coraçone [Khorasan, in northeast Persia] and many others, who honored us with gifts of clean cinnamon water and brandy. Many fruits were offered for sale, as radishes, onions, leeks, etc.

The Web of Batik

Cloth was one of the most important imports into the Indonesian archipelago for much of the early modern period. Significant quantities of cloth came from India, and there is good evidence that trade in this item was being carried out on a vast scale long before Europeans became involved in it, after the Portuguese conquest of Malacca in 1511. Cloth was particularly important in connecting south Indian weavers with Sumatra and Sulawesi, and fine specimens of patolas *and other textiles have turned up in grave sites from very early times. Yet by the seventeenth century, a large percentage of this cloth was going to Java, where both indigenous elites and commoners used it for sarongs. Batik, the process of wax impression with designs that allowed dyes to be pressed into cloth in ever more elaborate patterns, became popular throughout the Indonesian archipelago in a range of forms and styles. It eventually became one of the most recognizable crafts connoting cloth of Indonesian origin and artisanship. On Java, browns and golds were prized, particularly in the courts of Solo and Yogyakarta, where individual pieces could be worth huge sums. Batik stands as one of the true symbols of Indonesian life—a batik-clad man or woman can be found among the elite or lower classes, on Java or elsewhere in the archipelago, historically and today.*

Batik pattern. Photo by Eric Tagliacozzo.

An Englishman in Banten

Edmund Scott

Ten years after de Houtman's account of Banten in 1596, and on the other side of the fin de siècle divide, Edmund Scott's description of the port shows how quickly things had moved along from the point of view of internationalization. Banten is now identified as part of a string of cosmopolitan trading towns along the northern Javanese coast. This narration of the rise of the pasisir is important because it heralds European cognizance of the ascendance of the maritime littoral as the engine of change in Java, rather than the interior courts, which had been the locus of power for centuries. Banten, Scott tells us, was very populous; its ruler practiced absolutism. Yet the fact that the Dutch were starting to build structures not out of perishable wood but out of brick gives a sense about European designs on permanency in their dwellings and their plans for the future. A simple architectural reference such as this can help us understand how nearly imperceptibly things were changing on the ground, until the local ruler realized that dislodging a trading community such as the Dutch—who had arrived in small numbers at first, but whose numbers were ever expanding—might prove more troublesome a proposition than had first appeared.

Edmund Scott Describes Bantam, Java Major, 1606

Java Major is an island, which lyeth in 140 degrees of longitude, from the middle part of it, and in 9 degrees of latitude; being also about 146 leagues long, east and west, and some 90 broade, south and north. The middle part of which land is for most part all mountaines, the which are not so steepe but that people doe travaile to the toppe of them, both on horsebacke and on foote. Some inhabitants dwell uppon those hills which stand next [i.e., nearest] to the sea; but in the verie middle of the land (so farre as ever I could learne) there is no inhabitants. But there are wild beasts of divers sorts, wherof some doe repaire neere the valleys adjoining to the sea, and devoure many people. Towards the sea for most part is low moorish [i.e., marshy] ground, wherein stand their principal townes of trade; the chiefest whereof lye on the north and north-east side of the island, as Chiringin [Ceribon],

Bantam [Banten], Jackatra, and Jortan or Gressey [Gresik]. The which lowe ground is verie unwholesome and breedeth many diseases, especially unto strangers which come thether; and yield no marchandise worthy trading for, or speaking of, but pepper; the which hath been brought in times past from all places of the land to Bantam, as the chiefe mart towne of that countrey. The which towne for trade doth farre exceede Achin or any towne or citie thereabouts. And pepper was wont to be brought thether from divers other countreys; which of late yeeres is not, by reason that the Dutchmen trade to every place to buy it up.

This towne of Bantam is about three miles in length; also very populous. There are three great markets kept in it every day, one in the forenoone and two in the afternoone. That especially which is kept in the forenoone doth so abound with people that they thronge together as in many faires in England. Yet I never saw any kinde of cattell to sell, by reason that there are verie few tame in the countrey. Their foode is altogether rise, with some hens and some fish, but in no great aboundance.

The Javans houses are altogether built of great canes and some few small timbers, being sleight buildings. In many of the principall mens houses is good workemanship shewed, as carvings, &c. And some of the chiefest have a square brick rowme, being built in no better forme than a bricke-kill[n]; which is onely to put in all their household stuffe when fier commeth; but they seldome or never lodge not eat in them.

There are many small rivers running thorough the towne. Also there is a good rhode for ships; whereby, if they were people of any reasonable capacitie, it would be made a verie goodly citie. Also it is walled round with a bricke wall, being verie warlike built, with flankers and turrets scowring everie way. I have been told by some that it was first built by the Chineses, and by others that it was first built by the Portingales; wherefore I cannot say certainely by which of them it was first built; but it is most likelye by the Chineses, be reason of the oldnesse of it, for in many places it is fallen to decay for want of repayring.

At the verie west end of this towne is the China towne; a narrow river parting them, which runneth crosse the end of the China towne up to the Kings court, and so through the middle of the great towne, and doth ebb and flowe, so that at a high water both galleys and junckes of great burthen may goe up to the middle of the great towne. This China towne is for the most part built of bricke; everie house square and flat overhead, having bordes and smale timbers or split canes layd over crosse, on which is layd bricks and sand, to defend them from fire. Over these bricke warehouses is set a shed, being built up with great canes and thatched; and some are built up with small timbers, but the greatest number with canes onely. Of late years, since wee came thether, many men of wealth have built their houses to the top all fire-free; of the which sort of houses, at our first coming, there was no more but the Sabindars house and the rich China marchants house; which nevertheless, by means of their windowes and sheds round them, have been consumed with fire.

In this [China] towne stand the English and Dutch houses; which are built in the same manner, only they are verie much bigger and higher than the ordinarie houses. And the Dutchmen of late, though with great cost and trouble, have built one of their houses up to the top all of bricke, fire-free, as they suppose.

The King of this place is absolute, and since the deposing and death of the late Emperour of Damacke [Demak] is held the principall king of that island. He useth always marshall law upon any offender whome hee is disposed to punish. More, if any private mans wife, or wives, bee taken with dishonestie (so that they have good proofe of it), they have power in their owne hands to cause them presently to be put to death, both man and woman. And for their slaves, they may execute them for any small fault. If the King send for any subject or stranger dwelling or being in his dominions, if he send a man, the partie may refuse to come, but if once he send a woman, hee may not refuse nor make no excuse. Moreover, if any inferiour bodie have a suit to a man of authoritie, if they come not themselves, they always send a woman; neither doe they ever come or send but they present the part they sue too with some present, be their suite never so small. To everie wife that a Javan (being a free man) marrieth, he must keep ten women slaves, which they as ordinarie use as their wives; and some of them keepe for every wife forty slaves, for so they keepe ten, they may have as many more as they will; but they may have but three wives onely.

The Javans are generally exceedingly proud; although extreame poore, by reason that not one amongst a hundredth of them will worke. The gentlemen of this land are brought to be poore by the number of slaves that they keepe, which eat faster than their pepper or rise growth. The Chineses do both plant, dresse, and gather the pepper, and also sowe their rise; living as slaves under them, but they sucke away all the wealth of the land, by reason that the Javans are so idle. And a Javan is so proude that he will not endure one to sit an inch higher in height above him, if hee bee but of the like calling. They are a people that do very thirst after blood. If any Javan have committed a fact worthy of death and that he be pursued by any, whereby he thinketh hee shall die, he will presently draw his weapon and cry *Amucke*, which is as much [as] to say: I am resolved; not sparing to murther either man, woman, or childe which they can possibly come at; and he that killeth most dieth with greatest honor and credit. They will seldom fight face to face with one another, or with any other nation, but do altogether seek revenge of their enemie cowardly albeit they are, for the most part, men of a goodlie stature. Their law for murther is to pay a fine to the King, and that but a small summe; but evermore the friends of the partie murthered will be revenged on the murtherer or his kindred. So that the more they kill one another, the more fines or profite hath their King.

Their ordinarie weapon which they weare is called a crise. It is about two foote in length; the blade being waved and crooked too and fro . . . and withall exceeding sharpe; most of them having the temper of their metall poysoned, so that not one amongst five hundred that is wounded with them in the bodie escapeth with his life. The handles of these weapons are either of horne or wood, curiously carved in the likenesse of a divell, the which many of them do worship. In their warres their fight is altogether with pikes, darts, and targets. Of late some few of them have learned to use their peeces [i.e., muskets], but verie untowardly.

The gentilitie, both men and women, never goe abroad but they have a pike borne before them. The apparell of the better sort is a tucke on their heads, and about their loynes a faire pintado [printed or painted cloth]; all the rest of their bodies naked. Sometimes they will weare a loose coate, somewhat like a mandillion [a loose overcoat], of velvet, chamlet cloth, or some other kind of silke; but it is but seldome, and uppon some extraordinarie occasion. . . .

The men, for the most part, have verie thicke curled haire on their heads; in which they take great pride, and often will goe bareheaded to shew it. The women goe all bareheaded; some of them having their haire tucked up like a carthorse tayle, but the better sort doe tucke it up like our riding geldings tayles. About their loynes they weare of the same stuffes which I have before mentioned; always having a faire girdle or pintado of their countrey fashion throwne over one of their shoulders, which hangeth downe loose behinde them.

The principallest of them are most religious; but they very seldome goe to church. They doe acknowledge Christ to be a great prophet, whom they call *Naby Isat* [Nabi Isa, the prophet Jesus]; and some of them do keepe of Mahomet priestes in their houses. But the common people have very little knowledge in any religion; onely they say there is a God which made heaven and earth and them also. Hee is good (they say) and will not hurt them; but the Divell is naught [i.e., bad] and will doe them hurt; wherefore many of them, for want of knowledge, doe pray to him onely, for feare least he should hurt them. And surely, if there were men of learning (which were perfect in their language) to instruct them, a number of them would be drawen to the true fayth of Christ, and also would be brought to civilitie. For many which I have reasoned with concerning the lawes of Christians have liked all well, excepting onely their pluralitie of women, for they are all lasciviously given, both men and women.

The better sort, which are in authoritie are great takers of bribes, and all Javans in generall are badd paymasters when they are trusted. Notwithstanding, their lawes for debts are so strict that the creditour may take his debtour, his wives, children, and slaves, and all that hee hath, and sell them for his debt. . . .

They delight much in ease and musicke. And fir the most part they spend the day sitting crosse-legged like a taylor, whitling of stickes; whereby many of them become very good carvers to carve their cryse handles; and that is all the worke the most of them indevour to doe.

They are very great eaters; but the gentlemen allow their slaves nothing but rice sodden in water, with some rootes and hearbes. And they have a certaine hearbe called *bettaile* [betel], which they usually have carried with them wheresoever they goe, in boxes or wrapped up in cloath, like a sugerloafe; and also a nutt called pinange [areca-nut]; which are both in operation very hott, and they eate them continually, to warme them within and keepe them from fluxe. They doe likwise take much tobacco and opium.

A "Harem" in Aceh

*Aceh may well have been the most flourishing, crowded polity in the entire archi-
pelago in the sixteenth and seventeenth centuries. Sixteenth- and seventeenth-century
Aceh was a very cosmopolitan place when measured purely by contacts and exchanges
with other kingdoms and countries. Islam came to the Indies in this general region at
the end of the thirteenth century, and by the seventeenth century Aceh was a bulwark
of the religion and one of the most Islamized courts in these waters. Though Aceh
professed a comparatively strict version of Islam in comparison to other polities of the
archipelago, it did not stop the former from having several female rulers, as well as
a history of female military leaders who figured prominently in Acehnese wars over
the course of the centuries. The majority of elite Acehnese women, however, probably
led fairly circumscribed lives, as evidenced by the Gunongan, a strange but eerily
beautiful building made of stone by Sultan Iskandar Muda, who ruled Aceh between
1607 and 1636. In this unusual edifice he housed his "harem" so that his female retinue could relax in privacy under the watchful eyes of only the sultan himself. The
Gunongan became one of the architectural symbols first of Aceh's special status in
the Dutch Indies and then later in independent Indonesia, serving as a marker of the
autonomy of this kingdom under successive regimes (both Western and Indonesian)
of occupying rule.*

A "harem" in Aceh. Photo by Eric Tagliacozzo.

Contract with Banjarmasin

Anonymous

Although the initial Dutch presence in the archipelago was limited to Java and a few island outposts, mostly in the Moluccas, gradually the VOC came into contact with more and more indigenous polities and began to close contracts with these polities' rulers for the mutual benefit of both parties. Typically, the contracts stipulated how commerce was to be carried out, who was to be involved, and the mechanics of getting commodities to markets. Yet these treaties were also political in nature and described the rights and responsibilities of both the Dutch and the local sultanates and rajas whereby all future relations were to be judged. In the early centuries of the VOC, these documents tended to be more or less egalitarian; the Dutch were not yet in a position to fully dictate the terms of power and exchange. Treaties with the sultanate of Banjarmasin in southeastern Borneo, dated 1661 and 1664, show this fairly clearly. Yet as time wore on, such treaties—later called "short and long contracts" in the nineteenth century—tended to constitute less mutually beneficial partnerships. Rather, they represented symbols of a rapidly diminishing equality in the archipelago.

Articles of Agreement June 2, 1661

Articles of agreement and continuous Friendship agreed between the Pangeran Ratou of Martapoura and the Governor General Joan Maetsuijker and the council of the Indies at Batavia, closed under the date 2nd of June, 1661, in Batavia's dagh-register is written as follows.

First, it is agreed, that all the pepper in Banjarmasin will only be delivered to the Company and nowhere else.

Second, a fixed price for pepper has been agreed, one hundred and eighty *gantangs* of gold for a bucket, or sixteen reals (or other merchandise) that will approximate this value in this manner.

Third, it is agreed that merchandise is allowed to be brought to Martapoura, but only to Martapoura and to Banjarmasin and not elsewhere.

Fourth, it has been determined that, according to custom, for the imports and exports of merchants a toll will be paid.

Fifth, if one of the servants of the East India Company is found guilty of a crime, that the Pangeran Ratoe will not be allowed to punish him, but rather he will be delivered to the head of Martapoura.

Sixth, in the event of abscondances by Company men, either free men or slaves, to Martapoura or somewhere else, then the Pangeran Ratoe will not persecute them, but hand them over to the head of Martapoura.

Seventh, the head, who is at Martapoura, is left in continuous protection of the Pangeran Ratoe, and will remain untouched, so that all the mentioned articles of the agreement can be acted on.

Written on Tuesday, December 18.

Translation of the Contract, 1664

The Governor General Joan Maetsuijker has, with the Pangiran Ratu of Banjarmasin, a contract sealed in which the Pangiran Surjanata, Prince of Banjarmasin, in all parts will follow. He is to sell all of his pepper to the Company without being allowed to sell anything to other nations or Banjars.

The second article, which is also included in the contract says, that we will pay for one hundred and eighty *gantangs* pepper a *tahil* of gold or equivalent merchandise.

The third article is that we, the voc, it is agreed will be allowed to negotiate in Martapoura or Banjarmasin, either in a ship or in a lodge that may be found there.

The fourth article is agreed vis-à-vis tolls, that the Company will pay five ten hundreds *gantangs* in import as well as in export, without this being changed unless by prior agreement.

The fifth article is that if some Dutchmen commit crimes they are to be delivered to the Company, and they will not be tried by the Sultan of Banjarmasin.

The sixth article is that any slave or servants of the Company near or in Banjar, or Martapoera, who abscond shall again be delivered to the Company, and not to the king.

The seventh article is that the Sultan of Banjarmasin must protect all in his land, great as well as small, without molestation.

The time when this agreement was written is on a Friday the first day of the month Safar in the year 1664.

Translated from Dutch by A. van de Rijt and E. Tagliacozzo

General Missives of the voc

Anonymous

The voc started off as a small confederation of investors and ships in the early seven-teenth century, but it later developed into one of the most powerful quasi-state forces of political, economic, and military might anywhere in the world. The voc had trade outposts throughout the globe, but the core of Dutch power and Dutch profit resided in Indonesia. Though the Dutch were not the first Europeans to "find" the Indies, they were the first to consolidate their foothold there into something larger than the sum of its parts. Dutch trading posts began to slowly appear throughout the myriad islands of the Indies; voc merchants dealt in a great variety of commodities and were engaged in exchanges with a wide variety of peoples. The generale missieven, *or general dispatches, chronicled the day-to-day and week-to-week affairs of the com-pany, keeping track of which company servants and which ships were at which out-posts, what they were doing there, and how much profit they were contributing to the overall Dutch cause. These dispatches are one of the main sources that allow us to see the functioning of Indies trade and diplomacy on both a pan-archipelagic and a local scale.*

(*Compare* Daghregisters *1675; all ships of the return fleet back to Holland have passed the Cape except the* Free Sea, *which we hope has done so.*)

Severe disease has for some time reigned in the islands and has already taken away a large number of indigenes from our nation.

(*Marten Roos, after the death of W. Maetsuyker, stands in as the governor of Banda; a storm damages the nutmeg trees.*)

The same province and surrounding lands were also visited by Heaven with severe disease and death, by which many people have been pulled away, among whom are even the King Sultan Mandarsaha, who died January 3rd.

(*His descendant has approved the contract.*)

How the prince Calmatta (of Makassar) will judge these elections, time will learn, though hopefully, the benefits that he enjoys from the Company will keep him from breaking out into revolt.

The allies now and then have quarreled, which previously could not be completely avoided. There have been some months of drought causing the rice yield to be low this year.

The preacher Jacobus Rijnsdijck has returned with the fleet, having baptized there a decent number of children as well as the elderly.

(*The warehouses in Palembang and especially in Djambi are packed with pepper; money is flowing in well. Ordered rice from Siam; for data on Japan, compare* Beschrijvinge *ii, i, p. 451. In Bengal many ships are needed for transport for much silk that is stored in the warehouses; rice from Bengal and from Coromandel is in demand; no agreement has been made on a large cargo of silk from Persia; the office in Muscat will be informed.*)

While the Arabs have sought contact with us more for their own benefit than to allow us any kind of prominence in their country, we continue our war with the Portuguese, whose aggression against us is so great, that some of her ships, traveling from the Persian Gulf, met with some of our ships out in the sea near Diu (India). The ship the *Gecroonde Vreede* (leading the fleet) was attacked by cannon fire.

(*The relations at Surat remain good; the Portuguese are not making headway in Goa.*)

We have now been plagued four years in a row by the Muscat (Omani) Arabs. They have been presented with two thousand *thoman*, or about seventy thousand guilders toll, but they did not find this sufficient, so that, after having declined some of our offers, they took nothing and left in irritation.

(*Plans to transfer one Indian factory elsewhere, where there is already an English station; trade in Malabar goes badly.*)

The Raja of Cochin has complained with some other rajas to superintendent Van Goens; most of the difficulty lies in the transportation of goods. The governor and the Company would only give rights to diving for pearls, and other materials at sea without anyone else participating. We will also not allow native and foreign vessels without Company agreement to pass, and thus we will monitor all vessels that without the Company's consent travel in these waters. This has also long been a law that the Portuguese put into practice, however one commander, Van Rheede, is against these coercions, and thus a discussion has arisen about it.

(*Van Goens sr. has because of this discussion come to Batavia; he wants Malabar to be placed again under Dutch authority in Ceylon.*)

On the coast of Madura the whole land is in a chaotic mess because of revolts against de Neyck, without anyone knowing who the lord of the land is in reality. This is because of robberies by the lords of Mysore and other

Malabar princes because of trade. For the Company, otherwise things would be favorable and the trade considerable. The stations of the Company have on multiple occasions been attacked by robbers and native enemies, so the superintendent has ordered the parruas to be sealed off with a canal of eighteen feet and a force of about one hunded white men, who currently reside there, at the expense of the Company. The voc will also hire another 100 native soldiers, and at the cost of the parruas, another 150 to protect their own quarter. His Excellency has at our command stopped the building of a fortress, and we will discuss whether or not this slight improvement of the station by closing it in a half circle at the beach, will be enough to defend it.

(*At Ceylon things are relatively quiet.*)

The situation here appears to be favorable, despite the arrival of someone who lives as a *brahmin* and pretends to be a prince (faking this very well), so that the governor and my council thought that this could be the true prince who a long time ago was killed. We continue to discuss this. Whether he is with certainty the murdered prince, we have reasons to seriously doubt. This man has at his own initiative come to us and to the Company to ask for protection. One other man, who now has been at Batavia and is believed to be a faker, we have found necessary to send with the fleet to Ceylon for further examination and interrogation. We will treat both well, in the meantime.

(*One assumes that 100 to 120 soldiers have been sent from the fatherland to Ceylon, and that 225 men arrive from Batavia. For the eastern quarters six to seven hundred men are needed. Trade in Ceylon is growing.*)

So many people are needed for the protection of the rivers here, and once that is taken care of for the first time we will not have to think about permanent outposts or expansions. All of the lower lands here will be under our devotion.

Translated from Dutch by A. van de Rijt and E. Tagliacozzo

Negara: The Theatre State in Bali

Clifford Geertz

The anthropologist Clifford Geertz was for decades one of the most perceptive West-
ern scholars of Indonesian culture and society. In the second part of his career, he
outgrew Indonesian studies and in fact became one of the most important anthro-
pologists of the second half of the twentieth century. Geertz was interested in many
aspects of Indonesia: some of his more widely read work dealt with social relations
in a Javanese village, with the acculturation of Islam in the archipelago, and perhaps
most famously, with the "status bloodbath" of the Balinese cockfight. In this section,
Negara: The Theatre State in Bali, *he dwells on the intimate connection between*
status and power in classical Bali, as exhibited through the grandeur of public cer-
emony. The spectacular rituals of local life, explains Geertz, mirrored what the Ba-
linese believed to be the cosmic order: everyone had their place on earth, and this
worldly station directly correlated with a person's status in the larger universe.

The ceremonial life of the classical *negara* was as much a form of rhetoric as it
was of devotion, a florid, boasting assertion of spiritual power. Leaping alive
into flames (and, so it was thought, directly into godhood) was only one of
the grander statements of a proposition that royal tooth filings, royal temple
dedications, royal ordinations, and, in the *puputans*, royal suicides made in
other, no less categorical ways: there is an unbreakable inner connection between social rank and religious condition. The state cult was not a cult of
the state. It was an argument, made over and over again in the insistent vocabulary of ritual, that worldly status has a cosmic base, that hierarchy is the
governing principle of the universe, and that the arrangements of human life
are but approximations, more close or less, to those of the divine.

Other aspects of Balinese ritual life had other statements to make, some of
them in partial conflict with the point that the state ceremonies made: Status
is all. As the *negara* was but one among many social institutions in classical
Bali, so its obsession, rank, was only one among many obsessions. But that
obsession, and the cluster of beliefs and attitudes that grew up around it, was
about as pervasive in the general population as it was in that small part of it

immediately absorbed in the affairs of the *negara* as such. "The king was the symbol of the peasantry's greatness," Cora Du Bois has written about Southeast Asian Indic monarchs generally; and, somewhat more carefully phrased, the comment applies with special force to Bali. The ritual extravaganzas of the theatre state, its half-divine lord immobile, tranced, or dead at the dramatic center of them, were the symbolic expression less of the peasantry's greatness than of what its notion of that greatness was. What the Balinese state did for Balinese society was to cast into sensible form a concept of what, together, they were supposed to make of themselves: an illustration of the power of grandeur to organize the world.

The Balinese, not only in court ritual but generally, cast their most comprehensive ideas of the way things ultimately are, and the way that men should therefore act, into immediately apprehended sensuous symbols—into a lexicon of carvings, flowers, dances, melodies, gestures, chants, ornaments, temples, postures, and masks—rather than into a discursively apprehended, ordered set of explicit "beliefs." This means of expression makes any attempt to summarize those ideas a dubious business. As with poetry, which in the broad, *poiesis* ("making") sense is what is involved, the message here is so deeply sunk in the medium that to transform it into a network of propositions is to risk at once both of the characteristic crimes of exegesis: seeing more in things than is really there, and reducing a richness of particular meaning to a drab parade of generalities.

But whatever the difficulties and dangers, the exegetical task must be undertaken if one wants to be left with more than the mere fascinated wonderment—like a cow looking at a gamelan orchestra, as the Balinese put it—that Helms, for all his responsiveness and powers of description, displays. Balinese ritual, and most especially Balinese state ritual, does embody doctrine in the literal sense of "teachings," however concretely they are symbolized, however unreflectively they are apprehended. Digging them out for presentation in explicit form is not a task in which the Balinese, aside from a few modernists nowadays, have ever had any interest. Nor would they feel, any more than a translated poet ever feels, that any such presentation really gets to the heart of the matter, gets it really right. Glosses on experience, and most especially on other people's experience, are not replacements for it. At the very best they are paths, twisted enough, toward understanding it.

Practically, two approaches, two sorts of understanding, must converge if one is to interpret a culture: a description of particular symbolic forms (a ritual gesture, an hieratic statue) as defined expressions; and a contextualization of such forms within the whole structure of meaning of which they are a part and in terms of which they get their definition. This is, of course, nothing

Balinese offering. Photo by
Tineke Hellwig.

but the by-now-familiar trajectory of the hermeneutic circle; a dialectical
tacking between the parts which comprise the whole and the whole which
motivates the parts, in such a way as to bring parts and whole simultaneously into view. In the case at hand, such tacking comes down to isolating
the essential elements in the religious symbolic suffusing the theatre state,
and determining the significance of those elements within the framework of
what, taken as a whole, that symbolic is. In order to follow a baseball game
one must understand what a bat, a hit, an inning, a left fielder, a squeeze
play, a hanging curve, or a tightened infield are, and what the game in which
these "things" are elements is all about. In order to follow the cremation of a
Balinese king, one needs to be able to segment the torrent of images it gener-
ates—cloth snakes, arrows turning into flowers, lion shaped coffins, pagodas
on litters, doves rising from the brows of suiciding women—into the significant elements of which it is composed; and one needs to grasp the point of
the enterprise to begin with. The two sorts of understanding are inseparably

dependent upon one another, and they emerge concurrently. You can no more know what a *badé* tower is (as we shall see, it is an *axis mundi*) without knowing what a cremation is than you can know what a catcher's mitt is without knowing what baseball is.

The state ceremonials of classical Bali were metaphysical theatre: theatre designed to express a view of the ultimate nature of reality and, at the same time, to shape the existing conditions of life to be consonant with that reality; that is, theatre to present an ontology and, by presenting it, to make it happen—make it actual. The settings, the props, the actors, the acts the actors perform, the general trajectory of religious faith that those acts describe—all need to be set against the background of what the devil was going on. And that background can only be perceived, and perceived in the same measure, as those theatrical components are perceived. Neither the precise description of objects and behavior that is associated with traditional ethnography, nor the careful tracing of stylistic motifs that is traditional iconography, nor the delicate dissection of textual meanings that is traditional philology are in themselves enough. They must be made to converge in such a way that the concrete immediacy of enacted theatre yields the faith enclosed within it.

Behind the tendentious dramaturgy of state ritual, then, and in fact behind the unchanging plot that animated it, lay two fixed conjunctions of imaged ideas. First, *padmasana,* the lotus seat (or throne) of god; *lingga,* his phallus, or potency; and *sekti,* the energy he infuses into his particular expressions, most especially into the person of the ruler. Second, *buwana agung,* the realm of being; and *buwana alit,* the realm of sentience; the "big world" of what there is and the "little world" of thought and feeling.

Surrounded by a swarm of related, ancillary ideas, also deeply sunk in the pomp and ornament which Helms describes, these two symbol packets formed the content of what is usually all too casually referred to as "divine kingship" in Bali. The message the *negara* was designed to convey, and in its ritual life did convey, is ill-described by the mere statement, correct enough in itself, that the king was a kind of corporeal god. To the degree that it can be abstracted at all from the vehicles of its expression, the message was that the king, the court around him, and around the court the country as a whole, were supposed to make themselves into facsimiles of the order their imagery defined.

Like dream symbols, religious symbols are richly polysemic (that is, have multiple senses), their significance spreading out profusely in an embarrassment of directions. And this is as true for Balinese religious symbols as for any in the world. They reek of meaning.

Literally, *padmasana* means "lotus seat." It is used to refer to the throne of the supreme god Siva (or Surya, the Sun), who sits unstirring in the center of a lotus (*padma*) surrounded on four petals to the north, east, west, and south by Wisnu, Iswara, Mahadewa, and Brahma, each associated with a particular color, day of the week, part of the body, weapon, metal, magical syllable, and form of supernatural power. It is used to refer to the small stone column, surmounted by a high-back chair (also of stone) set cater-cornered on the most sacred spot in Balinese temples, upon which offerings to the supreme god are placed during temple ceremonies, when, enticed out of one version of heaven into another by his dancing worshipers, he comes there to sit. It is used to refer to the posture, a kind of infolded squat, one adopts when meditating upon the divine. It is used to refer to the act and the experience of meditation itself. It is a coital position, it is the base of a lingga, it is one of the many names of the supreme god, it is an iconic picture of the cosmos, it is the receptacle upon which the remains of a high priest are conducted to his cremation. And it is the innermost reaches of the human heart.

Lingga is a symbol no less ramifying. Strictly, of course, it refers to Siva's phallus—the "marvelous and interminable" one by which he established his superiority over Brahma and Visnu. Beyond that, it refers to the rough-hewn stone representations of that phallus—mere oblong rocks, suitably rounded at the top—found in temples and other sacred spots all over Bali. More abstractly it is the prime symbol of divine kingship as such. Not only is the king referred to as the lingga of the world; but also, since "on earth, the ruler acts on behalf of Siva, and the essence of his royal power is embodied in the lingga [which] the Brahman . . . obtains . . . from Siva and hands . . . over to the founder of the dynasty as the palladium of his royalty," the image summarizes the deep spiritual connection (Hooykaas calls it an "indivisible trinity") between the supreme god, the reigning king, and the state high priest. The small, whisk-like sprinkler made of grass stalks and plaited leaves from which priests shake drops of holy water over worshipers at the sacramental high point of practically all Balinese rituals is also addressed as a lingga. The kris (dagger) all noble personages wear thrust into the back of their sarongs, the crystal bar set into the ceremonial headdress of a high priest, the upper tip of a noble's cremation tower, the vehicle that transports the cremated soul to heaven, and the scaffold from which those widows throw themselves so dutifully onto their lord's pyre are also conceived to be linggas.

Finally, *sekti* is the Balinese word for the sort of transordinary phenomenon that elsewhere is called *mana*, *barake*, *orenda*, *kramal*, or, of course, in its original sense, charisma; "A divinely inspired gift of power, such as the ability to perform miracles."

At the bottom, however, *sekti* rests on a distinctive view of how the divine gets into the world; and most particularly on an elusive and paradoxical conception (and not only to external observers) of the relation between, on the one hand, the subsistent "forms" or "shapes" the divine takes (the Balinese word is *murti,* "[a] body," "bodily," "physical" from the Sanskrit *mūrta,* "settled into any fixed shape") and, on the other hand, the dynamic "manifestations" (the Sanskrit is *śakti,* "the energy or active part of a deity") that, in those forms and through those shapes, it variously has. Brahma and Visnu are said to be *sektis*—that is, roughly, "activations"—of Siva. So is Siva's wife. So indeed, are all the gods and goddesses. The king, the lord, the priest, and the ascetic are all said to be *sekti* (*not,* as often has been said, "to possess" it) to the extent that they are, in turn, instances of what they adore. Royal regalia, priestly ritual objects, sacred heirlooms, and holy places are all *sekti* in the same sense: they display the power the divine takes on when it falls into particular shapes. *Sekti* is "supernatural" power well enough—but supernatural power which grows out of imaging the truth, not out of believing, obeying, possessing, organizing, utilizing, or even understanding it.

Cultures in Collision

Although voices from the medieval and early modern periods of Indonesian history do survive, for the most part these are only scattered fragments of archipelago thought and opinion produced in these early centuries that were ultimately lost. By the nineteenth century, voices from the region became more numerous, and they are better preserved; in some ways this period can be seen as a golden age of Malay and Indonesian literary forms. A wide range of authors were writing in several different languages, recording both traditional concerns of court life, such as status and genealogy, and new phenomena, such as the collision of colonial and autochthonous worlds. Some of these authors were better placed than others to record the changes, but all brought regional and particular experiences to bear on the evolving political world of the archipelago, as well as a common cultural context or understanding that helped shape their worldviews.

Texts such as the *Tuhfat al-Nafis* and the *Hikayat Abdullah* record the fluidity of archipelago political life, as princes, pretenders, and adventurers were still very much in motion, circulating among a number of regional ports where they might consolidate or even expand their power. These accounts to some degree represent a pan-Malay consciousness, one commonly shared among many of the lowland, coastal, and seafaring people of the archipelago. These are aristocratic texts, and they embody a class-based worldview, expressing the concerns and predilections of elites, but the messages woven into them would have been understood even by nonelites, who shared a common cultural idiom with the authors. These two accounts are noteworthy in part because they show that indigenous Malay elites maintained their networks through travel and through the written word. They further suggest that European powers had not yet fully circumscribed traditional permeabilities of movement, even if this cultural moment was not far off.

The texts included here from Java, Bali, and Lombok represent slightly different concerns. These places eventually became core areas of Dutch control in the Indies, so much so that the colonial authorities coined a word,

Buitenbezittingen, or "outer possessions," for all islands beyond Java and its immediate neighbors. Here, the Dutch were already well entrenched, and though expansion still continued throughout the nineteenth century in parts of all these islands, by the middle decades of the century it was clear that Java would become the fulcrum of Dutch control. The *Babad Diponegoro* offers an account of the last great stand on Java against the aggressive and widening occupation of the Dutch, a war that lasted five years and cost hundreds of thousands of lives. With the end of the Java War (1825–30), all hopes that Java could rid itself of imperial control anytime soon were shattered. The war broke the Javanese aristocracy to Dutch bidding, and it broke the Javanese landscape as well, furthering the new policy of the *cultuurstelsel* (cultivation system), which eventually turned the island into an export-crop plantation under Holland's rule. Bali and Lombok took longer to subjugate, as they were ultimately less important to the Dutch, but many of the concerns in indigenous voices resembled those in Java, although plenty of local issues (competition, coercion, and collaboration) existed as well.

Dutch voices during this period expressed a range of concerns. Ideas about exploring the archipelago (more fully examined in the following chapter) and notions about the lack of social justice created by the new, evolving political economies of the Indies representing only two of the most important ones. Although military expeditions traversed large parts of the archipelago, scientists and particularly naturalists also proved crucial in the "discovery" of new landscapes, as well as in recording lifeways, folk traditions, and the incredible diversity of the islands' flora and fauna for a wide, ultimately global, audience. These processes of inquiry took place predominantly in the *Buitenbezittingen*, and these voices were important in giving a shape to the Indies as a discovered place, one that could be cordoned off and drawn on a topographical (and political) map. In the areas of strongest Dutch control, however, where plantations and the export economy were becoming the lived reality of millions of people, voices also began narrating and chronicling the struggles of indigenes under Dutch rule. *Max Havelaar* may be the most sensitive and heart-rending account of such processes available from this period, not just in the Dutch East Indies but in colonial Southeast Asia and perhaps even in the colonized world as a whole.

A final concern of authors from this period might best be described as subaltern; for the first time, perhaps, the written record manifests the thoughts and opinions about life and change in the archipelago from a range of interested actors who often do not get to speak at all. For women, who made up half of the population of the Indies at this time, but only a tiny percentage of its *written* voices, no better an advocate could have been hoped for than Raden

Ajeng Kartini, a Javanese woman of noble birth whose letters and thoughts on modernity, gender, and colonization became world famous. Kartini died very young—just after childbirth—but not before she had left her imprint on Indonesian consciousness; she is still considered one of the most important figures Indonesia has ever produced. Others—such as Chinese coolies in Sumatran labor camps—never meant to have their voices recorded, but their thoughts survive in court records and other documents that required their viewpoints in criminal investigations. These voices are harrowing and emotional partly because of the chance nature of their recording; had something not gone terribly wrong, they would never have been written down at all. Yet these instances of scandal, abuse, and mistreatment are doubly important because they also represent the lives of millions of poor workers trafficked to Indonesia over many decades, but never able to tell of the grim reality of their lives.

The selections presented here offer only a small cross-section of the "cultures in collision" that might have been selected. Yet together they indicate the vast diversity of experiences in the archipelago at the time, and show how atomized and particular people's lives could be, even those existing in close proximity to one another. This holds true geographically and from a class perspective; it is also true in representing schisms along ethnic and gender lines. Yet many of the voices also exhibit a curious unity, a shared concern with forms of coercion and control in archipelago waters that—if not wholly new—were now being exercised on a far larger scale, and in a far more concerted fashion, than ever before. As such, the voices presented here do seem to hold together, if only as harbingers and distant echoes of still greater changes soon to come.

The *Tuhfat al-Nafis*

Raja Ali al-Haji Riau

The Tuhfat al-Nafis (Precious Gift) *was written in the islands of Riau sometime in the nineteenth century, though it tells the tale of earlier events in this part of the archipelago stretching back several centuries. The Riau Sultanate was a powerful and important polity and one of the inheritors of the Malacca Sultanate, the most vibrant maritime kingdom of the fifteenth and early sixteenth centuries, finally destroyed by the Portuguese entrance into Southeast Asia in 1511. The rulers of Riau were not indigenous to this small cluster of islands. Rather, they were Bugis princes, part of the diaspora of sea-based peoples from south Sulawesi that developed from the seventeenth century onward as Dutch power was established in that place and local nobles fled elsewhere to carve out new kingdoms. The* Tuhfat al-Nafis *gives a very clear and detailed portrait of political power and court culture in Riau, linking the story of this place with other Bugis satellite communities in the wider archipelago. Beyond this, however, the* Tuhfat al-Nafis *also gives us a sense of how fluid archipelago sultanates could be, drawing manpower, material, and cultural inspiration from a number of scattered sites.*

According to the story, not long after this, in the hijra year 1225 on Thursday, 15 Zulhijjah at midday, Sultan Mahmud summoned Yang Dipertuan Muda Raja Jafar, who was at that time in Lingga, and called together the elders, the dignitaries, and the prominent nobles. When they were all present, he said to his cousin Raja Jafar, the Yang Dipertuan Muda, "Jafar, if it is the wish of Allah Almighty that I die in a few days, or shortly after that, I entrust Komeng (that is his son Tengku Abd al-Rahman) to you, and my last testament is that if I die, you are to make Komeng my successor in the kingdom." When the Yang Dipertuan Muda Raja Jafar and the elders and the dignitaries heard this, they all wept a little. The elders present at the time were first, Encik Abd al-Manan, a locally born Bugis; second, Encik Kaluk, also a locally born Bugis; third, the Panglima Dalam; fourth, Panglima Perang Jamal; fifth, Suliwatang Ibrahim; sixth, Syahbandar Muhammad; and there was a Lord Sayid, Engku Sharif Muhammad Zain al-Kuds.

According to the story, when Sultan Mahmud had finished appointing his executors, and had given his last testament, Yang Dipertuan Muda Raja Jafar returned to administer Riau, and there he remained. Shortly afterwards, Sultan Mahmud became ill, and his condition deteriorated daily. The people of the country were greatly distressed, especially the elders and the dignitaries, who all gathered within the palace to keep watch during His Majesty's illness. When his condition worsened, the elders sent a messenger to Riau inviting the Yang Dipertuan Muda Raja Jafar to come. On arrival, the messenger presented himself before Yang Dipertuan Muda Raja Jafar, and informed him that His Majesty was gravely ill. When Raja Jafar heard his news he was shocked and overwhelmed by sorrow. Impatient to leave for Lingga, and with no time to make vessels ready, he had a Chinese *pukat* row him and one or two attendants to Lingga while his brother Raja Ahmad followed. Not long afterwards they reached Lingga, where he went ashore to present himself before His Majesty Sultan Mahmud, whom he found in a serious condition. When Sultan Mahmud saw his cousin, he struggled to say, "Jafar, Komeng, Jafar, Komeng . . ." several times. Those were his words. Yang Dipertuan Muda Raja Jafar wept, and maintained a vigil close by His Majesty.

According to the historians, on Monday night, 18 Zulhijjah, at the time of the dawn prayers, His Majesty Sultan Mahmud left this transitory world to return to that which is eternal. *Verily we belong to Allah and to Him we return.* This was in the year of the hijra of the Prophet (*may Allah bless him and grant him peace*) 1225. A great uproar broke out in Lingga because of His Majesty's death, with those in the palace and the town lamenting and weeping. All the people of Lingga, the honoured and humble, high and low, old and young alike shaved their heads. They gathered inside the palace to carry out the Yang Dipertuan Muda's commands concerning the preparation of Sultan Mahmud's body. When all the customs traditional at the funeral of a great king were complete, His Majesty's body was taken into the audience hall, where all the dignitaries, the princes, the elders, the nobles, and the inhabitants of the country gathered. The Yang Dipertuan Muda invited Tengku Besar Abd al-Rahman to come into the audience hall. Then the Yang Dipertuan Muda ordered one of the princes to make a proclamation to the multitude present, so that all the people of the country, the sea-people and the soldiers would truly know that Tengku Abd al-Rahman, with the title Sultan Abd al-Rahman Syah, was the successor to his father the late Sultan Mahmud in the kingdom. And the multitude responded in agreement, "May his sovereign power increase!" According to one established account, Sultan Abd al-Rahman Syah was invested as successor to the kingdom even before Sultan Mahmud's interment.

When the public proclamation of Sultan Abd al-Rahman Syah had been completed, the Yang Dipertuan Muda ordered the late king's body to be carried to the grave with all the royal ceremonial funeral appurtenances, the drums, trumpets, and so forth, and the regalia. When they reached that side of the Lingga mosque facing Mecca—the Tanda side—they buried him there, and then all the people returned and donned court mourning according to the custom when a great Malay king dies. The Yang Dipertuan Muda ordered the Lord Sayids, hajis, and *lebai* to recite the creed every night. He distributed alms to them all and to the poor for forty days, and also on the hundredth day after the funeral.

According to the story, Raja Husain, a son of His Majesty the late Sultan Mahmud, came to Lingga and there met his brother Sultan Abd al-Rahman and the Yang Dipertuan Muda of Riau, Raja Jafar. The three princes wept, and Raja Husain then left to visit his late father's grave. Not long afterwards, Raja Husain left for Riau. Yang Dipertuan Muda Raja Jafar also returned there where he remained with Raja Husain, Temenggung Abd al-Rahman, and all the Bugis and Malay princes. Riau became prosperous, as many traders came from Java and from Siam, as well as the Chinese *wangkang* and Bugis *perahu*, because Engku Karaeng Talibak was in Riau and because it suited them to trade using Riau as a base.

During Sultan Abd al-Rahman's reign, the administration of the kingdom was carried out by Yang Dipertuan Muda Raja Jafar. With his Majesty on Lingga were Sayid Kuning (that is, Engku Sayid Muhammad Zain al-Kudsi); Suliwatang Ibrahim, the Lingga representative of the Yang Dipertuan Muda; his brother Syahbandar Muhammad; an elder, Encil Abd al-Manan; the chiefs of Kampung Bugis, and so forth. Lingga was peaceful, drawing revenues from Singkep. The country's fortification and Sultan Abd al-Rahman's palace compound were improved, and the fleet of war *penjajab* and the artillery made ready. The person responsible for all this was Encik Kaluk. The Yang Dipertuan Muda hoped that these measures would protect Lingga. Messengers, particularly Engku Sayid Muhammad Zain al-Kudsi and Encik Kaluk, were continually sent to Riau to present themselves before the Yang Dipertuan Muda. Nothing done in Lingga was kept secret, and if there was any matter of some importance, the Yang Dipertuan Muda himself came to Lingga. When it had been resolved, he would return again to Riau. That was the situation.

On Lingga Sultan Abd al-Rahman enjoyed performing devotional rites day and night. Indeed, His Majesty was very pious, and on Thursday nights he never slept, but was completely absorbed with his devotions. At daybreak he would attend the Friday prayers, dressed in the Arab manner, in a turban and a long gown. Afterwards His Majesty and the state officials would pause at the grave of his father, the late Sultan Mahmud, to read the Koran and recite the creed. Only when this was finished would he return, with all the people of the country following him. Reaching the audience hall, the procession would halt, and the people would be offered food—bread with chicken sauce or rice soup. After this everybody would return home. However, those who had their own obligations to their relatives or friends, or had a private concern, or were prevented by some other reason, did not accompany His Majesty. And so it was every Friday.

Furthermore, His Majesty Sultan Abd al-Rahman enjoyed the company of Lord Sayids and Lord Sheikhs, and liked to join with them for meals and prayers. He also enjoyed appointing wise men as imams and himself calling people to prayers. His Majesty's voice was extremely powerful and impressively strong, and when he gave the prayer call his voice could be recognized from far away. In addition, His Majesty enjoyed visiting the homes of his relatives and those of the elders and dignitaries. Occasionally he asked them for a meal. He was very jolly, not only with his relatives but with his servants and slaves, because he liked to amuse them and enjoyed eating and associating with them. His Majesty frequently wept because of his feelings of humility before Allah Almighty, particularly when the preacher read the prayers. That was how it was. His Majesty's wife, Raja Antiah, daughter of Raja Buntit (the wife of Raja Sulaiman) had already had a son, named Tengku Besar Raja Muhammad, who had been born when the late Sultan Mahmud was alive.

The *Hikayat Abdullah*

Abdullah bin Abdul Kadir Munshi

Munshi Abdullah was a man of mixed Tamil and Malay descent from the Malay Peninsula who left an account of his archipelagic travels called the Hikayat Abdullah. *He had an eye for detail, and he knew how to tell a good story; he often figured in many of his narratives himself (writing autobiographically at the time was quite unusual), which has left him open to the perhaps unfair accusation of being egotistical and self-promoting. It might be more just to see Abdullah as a "man of the world" during this epoch; he knew quite a few Europeans, as well as a great variety of princes, royals, and various other hangers-on throughout the Malay world. It is clear that he felt a sense of kinship and fraternity with many of his own class in this fluid maritime world, despite the fact that they were separated by evolving colonial spheres ruled by different flags. In this selection, he talks about Sir Stamford Raffles, the English ruler of Java during the so-called British interregnum between 1811 and 1816, a man who had employed Abdullah as a scribe. Abdullah here is concerned with the news that Raffles's ship had caught fire, and though the Englishman himself was safe, a host of the Malay-language manuscripts that he had collected, referencing the unity of the Malay world crossing both colonial spheres (English and Dutch), had irrevocably been destroyed.*

After some days I was still feeling unsettled because I was always thinking about Mr. Raffles. So I went back to Malacca. However some two months later I again returned to Singapore, and when I arrived I received news from Colonel Farquhar who told me "The ship carrying Mr. Raffles home to Europe sailed from Bencoolen one afternoon, and the same evening it caught fire with the loss of all the goods on board. Nothing was saved. But Mr. & Mrs. Raffles are safe, having escaped with only the clothes in which they stood." On hearing this my imagination reeled to think of all the works in Malay and other languages, centuries old, which he had collected from many countries, all utterly lost. Not a trace of them was left, for they were all in manuscript. Had they been printed there would still be a record of them. I thought too of all the remarkable objects Mr. Raffles had, to say nothing of his personal belongings. I recalled Mr. Raffles's promise that he would write books about the countries of this part of the world and that he would mention my name in them. All his material was lost. The more I thought about these things the more depressed I became. For it was a great loss indeed to European scholars because it had been Mr. Raffles's intention to write many books, one about Celebes, one about Borneo, and one about Singapore and to give an account of many matters of great importance. Now all the manuscripts and his English translations were lost. But then I recollected how thankful we should be to Allah that at least his life had been saved. Allah exercises His power over His servants in diverse ways. Sometimes the unforeseen occurs and sometimes the expected does not come to pass. Allah fulfils His purpose in His own way.

The *La Galigo* as Bugis History

Sirtjo Koolhof

One of the greatest (and longest) epics written in any language, the La Galigo *is the literary touchstone of the Bugis people of south Sulawesi, comprising history, gene-alogy, and worldview in a single, sprawling tale. The* La Galigo *has something for everyone: magic formulations of efficacy and power; tales of incest and exile; poetry, medical pronouncements, and stories of the Bugis peoples themselves, both semimyth-ical and historical in nature. The* La Galigo *questions and answers where the Bugis as a people come from—it also provides lessons for acceptable behavior and binds the community as a whole through its referrals to a common tradition and to common concerns. Only parts of the epic take place in southwestern Sulawesi, and this seems significant. Satellite communities of Bugis can be found scattered all over Indone-sia—in Sumatra, Borneo, Riau, and in the Moluccas, and in all these places Bugis descendents know the stories of* La Galigo. *The stories of* La Galigo *were originally handed down on lontar palms, but today—as with the selection provided here by the Dutch scholar Sirtjo Koolhof—almost all copies survive on paper manuscripts.*

Besides telling how and why the first human being came into existence, the *La Galigo* also describes how the narrow, vertically organized universe of Up-perworld, Middleworld, and Underworld gradually expands horizontally to encompass the regions on the earth known to the Bugis. Initially centered on Luwuq, the country where Batara Guru descended from heaven, the protag-onists' journeys to other lands introduce the audience to an ever-expanding world. While Batara Guru traveled only in a vertical direction to the realms of Upper- and Underworld, his son Batara Lattuq sets sail for Tompoq Tik-kaq, "Land of the rising sun," to meet his bride. Along the way he introduces other countries he passes through. Sawérigading, Batara Guru's grandson, continues the expansion of the world to even more regions, as does his son I La Galigo. In this way the *La Galigo* provides its audience with a picture of the world, of which the Bugis community is only a part. No description, however, is given of most of these countries: the protagonists merely pass

by—eventually marrying one of the princesses—and continue their journey.
The main message seems to be that the Bugis domains—Luwuq, Cina, Tompoq Tikkaq, and Wéwant Nriuq—are part of a larger world, a world which
sometimes intrudes into the land of the Bugis, and at which the heroes can
direct their heroic journeys and deeds.

It is against this background that the actions of the characters take place
and are described in detail, thereby explaining to the audience how various
customs came into being. For example, in the first episode, *Mula tau*, "the first
human being," or *Riuloqna Batara Guru*, "Batara Guru's descending,"—by far
the most popular and well-known—it is told how rice originated from the
body of Wé Oddang Nriuq, Batara Guru's daughter with one of his concu-
bines, who died seven days after her birth. Her father buries her body in the
hills and three days later, when he visits the gravesite Batara Guru discovers
to his astonishment that the hills are covered with a kind of grass of various
colors. He ascends to the Upperworld to ask his father, Patotoqé, what the
meaning of this all is and receives the following answer.

> That child is named Sangiang Serri,
> your child has become rice.
> Just descend to earth, Batara Guru,
> take it, and bring it into your palace.
> Do not, however, eat it,
> just eat wheat and corn,
> to keep your spirit alive during your stay in the world.

And if this short explanation from Patotoqé that the rice in fact is his granddaughter is not enough for people to understand that they should treat it with
the utmost respect, in another episode the disastrous consequences of a lack
of respect are described. When the ruling couple of Tompoq Tikkaq, Wé
Pada Uleng and La Urung Mpessi, want to perform one of the rites of passage
for their daughters, they prepare food for a large amount of guests. However,
no one shows up, and in an angry mood La Urung Mpessi throws away the
cooked rice and other dishes. When that news reaches Patotoqé he declares:

> We will destroy
> the country of Tompoq Tikkaq,
> we will take the breath
> of La Urung Mpessi, Wé Pada Uleng, and their fellow-leaders.

Three months later he sends some of his servants to the earth to make his
words come true:

A Bugis ship. Photo no. 3807, courtesy of KITLV, Leiden.

> Manifold were the plagues of To Palanroé [Patotoqé].
> Destroying the country of Tompoq Tikkaq
> and all of its surroundings.
> The country men's harvest did not succeed,
> potatoes turned into stones,
> corn turned into reed,
> millet turned into grass,
> Sangiang Serri became yet another kind of grass,
> none of the crops flourished.

Some time after this, after another insult of the gods, Patotoqé strikes Wé Pada Uleng and La Urung Mpessi with a serious disease from which they both die. A strong reminder for the audience to present Sangiang Serri with the respect she deserves.

While these—in *La Galigo* terms relatively short—sections relating to the rice goddess Sangiang Serri are quite well-known among the people, they differ from other important subjects treated in the *La Galigo*, of which those of love, marriage, and its regulations stand out as ubiquitous. Mattulada has defined the central theme of the *La Galigo* as "the social structure of the community and the power that regulates it" (Mattulada 1978: 129). And it is precisely in the rituals on the occasion of marriages that the social and power structures of Bugis society are articulated, both in the texts of the *La Galigo* and in Bugis daily life. Weddings are the most important of life cycle rituals, and excellent events to (re)define and display social relationships between individuals and groups (Millar 1989; Acciaioli 1989: 223–24). And this has been the case for centuries if we may extend Nicholas Gervaise's late seventeenth-century description of the Makasar people to their close kin the Bugis:

> There are no People more cautious than the Macasarians in the Marriages which they contract, nor that solemnize 'em with more Pomp and Ceremony; as believing it to be the most Important Act of civil Life, and the most Sacred of their Religion. (Gervaise 1971: 103)

Stories centering on the marriage of one of the characters make up a large portion of the existing episodes. Already in the very beginning of the first episode, before Patotoqé can let his son Batara Guru descend to earth, efforts have to be made to find a suitable marriage partner to accompany him—and thus provide the gods with offspring—during his life in the Middleworld. This marriage is the first of a long series of descriptions of weddings and their preparations, of which the most important is that of the *La Galigo*'s hero Sawérigading. He grows up in the palace in Luwuq, separated from his twin sister Wé Tenriabéng, of whose existence his parents keep him unaware. On one of his journeys he is informed by a cousin that he has a twin sister who lives in a separated half of the palace in Luwuq. Some time after his return Sawérigading climbs the roof beams of the palace, sees his sister, and immediately falls passionately in love with her. Of course this incestual love is strictly prohibited, and despite his efforts he is unable to convince his parents (and his sister) to allow him to marry Wé Tenriabéng, his mother telling him:

> It is forbidden to become a couple
> for people who are siblings.
> Obviously you would call down disaster upon your country.
> The people will die,
> the country destroyed.
> Be it for half a day, an eyeblink,
> siblings cannot become a couple,
> because the country will submerge,
> it will be ruined
> none of the people in the world will be saved.

Sawérigading replies:

Let the people die,
let the villagers be exterminated,
as long as my wish comes true,
my hopes are fulfilled.

After many more explanations by other people, and even by his own twin
sister, Sawérigading is convinced that he has to satisfy himself with another
wife. He, of course, is not the only one to be convinced; the audience also
should realize the dangers of such behavior. And they do. As an old woman
from Luwu explained to Shelly Errington: "Sawerigading and Tenri Abeng
were not allowed to marry, and therefore we may not. If they had been permitted, we could, too" (Errington 1989: 266). Up till the present day the birth
of a *dinrulawent*, "lit. golden twin, a twin of both sexes," is considered inaus-
picious. To prevent the undesirable consequences some villagers come to the
house of Petta Ballasari, daughter of one of the last rulers in Wajo, to sell
one of the children to her symbolically. Usually an amount of less than half a
dollar is paid to the parents. If then one of the children is sold, in a sense they
are not siblings anymore, and thus the danger of an incestuous relationship is
avoided. How important this is can be seen once more from Sawérigading's
case. Although a long-term, officially sanctioned relationship between him
and his sister is not established—and no mention is made of short, but physically intimate contacts—the context makes clear that something went funda-
mentally wrong. Sawérigading leaves Luwuq behind to find himself another
spouse overseas in Cina. For this journey the term *ripaliq* is used, meaning
"to be expelled (drifting on a raft of banana trunks) after committing incest"
(Matthes 1874: 870). His sister ascends to the Upperworld, and is thus effec-
tively dead. Both sanctions are explicitly mentioned as the proper punish-
ments for committing incest (Matthes 1885: 182–83; Mattulada 1985: 202). That
the relationship between Sawérigading and Wé Tenriabéng apparently went
too far is furthermore seen in one of the following episodes in which I La Galigo, Sawérigading's son, travels to Luwuq. Upon his arrival he is told that the
land is barren and that the harvests were destroyed by fire since his father left
the country (Kern 1939:3 95). After I La Galigo's visit to Luwuq, the curse on
the country of Luwuq is lifted. However, in the village of Cerekang—the area
where according to tradition the palace of Sawérigading once stood—the villagers believe up till the present day that their region's relative poverty is to be
blamed on the incestuous affair that took place between Sawérigading and his
twin sister in *La Galigo* times.

Following these events Sawérigading has to leave his native country Luwuq, to find himself another wife overseas. With the help of his sister the

giant sacred tree Wélenréng is felled, and transformed into a fleet of ships that will bring him to Cina. A widely known episode of the *Sureq Galigo*, "The felling of the Wélenréng tree," was mentioned to me more than once as the source for environmental awareness. The respect shown in the text for the sacred tree and its inhabitants should extend to all the products of nature until the present day.

Sawérigading then arrives in Cina, after a journey during which he had to fight seven enemies at sea. During the first three months there he pretends to be on a trading mission. On this occasion the customs regarding trade in a foreign country are explained: the ruler has primary rights to buy at favorable prices (*mabbaluq sala*, "wrong trading"), and only afterwards the common people can make their choice and buy (*mabbaluq samaq*, "common trading") (Kern 1939: 224–25). After that period Sawérigading sends the birds he brought with him to the Cina palace, to observe if Wé Cudiaq really looks like his sister as described. As could be expected, this is the case. We are then told quite extensively how Sawérigading acts to catch a glimpse of her himself, and how his servants visit the palace to propose to Wé Cudiaq's family, an occasion at which the customs that govern marriage proposals are described in detail.

The *Babad Dipanegara* in Java

Peter Carey

Alongside the hikayats and sejarahs, two Malay types of historical narrative, the babad is a Javanese chronicle-based form that has given scholars a sense of the royal genealogies, lineages, and stories of the ruling houses of the archipelago. One of the most famous of this genre of historical epics has been the Babad Dipanegara *(Ballad of Prince Dipanegara).* Dipanegara was a Javanese prince who led the last significant uprising against the Dutch in Java, predating the high colonial period; the war cost hundreds of thousands of lives and laid to waste a huge section of Java's fertile soil for years afterward. The conflict lasted five years (1825–30), and with its end any real chance of resistance against the occupying colonial regime had passed on this island. By all accounts Dipanegara was a very brave leader and a shrewd tactician; with a far less technologically sophisticated force than what the Dutch could bring to bear, he kept the Europeans at bay for years through a combination of direct pitched battles, guerilla warfare, and jihad. A translation of part of the* Babad Dipanegara *by the British historian Peter Carey follows.*

Verses 18–26

18. Pangeran Dipanagara said calmly:
    "if you are afraid to oppose
    the Dutch, from now on
    once and for all become (my) enemy!"
    Pangeran Mangkubumi was silent
    observing his nephew's
    great wrath.
    He resigned himself to his fate, leaving everything to God.
    Not long afterwards someone came to make an announcement,
    performing a *sĕmbah* before him:
19. "Lord, there are visitors outside,
    Mas Tumĕnggung Sindupraja
    accompanied by two Dutchmen."

Prince Dipanegara.
Drawing no. 2505,
courtesy of KITLV,
Leiden.

The Pangeran said pleasantly:
"Summon them to come in immediately!"
He made a *sĕmbah* in agreement (and) left.
Already (the guests) were ushered in.
Tumĕnggung Sindunagara
and the two Dutchmen sat down on chairs.
(Sindunagara) spoke slowly
20. with his hands clasped in front of him:
"I have been sent by
Resident Smissaert, my son.
First, he gives
his greetings to Your Lordship
(and) secondly I
am instructed
to present you with a letter."

The letter was received (and) read attentively
right through to the end.

21. After it has been read, (Dipanagara) quickly
handed it over to his uncle,
saying slowly
"Here my Lord!"
Pangeran Mangkubumi received
the letter. After he had read it,
he was startled at heart.
Pangeran Mangkubumi said:
"It is up to you what you write in reply,
choose (one of) the two courses."

22. Pangeran Dipanagara said calmly:
"Sindunagara, my reply is this;
tell the Resident
that as it concerns his calling me,
even if he waits till the roads turn to mud
under no circumstances would I be willing
to enter the Residency.
If the Resident wants
to bring an army complete with weapons of war
to mistreat me,

23. no matter whether he orders or does not forbid (it),
life (and) death will certainly not occur
(for) they are at the discretion of the Lord Allah.
If Smissaert pretends
that he can ordain life and death
(and) not Allah the Almighty,
then in my view
the Dutch have evil hearts
(and) are not fitted to exercise law and justice.
(Go) quickly (and) tell that

24. to the smooth bald-headed one! In my childhood
people used to make me afraid when giving an order,
(but) all this bragging
about going to war is just idle talk.
Now I am not cowed any more.
Quickly Sindunagara
tell him that I
will just await him here.

If it comes to battle, the bald-headed one will be disappointed
if I am not present (too)!"

25. Both Dutchmen sat staring in amazement,
neither could speak.
Then Sindunagara swiftly
begged permission to depart.
Hurriedly they went on their way,
three in number inclusive of the Dutchmen.
On horseback hastening along
at a gallop, they soon arrived
at the (Residency) office. All the *Nayakas* were waiting.
Sindunagara spoke,

26. informing them about everything;
beginning, middle, (and) end, nothing was omitted from
the Pangeran's replies.
All of them were brought to the knowledge
of the Resident, Mr. Smissaert,
(who), when he heard the words
of the Mas Tuměnggung,
was exceedingly angry as though he had been slapped;
his face was hot, glowing with wrath,
(and) his heart was afire.

Sasak Literature of Lombok

Geoffrey Marrison

The babad *(historical chronicles) of Lombok are another group of indigenous literary documents that give us an interesting view into the particularities of the historical experience in a less-traveled part of the archipelago. Lombok was a battleground
between warring, rival cultures. The Balinese (and even the Javanese, who resided
for the most part one island over further to the west) held periodic sway there, and
indigenous Sasak culture, which was stronger on the eastern half of this small island,
continually fought to assert itself against these foreign influences. The historical epics
of Lombok—such as the one presented here by the scholar Geoffrey Marrison—reflect
this cultural duality, echoing at times the concerns of the Sasak princes and sultans,
and at other times portraying the Hinduized point of view of the nearby Balinese
conquerors. Because the Javanese were occasionally also involved in these struggles,
and Bugis princes and Chinese merchants weighed into the delicate balance of power
as well, Lombok makes for a particularly interesting place to look at the cross-currents
of power, diaspora, and influence at work in the central waters of the archipelago.*

The *Babad Congah Sakra III* begins with the rebellion at Sakra in 1826 instigated by Radèn Suryajaya, an impetuous young man, unwilling to heed the
advice of his elders, who nevertheless attracted a popular following. The Balinese ruler demanded the sending of young women from Sakra for the palace, which was much resented. Envoys returning from this mission brought
a summons from the ruler of Sakra to go to the capital. Suryajaya urged
Komaladewa Mas Panji to rebel against the Balinese. He came with his father,
Manajahi, to say that not only were the Sasak ready, but also that the minor
Balinese courts of Mataram, Pegasangan, and Pagutan were then inclined to
resist the hegemony of Karangasem Lombok. Mas Panji urged the nobles of
Sakra, Dèn Nuna Lancung, and Dèn Hormat, to take part, the latter being
reluctant. News of the Sasak preparations reached West Lombok and a first
skirmish near Rarang went against the Sasak. Then the men of Kopang and
Batu Kliang marched westwards, pretending to be escaping from Sakra, but
they were engaged and surrounded by the Balinese. Sasak reinforcements

from Praya and southern villages then came up, but Mas Panji was wounded, and Radèn Suryajaya and the Sasak fell away. The Balinese failed to follow and all the Sasak returned to Sakra. Meanwhile, Manajahi, in the village of Surabaya in South-East Lombok, gathered forces from nearby to help Mas Panji. At this point, the Balinese had invested Jerowaru in the South-East. Manajahi was sent to help, but the Balinese, aided by Sasak from Suradadi, intercepted them. The men of Jerowaru were not able to withstand the Balinese pressure. The Balinese turned first against Surabaya, then against Sakra.

Sumbawanese visitors were expected at Sakra and landed on the East Coast of Lombok at Rambang, but when Manajai with a party under white flags went to meet them, they were suspicious and sailed away. Meanwhile, the Balinese repeatedly attacked Sakra, but for a time Mas Panji held them off. Then he took respite to attend a cockfight. The Balinese renewed the attack, which caused panic. Radèn Suryajaya and Radèn Hormat were killed, and Mas Panji was hit by a bullet, and took no further part in the struggle. The Balinese fired the mosque of Sakra, and there was renewed panic, and Sakra was soon subdued.

Next follows an account of the Balinese dynastic quarrels of 1839–40. This arose because the wife of the ruler of Mataram, who was the sister of the ruler of Karangasem Sasak, had left her husband for a man called Gedé Dangin. Mataram attacked Karangasem, and in spite of lesser numbers prevailed against them, and the Sasak who had been clients of Karangasem went over to Mataram. In 1843, the son of the ruler of Mataram wanted to marry the princess of Pagutan, but the ruler of Koripan persuaded Pagutan that he would make a worthier husband. Pagutan rose against Mataram, Koripan did not help, and the ruler of Pagutan was killed. The ruler of Koripan had married a woman of Sakra, but when Mataram attacked him, Sakra failed to help and Koripan chiefs in Mataram were murdered.

In 1855, there was a quarrel between Mataram and Praya. The Balinese ruler had demanded the daughter of the ruler of Praya to be brought to Mataram, but he refused. Later, three Hajis were killed and Praya was subjected. A new palace at Cakranegara, the Mayura, with water gardens was built for the Balinese Raja. In Karangasem, Bali, at a cremation at which Cakranegara was represented, the theft of a ceremonial kris by a man of Klungklung led to an altercation and the Déwa Agung of Klungklung attacked Karangasem, who asked for help from Lombok, which was offered against Klungklung.

The final struggle of the Sasak against their Balinese rulers broke out at Praya in 1893. A stand was made at Kediri, but the Balinese prevailed, and also managed by devious means to impress Sakra to take action against Praya, but the Sakra men later returned home. The Balinese general, Ida Wayan, captured men from Sakra and exiled them to the island of Trawangan on the North-West coast. When he passed through Central Lombok he found all the Sasak in revolt and fled, while another Balinese leader, Gusti Belosok, was killed by Sasak at Pohgading in East Lombok. All East Lombok now stood with Sakra, and more and more villages joined in the cause. But at a great battle near Kediri in West Lombok, the Sasak were beaten and the Tuan Guru of Sakra was slain. Risings in Gerung and Sekerbéla showed the Balinese that West Lombok Sasak were now also against them. A major battle round Praya remained inconclusive, and Sasak prisoners escaping from Trawangan met disaster. The Sasak effort lost momentum and the Balinese regained much of Central Lombok, and advanced on Masbagik in East Lombok, but the on-slaught was indecisive.

Now follows an episode of a supposed prince of Makassar who came to help Sakra. He led Sasak forces to attack the Balinese headquarters at Kota-raja and neighbouring villages, but without success. It was after this that the Dutch intervened. Their envoy was Liefrinck, who came to Sakra, and was able to arrange relief supplies, and later a force of eight warships was sent to Ampenan. He was able to get partial withdrawal of the Balinese forces, but was persuaded to spare the palace. One night the Balinese fell on the Dutch who were encamped by the Meru temple in Cakranegara, and two thousand were killed, while others had to retreat, and others were killed in an engage-ment at Narmada. A new expedition was sent from Europe and Batavia. Ten ships were sent, which bombarded the Balinese positions, and fifty thousand soldiers were landed. The Anak Agung in Mataram was the first to die, the ruler of Cakranegara was taken prisoner and exiled, Cakranegara was pil-laged and burnt, and the Balinese fled hither and thither.

Max Havelaar

Multatuli

Multatuli (the pen name of Eduard Douwes Dekker, a Dutch writer and colonial administrator of the mid-nineteenth century in Java) caused an immediate stir with the publication of his book, Max Havelaar; Or, The Coffee Auctions of the Dutch Trading Company, *in 1860. Though the Dutch had been exploiting Java's natural wealth and its people for centuries by the time of the book's publication, the Netherlands itself viewed its own colonial project as comparatively benign alongside other European regimes in Asia.* Max Havelaar *told a very different story and demanded answers for a system it described as so exploitative that its collective accusations shocked the Netherlands. Though written under a pseudonym, it was clear that the book's author knew his subject. For example, the Dutch mandated the cultivation of coffee and sugar in huge quantities on Java instead of that of rice, to meet and even exceed global market demand for these export products. While this enormous agricultural enterprise rested on the labor and sweat of Javanese farmers, its financial rewards did not trickle down to them.* Max Havelaar *offered one of the first major indictments of the so-called* cultuurstelsel, *and it painted a damning picture of a colony that many Dutch colonials portrayed as a paradise on earth.*

At Serang, when Havelaar was staying in the Resident's house, he had spoken to Mr. Slymering about the abuses in Lebak, and had been told "that this was more or less the case everywhere." That, of course, Havelaar could not deny. After all, who would maintain that he had seen a country where no wrong was ever done? But Havelaar held that this was no reason for allowing abuses to continue where one found them, especially when one was explicitly called upon to resist them; also that from everything he knew of Lebak, there was no question of *more* or *less* there but of *an excessive degree.* To which the Resident replied, amongst other things, that in the Division of Chiringien, also belonging to Bantam, things are still worse.

Now assuming, as may be assumed, that a Resident derives no direct advantage from extortion and from arbitrary use of the population, the question arises: what, then, induces so many people, contrary to sworn oath and duty, to allow such abuses to persist without notifying the Government of them? And anyone who reflects on this question must find it very, very strange that the existence of these abuses is so calmly recognized, as though it were a matter beyond any man's reach or competence to remedy. I will endeavour to unfold the reasons for this.

In general, the mere task of carrying evil tidings is an unpleasant one, and it really seems as though something of the unfavourable impression they make sticks to the man whose depressing duty it is to convey them. Now, if this fact alone is sufficient reason for some people to deny, against their better knowledge, the existence of something disagreeable, how much more must it be the case where there is a risk, not only of incurring that disfavour which seems to be the lot of the bearer of ill news, but of being actually looked upon as the *cause* of the adverse situation which duty compels one to reveal!

The Government of the Dutch East Indies likes to write and tell its masters in the Motherland that everything is going well. The Residents like to report that to the Government. The Assistant Residents, who, in turn, receive hardly anything but favourable reports from their Controleurs, also prefer not to send any disagreeable news to the Residents. All this gives birth to an artificial optimism in the official and written treatments of affairs, in contradiction not only to the truth but also to the personal opinion expressed by the optimists themselves when discussing those affairs orally, and—stranger still!—often even in contradiction to the facts in their own written statements. I could quote many examples of reports which extolled to the skies the favourable conditions in a Residency and belied themselves in the same breath, especially when the *figures* spoke. If the ultimate consequences did not make the matter too serious, these examples would arouse laughter and ridicule, and one can only be amazed at the naïveté with which, in such cases, the grossest lies are often maintained and . . . accepted, although the writer himself, a few sentences further on, proffers the weapons for combating those lies. I shall confine myself to one single instance—which, however, I could multiply many times over. Among the documents before me I find the Annual Report of a Residency. The Resident speaks in glowing terms of the flourishing trade there, and asserts that the greatest prosperity and activity are to be seen throughout the whole region. But a little later, he has to talk about the slender means at his disposal for foiling smugglers, and acts immediately to prevent a disagreeable impression from being made on the Government by the conclusion that a great deal of import duty is therefore evaded in his Residency:

"No," he says, "there is no need to fear that at all! Little or nothing is smuggled into my Residency, because . . . there is so little doing in these parts that no one would risk his capital in commerce here!"

I have read a similar report which began with the words: "During the past year the peace in the area has remained peaceful." Such sentences certainly bear witness to a very confident confidence in the Government's indulgence towards anyone who spares it unpleasant news or who, as the saying goes, "does not embarrass it" with depressing reports!

Where the population does not increase, the fact is attributed to the inaccuracy of the censuses of previous years. Where the revenue from taxes does not rise, it is counted as a merit: the intention is to encourage agriculture by low assessments, since it is only *now* beginning to develop and will soon— preferably when the writer of the report has left the district—yield fabulous results. Where riots have taken place that *cannot* remain concealed, they are the work of a few ill-disposed persons, who need no longer to be feared, since there is now *general* contentment everywhere. Where distress or famine has thinned out the population, it is owing to failure of crops, drought, heavy rains, or something of the sort, but never to mis-government.

Before me lies the note by Havelaar's predecessor in which he ascribed "the decline in the population of Parang-Kujang" to *"outrageous"* abuses. That note was *un*official, and contained points which the writer was to *talk* over with the Resident of Bantam. But in vain did Havelaar search in the records for evidence that he had frankly reported the matter in so many words in an *official memorandum*.

In short, the official reports from the functionaries to the Government, and consequently also those based upon them which the Government sends to the Motherland, are mostly and for the most important part *untrue*.

I know this is a grave charge, but I stand by it, and am in a position to support it with proofs. Anyone who is put out by my expressing my opinion so uninhibitedly should consider how many millions of pounds and how many human lives in England would have been spared if someone there had succeeded in opening the eyes of the nation to the true state of affairs in India, and how beholden everyone would have been to the man who had had the courage to be a Job's messenger before it was too late to repair the damage in a less sanguinary manner than subsequently became inevitable.

I have said I can prove my charge. Where necessary, I can show that there was often famine in regions which were praised as models of prosperity, and that frequently a population which was reported to be peaceful and contented was on the point of exploding in revolt. It is not my intention to produce these proofs in *this* book, though I feel sure that no one will lay it down without believing that they exist.

For the moment I will confine myself to one more example of the absurd optimism of which I have spoken—an example which anyone, whether he is *au fait* with Dutch East Indian affairs or not, can easily grasp.

Each month, every Resident renders a return of the amount of rice imported into or exported from his Residency. In this return, trade is split into two parts, namely, that with the outside world and that with the rest of Java. Now, if one takes note of the quantity of rice exported according to the latter returns *from* Residencies in Java *to* Residencies in Java, it will be seen that the quantity amounts to many thousands of pikols *more* than the rice which, according to the same returns, is imported *into* Residencies in Java *from* Residencies in Java.

I shall at present refrain from saying what one must inevitably think of the intelligence of a Government that accepts such statements and publishes them. I only wish to draw the reader's attention to the *object* of this deceit.

The percentage bonus paid to European and native functionaries for products to be sold in Europe had such a detrimental effect on rice cultivation that some regions were ravaged by a famine which could *not* be conjured away from the sight of the Motherland. I have already said that instructions were then issued to the effect that things must not be allowed to go quite so far again. The many consequences of these instructions included the returns of imports and exports of rice I have mentioned, so that the Government could constantly keep an eye on the ebb and flow in supply of that article of food. *Export* from a Residency means prosperity; *import* into it means want.

Now, when those returns are examined and compared, it will be seen that rice is so abundant everywhere *that all Residencies combined export more rice* than *all the Residencies combined import*. I repeat that here there is no question of export overseas, for which a separate statement is rendered. The conclusion of all this is therefore the absurd thesis *that there is more rice in Java than there is*. That's prosperity, *if* you like!

I have already said that the desire never to send other than good news to the Government would be comic if the results of it all were not so tragic. For what correction of so much wrong can be hoped for in the face of a predetermined purpose to twist and distort everything in the reports to the authorities? What, for instance, may be expected from a population which, by nature gentle and submissive, has complained of oppression for years and years, when it sees one Resident after another retire on furlough or pension, or be called away to another post, without the *slightest thing* being done to redress the grievances under which it suffers? Must not the bent spring eventually recoil? Must not the long-suppressed discontent—suppressed so that the Government can continue to deny its existence!—finally turn to rage, desperation, madness? Is there not a *Jacquerie* at the end of this road?

And where, then, will the officials be who succeeded one another for so many years without ever stumbling on the idea that there might be something higher than the "favour of the Government"? Something higher than the "satisfaction of the Governor-General"? Where will they be then, the writers of empty reports who throw sand in the eyes of the administration with their untruths? Will they, who previously lacked the courage to put one bold word on paper, suddenly fly to arms and save the Dutch possessions for the Netherlands? Will they restore to the Netherlands the treasure that will be required to quell insurrection, to prevent revolution? Will they restore to life the thousands who will have perished through *their* guilt?

A Naturalist Climbs a Mountain

Alfred Russel Wallace

Alfred Russel Wallace was a British naturalist who traveled ceaselessly, often alone, in the Dutch East Indies in the middle decades of the nineteenth century. He mapped out an astonishing number of flora and fauna species previously unknown to Western science. Wallace demarcated a line (called the "Wallace Line" after him) along which Asian and Australasian life forms seemed to diverge: it ran just east of Borneo and Bali, and his conclusions about this deep structural channel separating realms of wildlife still hold true today. Most famously, he came upon the building blocks of the theories of natural selection and evolution quite independently—and concomitantly—with Charles Darwin, who was working on the other side of the earth off the Galapagos Islands. Darwin's publicist claimed most of the credit for his client; Wallace went back to his butterflies. He traveled by indigenous boat to some of the most remote islands of the Indonesian archipelago in his quest for knowledge about little-known species, and he eventually alerted the world that the Indies provided a naturalist's paradise. The selection printed here comes from one of his less exotic journeys—to the upper slopes of a mountain on Java—but it is nevertheless representative of the man and his sensibilities.

By far the most interesting incident in my visit to Java was a trip to the summit of the Pangerango [Pangrango] and Gedeh [Gede] mountains; the former an extinct volcanic cone about ten thousand feet high, the latter an active crater on a lower portion of the same mountain range. Tchipanas [Cipanas], about four miles over the Megamendong Pass [Puncak], is at the foot of the mountain. A small country house for the Governor-General and a branch of the Botanic Gardens are situated here, the keeper of which accommodated me with a bed for a night. There are many beautiful trees and shrubs planted here, and large quantities of European vegetables are grown for the Governor-General's table. By the side of a little torrent that bordered the garden, quantities of orchids were cultivated, attached to the trunks of trees, or suspended from the branches, forming an interesting open-air orchid-house. As I intended to stay two or three nights on the mountain I engaged two coolies to carry my baggage, and with my two hunters we started early the next morning. The first mile was over open country, which brought us to the forest that covers the whole mountain from a height of about five thousand feet. The next mile or two was a tolerably steep ascent through a grand virgin forest, the trees being of great size, and the undergrowth consisting of fine herbaceous plants, tree-ferns, and shrubby vegetation. I was struck by the immense number of ferns that grew by the side of the road. Their variety seemed endless, and I was continually stopping to admire some new and interesting forms. I could now well understand what I had been told by the gardener, that three hundred species had been found on this one mountain. A little before noon we reached the small plateau of Tjiburong [Cibeureum] at the foot of the steeper part of the mountain, where there is a plank-house for the accommodation of travelers. Close by is a picturesque waterfall and a curious cavern, which I had not time to explore. Continuing our ascent the road became narrow, rugged and steep, winding zigzag up the cone, which is covered with irregular masses of rock, and overgrown with a dense luxuriant but less lofty vegetation. We passed a torrent of water which is not much lower than the boiling point, and has a most singular appearance as it foams over its rugged bed, sending up clouds of steam, and often concealed by the overhanging herbage of ferns and lycopodia, which here thrive with more luxuriance than elsewhere.

At about seventy-five hundred feet we came to another hut of open bamboos, at a place called Kandang Badak, or "Rhinoceros-field," which we were going to make our temporary abode. Here was a small clearing, with abundance of tree-ferns and some young plantations of Cinchona. As there was now a thick mist and drizzling rain, I did not attempt to go on to the summit that evening, but made two visits to it during my stay, as well as one to the active crater of Gedeh. This is a vast semicircular chasm, bounded by black perpendicular walls of rock, and surrounded by miles of rugged scoria-covered slopes. The crater itself is not very deep. It exhibits patches of sulphur and variously-coloured volcanic products, and emits from several vents continual streams of smoke and vapour. The extinct cone of Pangerango was to me more interesting. The summit is an irregular undulating plain with a low bordering ridge, and one deep lateral chasm. Unfortunately there was perpetual mist and rain either above or below us all the time I was on the mountain; so that I never once saw the plain below, or had a glimpse of the magnificent view which in fine weather is to be obtained from its summit. Notwithstanding this drawback I enjoyed the excursion exceedingly, for it was the first time I had been high enough on a mountain near the Equator to watch the change from a tropical to a temperate flora. I will now briefly sketch these changes as I observed them in Java.

On ascending the mountain, we first met with temperate forms of herbaceous plants, so low as three thousand feet, where strawberries and violets begin to grow, but the former are tasteless and the latter have very small and pale flowers. Weedy Compositæ also begin to give a European aspect to the wayside herbage. It is between two thousand and five thousand feet that the forests and ravines exhibit the utmost development of tropical luxuriance and beauty. The abundance of noble Tree-ferns, sometimes fifty feet high, contributes greatly to the general effect, since of all the forms of tropical vegetation they are certainly the most striking and beautiful. Some of the deep ravines which have been cleared of large timber are full of them from top to bottom; and where the road crosses one of these valleys, the view of their feathery crowns, in varied positions above and below the eye, offers a spectacle of picturesque beauty never to be forgotten. The splendid foliage of the broad-leaved Musacæ and Zingiberaceæ, with their curious and brilliant flowers, and the elegant and varied forms of plants allied to Begonia and Melastoma, continually attract the attention in this region. Filling up the spaces between the trees and larger plants, on every trunk and stump and branch, are hosts of Orchids, Ferns and Lycopods, which wave and hang and intertwine in ever-varying complexity. At about five thousand feet I first saw horsetails (Equisetum), very like our own species. At six thousand feet, Raspberries abound, and thence to the summit of the mountain there are three species of eatable Rubus. At seven thousand feet Cypresses appear, and the forest trees become reduced in size, and more covered with mosses and lichens. From this point upward these rapidly increase, so that the blocks of rock and scoria that form the mountain slope are completely hidden in a mossy vegetation. At about eight thousand feet European forms of plants become abundant. Several species of Honeysuckle, St. John's-wort, and Guelder-rose abound, and at about nine thousand feet we first meet with the rare and beautiful Royal Cowslip (Primula imperialis), which is said to be found nowhere else in the world but on this solitary mountain summit. It has a tall, stout stem, sometimes more than three feet high, the root leaves are eighteen inches long, and it bears several whorls of cowslip-like flowers, instead of a terminal cluster only. The forest trees, gnarled and dwarfed to the dimensions of bushes, reach up to the very rim of the old crater, but do not extend over the hollow on its summit. Here we find a good deal of open ground, with thickets of shrubby Artemisias and Gnaphaliums, like our southernwood and cudweed, but six or eight feet high; while Buttercups, Violets, Whortle-berries, Sow-thistles, Chickweed, white and yellow Cruciferæ, Plantain, and annual grasses everywhere abound. Where there are bushes and shrubs the St. John's-wort and Honeysuckle grow abundantly, while the Imperial Cowslip only exhibits its elegant blossoms under the damp shade of the thickets . . .

In my more special pursuits, I had very little success upon the mountain, owing, perhaps, to the excessively unpropitious weather and the shortness of my stay. At from seven thousand to eight thousand feet elevation, I obtained one of the most lovely of the small fruit pigeons (Ptilonopus roseicollis), whose entire head and neck are of an exquisite rosy pink colour, contrasting finely with its otherwise green plumage; and on the very summit, feeding on the ground among the strawberries that have been planted there, I obtained a dull-coloured thrush, with the form and habits of a starling (Turdus fumidus). Insects were almost entirely absent, owing no doubt to the extreme dampness, and I did not get a single butterfly the whole trip; yet I feel sure that, during the dry season, a week's residence on this mountain would well repay the collector in every department of natural history.

After my return to Toego [Tugu], I endeavoured to find another locality to collect in, and removed to a coffee plantation some miles to the north, and tried in succession higher and lower stations on the mountain; but I never succeeded in obtaining insects in any abundance, and birds were far less plentiful than on the Megamendong Mountain. The weather now became more rainy than ever, and as the wet season seemed to have set in in earnest, I returned to Batavia, packed up and sent off my collections, and left by steamer on November 1st for Banca and Sumatra.

Surveilling the Arabs

Consulate Officials

One population group the Dutch watched very carefully in the Indies were Arabs—both people actually from the Middle East and those Indies subjects of Arab parentage or extraction. Many Indonesians prized Arab bloodlines because they provided religious legitimacy as well as social distinction, particularly if the bloodlines in question were said to stretch back to the Prophet Muhammed himself. Though Arab families had prestige in local communities, they were also thought by the Dutch to be particularly resentful of the expansion of European hegemony over the islands. Most Arab families had nothing to do with any intrigues or plots against Dutch power in the archipelago. Yet there were some members of this community who did travel widely outside the Indies, where they agitated against growing Dutch control over the islands. The Dutch were very careful to set up an espionage network tracking Arab movements across their borders, particularly to Penang and Singapore, where other Arab communities occasionally provided cash and even guns for revolts. These two letters between the Dutch consul in Penang and a British steamship owner show the process of tracking Arab individuals, as these men slipped in and out of the Indies' boundaries, their intentions often unknown to the colonial state.

Netherlands Consulate

Penang, 20th March 1876:

Sir,

I am informed that among the passengers on board the steamer "Batara Bayce Sree," that sailed from this port on the 7th instant, was a certain Arab, well known at this place, called Sayd Habib Abdul Rachman. Not only does this name not appear on the list of passengers handed to the harbour master, and also to this consulate, but upon your employé being questioned whether there were any Arabs among the passengers, he dishonestly answered in the negative, and stated that the three Seyds mentioned on the passenger list,

An Arab in Indonesia,
1901. Photo no. 19795,
courtesy of KITLV, Leiden.

were natives of Penang and "bona fide" traders. I therefore request you to fur-
nish me with some explanation in the matter, with as little delay as possible.

To the managing owner of the British steamer
Batara Bayce Sree, Penang.

From Netherlands Vice Consul . . .

★ ★ ★

Penang, 24th March 1876:

Sir,

I have the honour to acknowledge yours of the 20th instant. I was unaware
that Syed [*sic*] Habib Abdul Rachman had proceeded to Acheen in the "Batara

Bayce Sree" and on making enquiries after the receipt of your letter among my employees, I was told that only the three Seyds mentioned in the Passenger list furnished to you and the Harbour master, had sailed as Passengers in my vessel. I however directed my agents to discover from the Achinese here, without exciting suspicion, whether or not Abdul Rachman had left Penang, and after some equivocation and beating about the bush on their part, I was informed that Abdul Rachman had really left Penang in my vessel, and in order to do so had taken his passage in a false name and had cut his beard and otherwise disguised himself in order to escape detection. I shall make further enquiries in the matter and shall be most happy to offer you every assistance in my power in any steps you may think necessary to be taken. I beg to assure you that the man did not go in my vessel with my knowledge or privity, nor, so far as I can learn, with the knowledge or privity of any of my employés, and had I had any suspicion of what was taking place, I should for the protection of my own interest alone, have immediately prevented it and informed you thereof. I extremely regret the occurrence but hope you will exonerate me from any blame in the matter.

I have the honour to be

Sir

Your most obedient Servant . . .

A Pioneer of Women's Rights

Raden Ajeng Kartini

Raden Ajeng Kartini was the daughter of a lesser Javanese aristocrat, born in Java in 1879. In this era, Javanese women were very cloistered by the males in their families and lived knowing few people except the members of their and their eventual husband's households. Kartini's father was an exception to this general pattern and allowed his daughter to receive an elementary school education, with her flourishing under such tutelage. Kartini befriended several Western women, and her correspondence with them (published in book form after her death) eventually made her an icon for many other women who wished to have less circumscribed lives. Kartini wrote about the societal changes she witnessed, and she understood that many of Java's old traditions had come under siege from aspects of the Western presence there, particularly from forces of modernization. Kartini eventually became the central female figure of Indonesian nationalism in the twentieth century, though she was rarely a "nationalist" in any real sense herself. Her plight and the sensitivity of her voice spoke to millions, however, and not just in the Indies—Kartini symbolized hope and conscientiousness to many throughout a changing world.

TO STELLA ZEEHANDELAAR

Japara, May 25, 1899

I have been longing to make the acquaintance of a "modern girl," that proud, independent girl who has all my sympathy! She who, happy and self-reliant, lightly and alertly steps her way through life, full of enthusiasm and warm feeling; working not only for her own well-being and happiness, but for the greater good of humanity as a whole.

I glow with enthusiasm towards the new time which has come, and can truly say that in my thoughts and sympathies I do not belong to the Indian world, but to that of my pale sisters who are struggling forward in the distant West.

If the laws of my land permitted it, there is nothing that I had rather do than to give myself wholly to the working and striving of the new woman in

Europe; but age-long traditions that cannot be broken hold us fast cloistered in their unyielding arms. Some day those arms will loosen and let us go, but that time lies as yet far from us, infinitely far. It will come, that I know; it may be three or four generations after us. Oh, you do not know what it is to love this young, this new age with heart and soul, and yet to be bound hand and foot, chained by all the laws, customs, and conventions of one's land. All our institutions are directly opposed to the progress for which I so long for the sake of our people. Day and night I wonder by what means our ancient traditions could be overcome. For myself, I could find a way to shake them off, to break them, were it not that another bond, stronger than any age-old tradition could ever be, binds me to my world; and that is the love which I bear for those to whom I owe my life, and whom I must thank for everything. Have I the right to break the hearts of those who had given me nothing but love and kindness my whole life long, and who have surrounded me with the tenderest care?

But it was not the voices alone which reached me from that distant, that bright, that newborn Europe, which made me long for a change in existing conditions. Even in my childhood, the word "emancipation" enchanted my ears; it had a significance that nothing else had, a meaning that was far beyond my comprehension, and awakened in me an ever growing longing for freedom and independence—a longing to stand alone. Conditions both in my surroundings and in those of others around me broke my heart, and made me long with a nameless sorrow for the awakening of my country.

Then the voices which penetrated from distant lands grew clearer and clearer, till they reached me, and to the satisfaction of some who loved me, but to the deep grief of others, brought seed which entered my heart, took root, and grew strong and vigorous.

And now I must tell you something of myself so that you can make my acquaintance.

I am the eldest of three unmarried daughters of the Regent of Japara, and have six brothers and sisters. What a world, eh? My grandfather, Pangeran Ario Tjondronegoro of Demak, was a great leader in the progressive movement of his day, and the first regent of middle Java to unlatch his door to that guest from over the Sea—Western civilization. All of his children had European educations; all of them have, or had (several of them are now dead), a love for progress inherited from their father; and these gave to their children the same upbringing which they themselves had received. Many of my cousins and all my older brothers have gone through the Hoogere Burger School—the highest institution of learning that we have here in Indië; and the youngest of my three older brothers has been studying for three years in

Kartini (left) and her sisters Kardinah and Roekmini, 1902. Photo no. 15467, courtesy of KITLV, Leiden.

the Netherlands, and two others are in the service of that country. We girls, so far as education goes, fettered by our ancient traditions and conventions, have profited but little by these advantages. It was a great crime against the customs of our land that we should be taught at all, and especially that we should leave the house every day to go to school. For the custom of our country forbade girls in the strongest manner ever to go outside of the house. We were never allowed to go anywhere, however, save to the school, and the only place of instruction of which our city could boast, which was open to us, was a free grammar school for Europeans.

When I reached the age of twelve, I was kept at home—I had to go into the "box." I was locked up, cut off from all communication with the outside world, toward which I might never turn again save at the side of a bridegroom, a stranger, an unknown man whom my parents would choose for me, and to whom I should be betrothed without my knowledge. European friends—this I heard later—had tried in every possible way to dissuade my parents from this cruel course to me, a young and life-loving child; but they were able to do nothing. My parents were inexorable; I went into my prison. Four long years I spent between thick walls, without once seeing the outside world.

How I passed through the time, I do not know. I only know that it was terrible. But there was one great happiness left me: the reading of Dutch books and correspondence with Dutch friends was not forbidden. This—the only gleam of light in that empty, somber time, was my all, without which, I should have fallen, perhaps, into a still more pitiable state. My life, my soul even, would have been starved. But then came my friend and my deliverer— the Spirit of the Age, his footsteps echoed everywhere. Proud, solid ancient structures tottered to their foundation at his approach. Strongly barricaded doors sprang open, some as of themselves, others only painfully half way, but nevertheless they opened, and let in the unwelcome guest.

At last in my sixteenth year, I saw the outside world again. Thank God! Thank God! I could leave my prison as a free human being and not chained to an unwelcome bridegroom. Then events followed quickly that gave back to us girls more and more of our lost freedom.

In the following year, at the time of the investiture of our young Princess, our parents presented us "officially" with our freedom. For the first time in our lives we were allowed to leave our native town, and to go to the city where the festivities were held in honor of the occasion. What a great and priceless victory it was! That young girls of our position should show themselves in public was here an unheard-of occurrence. The "world" stood aghast; tongues were set wagging at the unprecedented crime. Our European friends rejoiced, and as for ourselves, no queen was so rich as we. But I am far from satisfied. I would go still further, always further. I do not desire to go out to feasts, and little frivolous amusements. That has never been the cause of my longing for freedom. I long to be free, to be able to stand alone, to study, not to be subject to any one, and above all, *never, never* to be obliged to marry.

But we *must* marry, must, must. Not to marry is the greatest sin which the Moslem woman can commit; it is the greatest disgrace which a native girl can bring to her family.

And marriage among us—miserable is too feeble an expression for it. How can it be otherwise, when the laws have made everything for the man and nothing for the woman? When law and convention both are for the man; everything is allowed to him?

Love! what do we know here of love? How can we love a man whom we have never known? And how could he love us? That in itself would not be possible. Young girls and men must be kept rigidly apart, and are never allowed to meet. [. . .]

I am anxious to know of your occupations. It is all very interesting to me. I wish to know about your studies, I would know something of your Toynbee evenings, and of the society for total abstinence of which you are so zealous a member.

Among our Indian people, we have not the drink demon to fight, thank God!—but I fear, I fear that when once—forgive me—your Western civilization shall have obtained a foothold among us, we shall have that evil to contend with too. Civilization is a blessing, but it has its dark side as well. The tendency to imitate is inborn, I believe. The masses imitate the upper classes, who in turn imitate those of higher rank, and these again follow the Europeans.

Among us there is no marriage feast without drinking. And at the festivals of the natives, where they are not of strong religious convictions (and usually they are Moslem only because their fathers, grandfathers and remote ancestors were Moslem—in reality, they are a little better than heathen), large square bottles are always kept standing, and they are not sparing in the use of these.

But an evil greater than alcohol is here and that is opium. Oh! the misery, the inexpressible horror it has brought to my country! Opium is the pest of Java. Yes, opium is far worse than the pest. The pest does not remain for ever; sooner or later, it goes away, but the evil of opium, once established, grows. It spreads more and more, and will never leave us, never grow less—for to speak plainly—it is protected by the Government! The more general the use of opium in Java, the fuller the treasury.

The opium tax is one of the richest sources of income of the Government—what matter if it go well or ill with the people?—the Government prospers. This curse of the people fills the treasury of the Dutch East Indian Government with thousands—nay, with millions. Many say that the use of opium is no evil, but those who say that have never known India or else they are blind.

What are our daily murders, incendiary fires, robberies, but the direct result of the use of opium? True, the desire for opium is not so great an evil as long as one can get it—when one has the money to buy the poison; but when one cannot obtain it—when one has no money with which to buy it, and is a confirmed user of it? Then one is dangerous, then one is lost. Hunger will make a man a thief, but the hunger for opium will make him a murderer. There is a saying here—"At first you eat opium, but in the end it will devour you."

It is terrible to see so much evil and be powerless to fight against it.

That splendid book by Mevrouw Goekoop I know. I have read it three times. I could never grow tired of it. What would I not give to be able to live in Hilda's environment. Oh, that we in Indië had gone so far, that a book could cause such violent controversy among us, as *Hilda van Suylenburg* has in your country. I shall never rest till *H. v. S.* appears in my own language to do good as well as harm to our Indian world. It is a matter of indifference whether good or harm, if it but makes an impression, for that shows that one is no longer sleeping, and Java is still in deep slumber. And how will her people ever be awakened, when those who should serve as examples, themselves love sleep so much. The greater number of European women in India care little or nothing for the work of their sisters in the fatherland.

Will you not tell me something of the labors, the struggles, the sentiments, of the woman of today in the Netherlands? We take deep interest in all that concerns the Woman's Movement.

Chinese Coolies to Sumatra

William Pickering

*Some commentators have estimated the Dutch plantation and mining sectors of Suma-
tra to have constituted the most profitable colony in the history of global colonialism;
rubber, oil palms, and coffee, among other products, all grew there in near-perfect conditions. Because there were not enough local Sumatrans to do the labor of forcing these
commodities from the ground, the Dutch brought in coolies from various places—Java,
India, and especially China—to make their profits. Over decades Chinese laborers came
by the millions to help make the Dutch dream of record profits a reality. Much of this
traffic took place aboveboard, sanctioned both by the colonial Dutch and by the Chinese
authorities themselves, but this "official" moniker did little to lessen the abuses that
constituted a normal operating part of a complicated system of human procurement.
Many thousands of Chinese also found their way to the Sumatra plantations by way
of illegal procurement, and these laborers had no protection under the law at all. Occasionally the illicit voyages were intercepted, and it was at those moments that Chinese
coolies—poor, illiterate, and usually among the most forlorn of "voiceless" populations—spoke into the official record, usually in the courts. This selection memorialized
by the "Protector of Chinese" in Singapore shows these forces at work.*

"Cheah Sin Ng":

I am manager to Mr. Hermann, a proprietor of tin mines at Siak. . . . I had
chartered three tongkangs to take the coolies to Siak as my boat is undergoing
repairs. This morning about 9:30 . . . eighteen coolies had gone on board, the
remainder said, "we won't go" . . . "you will sell us as little pigs to another
country."

"Lim Shit":

I am from the . . . province of Canton, and am a farm labour [sic]: I was
induced . . . to leave my home, they told me that if I would follow them
to Singapore, they would find me good employment as a sawyer or brick-

Chinese coolies and their supervisors, 1870. Photo no. 10456, courtesy of KITLV, Leiden.

maker. . . . From our village, nine men besides me were induced to come away, and on the 15th of the 12th moon we were put on a Hainan junk . . . this morning I asked Chin-Sam for money to send to China, but he said we should get no money till we arrived at the place we were going to. Hearing that we were being taken away from his country, we refused to go on board the boat; Hiap-tye's man attempted to force me, so I ran away, as I had seen others beaten.

"Chew Ah Nyee":

Chaing-See and Kuai-leong told me they could get me plenty of work at Singapore as a clerk, and that wages here were very good; I believed them, and was put on board a junk and brought to this place, where I was sold to a shop . . . there were ninety men from my district, the strong men were sent to sawyards I believe, but I was sold as a "little pig," being weak. This morning I was being taken to a boat with many others. I don't know where they were taking us to, but we heard that the place is eleven or twelve days' sail from this end, and that we had to work in tin-mines.

"Hang Ship Ug":

We were all locked up within three doors, and never allowed to go out,—we were told that we should be locked up in the timber-yards.

"Leong Ship Sam":

We were kept in ignorance and could not see the sky, until to-day [*sic*], when we were told that we must work in some tin mines. . . . I and fourteen others were sent on board a boat, and if the gentlemen had not come and delivered me, I should have been stolen away in ignorance.

"Lew Ship Yit":

I was being taken on board a boat with a lot of others, and if any refused to go they were beaten by the Kheh-tows, there was a row and I got a blow during the struggle. I don't wish to go past Singapore, this is the place I agreed to come to.

IV

Through Travelers' Eyes

For a very long time, the Indonesian archipelago has inspired travelers of various descriptions to pass through its far-flung island world. Though early descriptions of "the lands beneath the winds" are scattered (such as those of the Chinese monk I-Ching, Marco Polo, and the Arab adventurer Ibn Battuta), by the eighteenth and especially the nineteenth centuries, such accounts were becoming more common. These narratives sketch a strange yet wonderful world, one at once full of danger and opportunity—an irresistible combination for many stout-hearted sojourners of the time. Travelers sometimes exaggerated the things they saw in Indonesia because the islands were remote and difficult to visit and few readers could check the accuracy of their descriptions. Yet many accounts of the archipelago during this period are remarkably accurate; often subsequent travelers visited specific locations in the Indies decades or even centuries later and were able to find specific aspects of earlier visitors' descriptions still intact.

This is not to imply that the archipelago resisted change in a wholesale manner over time, for it certainly did not. Yet in the eighteenth and even in the nineteenth centuries, large parts of the Indies remained sufficiently isolated from the larger currents of global events for travelers to describe locales as "primordial" or "unchanging." Changes and the echoes of distant events trickled slowly into many of the far-flung islands. Distant archipelagos of tiny atolls received word of regional or transregional events in the form of the occasional ship that might touch its shores. This was equally true of mountain populations who were cut off from their neighbors by altitude and difficult topography, so that the occasional traveler who made the trek offered an unusual but often very welcome sight. Communities of separated "Indonesians" knew that there was a wider world beyond their horizons, but it was only in the eighteenth and nineteenth centuries that this world increasingly started to show up at their doorsteps.

Some parts of the archipelago had been receiving visitors for a longer period of time than others. In parts of the Moluccas, the fabled Spice Islands, the arrival of travelers did not mark an especially noteworthy event. Visitors had been coming for centuries, perhaps millennia, to try to procure the nutmeg, clove, and mace that grew nowhere else in the world. Bugis communities such as those at Makassar and from further afield were also accustomed to a certain amount of visitation and foreign influence, since the Bugis and Makassarese peoples traded widely in archipelago seas and to places like the Philippines and Australia. Even Banjarmasin, a comparatively new addition to the panoply of ancient harbors scattered throughout the islands, made for a cosmopolitan place at an early date: Chinese junks and European square-rigged ships, indigenous *prahu* and Melanesian *kora-kora* could all be found in its roads. The narratives about places such as a Ternate, Tidore, Makassar, and Banjarmasin often reflect these histories of trade and contact, painting these locales as distant but simultaneously connected to broader systems of travel, commerce, and influence in the world.

Other parts of the archipelago were seen differently through travelers' eyes. Thomas Forrest's account of the coasts of New Guinea (parts of the contemporary Indonesian province of West Papua) tells of a place little touched by the outside world. People here lived in the wood age: the vast swamps of New Guinea provided almost no stone and certainly no metal, which rendered the latter an important item of trade. Likewise, many of the islands in Nusa Tenggara, such as Flores, were seen as nearly wholly off the grid of modern events. The notion of an even greater remoteness in this sense clung to interior populations, which, according to some visitors of the time, were little better than animals, clad in bark or leaves or often wearing no clothing at all. Even the uplands of Palembang, which had engaged in active exchange with the Dutch and certain other visitors for a very long time, was painted as terra incognita by sojourners passing through this region as late as the early twentieth century. Descriptions of the landscape and the people of this region leave little doubt as to European notions of superiority over local populations, who were deemed "primitive"—and therefore conquerable—like almost everyone else in Indonesia.

Yet we also have accounts of other travelers passing through the Indies, those who came from different shores or who were not necessarily concerned with exploration, conquest, or trade. Letters from Chinese merchants trading with Dutch Batavia form one of these interesting sources. They record not European sensibilities but rather those of another outside group trading with the Dutch, who were fast becoming the most important commercial clique in the archipelago. Descriptions of piratical attacks in the waters off Java show that the process of attaining regional supremacy based on trade and political control was an uneven one. The contours of a burgeoning Dutch hegemony were still being challenged, even in the core areas of European control such as the *pasisir* coasts of northern Java. Travelers to the region also included scientists, who looked at the Indies not as a field for conquest or profit but rather as a source of knowledge. The travelers' various agendas implied different visions of locations, peoples, and environments, based not only on what was being seen but on who was doing the seeing.

This crucial importance of the "eye of the beholder" was something that travel narratives from Indonesia shared with accounts given by other voyagers around the world. Everywhere on the globe territory was being conquered by Europeans; by 1914 nearly 90 percent of the world's land surface was planted with European flags. Yet these conquests included processes of knowing and describing, as well as actual military feats: travelers generally came before armed might, and the descriptions of their sojourns often conditioned the political events that followed their voyages. In Indonesia as elsewhere a fascinating dialectic of travel and observation fed into a larger narrative of economic expansion, and ultimately, of political control and conquest. The voices presented here tell some of that story for the eighteenth and nineteenth centuries, which was not the first time that travelers had traversed the archipelago. Yet at this moment description, for the first time on a large scale, started to phase into something more sinister and coercive.

Visiting Banjarmasin

Daniel Beekman

The Dutch traveler Daniel Beekman's narrative of life in the port of Banjarmasin in 1714 is one of the best accounts available of eighteenth-century life on Borneo. Banjarmasin constituted an important sultanate, and its harbor welcomed ships from around the Indonesian archipelago and beyond. It was the channeling point for a range of commodities that entered the Borneo interior from the city, and in turn Banjarmasin funneled much natural produce from the forest to the outside world. Beekman made a distinction between the Banjars of the coast, who had embraced Islam, and the Dayaks of the interior, whom he described as more warlike and fearsome. He also left an impression of life in Banjarmasin as one of comparative comfort and ease. Though Beekman found the local inhabitants to be "lazy" by his standards, the wealth of rice, fish, and fruit easily available to them made such proclivities understandable to his sensibilities, if not to his own moral code. This trope of the "embarrassment of plenty" would be one repeated by many other travelers in Indonesia's islands.

The Natives are of two sorts, *viz.* those that inhabit in or near the Ports of Trade (as particularly the Banjareens) and the Inhabitants of the inland Country; for the former are of a middle Stature, rather than over, well shap'd and clean limb'd, being generally better featur'd than the Guinea Negroes: Their Hair is long and black, their Complexion somewhat darker than Mulattos, but not quite so black as the aforesaid Negroes; they are affronted if you called them black Men. Both Men and Women value themselves in a particular manner, if they are whiter than ordinary. They are very weak of Body, which is occasion'd chiefly by their lazy unactive Life, and mean Diet not having the opportunity of Walking, or of any Land Exercise, and working seldom, but are always in a sitting posture, either in their Boats or Houses; neither do they stir without it be out of absolute necessity. They us'd to laugh at us for walking about in their Houses, telling us that it looked as if we were mad, or knew not what we did: If, say they, you have any Business at the other end of the Room, why do you not stay there; if not, why do you go thither; why always stalking backwards and forwards? If the Banjareens have but a quantity of Rice and Salt, they think themselves very rich, for if they throw a casting Net at their Door, they need not fear the want of a Dinner, so great abundance of Fish is in the River.

The Women are very little, but very well shaped, having much handsomer Features and better Complexion than the Men; they walk very upright, and tread well, turning their Toes out, which is contrary to the Purchase of most Indians. I believe it is a Custom forced upon them by their walking on the Logs that float upon the River before their Doors from House to House, as I shall explain more at large by and by. They are very constant when married, but very loose when single; neither is her former Compliancé counted a Fault in a Wife; and the Mothers do often prostitute their Daughters at eight or nine Years of Age for a small lucre. They generally marry at that Age, and sometimes under; but as they are soon ripe for Matrimony, their Fertility soon decays, for they are generally past Child-bearing at 20 or 25; it is rare that a Woman holds till 30. They live to a tolerable good Age, and use daily Bathing in the Rivers, and are expert Swimmers. Every Day whilst we remained at Tatas, we saw the River full of Men, Women, and Children, even some in Arms, which they carry in for Health's sake, to which this way of Bathing must needs be very beneficial and refreshing in so hot a Climate.

In burying their Dead they take care to lay their Heads towards the North, and put into the Grave with them a great deal of Camphire, and several things necessary for the support of Life; for what end the Camphire is deposited there I know not; but the latter is according to an old Pagan Custom, that has been handed down to them, as believing that those Provisions were useful to them in their Journey to the other World. But now being Mahometans they say they do it only as a mark of Respect. They carry them in Boats as near as they can to the Burying-place, attended by their Friends in great Order and Ceremony, being dress'd all in White, with lighted Torches in their Hands, tho' it be in the Day-time.

The inland inhabitants are much taller and stronger bodied Men than the Banjareens, fierce, warlike, and barbarous. They are called Byajo's, an idle sort of People, hating Industry or Trade, and living generally upon Rapine and Spoil of their Neighbours, their Religion is Paganism, and their Language different from that spoken by the Banjareens. They go naked and only have a small piece of Cloth that covers their private Parts; they stain their Bodies with blue, and have a very odd Custom of making Holes in the soft part of their Ears when young, into which they thrust large Plugs, and by continual pulling down these Plugs the Holes grow in time so large, that when they come to Man's Estate, their Ears hang down to their very Shoulders. The biggest end of the Plug is as broad as a Crown piece, and is tipt with a thin Plate of wrought Gold. The Men of Quality do generally pull out their fore Teeth and put Gold ones in their room. They sometimes wear, by way of Ornament, Rows of Tygers Teeth strung and hung round their Necks and Bodies. Those of them that were subject to the Sultan of Caitangee (whom I shall have occasion to mention often hereafter) are now in Rebellion against him; he that headed them made Pretences to the Crown, and was set up by these Mountaineers against the present Sultan (to whose Government they are very averse) who was chosen by the general Consent of the People, at least of the civiliz'd trading part of them. But this Pretender,—before I came away, was dispatch'd by Poison. However, some of those People, *viz.* those that live near the Ports of Trade, are in subjection to their different Kings or Sultans; the others live in Clans by themselves, without Kings, or any Form of Government. I have seen some of the former come down the River to the Port of Banjar Masseen in very ill-shap'd Praws; and bring down Gold Dust Diamonds, Bezoar-stones, Rattans, and sundry other Merchandizes. The Banjareens will not suffer the Europeans to have any Acquaintance or Trade with them, but do purchase the Goods from them, which they sell to us at a greater Price. And I do verily believe, that the many frightful Stories they tell of those People's Barbarity and Cruelty, are only invented on purpose to deter us from having any Acquaintance or Commerce with them, which would be a great disadvantage to the latter; tho' some of these Reports may be true: As to their Women I never saw any of them, and so can give no Account of them. The Island is divided into different Kingdoms, having their particular Kings or Sultans, whom they called Raja's.

I shall only say that there are several Kings or Raja's in the inlands Country; as also the Cities of Borneo, Succadanam and Passeer have each of them one; that formerly all the other Raja's (as well as he to whom Banjar Masseen belongs) were subject to the Raja of Borneo, who was a Supreme King over the whole Island; but now his Authority is mightily decreased, and there are other Kings equal, if not more powerful than himself, particularly the Sultan of Caitangee. His Name is Pannomboang, and stiles himself Sultan of Caitangee, which is the City where he resides, situated within one hundred Miles of the Port of Banjar Masseen. His Brother is another King, and stiles himself Sultan of Negarree, a City about three hundred Miles up the main River, where he resides. But the former is the greatest, by reason of the Trade and the Customs he receives from this Port, which may be computed to amount to six or eight thousand Pieces of Eight per annum. But I think I have said enough of these general Matters, and it is time to give an Account of our particular Proceedings after our arrival in the River.

After we cast Anchor as aforesaid, we espy'd a small Praw or Boat under the Shore; we sent in a very civil manner to the Persons that were in it, and intreated them to come on board. We lay then with our English Colours flying, at which they were much surprized, knowing how severely they had used our Countrymen, when last among them. However, partly thro' Fear, and partly thro' our kind Invitation, they came on board. They were very poor-look'd Creatures, that had been at Tomberneo [Tabanio], and were returning to Tatas. We express'd all the Civility imaginable towards them, gave them some small Presents, and desired that they would acquaint their King or Grandees in the Country, that there were two English Ships come to buy Pepper of them; that we were not come to quarrel, but to trade peaceably, and would pay them very honestly, and comply with all reasonable Demands according to what should be hereafter agreed on. They inquir'd whether we were Company Ships, to which we did not readily answer them; but before we did, they proceeded and said, that if we were, they, as Friends, would advise us to depart the Port forthwith, because their Sultan and their Oran-Cays, or great Men, would by no means have any Dealings with us. We design'd to have sent our Boat that Night to their Town call'd Tatas (which is about thirty Miles above the Place where we lay) that she might arrive there by Day-light the next Morning; but those Persons dissuaded us from it, assuring us that we should soon have News from their Sultan; and that some of their Men would not fail to be down with us the next Day. Then they took their leave of us, returning us many Thanks for our Presents.

The next Day came on board of us a Boat, with one Cay Rouden T'acka, and Cay Chetra Uday, being Messengers from the King. We received them as civilly as possible. The first thing they inquired, was whether we were Company Ships or separate Traders; that if the former, we need not wait for an Answer, and that it would be our best ways to be gone; desiring earnestly that what Answer we should return them might be sincere; for that whatever we said to them should be told the Sultan. Finding no other methods to introduce ourselves, we were forc'd to assure them that we were private Traders, and came thither on our own Account to buy Pepper. This we did, believing we might in time have a better Opportunity of making our honorable Masters known, and of excusing the heavy Crimes laid on their former Servants, whose ill Conduct has been the Cause of the Factory's being destroyed. They ask'd us why we came thither rather than to any other Place, since our Countrymen had so grosly abused them? We answer'd, that we were Strangers to that Affair; and that at first we design'd to go to Pallambam; but being inform'd that Pepper was much cheaper here, we were willing first to try this Market. They also enquir'd what number of Men and Guns we had, and cast their Eyes slyly about to endeavour to guess of what strength we were; for they were exceedingly jealous of all Europeans.

Towards Night they departed, and we gave them some Guns. They left two Persons on board, with whom they desir'd our Linguist would come up to the Town next Day, to give answer to such other Questions as might be ask'd. We gave Instructions to our Linguist to tell them, that we were two small separate Stock-Ships; that we were informed at Batavia, that Pepper was very cheap at this Port, so chose rather to come hither than to Pallambam: We order'd him to learn on what Conditions they would offer to trade with us, and who were the properest Person to apply to; to press a speedy Meeting: And if they ask'd what we had to purchase Pepper with, to tell them Mexico Pieces of Eight; (for Pillar-dollars they will not take); to give them kind Invitations to come on board; to write down all Questions and Answers: And if any thing of Consequence should be further ask'd, to give no Assurances or Answers of themselves, but to plead Ignorance, and to refer all to the Merchants (for so they were to call us, and not Supercargo's, which would have created a Jealousy that we belong'd to the Company;) to take care to keep the Sailors sober, and in good Order; with some other Instructions less material.

Having given them these general Directions, we sent them away the 2nd of July at two a Clock in the Morning. One of the Linguists was an Englishman, the other a Javan whom we hir'd at Batavia; but we put most Confidence in the first. They return'd that very Night, and told us, we should have an Answer in seven Days from the Sultan of Caytangee, and in eleven from the Sultan of Negarree. They also brought us a Caution from the Banjareens to beware of some large Pirate Praws mann'd with about a hundred of the Byajo Men, that lay skulking thereabouts. But before this Advice came, we were like to have felt some of the cruel Effects of their Barbarity through our own Inadvertency: For that Day about Noon we saw three large Praws under the Shore, which had shot up the River a little above our Ships: Whereupon, imagining they were Banjareens, and hoping to get some better Information in relation to Trade, I went into the Longboat in Company with Mr. Bartholomew Swartz, chief Supercargo of Borneo, and Mr. John Beacher, chief Supercargo of my Ship, and Mr. John Gerard, our Assistant and Purser, with five Men and a Boy. We carried only two Muskets, and a small Fowling-piece, with two Cartouch-boxes; but had we thought of meeting with such Barbarians as we did, we should have been much better provided. We hoisted our Sail, and stood towards them; but they row'd with all their Might from us; and finding we were like to come up with them, they ran their three Vessels up a Creek among the Trees, which were exceedingly thick, hanging over the Water, and gave so great a Shelter that there was no Wind for us to sail up the Creek after them: However, we made in, thinking they were bound no further, but being come close to the Mouth of the Creek, we saw their Praws a little way up, and no men in them; For they, being about a hundred in number, were got ashore among the Trees, designing to draw us in, and destroy us all; which they might easily have done, had they all equal'd the Courage and Resolution of their Leader. For the Creek was not above ten Yards over, and they exceeded us in number above ten to one, being arm'd with Javelins, Sampits, and poison'd Arrows. We call'd aloud, and ask'd them what they had to sell, with some other Questions, but receiv'd no Answer 'till we were got up into the Creek; when on a sudden we heard a horrible Shout, after the manner of these Barbarians; and at the same time their Captain advanc'd boldly towards the Boat, threw a Javelin at us, and immediately after shot an Arrow.

It was fortunate for us that his Men were not so forward, and seem'd dismayed, keeping back among the Trees, but let fly a Shower of their poison'd Arrows among us, which however did us no Damage. We immediately put ourselves in a posture of Defence, and presented our small Arms, but were at first unwilling to fire, least such as Proceeding should frustrate our Design of trading in the Port. But seeing no other Remedy, and perceiving by their Dress and Language that they were not Banjareens, we discharged our Pieces at them, which put them to flight, scouring in among the Trees; tho' even in their Retreat they ceas'd not to let fly their Arrows at us, after the manner of the ancient Parthians. Whilst Mr. Gerrard was loading our Guns again we us'd our Pocket-pistols, firing wherever we saw a Bush wag. In the mean time the Sailors were in great Confusion, but not idle, haling the Boat by the means of the Boughs and Shrubs, until they got her out; before which we had discharged our Pieces a second time. But we saw no more of these Villains, they being frightened at the Noise, and Danger of our Fire-arms. We were not a little pleased at our narrow Escape. What loss the Enemy had we know not; but our good Fortune brought us off without so much as one Wound. We brought away some Darts that stuck in the side, and Sail of our Boat. These People go naked, having only a Chawat, or small Piece of Cloath, about the breadth of a Hand, to cover their Privy-parts. Their Bodies were all over stain'd with Blue; and they seem'd to be strong, tall Men, like the Mountaineers spoken of before.

The Lure of Spice in the Moluccas

One of the most blessed sights for all early traders to the Indies was the far-off vision of Moluccan volcanoes—here, the spice-bearing cone of Ternate. On Banda, a small volcanic island in the central Moluccas, most of the world's nutmeg and mace, two of the spices most sought after by Europe in the so-called age of discovery, grew naturally. Ternate and a few other small islands in the northern Moluccas were home to most of the world's cloves. Due to these three spices—and to a number of other enticing products indigenous to these tiny islands in Eastern Indonesia, including bird of paradise feathers, cassowary claws, and edible sea cucumbers—the Moluccas became one of the most fabled and eagerly sought-out destinations in the early modern world. This desire had its price, however. The Dutch tortured and killed many of their competitors for spices and then repopulated parts of the islands with slaves thought to be loyal to Holland's colonial ambitions. Even then, however, the maddening desire for these rare eastern Indonesian items often proved to be too much. Smuggling, for example, was always a problem. Ironically, the VOC monopoly on cloves was finally broken in the mid-eighteenth century by a Frenchman named Pierre Poivre (or roughly, "Peter Pepper"), who smuggled out clove seedlings to be replanted in French Mauritius, all the way across the Indian Ocean.

The lure of spices, the Moluccas. Photo by Eric Tagliacozzo.

An Englishman in New Guinea

Thomas Forrest

Thomas Forrest, an Englishman, completed a series of epic voyages in eastern Indonesia and Australasia in the latter decades of the eighteenth century. His journal entries offer some of the most detailed descriptions that we have of eastern Indonesia in this period, when the Dutch were still isolated in comparatively few settlements. Forrest had trading interactions with Papuans along the coasts of New Guinea; his narrative of these meetings shows that outsiders were already starting to have some limited ideas about Papuan life, and that Papuans—in language and in dress—already had a sense of the outside world as well. This shows that supposedly isolated places such as New Guinea were actually integrated into regional and transregional systems of commerce and exchange at a far earlier time than has been previously supposed. Forrest comments on several interesting cultural attributes of Papuan life, including the predilection to keep houses on stilts (to deal with the tides of the huge swamplands of the southern coasts) and the sequestering of male bachelors into separate dwellings close to the population's main settlements. Many cultures along the vast maritime littoral of New Guinea shared these and other customs.

1775 January

Off the mouth of the bay before the harbour, but out of the swell, a boat, with two Papua men, came on board, after having conversed a good deal with our linguists at a distance: satisfied we were friends, they hastened ashore, to tell, I suppose, the news. Soon after, many Papua Coffres came on board, and were quite easy and familiar: all of them wore their hair bushed out so much round their heads, that its circumference measured about three foot, and were least, two and a half. In this they stuck their comb, consisting of four or five long diverging teeth, with which they now and then combed their frizzling locks, in a direction perpendicular from the head, as with a design to make it more bulky. They sometimes adorned their hair with feathers. The women had only their left ear pierced, in which they wore small brass rings. The hair of the women was bushed out also; but not quite so much as that

A Papua man, 1920.
Photo no. 28554,
courtesy of KITLV,
Leiden.

of the men. As we were rowing along, one of my crowned pigeons escaped from its cage, and flew to the woods.

We anchored about four in the afternoon, close to one of their great houses, which is built on posts, fixed several yards below low water mark; so that the tenement is always above the water: a long stage, supported by posts, going from it to the land, just at high water mark. The tenement contains many families, who live in cabins on each side of a wide common hall, that goes through the middle of it, and has two doors, one opening to the stage, towards the land; the other on a large stage towards the sea, supported likewise by posts, in rather deeper water than those that support the tenement. On this stage the canoes are hauled up; and from this the boats are ready for a launch, at any time of tide, if the Haraforas attack the land; if they attack by sea, the Papuas take to the woods. The married people, unmarried women, and children, live in these large tenements, which, as I have said, have two doors; the one to the long narrow stage, that leads to the land; the other to the broad stage, which is over the sea, and on which they keep their boats, having outriggers on each side. A few yards from this sea stage, if I may so call it, are built, in still deeper water, and on stronger posts, houses where only the bachelors live. This is like the custom of the Batta people on Sumatra, and the Idaan or Moroots on Borneo, where, I am told, the bachelors are separated from the young women and the married people.

At Dory, were two tenements of this kind, about four hundred yards from each other, and each had a house for the bachelors, close by it: in one of the tenements were fourteen cabins, seven on a side; in the other, twelve or six on a side. In the common hall, I saw the women sometimes making mats, at other times forming pieces of clay into earthen pots; with a pebble in one hand, to put into it, whilst they held in the other hand, also a pebble, with which they knocked, to enlarge and smooth it. The pots so formed, they burnt with dry grass, or light brushwood. The men, in general, wore a thin stuff, that comes from the cocoa nut tree, and resembles a coarse kind of cloth, tied forward round the middle, and up behind, between the thighs. The women wore in general, coarse blue Surat baftas, round their middle, not as a petticoat, but tucked up behind, like the men; so that the body and thigh were almost naked: as boys and girls go entirely. I have often observed the women with an ax or chopping knife, fixing posts for the stages, whilst the men were sauntering about idle. Early in the morning I have seen the men setting out in their boats, with two or three fox looking dogs, for certain places to hunt the wild hog, which they call Ben: a dog they call Naf. I have frequently bought of them pieces of wild hog; which, however, I avoided carrying on board the galley, but dressed and eat it ashore, unwilling to give offence to the crew.

At anchor, I fired some swivel guns: the grown people did not regard this, or seem frightened, while the boys and girls ran along the stages, into the woods. *Saturday* the 28th. Fresh winds, with squalls, but no rain. The clouds seemed to gather, and settle over the mountains of Arfak, which lie south of this harbour; they are exceeding high; higher than any of the mountains we had hitherto seen, to the westward, on this coast.

After passing the Cape of Good Hope, the promontory of Dory, from a large ship's deck, may be seen fifteen or sixteen leagues off, disjunct from New Guinea, and like an island. To get into Dory harbour, coast it along, at a reasonable distance: the flat points and the island Yowry will appear very plain. Having got beyond the last Flat Point, which is near the easternmost part of the promontory, you suddenly perceive an island (Manaswary): this must be kept on the left. Steer mid channel, in fourteen and fifteen fathom water, sandy ground. Farther in, and to the westward of Manaswary, is a smaller island, called Masmapy; which must also be left on the same hand. When abreast of the island Masmapy, that is, when the body of it bears about south, you will have fourteen fathom water, sandy ground: then look out for a sunk shoal of coral rocks, two foot deep, at low water, and at high water fix: it is bold to. Keep it also on the left, and steer into the inner harbour, which will hold any number of ships, in soundings from twelve to five fathom water, muddy ground. Fresh water may be had in many places; wood everywhere. Dory harbour lies in latitude 00° 21 s. longitude 131° E.

Schouten's island, is laid down by Dampier, bears E.S.E. from the Cape of Good Hope, and has its south coast undetermined by a dotted line. The coast of New Guinea opposite to it is undetermined also.—As the promontory of Dory bears from the Cape in the same direction, and I can find no voyager has gone to the south of Schouten's island, I am apt to think that it is the same land, which time alone will show.

Having opened the hold, about which we lately had been in great pain, we found our provisions greatly damaged. A tight chest saved many of my piece goods. The damaged I washed directly in fresh water, and was lucky in getting them well dried. It often threatened to rain, but did not; unlike the climate of Waygiou, where, as has been said, the clouds often break, and fall in rain unexpectedly.

Letters from Chinese Merchants to Batavia

Leonard Blussé

Letters in Chinese showing the connections between coastal southeastern China and the Dutch Indies are comparatively rare, but those that do survive show how important these trading voyages were to both sides. Though Chinese merchants had been sailing to the Indonesian archipelago for centuries, the Dutch imposition of rust en orde (peace and control) over increasing stretches of the islands by the early nineteenth century made trade ever more profitable. The Dutch needed the Chinese navigators and merchants as an outlet for the Indies' goods; many of these were natural products (such as resins, spices, and animal parts), though increasingly they were farmed commodities as well. The Chinese also wished to sell silk, porcelain, and tea to the Dutch, as well as a wide variety of other items, some of them going to the indigenous populations of the Indies themselves. Commerce between the two sides was highly orchestrated, and the communication between Chinese merchants hoping to trade in the Dutch-controlled islands and their Dutch "hosts" was ritualized in character. The giving of tribute gifts—here satin, linen, gold foil, and tea in a selection translated by the Dutch historian Leonard Blussé—was a mark of respect, but it was also a device to oil the wheels of exchange toward a favorable reception of traders from afar.

Letter of Jiaqing Year 7, Tenth Day of the Twelfth Month [January 4, 1803]

The Li Kunhe Ocean *Hang* of Xiamen respectfully addresses Your Royal Highness:

We have the honour to inform You that this unskilled, humble merchant is fitting out ocean vessels to engage in trade. We have often benefited from Your great Benevolence and many times we have rejoiced in Your gracious Protection. Your Majesty is a scion of Ge-la-ba's illustrious families. You are the Powerful Sovereign of the Sea.

Trade in the Eastern and Southern regions must be carried our in an honest and trustworthy manner!

The hub of land and sea traffic is managed in perfect order.

Even though we are far away and deprived of your Eminence and Instruction, we have in fact been the recipients of Your Benevolence over many generations.

This year we have established the [Li] Kunhe Ocean *Hang* and specially fitted out a vessel, the Rong fa to trade with Your Country. The shipmaster, Huang Jiguan, is not well acquainted with the people and local conditions there. He is not yet familiar with all matters of business. Nonetheless, we hope You will show solicitude to him so that the accounts can be settled promptly in order to allow for the speedy return of the vessel. If that is possible, the itinerant merchants of the coastal regions have received Your unbounded, beneficent Protection.

Because our vessel is bound for Ge-la-ba we are sending a letter of exceptional respect and wish You happiness and peace. Furthermore, we have added local products, noted down on a separate list of commodities, to present to You.

Presents:

two bolts of top quality white Chinese linen
two chests of top quality Xihe scented tea
two chests of top quality gold foil for gilding
two bolts of top quality black tribute satin.

The Li Kunhe Ocean *Hang* prostrates itself a hundred times.

Blussé: The flattering introduction of Li Kunhe's letter is part and parcel of a long tradition in Chinese commercial correspondence. Two points in the letter require further explanation: it is noteworthy that the supercargo in charge of the shipowner's affairs, Huang Jiguan, had no experience in the Xiamen-Batavia trade. Li Kunhe begged the Governor-General to ensure that the trading accounts would be settled promptly. He feared that if his junk could not sail in time, it might not be able to reach its Fujian homeport during the southern monsoon. We shall find this particular concern again in all his letters.

Li Kunhe's second letter shows that his requests had been complied with.

Letter of Jiaqing Year 8, Twelfth Month [January–February 1804]

Your Majesty, great wide and able ruler of Ge-[la-ba]

Please permit me to state respectfully that Ge-la-ba is a prosperous place, renowned among maritime countries. In the northern islands and southern ports, ships throng the navigation routes, merchants flock together like clouds knowing that You move and inspire the people by Your virtuous Conduct.

Your Fame is unique like that of the Great Wall. From afar, like sunflowers eagerly facing the sun, we look up to Your glorious radiance.

Last year [our] vessel, the *Rong Fa*, came to Ge-la-ba. We entrusted the command of the ship to Huang Jiguan and were the recipients of Your Benevolence and Protection yet gain, so that our people returned [to Xiamen] singing and on time. Moreover, I have taken note of Your gracious gifts. I am ashamed of not possessing precious gems to repay you for them. This time I am sending the same ship again and the same people to cross the seas to your Domain. We cannot guarantee the time of our arrival, but if we return home in time then the merchants, as well as our Ocean Trading Company, will rejoice.

The problem is that we had originally planned to send three ships to Ge-la-ba, but unexpectedly the ships bound for Melaka, Bing-lang [Penang], and Sulu were all lost at sea, and there are few ships from Xiamen that spent the winter in Luzon. Therefore I am sending only two ships to Ge-la-ba this time. All the passengers arriving from several thousand miles away had been told that three ships would be sailing for Ge-la-ba. But they did not know that this year only two ships would sail. The passengers that were to be transported on three ships are now to be carried on two ships, and consequently the number of people [on each ship] is too high. Our company knows that the [Dutch East India] Company regulates the number of migrants. The law is very severe on this point. Strictly speaking we should adhere exactly to the quota. Yet, we should allow for the fact that the passengers who have traveled from afar to Xiamen with slender purses have made a long and difficult journey. If we were not to respond leniently to their requests to be allowed to go aboard, then those from afar would run out of money and find themselves unable to return home. The dilemma was whether to proceed or turn back. These were extremely distressing circumstances! They [the passengers] earnestly implored us to take pity. We had to accede to their entreaties. In truth they were to be pitied. Our company had no choice but to let them embark. Consequently, there are more than one hundred excess passengers.

Naturally I had to write and explain this matter to You. We hope Your Excellency will grant us a favour and permit them to go ashore. Our company will be so moved by such a decision that it will be engraved on our hearts. It goes without saying. Moreover, all our compatriots in China will be infinitely grateful. If You graciously deign to give my letter your full consideration, I would be most happy.

How my thoughts reach out to You who are so far way as I write this letter! The worthless items I am presenting to You are noted on a separate list. I hope You will accept them and I look forward to seeing You with eager anticipation.

Blussé: Because members of the Fujian gentry engaged in trade only covertly, their "tradenames" were not the same as the names they used in public life. In this letter, Li Kunhe unveils his real name, Li Qingen, to the Governor-General, whom he may have met in Batavia at some time in the past, and reveals that the *Nanyang* trade had suffered severe losses in 1803. The main theme of this letter is how to solve a possible infraction of the immigration procedures in Batavia. The immigration of Chinese settlers was a perpetual source of concern to the Dutch colonial authorities in Java, especially after the Chinese uprising of 1740. In order to avoid internecine strife between Chinese from different provinces, immigration was allowed from Xiamen only. According to the *plakaat* (edict) promulgated by Governor-General in Council on 31 March 1761, small junks were allowed to carry a total of 200 crew members and passengers, whereas large junks were allotted a quota of 250 people. As the *plakaat* of 10 July 1800 makes clear, there were administrative problems with the registration of Chinese immigrants. While generally some 1,500 "permissie-briefjes," or licences to settle, were issued every year, only 185 people had applied for a licence in the first six months of 1800. (From the information provided by IJesseldijk we know that 1,338 newcomers had actually arrived in Batavia during that same year. Many of these people must have entered as illegal immigrants or may have immediately travelled on to other ports elsewhere in the Archipelago.) Because the intake of Chinese immigrants was considered to be insufficient, measures were taken in to encourage Chinese legal settlement in Batavia.

In response to a report that the sugar mills in the vicinity of Batavia found themselves short-handed, on 27 July 1802 the Governor-General in Council decided to increase quotas for junks from Xiamen to four hundred people for small junks and six hundred for large ones, with half of the passengers being granted a residence permit valid until further notice. Two days later, on 29 July, new regulations were issued that again limited immigration to the Chinese from Xiamen. Junks from other Chinese ports were forbidden to bring in immigrants. In these circumstances, the decision of Li Kunhe to transport all those who were awaiting passage to Batavia on two junks could not have been a happier one. This becomes apparent from the third letter in which Li Kunhe expresses gratitude that his *nachodas* were not fined for bringing in too many people.

Letter of Jiaqing Year 9, Twelfth Month [January 1805]

The Li Kunhe Ocean *Hang* of Xiamen respectfully addresses itself to Your Majesty,

We have the honour to inform You that these humble merchants have with their meagre capital fitted out a ship to sail to Your country to engage in trade. Even with the rivers of ink and mountains of paper, Your Protection and great Benevolence towards us could not be adequately described.

Last winter when our vessel, the *Rong Fa*, arrived in Ge-la-ba with excess passengers on board, we were not fined, thanks to Your great Humanity. This adequately demonstrates that Your Generosity is as deep and wide as the ocean. You have treated the merchants from far away with beneficence. We rest our brush for a while, as there is still so much that might be said. Our ship returned with the precious presents You have again bestowed on us. As we note them down, we feel even more honoured.

This winter we have again fitted out the *Rong Fa* to sail to Your Territory. The shipmaster, *Huang Jiguan* has often been the recipient of Your vast Benevolence. The longer he is in receipt of it, the more profoundly he appreciates it. We would be grateful to Your boundless Benevolence in protecting him as before in all respects, arranging for early clearance of payments to allow his prompt return. We have a further request:

For several years, Chinese vessels have been few in number. For ports like Machen [Banjarmasin], Ruofu [Johore], and Lungya [Lingga Archipelago], for example, no ships have been fitted out for a long time. All those Chinese seeking to join their kinfolk and friends there must therefore go via Your Territory. The number of passengers consequently exceeds the normal quota. Out of Your kind Consideration You have magnanimously forgiven this. But this year the East India Company has informed us that, in addition to the two *wen* [*rijksdaalder*], three *chao* [*stuiver*] that have to be paid by each sailor and passenger according to the original regulation, all five hundred passengers who are allowed to enter each year will have to pay an additional fee of two *wen*, two *chao* according to the new regulations. But in the past there has never been a regulation such as this new one!

We beseech Your Majesty to bestow upon us your unchanging benevolence and to apply Your Policy according to precedent, so that our ship will not incur a loss. If there has been an unexpected excess number of passengers, our ship had no choice, as more than half of the passengers are too poor to earn a living! They stole on board after our departure! When we hoisted sail, availing ourselves of the tide, and passed [Da] an island [near Xiamen], we had no time to check the passengers. Once a sea, on checking the list of names we discovered that there were more people on board. On the open sea there were no boats to take them back. We felt that they were most pitiful. We had [no choice but] to bow to circumstances and transport them. We hope, more-over, that You will sympathize and show Your Magnanimity by forgiving us and then making an exception so that Your Great Virtue will draw praise not only from us but from all quarters.

On our ship we are respectfully sending You some presents unworthy of You to express our sentiments towards You. We wholeheartedly hope You will accept them and wish You peace and happiness. Respectfully submitting this letter for Your perusal.

List of presents on the envelope:

tribute satin, 2 bolts
Xihe scented tea, 2 chests
Chinese white linen, 2 bolts
gold foil, 2 chests

Blussé: From this letter, received by the Batavian authorities in early 1804, it becomes clear that Chinese shipping to Southeast Asia was indeed going through a slump. Travellers to the Malay Peninsula and its vicinity were forced to travel via Batavia. As I have demonstrated elsewhere, the VOC also forced Chinese merchants destined for other ports in the Archipelago to pass through Batavia. The worries about exceeding the existing quota of passen-gers exposed by Li Kunhe in his letter are corroborated by the *syahbandar*'s report that in February 1804 the *Rong Fa* had brought in 998 passengers, no less than 498 persons above the set quota. Clandestine boarding of the Chi-nese junks after their departure from Xiamen had also been described in the *plakaat* of 31 March 1761 quoted above. The poll tax of two *wen* and three *chao*, however, does not tally with the figures given in the *Plakaatboek*.

Letter of Jiaqing Year 12, Twelfth Month [January 1808]

The Li Kunhe Ocean *Hang* of Xiamen respectfully addresses a letter to Your Highness, the Vice-Roy of Ge-la-ba.

We are convinced respectfully that Ge-la-ba is a prosperous country, famous among the maritime countries. Its scenery is extraordinarily beautiful. People from far and near look up to You with respect. Trading ships ply the waters of this hub of sea and land transport. You protect the countries of the southern seas; Your heroic vassals respect Your sovereign laws and regulations. Your benevolence extends to the Orient. Those from afar are bathed in Your Kindness. We know that like the sun, which sheds it radiance everywhere over the three mountains Your Light leaves no place untouched.

Last year, our humble company fitted out two ships to trade with Your Country. This autumn one returned to Guangdong and the other to Xiamen. Because of the high prices being asked on merchandise [in Batavia], many business losses were incurred. This winter we are once again sending the *Shi-san-wan-sheng* to Your Country. The ship's master, Ma Huaguan, has already benefited from Your great Kindness. We merely hope You will continue to favour him and allow him to trade promptly so that he can leave on schedule.

As regards to trade, we also hope that You will order Your subjects to trade fairly at reasonable prices, so that the goods brought home can reap a small profit when they are sold. When the merchants hear about this they will eagerly flock to You. It will be even proof of how great is Your Kindness in accommodating foreigners.

This year the person who issued the licence for Makassar told us that Your Country wants to use copper coinage. We had intended to send this to You, but this commodity is looked upon as a necessity in our country, and the authorities have always forbidden it to be exported. It is difficult to defy the law of the land. Our company has employed every possible means to try and purchase some, but if the custom officials were to hear about this, they would make serious efforts to prevent it. It is too difficult to export it, instead, in accordance with Your Order, we shall try to recruit craftsmen [to make copper coins] and send them to Your country to enter Your service. We shall be grateful if You welcome them when they arrive.

We have received Your opulent Presents. We have recorded them all, one by one. Now, as this ship prepares to depart, we are sorry that we lack suitable gifts to reciprocate Your presents. We have prepared some trifling articles of four kinds. We offer them as a paltry expression of our respect. While writing this letter our thoughts reach out to you. We pray You will peruse this letter carefully and we hope it brings You joy.

2 rolls of tribute satin
2 bolts of Chinese white linen

2 chests of gold foil
2 chests of Xihe scented tea.

Blussé: The export of copper was traditionally forbidden by Chinese law. Yet Chinese copper coins (cash or *picis*) were in great demand in Southeast Asia. Because the Napoleonic Wars had brought the import of Japanese copper into Java into a sudden halt, the Batavian government had sought to replace the locally minted or molded copper coins with Chinese *cash*.

Pirates on the Java Sea

George Earl

Though many Europeans traveled throughout the vast Indonesian archipelago by ship, piracy was a real problem, even in waters very close to the Dutch colonial center at Batavia. Many Europeans thought that piracy was endemic to maritime Southeast Asia, and to the Indies in particular. This was untrue: piracy was conditional, often utilized in conjunction with trade or in place of it if a ship met on the high seas was deemed to be unable to defend its own cargo. Corsairs also sprang up to take advantage of new opportunities generated by advancing trade or by liminal spaces neglected by newly powerful regimes like the Dutch. What Europeans such as the English traveler George Earl called piracy proved common in certain seascapes, most notably in the Sulu Sea, off New Guinea, and in the Straits of Malacca. The sight of ships approaching one's own craft uninvited was a universal sign for caution in the region. Maritime Southeast Asia, and Indonesia in particular, still stands as one of the world's most common places to hear of piratical attacks, though the tools and methods of such attacks have changed considerably since the nineteenth century.

The schooner in which I made my voyage, had been in the first instance bound to Surabaya, the capital of the eastern districts of the island, being in want of repairs, which could be effected at a cheaper rate at that port than at any other belonging to Java. We should not have visited Batavia had the monsoon permitted us to enter the Java sea by the straits to the eastward of the island. On the 27th December we weighed and stood out of Batavia roads with a strong land wind, and at eight o'clock, having gained an offing of several miles, we found ourselves in the midst of a fleet of fishing-boats, the crews of which were hauling their nets. In addition to these implements, they were provided with fish traps made of basket-work, which are baited with small fry, and afterwards sunk by means of stones, their position being indicated by long bamboo fishing-buoys. The traps are left in the sea all night, and are raised in the morning for the purpose of taking out the fish; and as each bamboo is furnished with a large bunch of grass fastened to one end, which is made to stand high out of the water by means of a weight attached to the other, the fishermen can readily find them.

The easterly monsoon which prevailed was directly contrary, so that we were only enabled to progress by taking advantage of the land and sea breezes. The land breeze in general commences about midnight, and as it blows directly from the shore, a vessel is able to steer her course the greater part of the night, but after sunrise, the wind always draws round to the eastward, and she is consequently forced off the shore. At about nine a.m., when seven or eight miles distant from the land, the anchor is dropped, and towards noon, when the sea breeze sets in, it is again weighed, and the ship is run in and anchored as near the shore as possible, to await the return of the sea-breeze.

In some parts of the world this mode of navigation would be tedious, but here the voyager is constantly amused by the contemplation of the ever varying landscape; and vessels of all descriptions, from the stately ship to the lively canoe, are always passing and re-passing, adding interest and gaiety to the scene.

There are great varieties of native *prahus*, some being built after a European model, and carrying sails similar to those of our English luggers: others are of native construction with lateen sails, and many built with high stems and sterns, skim along under the *lyer tanjong*, or square mat sail of the Batavian fishing *prahus*.

On the 30th, we were off Indramayo point, and near a spot which a few years before had been the scene of a most atrocious act of piracy, the circumstances of which were related to me in the following manner. An English merchant, who had resided during several years in Java, embarked at Batavia on board one of his vessels, a large brig, for the purpose of visiting Samarang, taking with him a considerable sum of money for the purchase of the produce of the eastern districts. These facts having reached the ears of a famous piratical chief, he determined to waylay the vessel, and accordingly, mustering a sufficient number of *prahus*, cruized about in the neighbourhood of Indramayo, and meeting with the brig as he had expected, commenced an attack upon her. The crew of the latter vessel consisted of two Englishmen, the captain and the chief officer, and about thirty Javanese seamen, who, together, with the owner, defended the vessel for some time. Towards the evening, however, the unfortunate merchant was killed by a spear fired from a musket, and the pirates taking advantage of the confusion produced by this event, immediately boarded. The two remaining Englishmen, being well aware that certain death awaited them should they remain, threw themselves into the sea, and succeeded in reaching a bamboo fishing–buoy, such as I have before described. The pirates, too busily employed in plundering their prize to think of anything else, did not perceive their place of refuge, and the vessels soon drifted away out of sight. The condition of the persons who had thus escaped had improved very little for the better; they were immersed to the neck in water, dreading every moment the attack of sharks, nor had either, during the whole of the night, the comfort of knowing that his companion was still in existence. Soon after day-light some fishermen appeared, by whom they were perceived, but instead of rescuing them immediately from their peril-ous situation, the Javanese consulted together for a few minutes, and then approached the sufferers and demanded who they were. On being told they were Englishmen whose vessel had been attacked and captured by pirates, they were taken on board, treated kindly, and conveyed to the Dutch settle-ment at Indarmayo. Had they belonged to one of the Dutch cruizers, their fate would probably have been different, for the fishermen are on bad terms with the officers of the government *prahus*, whom they accuse of robbing them of their fish.

I never could learn the name of the piratical chief, but I have every reason to believe that it was the famous Rajah Raga, whose successful acts of piracy rendered him the idol of the people with whom he was associated. He was (or rather is, for I believe that he is still in existence) the brother of the Sultan of Coti, on the east coast of Borneo, which place he made his head-quarters. He was often sought for both by the English and the Dutch, but always man-aged to elude pursuit. On one occasion, while cruizing with three large *pra-hus*, he was attacked by an English man-of-war, and two of the *prahus*, with their crews, were destroyed, but the one in which the Rajah had embarked escaped.

On another occasion, his own *prahu*, which carried upwards of 150 men, and mounted several large guns, was entrusted to his favourite *panglima* or captain, who sailed in her on a cruise. Within a day's sail of Macassar he fell in with a ship, and wishing to distinguish himself by her capture, he fired into her and made preparations to board. To his utter surprise and dismay, however, he saw a line of large ports opened in the side of the vessel, and he found himself under the guns of a British man-of-war. The *panglima* hailed, and endeavoured to make it appear that he had acted under a misapprehen-sion, but his subterfuge was of no avail: a broadside from the man-of-war sent his vessel at once to the bottom, and he and all the crew perished, with the exception of two or three, who clung to a piece of the wreck, and were picked up by a native *prahu*.

The pirates who infested the Archipelago consist wholly of the inhabi-tants of the free Mahommedan states in Sumatra, Lingin, Borneo, Magin-danao, and Sulu; those natives who have remained uncontaminated by the detestable doctrines of the Arabs never being known to engage in the like pursuits. The Europeans who are unfortunate enough to fall into their hands are generally murdered, while the natives who compose the crews of the captured vessels are sold for slaves.

On the first of October the peaked mountains of Taggal appeared in sight, although we were still a long distance from it; and on the afternoon of the third we anchored in Samarang Roads. I have always regretted that my stay at this place was so short that I could see little of the country in the vicinity. The river, or rather creek, is very shallow, and cannot be entered by loaded boats at low water. The roads also are exceedingly insecure: it owes its importance, therefore, solely to the industry of the natives in the adjacent districts, who raise large quantities of coffee, pepper, and rice. Many ship-loads of the latter are annually exported to China, and to different countries in the Archipelago.

In the shallow water near the mouth of the river are fixed a number of fishing-weirs, made of bamboo, each of which has a small watch-box attached to it, erected on piles. One of these weirs belonged to an old Javanese, who with his son kept watch alternately every night. A few nights before our arrival, some thieves in a canoe attempted to plunder the weir, but the old man wounded one of them with a spear, on which they all made off. When he came home the next morning, as his son was not in the way at the time, he did not mention the circumstance, and the young man took his station at the weir the following night without being aware that there was any necessity for keeping a better look-out than usual. Soon after midnight, when he was dozing on his post, the thieves came suddenly upon him and wounded him in several places with their kresses [i.e., knives]: he was found the next morning nearly lifeless, but although his wounds were of so dreadful a nature that they would have been mortal to an European, at the time of our arrival he was rapidly recovering. The natives living principally on vegetable food, a wound seldom becomes much inflamed.

Colonial Geography in Kei and Flores

C. M. Kan

As the Dutch expanded outward from Java into the rest of the archipelago, they came across more and more islands and increasing numbers of peoples who inhabited these places. Eastern Indonesia had seen some of the earliest Dutch activity in the archipelago, notably Holland's focus on the spice trade of the north and central Moluccas, but other landscapes existed to be explored as well. The Kei archipelago in the southern Moluccas and Flores island in Nusa Tenggara constituted two such places; both were fairly sparsely populated, but both held out the opportunity of riches—agricultural, mineral, or aquatic—that quickened the pace of Dutch exploration and mapping. Indies geographical societies pushed the agenda for these scientific incursions, but the colonial state was never far from the choosing and planning of subsequent destinations for "discovery." Teams of explorers and scientists were often outfitted with topographers, geologists, anthropologists, and/or linguists, and military personnel arriving in tandem. In such a way the "wild east" of the archipelago was eventually brought under Dutch sway by the early twentieth century, though small pockets of the region's peoples did not see white people until the mid-1900s.

Finally, concerning the voyages of exploration, the progress of the expeditions to the Kei-islands and Flores, outfitted by the Dutch Geographical Association, is described in the most recent issue of their association's journal "Reports and Announcements." It shows that the lieutenant at sea, Mr. H. O. W. Planten, who is in charge of the Kei-group's research after Mr. Posthumus Meyes's return, will start the hydrographic assessment with a sailboat belonging to the Langen firm. It also shows that the meteorological observations that had been performed regularly since July should be continued, and that the firm for that purpose has had an observatory built. From Mr. Wertheim, we know that many different geological expeditions were executed, for example on Kei-Doellan, which was traversed in two main directions and on which nothing but coral formations were found. A more in-depth geological investigation of this island will take place together with the topographic assessment by Mr. Planten. The months November and December, 1888,

Mr. Wertheim spent on an expedition at Hoog-Kei, where he hoped to find more variation in the formation. Due to new donations the carrying out of this expedition until the end of May 1889 is now secured.

Concerning the expedition to Flores, as is known, the topographic research there will be performed by Engineer R. van den Broek, and the geological research by Prof. Dr. A. Wichmann. Since both, according to the most recent messages, are still underway to their respective destinations, one can only say this about the Flores research at this point, namely that Mister Wichmann as well as Prof. Max Weber and his wife after their expedition through Celebes were planning on crossing the island Flores from its north shore to Sikko. Referring to Mister Wichmann's letter for the particularities of their journey through Celebes, we only remark that the peak of Bonthain, according to the explicit statement by Prof. Wichmann, "is without a doubt a real volcano," and that, against the expectation of the travelers, the areas that they visited belong to rather recent formations, which also the fauna suggest as well.

Concerning the expedition to the Aroe-bay (somewhat north of the Langkat-river, 4 degr. N.B.), Mister R. v. A. is very correct to make the following remark: "The intended region, that must once have housed the seat of an empire that in respect and power could challenge contemporary Pasei and the Melaka empire, but which belongs to part of the Indies Archipelago, and is frequently visited by persons, but unable to arouse much interest from the part of researchers, was in danger of being forgotten. This was so except for the clerks of the Indies Government, who because of their positions are persons responsible for informing the study of areas of land and people in the archipelago. They guard against "forgetting" through their publication of things that appear 'noteworthy' on their journeys. This will become even more necessary, when such clerks return from traveling (see the *Bijdragen*, 1889, p. 73, for example) with impression, 'that in these areas there still remains a rich opportunity for the development of industry and for the exploitation of wood, as well as the preparation of soil for tobacco culture.'

Translated from Dutch by A. van de Rijt and E. Tagliacozzo

Bugis Ships of Sulawesi

The Bugis and Makassarese peoples of southwestern Sulawesi are among the most famous maritime peoples not only of Indonesia but of Southeast Asia in general. Prior to the fifteenth century, the Bugis were not oriented primarily toward the water; most were farmers and herders in the rich but periodically dry landscape of what the first Europeans called the Celebes. Yet they took to the sea after this time and eventually built a maritime trading base at Makassar that stretched as far east as New Guinea and as far west as the Straits of Malacca. The Dutch conquest of Makassar in 1667 encouraged this far-flung diaspora even further, as many Bugis now sought their fortunes away from their ancestral homelands. Bugis ships have traditionally been built in several places in Sulawesi, but two sites for their construction—which use wooden pegs that swell with seawater and no nails whatsoever—were the villages of Bulukumba and Bira. The British were so afraid of these traders-cum-pirates that admonishments to watch out for the "boogeyman" entered our own language. Today Bugis ships—composites of original Bugis craft and partially Westernized designs from the age of sail and steam—can still be found around the Indonesian archipelago, including at Makassar itself and at Sunda Kelapa, Jakarta's historical harbor.

Bugis ships in Sulawesi. Photo by Eric Tagliacozzo.

Traversing the Interior of Palembang

H. H. van Kol

The residency of Palembang, in southern Sumatra, presented both opportunities and challenges to Dutch rule in the Indies. Dutch ships had been trading with this part of Indonesia for a long time, especially for tin and pepper, two commodities in high demand with the VOC. Though an armed Dutch presence had succeeded early in other parts of Sumatra, in Palembang and Jambi, "progress" had been slower in terms of pacifying local populations. In Jambi the situation proved particularly acute. For decades in the late nineteenth and the early twentieth centuries, the sultan there waged a war of resistance in the mountains. Palembang did not resist as long or as well, but still flare-ups against Dutch rule occurred throughout the period. Both Palembang and Jambi were rich agricultural domains in which crops grew readily; oil palms in particular flourished here, and the region became even more important with the discovery of petroleum at the fin de siècle. Trips by Dutch controllers and residents (such as H. H. van Kol) into the interior, thus, always inspired Dutch public interest—both in terms of what riches might be found next, and whether these expeditions would be met with smiles, or bullets, or a combination of both.

My Third Journey across Sumatra

7. THE RESIDENCY PALEMBANG

THE CHOSEN ROUTE

Of the three times that I traversed this big island—from Medan to Sibolga, from Padang to Djambi, and from Palembang to Benkoelen—the last time, despite a long detour, was the easiest one to do. Having arrived by the steamship *De Kock* in the capital Palembang, the *Ogan II* (also from the *Koninklijke Paketvaart Maatschappij* [KPM, a shipping company]), took me along the Lematang river to Blimbing, from where a short car-trip brought me to Moeara Enim, the center of cotton culture and the petroleum industry. The route proceeded past Lahat and Tebing Tinggi to Moeara Bliti, located on the Klingi, another branch of the Moesi-river. The Klingi valley was followed until Pasar Tjoeroep, from where Moeara Aman and Redjang Lebing were visited, I then returned via the same road, and, after having met Javanese emigrants at Kepahiang, I crossed for the third time the Barisan mountains and continued over sea to the harbor Benkoelen.

The large trading city of Palembang is thus factually not yet connected with the inland parts of the country through a land route, in which case the journey to Moeara Enim would take no more than seven hours compared to the current twenty-six to thirty-two hours. Ever since the automobile service was founded, the ferries across both rivers have improved, though they are still primitive, which often causes a long delay. The ferry at Tebing Tinggi, for example, across the Moesi (no wider than sixty to eighty meters) takes twenty to forty minutes and, at *bandjir* [flooding], it can be called extremely dangerous, if not impossible. The expensive governmental postal car goes until Moeara Bliti, from where one can then use the very cheap and excellent private car services from Mr. E. F. Schlüter for the remainder of the trip, whereby the pass of the Boekit Kaba (+/− 1,115 meters) must be crossed, to then descend at Pasar Tjoeroep. Until the border with the residency Benkoelen, the road remains flat and then quickly climbs along rather steep cliffs.

Thirty years ago a trip from Palembang to Moeara Enim in the Westmoesson took three weeks and longer. From there things went inland per horse or on foot, later in ox carriages, through regions where at night tigers scan for prey and elephants horde; nowadays these are only found in large numbers in the vicinity of Moeara Bliti. These days interior merchants move with bikes and cars across these regions with clear-cut roads. Nevertheless, decent roads cannot be spoken of yet once one has passed the swampy lowlands that separate Palembang from the seacoast.

The Boat Trip along the Lematang

From Palembang there exists, as already mentioned, no land connection with the interior. The part of the road that was being built by the Government was in progress, but the construction was delayed because of financial shortages. The fierce competition, however, makes the transport costs by water very low; a journey of more than twenty-four hours from Palembang to Moeara Enim, during which a meal was served twice, cost natives no more than seventy cents for a distance of 190 kilometers.

The boats from the KPM, nicely decorated for European travelers, make this journey worth it. The only problem is that at low tide, they cannot go beyond Penang-geran, about twenty-six kilometers below Moeara Enim.

On May 16, at 4 p.m., the *Ogan II* had freed itself from a true island of water plants. Higher upriver, as soon as the river water is clear, these no longer occur, so we floated steadily forward. The sea stream, however, can still be sensed at the pump station Soeka Ramei, no less than eleven hours by steamboat from the coast. Many indigenous boats passed especially in the morning, loaded with men and women, on their way to work on the *ladangs* (dry rice fields). Often these were navigated by the forceful hands of women, with giant hats on their heads for protection against the burning sun. Standing on the front, these rowers, *anak prahoe* ("children of the boats") know how to make the boat go forward with a nice move and a forceful swing of the triangular stick; due to their hard work and their many children many of these women look old only a few years into their marriages.

Multiple villages became visible along both banks, where apparently immunizations were attempted, though not without force, which was deemed necessary after a terrible cholera outbreak, which claimed in 1910 at Moesi Ilir about one thousand victims. These large rivers are the natural highways, along which the population settled and from where they penetrated the vast wilderness of the Palembang interior.

Original forest is rarely found along the banks of the Lematang. Between the *kampungs* (villages) one finds vast plantations of kapok and fruit trees and cultivated or deserted *ladangs*; the cultivated strip along the river, however, is small, and after it everything is covered with wilderness or jungle. Still, the valley of Lematang is one of the most cultivated parts of the residency, and one finds there many *sawahs* (wet rice terraces) in the valley and *ladangs* along the high banks and on the hill slopes. Ships are more numerous on this river than on the Moesi, despite the smaller area of current. From Lahat until above Palembang, where she ends in the Moesi, the river has a length of 180 kilometers, even though her backland consists of the plateau of Pasoemah, the plateau of Semendo, the terrain surrounding Lahat, and the current area of Moeara Enim. There is much petroleum and solid fuel in this area.

During the dark night a white man disembarked from the boat, who did not know a word of Malay, settling in the jungle to drill petroleum. A monthly income of six hundred guilders, as well as drill taxes per meter and premiums for the finding of earth oil, had made this man decide to leave Romania, trying his luck far from his wife (although marital faith of the Romanians is not known to be valued) in the interior of Sumatra.

Translated from Dutch by A. van de Rijt and E. Tagliacozzo

The Zoology of the Indies

L. F. de Beaufort

The Indonesian archipelago represented—and still represents—one of the most biodiverse regions of the planet, both in terms of fauna and of flora. European naturalists were quick to catch onto this when they traveled in the region, from the time of the great German scientist Rumphius (1628–1702) to that of the Englishman Alfred Russel Wallace in the mid-nineteenth century (1823–1913). Naturalists saw the Indies as a kind of primeval garden in which the natural world could be studied without the sullying effects of humankind. This was a romantic view, but especially as the Industrial Revolution began to sweep over Europe, this vision also held some elements of truth. Though Rumphius and Wallace emerged as two of the giants of the evolving science of zoology in the Indies, they were followed by many other Europeans including Italians (such as Orlando Beccari), Norwegians (such as Carl Bock), and, of course, many Dutchmen. These scientists charted the natural history of the Indonesian archipelago, naming and studying thousands of birds, beetles, and mammals in the process.

It is no wonder, that the Indo-Australian Archipelago has always attracted zoologists, for here a number of islands with a rich and varied fauna are separated by seas, which are partly shallow, partly very deep and inhabited by a marine fauna of equal richness. From a zoogeographical point of view there is hardly any place in the world of greater interest than this chain of islands between the Asiatic and the Australian continent.

In the west, the Greater Sunda islands, situated on a common continental shelf, have a fauna very similar to that of Malacca; in the east New Guinea and neighbouring islands, connected with Australia by the Sahulshelf, show the same affinity in their fauna with that of the tropical part of the Australian continent and between those two the islands of the Moluccas, often separated by very deep seas, have an animal life which shows a remarkable and puzzling mixture of Asiatic and Australian affinity.

Every zoologist, who has visited these islands, has been impressed by the facts just mentioned. When the great naturalist A. R. WALLACE visited the archipelago, where he spent eight years studying and collecting the fauna, he was so struck by the affinities of the fauna of these islands, whilst at the same time each of them has its own peculiar species, differing slightly from the neighbouring ones, that his thoughts were continually at work to find an explanation. From Serawak he wrote his first contribution to the question of the origin of the species and later on, when in the island of Ternate, the principle of the survival of the fittest occurred to him and this made him write a paper at once, which he sent to DARWIN. The rest of the story is well known: DARWIN found his own ideas, which he had never published, expressed in WALLACE's paper. It stimulated him to publish his views, a joint paper by DARWIN and WALLACE was read at a meeting of the Linnean Society of London and caused great excitement: it was the birth of the evolution-theory, which has completely revolutionized biological science. We can therefore say without exaggeration that the biologist in the Indo-Australian Archipelago is on classic ground. If it is too much to say, that the evolution-theory was born there, one of the branches of this mighty stem, *viz.* genetic zoogeography, certainly sprouted in the Indo-Australian Archipelago, of which DARWIN wrote to WALLACE: "I think that the most interesting quarter of the globe in respect of distribution."

The fauna of Java is better known than that of the other islands, but it is decidedly less rich than that of Borneo and Sumatra. This may be partly due to the fact, that a great part of the island is cultivated. The original fauna, and especially that of the virgin forest, it therefore now restricted to what has remained of the immense forests, which must formerly have covered a great part of the island. Some of the species only adopted themselves to a life in the open. A vivid account, of how cultivation has changed the aspect of the fauna is given by KONINGSBERGER in his book: "Java zoölogisch en biologisch." The fauna is here treated from an ecological point of view, that of the different biocoenoses: the woods, the fields, the hills and mountains, streams and lakes, etc. are treated in succession and their characteristic forms of life are described. The book gives a comprehensive account of the Javanese fauna but does not aim at being a complete faunistical work. Such a work, though wanted badly, is still lacking. Some classes of animals, however, have been treated exhaustively.

Our knowledge of the birds of New Guinea has greatly increased since the island has been made more accessible through the Dutch scientific and military explorations and the same may be said of the Moluccas. Many of the smaller islands have been visited by naturalists, who collected for the Tring Museum, such as KÜHN, DOHERTY, DUMAS, and others. Many papers on the ornithology of different islands in the eastern part of the archipelago by ROTHSCHILD, HARTERT, AND STRESEMANN have been published in Novitates Zoologicae, the periodical of the Tring Museum.

VAN DEDEM's collections from Ceram and other islands have been studied by VAN OORT; and STRESEMANN, who collected there himself, has given us an account of the avifauna of this island. Quite recently a German expedition visited some of the Lesser Sunda-islands and several new forms have been described by RENSCH. The avifauna of Bali had previously been studied by STRESEMANN.

The monographs by MEYER and WIGLESWORTH and by SALVADORI are now antiquated. Not only because so many new discoveries have been made, but also because our views on the value of species and subspecies or geographical forms have changed so much since the publication of these works, that they would look quite different, had they to be rewritten now.

The avifauna of the Greater Sunda islands is also much better known, than twenty years ago. The only comprehensive work on the birds of Java is that by KONINSBERGER: "De Vogels van Java" ["The Birds of Java"] but this, too, belongs to a former period. In this island it is principally M. BARTELS who has made and is still making large collections and who has added much to our knowledge of the avifauna of this island, but many of his observations are as yet unpublished. The greatest advance perhaps has been made in our knowledge of the avifauna of Sumatra, through the collections of DEBUSSY, VAN HEYST, VAN HEURN, JACOBSON, BODEN KLOSS, ROBINSON, and others. The two last named ornithologists have amongst other things published a list of all species of birds, known to inhabit this island.

The literature on mammals is even more scattered than that on birds. Years ago, TJEENK WILLINK published a list, but since then our knowledge of this class has never been reviewed. Yet much and important knowledge has been done. Besides that of a remote period, such as that done by M. WEBER, whose anatomical studies on mammals of these islands (as e.g. that on *Manis*) are almost classical, much systematic work has been done by JENTINK, on material in the museum at Leyden: by MILLER, LYON, and others in the U.S. who studied collections made for the American museums and especially by OLDFIELD THOMAS, who wrote numerous smaller and larger papers on Indo-Australian mammals. As we mentioned above, the Greater Sunda-islands especially are rich in mammals. Those of Sumatra, Borneo and the smaller islands, such as those of the Riouw archipelago have been studied especially by Americans. The fauna of the interesting islands along the westcoast of

Sumatra has also been collected by an American, ABBOTT. Some of the islands have formerly been visited by MODIGLIANI and the mammological results were published by OLDFIELD THOMAS. JACOBSON made extensive collections in the island of Simalur and the Mentawei-islands were revisited by BODEN KLOSS.

As has been mentioned above, the species of mammals inhabiting the islands to the east of the Greater Sunda Islands are not numerous. The collections made by TOXOPEUS in Buru and those made by collectors of the Zoological Museum of Buitenzorg have been worked out by OLDFIELD THOMAS, who has also described many forms from other sources, amongst which *Rhynchomeles prattorum*, an endemic species of a new genus of marsupials from Ceram may be specially mentioned.

The mammalian fauna of New Guinea again is of greater interest. The few species of the monotreme genus *Zaglossus* are still imperfectly known. A survey of this genus has been given by KERBERT, the late director of the Zoological Gardens of Amsterdam, who gave some biological facts about these curious animals, specimens of which he studied in the Amsterdam Zoo. OLDFIELD THOMAS and ROTHSCHILD have more recently studied the same genus. The former also described many marsupials from this island, partly belonging to the collections of the British Museum, but recently also from those of the Zoological Museum at Buitenzorg, where extensive collections arrived from the last Dutch New Guinea expeditions to the Mamberamo river and the central mountains. Those of former Dutch expeditions have been studied by JENTINK, who also published a list of the mammals, then known to live in this big island. It is a well known fact that New Guineas is inhabited, not only by monotremata and marsupials but also by many curious rats of Australian affinity, which have related forms in the mountains of Luzon in the Philippines, as was long ago shown by OLDFIELD THOMAS, who is certainly the best authority on these rodents, and whose publications on this difficult group are numerous.

New Guinea, especially its interior, has long remained unknown. In 1902, a first Dutch scientific expedition was sent out; others followed and slowly but surely the white spots on the map disappeared. Large collections have been made, and the results published in "Nova Guinea," a work of which Vols v, ix, and xiii are entirely devoted to Zoology, whilst a new zoological volume is now being published. Besides these Dutch expeditions two British expeditions explored the Dutch part of the island. Several Dutch military surveys have made the interior of New Guinea more accessible and some naturalists, among whom was MEEK (who collected for the Tring Museum), have availed themselves of this opportunity.

The fauna of the central mountains, partly snow-clad, yielded many new species as might be expected, but we may safely say, that much still remains to be discovered.

From a zoogeographical as well as from an economical point of view the freshwater fish fauna of the Indo-Australian archipelago is of great importance, at least that of its western part. BLEEKER has already made us acquainted with a great number of species from the Greater Sunda islands, but much has been added to our knowledge since.

The Dutch Borneo expeditions at the end of the century made extensive ichthyological collections (which have been studied by VAILANT and MISS POPTA) and greatly increased our knowledge of the fish fauna of this island. WEBER and DE BEAUFORT described several new species from Sumatra. We may say, that the ichthyological fauna of these islands, as well as of Java, is fairly well known. As in the case of mammals the distribution of the true freshwater fishes shows the great affinity between the islands on the Sunda shelf inter se and with Malacca. Most families do not reach farther east than here: Celebes f.i. being totally deprived of Cyprinoidea, which are still abundant in Borneo. The difference between the fauna of these islands is striking and the Straits of Macassar are an important zoogeographical boundary. This part of the much discussed "line of WALLACE" has certainly *raison d'être*, as has been pointed out by the SARASIN's. The southern part, however, between Bali and Lombok, has not the same significance. Cyprinoidea do occur not only in Lombok, but even more to the east in Sumbawa, and the distribution of other animals, too, shows that the contrast which in WALLACE's opinion existed between the fauna of Bali and that of Lombok, is not so important as he thought.

An interesting study on the fish fauna of Borneo and Sumatra was made by M. WEBER. According to MOLENGRAAFF the sea level was so much lowered during the pleistocene ice-age, that the sea between Borneo and Java was transformed into a low land, where the streams of East Sumatra and West Borneo formed a large river, discharging itself into the South Chinese sea. If MOLENGRAAFF's views are right, the fauna of the rivers of East Sumatra and West Borneo must have mixed in pleistocene times. WEBER's object was now to investigate, if traces of these former conditions could be found in the recent fauna. He therefore compared the fish fauna of the river Kapuas of West Borneo, running into the Sunda Sea with that of the river Mahakam of East Borneo, which discharges itself into the Straits of Makassar. The result was, that out of the 142 species, which are known to exist in these rivers, only 52 occur in both. The Kapuas has 67 species, which do not live in the Mahakam and 75 percent of these are also found in rivers of East Sumatra. In accordance with what MOLENGRAAFF's views might lead us to expect, this shows that the Kapuas has more affinity in its ichthyological fauna with the rivers of East Sumatra than those of West Borneo. The Mahakam on the other hand, shows a great deal of endemism as a sign of its longer isolation.

The importance of the freshwater fauna for genetic zoogeography is clearly demonstrated by this example. Formerly it was often believed, that the freshwater fauna in the tropics did not show much variation. Although GÜNTHER, VON MARTENS, and others had already developed different views, it was especially M. WEBER who pointed out its importance, in connection with his own investigations on the freshwater fauna of Sumatra, Java, Celebes, and the Lesser Sunda islands.

Special attention was therefore paid to this part of the fauna during the Dutch New Guinea expeditions. The results were, with respect to fishes, that the typical freshwater fishes which we meet in the western part of the archipelago, do not occur here. This might be expected, as they are not found in the Moluccas either. The rivers and lakes of New Guinea are inhabited by marine immigrants, which we find elsewhere too, but also by others, which have Australian affinity. Among these may be mentioned *Scleropages leichhardti*, some sillurids of the family *Plotosidae*, and aberrant *Atherinidae*. Last named, although immigrants from the sea, live now exclusively in fresh or perhaps somewhat brackish water.

The Indonesian Hajj in Colonial Times

Travelers did not only come to Indonesia; they also left Indonesia to go to other places. One of the largest groups to do so were hajjis, Muslim pilgrims from all over the archipelago who first gathered and then left for the long sea voyage across the Indian Ocean to the Arabian Peninsula. The hajj constitutes one of the five pillars of Islam: every Muslim financially able to do so must try to undertake the pilgrimage at least once in his or her lifetime. Though Indonesia is about as far as one can get (in terms of Muslim-majority countries) from the holy cities of Mecca and Medina, very large numbers of Indonesians have undertaken this long journey across the centuries. A Dutch doctoral student, Johan Eisenberger, in Leiden in the 1920s was the first to write about these movements in great statistical detail; his dissertation chronicled the archipelago pilgrims making the trip and showed that the numbers were in the thousands, sometimes in the tens of thousands, every year. These were only the official figures: the true numbers were probably far higher, as not all pilgrims applied for passports and went through the official Dutch system of monitoring and surveillance. Dutch authorities felt ambivalent about the hajj: on the one hand, they genuinely tried to ameliorate some of the harsh conditions of the journey, while, on the other, they surveilled their subjects as potential conspirators in anticolonial behavior. Many Indonesian hajjis stayed in the Hejaz for a long time, studying religion, setting up businesses, and starting families in the process.

Pilgrims to Mecca from the Dutch East Indies

HAJJ YEAR	INDIES PILGRIMS	HAJJ YEAR	INDIES PILGRIMS
1850	71	1909	9,644
1852	413	1910	14,743
1855	1,668	1911	24,025
1860	1,420	1912	18,025
1866	2,212	1913	26,321
1870	3,258	1914	28,427
1875	5,655	1915	—
1880	10,179	1916	—
1885	4,760	1917	71
1890	5,785	1918	81
1895	11,570	1919	1,123
1900	5,068	1920	14,703
1901	7,421	1921	28,795
1902	6,092	1922	21,866
1903	5,679	1923	22,212
1904	9,708	1924	36,878
1905	5,205	1925	378
1906	6,675	1926	3,316
1907	8,514	1927	46,699
1908	9,169	1928	35,000

Source: "Indië en de bedevaart naar Mekka," by Johan Eisenberger (PhD diss., Leiden University, 1928), 204.

V

High Colonial Indies

Though scholars disagree about when such a designation might have come into effect, most do agree that the Dutch Indies experienced a high colonial period, which reached somewhere from the mid- to late nineteenth century to the middle of the twentieth, when Holland lost its colony, first to the Japanese and then to Indonesian independence. This period saw the fruition of many earlier patterns: an extension of colonial government over wider and wider sections of the archipelago; developments in technology and organization that allowed for an expansion of colonial influence not only in territorial breadth but also in depth (that is, in terms of how much of the indigenous population the Dutch were able to control); and the beginnings of a serious knowledge project through which the colonizers genuinely started to try to understand the colonized, employing means and methodologies we now ascribe to modern scientific disciplines and techniques. Many of these processes were evident before 1850–1950. Yet during much of this period they became the driving forces of Indies life, as the Dutch continually tightened their rule over the archipelago, only to lose their grip in an instant at the start of the Second World War in the Pacific.

The high colonial period marked a time during which many Dutchmen were absolutely convinced of the basic propriety of their right to rule—how could this not be so when they had brought railroads and schools to the Indies, as well as vaccinations, telegraphs, and a measure of peace (the *Pax Neerlandica*) to a constantly warring archipelago? A number of Indonesians believed this rhetoric too, seeing in their colonizers the truth of old prognostications (such as the Joyoboyo prophecy in Java) that the islands would eventually be ruled by a white race. Yet there were many others during this period too who started to feel a shadow pass through their hearts, indigenous and Dutch alike. Was it really beneficial to Indonesians that the Dutch ruled all their affairs and made such large sums on their labor? Was this pattern foreordained by the laws of modernity, so that Indonesians would remain in thrall to Europeans for an unspecified time into the future? Were these patterns of coercion and control really the natural order of things, and if they were not, how might matters change, and who was to change them?

These questions crossed the minds of a range of members of Indies society—civil administrators, churchmen, the laboring poor, and incipient nationalists. No one was sure about the answers to these queries; in fact, many people wondered which questions should even be asked. From the indigenous standpoint, it was clear that life in the Indies was not as "modern" and beneficial to the autochthonous inhabitants of the archipelago as their overlords sought to portray. Opium, for example, bought and then resold under government aegis at enormous profit, had various negative consequences. Islam came under challenge by the authorities, who had liberal and laissez faire policies on the books when it came to the archipelago's dominant religion, but still treated it as a threat across the colonial bureaucracy. Even the local environment was under siege, as a selection here about the shooting of a tiger by European officials makes clear. The perceived dissonances between Dutch rhetoric and aims and Dutch policies and realities were all too clear to many Indonesians, and though some fought these injustices only in their minds, others finally took up arms during this period in wars and rebellions aimed at throwing off Dutch rule.

From the European perspective, the high colonial period looked very different than this dark, cynical vision. As the selections here make clear, everywhere ruling European elites were studying, building, and "improving" Indies society—for Dutch benefit, to be sure, but also supposedly more philanthropically for the indigenous inhabitants of the archipelago themselves. Trade was encouraged and managed by the Dutch, often through local Chinese populations resident to the islands. The Dutch now controlled the latter, thereby supposedly protecting indigenes formerly cheated under the free reign of Chinese merchants. Anthropologists and explorers for the first time brought isolated parts of the archipelago into contact with "modern" life, simultaneously recording lifeways and rituals (such as marriages) that otherwise would have remained outside humanity's quest for all-encompassing knowledge. Most important, science—a near-holy word and concept of the time—was being used to better understand Indonesia both on its own terms and in an effort to improve local conditions for Indonesia's peoples. All of these projects, of course, also benefited from the background presence of the church, a self-described "benevolent" force that helped direct human progress as defined by the Dutch.

These contested visions of what was actually happening on the ground on the islands during the high colonial age show the tensions that modernity brought, even to places far removed from Europe, the purported epicenter of most modern change. It would be an oversimplification to imagine that Europeans only saw progress during this era, while indigenes only saw exploitation; rather, various perspectives existed on both sides of the color line. Clearly, however, both colonizer and colonized recognized that important forces were changing Indies society. Technology and the ways it could be utilized—or misused—constituted one of these forces. So, too, did religion, which was not modern in any real sense but which was being used in new and sophisticated ways, both to shore up colonial rule and to provide a challenge against it. Finally, concepts of race and human hierarchies were also undergoing a fundamental metamorphosis, changing from one factor among many in the classification of human beings to the single most important organizational index of colonial society.

The period of the high colonial Indies, however many decades it may have lasted, ended abruptly and very violently with the arrival of the Japanese. Yet before this time Indonesia arguably became a more vibrant and complicated place than it had ever been at any point in its previous history. The last remaining sultanates and kingdoms still opposing colonial rule were brought under the Dutch thumb in surprisingly little time. Cities were built and grew exponentially, and parts of the Indies that had experienced little or no communication with the outside world suddenly were brought into the currents of regional, transregional, and global life, sometimes very quickly and in very jarring ways. Agents of the colonial government—ethnographers, police officers, engineers, missionaries, and agricultural extension agents—crisscrossed the Indies as never before, and in far greater numbers. Holland's greatest colony was becoming modern in many senses, but these changes brought strife and agony alongside opportunity to a wide range of affected populations.

Chinese Traders in the Villages

M. R. Fernando and David Bulbeck

Although the Dutch rather depended on Chinese merchants living in the Indies to act as middlemen in their economic transactions with local populations, many Dutch looked on these Chinese with barely concealed disdain. Stereotypes of the Chinese as commercial parasites—as evident in this translation by the contemporary scholars M. R. Fernando and David Bulbeck—appeared in the high colonial era, though they were generated far earlier. Though pass and residency laws strictly controlled Chinese movements in the Indies, the realities of Chinese lives outside the main cities proved far more fluid than any statutes could enforce. Chinese merchants and revenue farmers indeed enjoyed a disproportionate share of wealth in the high colonial Indies, though for every success story within the community there were far larger numbers of Chinese who eked out meager livings as itinerant paddlers, fishermen, and craftsmen. In the vast hinterland of Java, where small economic transactions took place on a wide basis, the Chinese served as an all-important connective between local and colonial economies—linking the poorest peasant to larger administrative and exchange units in the Indies.

A Visit to a Javanese Market

Once while I was hunting, I happened to be near a village towards which many people were walking. I was curious and followed them until I came to a place where some three thousand people were assembled. It soon became evident that a market would be held there. I thought "let's wait, here is a good opportunity for me to ascertain how the extortions of the Chinese oppress the Javanese," a view which I have gained from reading this journal. I asked the man who was carrying fish how much he paid to the farmer for the market tax or *pasar pacht*; he replied ninety *duiten*. Upon being questioned, he said "I do not know exactly how much the farmer is entitled to collect, but some claim only fifty *duiten*." I persisted and asked "So why did you pay more?" The man said "My dear sir, if I tell you everything, I will not have time to sell my fish." The man had evidently become impatient with my questions. Then I talked to three women, one selling rice with vegetables and fish, another selling a sort of syrup, and the third one selling red pepper. The first one told me that the farmer had demanded twenty-five *duiten* from her, the second one twenty-two *duiten*, while the women selling red pepper had paid thirty *duiten* plus a handful of pepper to boot. I also asked them how much they thought they should pay. They said ten *duiten*, but quickly added that they dare not complain because the local chief was a good friend of the farmer, and anyway he lived far away so it was very difficult to go there and complain.

This was very bad, I thought and set about finding out how much this Chinese imposed on some rice sellers; I assumed he would not take anything from them. Well, he had taken four *duiten* from each of them. I remarked to the Chinese revenue farmer that he could not do this because the government had specifically forbidden it. The man looked at me and laughed saying "I do it to maintain the market." I went around the market. The place was a quagmire and there was nothing that looked like a building. This Chinese farmer was a buffoon and a thief. While walking around the *pasar* [i.e., market] I asked many other people about the tax and they all said things similar to what I have reported above.

It was getting late and time to go home. I approached the entrance of the market where someone unexpectedly grabbed me by the arm. I looked around and found a Chinese. When he looked at me closely he said, "I am sorry, sir, I thought you were a Javanese." I must admit that from hunting I was unkempt much like a coolie. But I asked the man, "Suppose I was a Javanese, what would you have of me?" His answer was, "Well, sir, then I would have to ask you to pay half a *duit* just like any other person who has come to the market." I asked him why it should be so and he said "To compensate for the trouble my colleagues and myself have taken to collect the market tax."

The joke had gone too far. I was very indignant about it and asked a man where the *controleur* lived so that I could talk to him. I was told that no *controleur* was living within ten *paal* of the area.

I came to the end of the road looking for a carriage I had ordered with a firm view of seeing, once I reached home, the Resident of Surabaya, within whose territory this incident had occurred. I hoped to achieve a favourable result from such a measure, because the Resident was known to be an upright and capable official who would not endure such things.

When I came to Surabaya, however, I calmed down because it would have appeared strange if I turned up at the Resident's door saying "I have found such goings on in your Residency," particularly as I have never met him. I decided to communicate my findings to this journal. Perhaps other Residents

Chinese shop in Bandung, 1920. Photo no. 4212, courtesy of KITLV, Leiden.

should be wary about this kind of problem lest a hunter turn up at a market again and defend these poor Javanese entrusted to the care of the officials.

The Chinese as Money-Lenders

The saying that the Chinese are the "blood suckers of Javanese" was first made by Governor-General van Overstraten and repeated in Parliament not long afterwards by the Minister of Colonies. We do not find it an elegant maxim, but it is true. Some proof of it has been conveyed to us recently, which we do not want to conceal from our readers. This proof involves the ways in which Chinese acquire the rice crop of natives by the so-called paddy trade.

The peasant needs a certain amount of money until his rice crop is harvested, bound into bundles, and safely stored. Then he must repay his debts. This is the right time of the year to meet most obligations including the initiation or marriage of his children or attending to such occasions of his relatives. This cycle of events returns every year. Now the peasant feels fortunate if he has enough for such expenses and no unforeseen contingencies such as the death of his first wife or children; if such, memorial feasts for the deceased will cost him more, if they do not occur at this stage. The new year is also an expensive time for him. Then he needs money to work his *sawah* [wet rice field]. If he does not have buffaloes or has sold them, he needs to buy them in addition to the other matters mentioned above. If he falls ill he must hire a *bujang* [hired labourer] to prepare his *sawah* for cultivation. If he has no paddy seed he must buy or borrow it from others. Once he has taken care of all these expenses, then he must replant his rice, weed his *sawah*, and guard it so that the birds do not eat his crop; if he cannot do any of these jobs by himself, he must engage his children. If the peasant concerned is poor, he needs from f50 to f60 for all the expenses involved. If he comes from the ranks of the well-to-do peasants in the *kampung* [semi-urban Indonesian settlement], sometimes a large sum of money, even up to f500 or f600, is insufficient for the purpose. Let us now discuss the situation in Buitenzorg and the environs of Batavia, because it is particularly well known to us in the light of new information.

"The peasant is most speculative and eager to buy things," our informant writes. "It is mostly the Chinese who provoke the peasant for such passions and make him speculate. The Chinese sell or barter their textiles for rice, at a price two or three times higher than the value of the goods themselves. The government has prohibited the natives from gambling but who cares about that? Think about the officials who are meant to enforce the law despite their meagre salaries."

How does the native find money to meet all his needs? "The first method is to borrow money to be repaid after the rice harvest, that is at the time when marriage and initiation festivities take place. The *sawah* that had not been worked immediately after the harvest now has to be prepared for cultivation. So the peasant may not be clear on where the money will come from. The Chinese understand this situation and take the opportunity to profit from it. They give no more than f5, to be repaid after the next harvest by a cart of paddy consisting of fifty bunches each weighing nine or ten *kati*. The Chinese exploit this transaction greedily; within six months the original f5 becomes f7.50, and in twelve months grows from f12.50 to f15.00. So the capital triples in two years. The whereabouts of this capital is uncertain, it has to be admitted, but the Chinese knows how to secure it."

"The second method by which the peasant obtains money is to borrow it as soon as one *petak* of land is ploughed and the seedlings are sprouting. The value of a *pedati* [cart-load] of paddy at the time is f7.50, and this will go up to f12.50 and f15.00 after six months, so the Chinese will have his capital doubled in half a year."

"The third mode is borrowing money on his *sawah* by a notary deed. In this case the plot of mortgaged *sawah* goes to the money-lender; he can cultivate it and reap its fruits until the debt is paid. This kind of loan generally involves a period up to ninety-nine years. The advantages the Chinese derive from this kind of transaction are great. They mostly take the landowners on as their *bujang* and let them work the *sawah* in return for half the crop. But the Chinese money-lenders know how to acquire the remaining half as well as making further loans available and selling textiles at high prices to the peasants, requiring repayments either in paddy or through the peasants' performing compulsory public labour services on a proxy basis."

"A fourth method available for the native to obtain money from a Chinese is to take a loan to be repaid in cash, with his *sawah* as the security and with the interest instalments to be paid in paddy. Such transactions also take place through the native intermediaries of the money-lenders. The Chinese provide money in June soon after the rice harvest. For a loan of f60, for instance, the interest should be paid in September the following year. This interest amounts to two *pedati* or cartloads, anything to one hundred bunches of paddy, each weighing from nine to ten *kati*. This becomes worth f24 or f30 by the following February-April period. So it goes on."

Is Opium a Genuine Evil?

J. Groneman

Perhaps no issue divided colonial public opinion in the Indies more than the so-called opium question. The Dutch regime brought opium from India, Turkey, and other places in enormous quantities; it was then shipped in Dutch and English bottoms to the colony, where it was auctioned off to opium "farmers" (usually Chinese syndicates), who paid for the right to retail it to people in a prescribed time and space. Revenues from Dutch opium sales brought in enormous sums of money to the government exchequer, but it also laid the administration open to accusations by reformers that the Indies colony was built on the misery and drug addiction of local populations. Chinese "coolies" bought opium in high quantities, often to the detriment of their health and well-being, but Javanese and other indigenous peoples of the archipelago also consumed it. Eventually, reformers forced the colonial administration to discontinue the farming system and to make at least a show of trying to cut down on consumption and addiction among local populations. The debate on the place of opium in Indies society continued for many decades, in fact until the Dutch lost their colony in the mid-twentieth century.

I could not respond in any pithier way to what I have read in the questions that the Government has asked in her well-known circular on opium.

I am not called in to answer those questions that are particularly put forward to civil servants of the regional and local governments and financial departments, because I am *not* a civil servant. But would it for this reason be conceited if I believe that I, as a layman, and as medical doctor, would probably even know more about this topic than a more privileged member of our Euro-Indies society? I believe, therefore, that I do have a certain right to express my opinion, and if the Government truly longs for a serious answer to the questions that were asked, then perhaps *my* opinion, too, could be welcome. It also might be that my opinion could be more conclusive than those of the civil servants who have to answer these questions in an uncomfortable situation, even when they know next to nothing or less about this issue.

I am not saying that this is the case in all, or even in most cases, but I do believe that someone, in order to evaluate the consequences of opium use correctly, must observe opium's consequences, and also its use, in the places where this has taken place. These are not in government or financial offices or along the main road, nor in the farms or warehouses for coffee or salt, that are every now and then inspected by civil servants. These *are* primarily in the opium-dens, and often in the houses and beds of the opium-smoker, and furthermore in courtrooms and prisons.

Regarding courtrooms, many civil servants who have as police-magistrates or presidents in district courts pledged about natives and Chinese can discuss this situation, but these decisions mostly concern whether the accused is guilty or not for the crime he committed; because people do not deal with the question of how the accused has reached this point, their experience is, therefore, insufficient to answer the real questions properly.

Hence I claim that these officials are not always the right people to ask these questions. For numbers, *not* the number of opium-smokers, but the number of those consuming opium *legally*, I make an exception. They have the most complete data on this, although the numbers are always too low, because these do not include illegal opium.

These numbers report, such as *Een Stem uit Indie* ["A Voice from the Indies"] in the March edition of the journal for this year, that in the residence of Kediri (Java), which only counts 700,000 inhabitants in total, that every year 2.5 million guilders are being consumed on opium, and likewise the value of an opium farm in the small residence of Jogjakarta is 57,000 guilders per month, and with the purchase-money of legal opium and the charges and profits of the farmer certainly not less than 12 hundred thousand gold per year, that is bought up by a part of the 460 thousand Eastern inhabitants, not including what has been spent on illegal opium.

Correct numbers and statistics of farm-values and purchase-money can be given by residential offices, and archives of the financial department. The expenses and profits of the farmer and smugglers that are also paid by opium-smokers cannot be given at all.

How many of the inhabitants of different nationalities use opium, and how much each person would use it on average—the maximum amount of the most serious smokers, and the minimum of new users—nobody knows, except for the farmer who would never tell such information easily.

Suppose that opium does *not* cause any *other harm*; how many good things have not gone by for households and for the whole population, who could have used their money to buy something else, even it were only better clothing and food and some harmless entertainment?

But opium *causes much more harm*.

I hold silence about the moral ruin (*zedelijke verderving*) of *everybody* who looks for profit in contraband and petty-sales in clandestine opium; others, who erode *legal* opium, and who encourage non-smokers to smoke and smokers to smoke *more*; and of still others, who work as spies for the farmers but too often try to catch not only smugglers but also innocent people and hand them over to a judge, whether it is because of disgusting profit-making, revenge, or even petty jealousy. Is it indeed really so easy, despite regulations that are not always followed, to hide . . . and find some opium on the farmland or in the house of the chosen victim. And it will seldom be discovered otherwise! Some civil servants are even mentioned, who have used this way to approach native or Chinese women who would otherwise be unapproachable for them. This could be untrue, but it is certainly not impossible.

I also hold silence of those victims (the fact that they exist can be proven through archives from several law-courts), who are punished while being innocent, but who through forced exchanges and relationships with guilty, punished people in prison become infected and ruined, while their families suffer outside prison.

I also hold silence for all those who, to a greater or lesser extent, become victims of gambling and swindling, of theft and robbery, of stealing and murder, caused by smokers, who were tortured by hunger for opium and therefore try to obtain those things through criminal ways that are not or not so easy to earn through honest work.

I wish, however, to say a little bit more about the smokers and their families, who are the first *immediate* victims of the indeed slow but therefore no-less-sure poison for society that is legalized by our government.

Here I speak out of my own experience, the experience of a doctor who has treated many opium-smokers on their request, and who has also healed some of them; a doctor who, fighting against the interest of the country's treasury, tried to reduce misery for those unfortunate people who are tired of their misery. The *only* thing that can save them in those cases, a way that often causes huge pain and therefore is so often neglected: namely, *abstinence*.

From that experience I learned that the majority of the smokers came to seek our opium for their salvation, because it was offered as a *remedy* by our farmers and their accomplices, or because they did not have the courage to turn down the politeness of the generous host who offered the lofty delight *for free*. Others became addicts because a friendly *baba* [i.e, Chinese Indonesian] had *offered* it to them as a greeting (after all, we know how open-handed the Chinese can be when it is in their interest). A few merely started out of curiosity or desire for pleasure or relief. All of them had after their first experiment tried it out for the second time, and being content of that, felt the need for the next dose. By this way, they have become smokers and slaves of a habit, that soon appears to be an *evil* habit that they can no longer live without.

Are there no civil servants who, by reading those questions, would say: *the Government knows that herself*, and she is not asking those questions so as to expect any true answers. But why is she doing this? . . . To receive *untrue* answers, with which she could make an excuse for her trade, which she can continue then? . . .

That would be indefensible, and that *cannot* and *may not be true*.

If the Government *knows* how pernicious opium is to become for the smoker and his family, and to the whole of Indies' society, then she, despite the interests of the treasury, would *have to* make an end of that evil, and, I totally agree with Mr. Jansz, that there is no other way for this then *forced withdrawal (abstinence)*.

Even though that abstinence would cost hundreds or even thousands of lives (and it won't be that much by far), hundreds of thousands of lives would be rescued or safeguarded from unbearable misery which is nothing else than a slow, torturous death.

Finally, one more question.

The treasury cannot lack these profits, it has been said.

What would we say to the Sultan of *Zanzibar*, or some other big driver of the slave trade, who we, out of Christian civilized humanism, wanted to persuade or force to end his barbaric trade? The answer: you are totally correct, alas, but my treasury cannot lack those incomes . . . ?

Would a civilized brother say: well, that changes the case then, go ahead as far as you can? . . .

Is that slave trade worse than our opium trade? . . .

Slaves can be fortunate, they can remain healthy and strong, and become old. Opium slaves *cannot*, for opium is always pernicious, even if it is consumed moderately. And because in the long run, using opium leads to abuse if the quantity that gives enjoyment or pleasure in the beginning is not satisfying in the long run, and the misery that replaces pleasure makes one desire for irresistibly new intoxication, that can only be extorted by increasingly *more* opium.

The former regent of Bandoeng, *Radèn Adipati* Wira nata Koesoemoe, once answered the question why *he* never drank wine like other regents from

Prijangan, to whom the *Koran* forbids misusing—but not using—wine. He answered: "If I drink wine, many of my subordinate chieftains would follow, and some would become *mis-users*. For this reason I do *not* use wine!"

He was only a follower of Muhammad.

Jogjakarta, 21 July 1882.

Translated from Dutch by Oiyan Liu

River Travel in the Padang Uplands

Anonymous

Although lying at a considerable distance from the Dutch seat of power at Batavia, Padang was one of the ports that the colonizers of Indonesia first identified as important as they began their expansion across the length and breadth of the archipelago. Padang became a crucial harbor and an important administrative outpost for the Dutch in Sumatra, but in the bovenlanden, *or uplands of this area, Dutch power and influence was far less assured than on the narrow ribbon of flatlands on the coast.* Controleurs, *or regional civil servants, were thus established there, and these men sent back regular reports about life in remote regions. In the Padang uplands, the stakes of a Dutch presence were deemed particularly important because of abundant coal deposits. This eventually led to significant mining in the highlands, as well as a railway service through difficult terrain to ferry the mineral to ships along the coast.* Controleurs *followed in the footsteps of some of the intrepid miners, traveling by boat on fast-moving rivers that transected the mountains of the interior. Dutch exploration of these liminal spaces continued into the early twentieth century, but knowledge occasionally came at the price of human life.*

The lines below are from the diary of a young clerk of the Indies government. To better orient the reader, Sidjoendjoeng, the place mentioned on the title page, lies about eighteen hours away from Padang in one of the many long valleys, which are so typical for the "high culture" of the entire region. At about half an hour's distance north of Sid is the lowest point of the valley. There, at Moeara, the small river of Sid and the southbound Sinamoe come together. East from there the river, called the Kwantan, and an even lower one called the Indragiri leaves the narrow valley.

SIDJOENDJOENG, MARCH 7, 1884

I am referring namely to a trip from our post to Doerian Gedang, a place close to the independent lands.

Quite a bit ahead of time, we, R. L. van W. and I, had decided to visit the place where in 1872 the well-known engineer de Greve in the Kwantanriver

Girls in festive costume, Lesung Batu, 1879. Photo no. 7081, courtesy of KITLV, Leiden.

found his death. That place is by foot difficult to reach; I estimate the distance from Moeara at about fourteen poles (eighteen minutes). Normally, and this is the rational way, one descends the river with the prauw (boat) and this makes the journey one of the most interesting ones of the Padang Highlands.

We left the 24th of February together from Sid, accompanied by some Malays, such as the warehouse master and the writer of Moeara, who, strangely enough, was a small hunchback Malay and carrying the curious name of Napoleon.

At Moeara we stepped into the quite spacious controllers-prauw, decorated by a tent and tons of flags. Five skilled navigators, from Silakat, and ready for their job, would bring us to our destination. The river was high those days. The water moved quickly, and the heavily loaded prauw moved with it. Soon we traveled between the high mountains, which are almost vertical, and at our feet, where there were large rocks, the banks of the river formed. Those rocks were of all kinds of shapes, in which one could often see animals or other objects. Of course, many of these were part of some Malay myth. One could see a stone ship; this once belonged to a young fellow, who left his parents and got rich from trade and traveled with his boat down the river. Because of his distinction, however, he wouldn't recognize his old mother—and as punishment his ship became stone! One could see a stone elephant, which fell from the sky—and so on and so on. Fantastic indeed, there in proud, lonely nature! Our vessel floated down the river, past the high rocks; it was beautiful, high, and mountainous . . . nevertheless all of it was dark and silent!

The first part of the river from Moeara to Moko-moko soon ended, and at the last mentioned place, where the banks are almost entirely closed in by rocks, we landed. At the right bank were the rocks, some hundreds of feet high in steepness; white quartz was visible between the green walls, which were largely grown with weeds. At the left bank, where we disembarked, one found the so-called Moko-moko, and this important place consisted of only one house. Close by was the main point of our tour—the cave of Moko-moko. The road, less than a footpath, really continued alongside the river and was very difficult to follow due to the many rocks, stones, and tree roots, which tested our feet. Between the varying shades of green one could see the current falling down, forming a ferocious ribbon which made it impossible to navigate the river.

Walking in a long line after one another, we and the coolies arrived finally at the cave. Several names carved into the walls proved regular visits of people, and was testimony to men being the same everywhere. It all looked fantastic.

Some large prauws were ready to bring us further. The river's current was quick though calm here between the heavenly high rocks. Halfway up the rock one could see large openings; these gave access to other caves that had never been visited by anyone, because they were practically impossible to reach.

After having eaten, we stepped onto the large prauw which was a little better prepared for the heavy task than the somewhat old controleur-prauw. The five rowers took their places and navigated, equipped with large pads, and calmly the light vessel moved over the current. With enjoyment we stared at the rocks that in their multicolored patterns surrounded the river. Then we went around the bend . . . and at that place there was a known current, one of the many that require a steady hand to traverse. Dangerous irregularities in the surface of the river, which fell with a terrible noise and high waves, made one think that any moment the vessel could be hit and turn upside down. Bouncing back and forth it floated through the mass; nearby were stones and rocks, which scared everyone. The vessel made many maneuvers between the rocks; one mistake and the vessel would certainly capsize.

There, in the middle of the current was a large rock; the prauw was heading right at it. We were scared about the speed; we would slam against the rock, and once in this water, the best swimming would not help. . . . Suddenly, close to the great stone, the vessel bucked; the stream fell in a large, descending water mass. Nevertheless calm and confident the rowers were standing and navigated the boat with their oars closely past the rock, almost gently through the ferocious waves! Just trust those men of Silakat; they know precisely how far they can go and that also their own lives are lost when they make a mistake.

New views were shown when we departed from the rocks. At our right-hand side we saw in the highest trees various *siamangs*—a monkey species with black skin. We noted little of the imitated screaming of a tiger, usually so often responded to, but now without response. We moved quickly and had to pass multiple currents before Silakat, but all were totally known to the rowers. Often the prauw took water in, but that was all. The rocky banks were now only visible very far away. At both sides there were now hills with heavy forests and to the left, where the village Silakat lies, one could also see rice fields. For a moment we stayed at this place, where the population was curious to see Europeans who almost never make it upcountry this far.

After some more time, we finally landed in front of a current that was too dangerous for us to pass; the prauw rowers, however brave, never risk this one.

It was a bit of a disappointment that at the other side there was no more vessel. We were thus forced to reach the end point of our trip, Doerian Gedang, on foot. Across the mountains, along dikes of rice fields, and along stone clogs, we walked on the small road for about half an hour. Finally we reached the opposite side of the kampung [i.e., village] where we had ourselves ferried. In the meantime our luggage, beds, etc. were carried as well; we could then sleep in the guest house.

At our arrival at Doerian Gedang, this place that has such a sad connotation because of the drowning of the engineer de Greve, we headed towards his grave. The final resting place of the able, much-loved engineer was very simple. We commemorated what the fatherland had lost in him, and we couldn't leave the place without a tear. Multiple times we heard about the peculiarities of his death. From brave to foolhardy he had put himself at risk in a boat upstream, and ignoring the severest warnings from natives from the region he had thrown out a led casting. When it got stuck, the vessel capsized in the quick current. Two officers sitting next to him barely saved their lives through frantic swimming.

For commemoration, the controllers Van Hoëvell and Twiss have put down a simply inscribed tombstone with much effort in the difficult-to-reach area. A leaf-roof and a thin demarcation protect the grave from animals and rain. It lies there in a lonely corner of the world.

Translated from Dutch by A. van de Rijt and E. Tagliacozzo

Ethnographic Notes on Sumba

J. J. van Alphen

Dutchmen who traveled or explored landscapes outside the colonial stronghold of Java often wrote pseudo-anthropological accounts of the peoples and cultures they encountered. By today's standards these accounts were almost invariably negative in their ascription of unsavory characteristics to local cultural practices and modes of living. Writings on Sumba, an island in Nusa Tenggara, eastern Indonesia, proved no exception: travelers there spoke of caste and slave systems that rendered large portions of the population completely powerless, and of a general "lawlessness" and "backwardness" that seemed to invite colonial occupation. These negative cultural attributes and localized systems of coercion were generally ascribed to lowland, coastal populations; the peoples of the interior were described as living in little more than the simplest state of nature. The Dutch eventually colonized Sumba in the early twentieth century, as local equines (called "sandalwood horses") were needed for Indies cavalry regiments. These same Sumba horses then helped in the conquest of other parts of the Indonesian archipelago as well.

Soemba and the Soembanese

Mr. J. J. van Alphen, missionary-teacher on the island of Soemba (residency Timor) has reported on that island and its inhabitants on February 5 in a public meeting in Kwitang. In an overview of this report the following is noteworthy:

The island Soemba is a very rocky, fertile land with clay ground and lots of water. Its primary product is the well-known sandalwood-horse. They live wild in the forests, which are considered sacred by the local inhabitants.

The population resembles in sight and character mostly those other societies of the South Sea islands; they are large and muscled, and have a light brown, sometimes olive-colored tint. This is because of their less pointed shoulder bones, their flatter noses, and their narrower foreheads, as compared with the Javanese and Malays. Van Alphen describes the inhabitants as very mistrustful, mean, cowardly, cruel, unashamed, impolite, dirty, industrious, religious, and welcoming (and bases this opinion on multiple facts, that he was a witness to during his time there). To mention a number of examples he says that a guest out of distrust does not dare to eat anything that is served by the host, before the latter has eaten it himself; that the Soembanese never washes, that he covers his entire body with old rags and leaves, wears the clothes on his body until they are entirely gone, and simply paints them black when they start to look dirty. He also says that he has the same ambition to kill a man as he would kill a chicken; but that his hospitality is so great that you can stay as long as you want. Especially a tendency toward power-hunger is a bad characteristic of the Soembanese, says the speaker, and he attributes the divisions on the island to this trait.

The clothes of the population in the interior are very primitive, as they cover their heads with tree bark, and are otherwise naked. Those who live closer to the coasts are better dressed, as they sell cotton products.

According to the speaker the land is divided in three castes, or rather classes, namely (1) the Merambas, or lords; (2) the Kapisoes, or free men and civilians; and (3) the Atas, or slaves. The Merambas are only lords in the sense that they have the right to plunder and steal all around the island. The Kapisoes are dependent on the lords, and—as van Alphen says—can be regarded as the milk cows of the former. The Atas are slaves by purchase or by birth. Although the latter belong to the lowest class, they are however well treated by their masters and eat with them at the same table. Their dependence just means that they are obligated to obey their masters in every way and are usually ordered to pillage; for the rest, their lives are in the hands of their masters.

On Soemba there exists a total anarchy. Those with the largest number of slaves are the most powerful; they wander to distant kampongs, steal from the inhabitants, and even carry away girls and little children with them.

There is no education on Soemba whatsoever; the children are, as soon as they can do without their mother's care, sent out to do labor. They must help their parents in cultivating the land. On Soemba people do not compute; numbers are indicated with fingers; for example a fist indicates five. No one ever discovered writing on Soemba; according to some saga, once, in the past, this was the case, but a large flood must have destroyed all present books. Furthermore, the speaker could not find a grave with inscriptions from which the existence of an alphabet could be deduced; he declared however, that also—due to insufficient funds—he was not able to investigate this further across the island.

There also seems to be no law in Soemba. The mighty can steal and plunder as much as they please; the weak, however, are punished for the same deeds with the loss of property, or with death.

An indigenous religion the Soembanese do not have; they worship only two invisible ghosts, namely the Omboe-awan, or lord of heaven, and the

Omboe-tanah, or lord of earth. Besides these stand a mass of earth ghosts, to which they sacrifice before battles, harvesting, or when going out to travel. These offerings consist of chickens, pigs, horses, and *karbouws* (water buffaloes). Noteworthy is that before the offering, the intestines of the chicken or the liver of the horses, pigs, and buffaloes are inspected to see if the good spirit accepts the offer. Temples are not found on Soemba, but altars are.

Matrimony resembles the customs of Java. Women are regarded as some kind of expensive commodity. Women are extremely rare, according to the speaker, a consequence of the slave trade. As an oddity the speaker reports that the women on Soemba, before marriage, lead a promiscuous life.

Very curious is what he reports with respect to ceremonial burials. The bodies are tightly bound up with cloth and put in a kneeling position, up against a pole. In front of the house of the deceased this is then stuck into the ground; the bodies of kings are left in that state until they have completely rotten away, while those of less important people are left two or three days above earth, after which they are placed in a grave, that has the form of a well, which is then sealed with a heavy stone. The clothes of the deceased, and his gems, are put next to him in the grave. During the days that the body is attached to the pole, friends and acquaintances come and bring gifts, consisting of textiles and other artifacts. The graves can be found in the middle of the kampongs and are well guarded by those who live there.

Translated from Dutch by A. van de Rijt and E. Tagliacozzo

Advice on Islam

C. Snouck Hurgronje

C. Snouck Hurgronje, or simply "Snouck," as he came to be known in many circles, was one of the foremost Indologists of his generation. These were scholars who took on the learning of the various Indies societies and their constituent peoples as the intellectual projects of their lifetimes. Snouck, however, also simultaneously served as an Indies colonial servant. This dual existence made him one of the more fascinating figures of his time, his life spanning several decades on either side of the twentieth century. Snouck lived in Arabia to learn about Islam and the transit of Indies students and pilgrims to that place, and he also wrote in period newspapers and scholarly journals about a wide variety of topics, most of them concerning the manner and practice of Islam in the Indies. Yet he became most known, perhaps, as one of the principle architects of the Dutch Aceh policy, as Holland tried to deal with the decades-long guerrilla war that raged in northernmost Sumatra toward the end of the nineteenth century. Though Snouck converted to Islam and in fact had two Indonesian wives and several children by them, many Muslims and Europeans doubted his trustworthiness as a convert because he was seen as a possible spy for the Dutch government. His knowledge of Islam, however, and of the Indies was never in question. In this selection from his administrative advice to the colonial regime, he talks about mosques and their functions in the Indies in the late nineteenth century.

Batavia, 11 September 1894

To the Director of Education

This advice can be regarded as collectively prepared by Sajjid Oethman bin Jahja and me. Since Sajjid Oethman cannot read European writing without assistance, I have kept him informed and updated him on the contents of the aforementioned pieces and given him the Arabic translation.

The matter that currently divides the Muslims at Negara in Amoentai recurs in other colonial areas, and led among other things recently in Palembang to considerable unrest. Therefore, Sajjid Oethman, when he last year

C. Snouck Hurgronje.
Photo no. 2510,
courtesy of KITLV,
Leiden.

published a Malay-language brochure about all kinds of legal determinations concerning the Friday Service, dedicated an important part (pages 31–50) of that to the discussion of the following: (under the title *Djam'oel-fawa'id*) those cases in which having more than one Friday service in the same city is allowed. Soon Sajjid Oethman wants to publish another brochure (this time in Arabic) with particular reference to the same matter, but for now he asks me to add to my advice here a copy of his thoughts.

This version Your Excellency will find under the appendices.

The application of generally recognized laws concerning this subject in the case of Negara, as far as this can be judged in the relevant writings, boils down to the following, according to me and Sajjid Oethman.

The proponents of holding a second Friday service in a new mosque at Negara use as argument that the distance between the two mosques is so far that one cannot hear the sound of the other mosque. Muslim law teaches that when one cannot hear under the most optimal circumstances the sound of another mosque, then it is allowed to establish a new one. In this case one would not take as baseline the distance between the mosques, but instead the distance of the old mosque from the border of the neighborhood in which one is building the new one.

Since these optimal circumstances, which the law demands, are rather rare, the lawmakers have determined this distance to be always 1 Arabic mile, which is 2,920 meters. At Negara the distance between the mosques measures along a swirling road, and is only 2,769 meters; so the Friday service cannot be allowed on the basis of this distance. Neither can they use the argument that the distance to the mosque is too far, because in the law books it says that only when such a trip is unbearable, a second service should be allowed. This excludes a distance of 2,769 meters, or as others indicate, a half-an-hour walk.

With regard to the complaint that the old mosque would provide too little space, it can be remarked that according to legal experts:

> 1. the space of the old mosque is sufficient as long as the standard number of people who visit under normal circumstances can fit inside;
> 2. if 1 is not the case, there should also not be any space left in the yard of the mosque.

From these points we must come to the conclusion, that Mekka and Medina have justly responded to the question, namely, that the current situation does not justify a double Friday service.

The consequence of breaking this law is, according to Muslim law, that one of the two services is declared invalid.

The pieces also report a party at Negara, who want to recognize as valid a double service, holding a service after the Friday service in the old mosque. They say that although this is not strictly legal, it is desirable. Rightly so, the *pangoeloe* (local rulers) wanted to forbid this.

According to the religious law (as specified on pages 34–35 of the added appendix) where such a double service is justified by the circumstances, the repetition of the service at the same place is forbidden.

Finally, it is perhaps useful to indicate here why in this Archipelago despite Muslim regulations that all recognize as valid, parties in different communities have several times sought to institute a new Friday mosque, although existing ones are sufficient according to the law, or could easily be made sufficient.

First, there are now and then religious *hadjis* (pilgrims) or *goeroes* (teachers), who gladly see the rising attendance of the Friday service as a consequence of their acts, but whose attempts to expand are fruitless for those who are further away from the mosque, even though distance does not justify a new mosque. Those teachers then search for texts, which, seemingly for them, justify the building of a new mosque. Because of their influence, they are able to bring funds together for construction and thus find satisfaction of their need for honor, or their striving for heavenly compensation in the attachment of their name to the erection of the new mosque.

Second, and no less important, is the custom of natives to shower all kinds of gifts, but especially their annual obligated *pitrah* (a certain amount of rice per capita) to the Friday mosque, where they speculate they will attend services.

Most of this profit is going to those who serve in the mosque.

Where a teacher who has a certain group of supporters outside the mosque stands outside the Friday mosque personnel, the temptation is for him to exploit a new mosque to the good of his and his intellectual followers. From the permission letter of the district head at Negara for the erection of a new mosque, one could conclude that the latter indeed had an incentive, since the head underscores that one does not entirely cancel one's gifts to the old mosque.

Translated from Dutch by A. van de Rijt and E. Tagliacozzo

Marriage in Minahasa

Anonymous

The Minahasa areas of northern Sulawesi were reached early on by Dutch ships, and a community of Dutchmen stayed there over the centuries, trading, mixing, and marrying into the indigenous population. Manado became one of the most friendly cities to Europeans in the Indies; eventually many autochthonous military conscripts came from here to serve in the colonial armed forces, partly because they were trusted by the Dutch and partly because the percentage of the Christianized population was higher here than almost anywhere else in the Indies. Because the Dutch had a comparatively easy time in this part of Sulawesi, Dutch writing about local culture and society is particularly voluminous and detailed about the ways of the Minahasa people, even if also sometimes condescending and judgmental. Descriptions of many local folkways, including marriages, were put to paper, and some of these descriptions even found their way back to a larger reading public in the Netherlands, in newspapers such as the Nieuwe Rotterdamsche Courant. *Marriages were important for cross-cultural contact and observation because they made for one of the few institutions that allowed the (mostly male) Dutch colonizers to spend time analyzing local gender relations at work.*

Many weddings have been taking place lately. This is evidence that the padi-harvest (rice-harvest) has not been too bad lately. Are marriages in these areas related to harvesting rice? No doubt. The number of marriages is greater when floors are stored with more rice, and the number and splendor of parties, too, is proportionate with this. For no marriages among Minahassa take place that are not accompanied by eating and dancing parties. The native is particularly keen on dancing. When one attends the wedding of an *imam*, where only music can be heard, and where there is no dancing, one should not attribute this to the disgust of the wedded couple, but attribute it to a certain fear of the community leader who does not want to fill the anger of the assistant minister/curate to whose jurisdiction he belongs. Clergymen strictly fight against dancing that, as an incorrect tendency, leads to immorality.

At Alfurese dancing parties, especially of those who are less well-off, things are therefore often not less rough and ready than those similar parties among farmers in Rotterdam. Those who belong to higher classes behave more properly. It seldom occurs that someone indulges excessively in arrack or wine. Minahassans, like almost every native from the Moluccas and Sunda islands, have great contempt for drunkenness and loudness.

Yet we deviate from our subject. Let us look at how it works regarding courtship among natives. The young man writes a letter to his chosen one, preferably on two-sided pages, in which he declares in great extent, and with meaningless sentences, his love, and in which he likes to bring up the name of *Tuhan Allah*. Truly, one is surprised about the eloquence and extensive synonymical expressions that the Minahassar possesses—even though he is not in love. When the girl has learnt of the letter, she writes back a couple of sentences, if she has learned how to write. If not, she would answer, which is often positive, through an acquaintance. But when the answer is negative the one who is rejected is seldom heartbroken.

If the girl has accepted the young man, then her family also needs to be notified, for if the family objects, a wedding will not take place. Family includes not only her parents, but also blood relatives such as brothers, uncles, and male cousins of varying degrees whose voices also count. Moreover, the veto of a grand-nephew, especially when he belongs to the nobility, could weigh as much that a rejection of the lover would be an inevitable result.

What could be the big obstacles that would hinder a wedding? In the first place: differences in social status: the girl, who belongs to a *bangsa* (a kind of indigenous noble), is not allowed to marry an ordinary native from the kampong, especially if he is not related to the government. Another objection could be that the young man had lived like a Don Juan. However, the most prominent objection is if the poor young man cannot fulfill the many requirements of the girl's parents. They ask for such a large *harta* (bride price), that fulfilling it is beyond the abilities of the young man or his family. *Harta* could consist of either a few pieces of white or colored cotton textiles and some *sarongs*, or a certain amount of rice and a few pigs, or a little house or a piece of land, and any other kind of valuable property to an indigenous inhabitant. Do not think that this *harta* is longed for to the benefit of the girl! Not even a fraction of it! Usually, these exclusively benefit elders, who want to take advantage of the future husband as much as possible.

The Alfurese customs are therefore again different from those of Europe. Whereas in Minahassa the elders of the bride are demanding, in Europe it is the young people who would first inform about the fortunes the girl would bring with her. Although one could not praise the attitude of the parents of the Minahassan daughters, nor that of present-day young men, both attitudes are understandable and perhaps somewhat excused. The very idea

Bride and groom in
Minahasa, 1910s. Photo no.
43136, courtesy of KITLV,
Leiden.

of a *struggle for life* (from the civilized world) is among the Minahassa totally
unknown. There are no poor people; every person owns a padi-field which he
maintains himself. We have to add that the Alfurese does not possess much
beauty and is not selective, so that the ugliest girls, even Albino's—for whom
one would generally shiver—would get married sooner or later. If so, is it
surprising that the girl's kin conscientiously look for a groom who would
bring as many advantages and benefits as possible? One does not have to fear
that a young virgin would remain unmarried.

Whereas during their engagement the young couple only had some limited
passion of love, during the bridal days the girl takes—at least in the public
eye—an even more reserved attitude. To sit next to each other and have a
private conversation, or lovemaking or courting is simply out of the question.
The native does not kiss; he finds this a silly habit of Europeans. In short, if

one would not know better, one would say that the two young people are strangers or had a dispute with each other. One understands it is impossible in a courtship as such, that the groom would know his girl, or that the bride would know her future husband. And what purpose would this serve anyway? Does the character and nature of one person really differ that much from another? Indeed no! And what are the topics they could talk about? About the future? Oh, how annoying. Everything will turn out well, won't it! "Do not worry about it now," thinks the native. Come on, there is nothing to talk about: wedding festivities are arranged by the family, and whatever needs to be said can also be said after the wedding.

About ten to fourteen days before the celebration of the wedding, the young couple takes horse ride or carriage with their witnesses to the post of the district-officer, whose division is located in the domicile of the girl, and where the paper-formalities take place. In the period between the civil marriage and the blessing of the church which is compulsory for Christians, activities take place in the kampong where the tender loved young woman lives. In one of the farm yards, preferably at the bride's parents, rises a spacious *sabuwa* (a kind of airy lean-to), and chickens, pigs, eggs, flour, and wine are all brought here by different family members. Friends and acquaintances help prepare the menu for the wedding day and alleviate the work of the bride's parents by keeping themselves busy with grilling poultry, cooking and roasting pigs, and baking cookies and cake.

In the meantime, the groom does not sit still either. He first looked for an elegant *pakean* (costume), consisting of a skirt or a long, black coat, pantaloons, dress shirt, shoes (socks are often removed), and a hat, all often borrowed from a comrade for the wedding day, willingly or hired for a small fee. Having all this, his heart is at ease, and so he hauls water or helps cutting wood, because a large banquet requires a lot of difficulties and energy.

The important day has finally arrived and the wedded couple makes their way in a procession to the church, where the wedding will be celebrated and solemnized by a missionary or a native parish minister. The witnesses follow a few steps behind the couple, followed by many small, dirty guttersnipes who are accompanying out of enjoyment. The young couple strides forward in an elegant and extremely slow manner. He holds a green or blue parasol above her head. If she is not too *maloe* (shy), she holds his arm which is the best way for her. She walks with much difficulty, for her skirt makes this impossible. Moreover, the legs are often tied up together far above the knee, so that the little feet are forced to take very little steps and so that the fine foldings remain intact. His gait is not smooth either; every now and then he peers at his feet with agony. He obviously does not feel comfortable wearing leather shoes.

There is not much interest for the church ceremony; even the parents and the close blood relatives are absent. How could they appear anyway? Everybody is too occupied with preparing for the feast. Generally speaking, the speech of the clergyman is not very long, and when the hymns are sung, everyone leaves the church, from which the short procession proceeds to the residence of the parents of the fresh bride. The married couple is greeted by neighbors and acquaintances. One consumes one or more glasses of arrack as refresher (for the upper class this would be sour Bordeaux) till the appetite is stimulated. Then, one walks down the stairs to the *sabuwa* where long, covered tables are equipped with borrowed plates, tin-made or leaded covers, and glasses in at least twelve different shapes and qualities.

The place of honor of the table is reserved for the young couple; well-to-do family members sit near them, the others are placed at the end of the table. The pious brother says a prayer and soon after that some men approach, who are often brothers and cousins of the newlyweds, with plates full of delicious dishes. One brings rice, the other brings chicken that has been prepared in tens of different ways, pork, several kinds of vegetables, and *sambals* (chili sauces). Everybody eats with an extraordinarily enormous appetite, except for the bride, for this is considered impolite. Perhaps, too, she may be moved, because of the emotions on that day. Nor does she talk, while the eloquence of her husband—either he could not find the right words because of his over-happiness, or perhaps he feels uncomfortable in his gala-costume and tight shoes—also leaves much to be desired. Tongues of guests, however, are loose. Their toasts in Alfurese and Malay stand out for their long-windedness and uniformity. The whole thing is literally repeating each others' empty phrases without ending and without meaning. It is therefore not surprising that at the end there is silence or loud yawning here and there.

Fortunately, everything comes to an end. When the last crumb of the cake disappears, and when the newly wedded groom has expressed his gratitude for everyone's participation and interest, the final prayer of gratitude takes place and everyone stands up. The tables are carried away, and after a break of a few quarters or hours (depending on whether the *rijsttafel*-feast (rice-table feast) took place in the evening or in the afternoon) the dancing-party commences. This is the most enjoyable part of the program. The musician starts to strike an old violin that releases piercing sounds so that it provokes one's desire to break the sorrowful musical instrument in two pieces. Before long the *kulintang* and the triangle, too, are waiting for their appearance. Now there stands an orchestra with overwhelming dissonance, to the extent that one soon notices how poorly the musical skills of the Minahassans are developed. Nevertheless, there is a certain cadence in music, so that it is possible for dancers to dance according to rhythm.

The party continues on the next evening. For this event women and girls again appear in rather tidy *sarongs* and *kabajas,* while men dress up in cotton pants and jackets, according to their social status. The music rings again and again, and small, wide, dark feet stamp around. But by this time, the wedding party has really ended, and men and women return to their padi-fields to pay the necessary attention to these fields. Very often the newlyweds stay and live with the bride's parents until they have bought their own house. And after a house-warming party is given for the new house, no enjoyment awaits except for the first, happy baptism party after one year.

H. E. K. (*Nieuwe Rotterdamsche Courant*)

Translated from Dutch by Oiyan Liu

Shooting a Tiger

Anonymous

Alongside Komodo dragons, tigers were the indigenous animals of the Dutch East Indies that had the greatest hold on the Dutch imagination, and the greatest capacity to elicit fear and wonder in the writings of travelers, administrators, and civil servants. Komodo dragons were located on a few isolated islands in Nusa Tenggara; tigers were far more widespread, however, particularly in Sumatra. Tiger attacks on humans and beasts of burden were fairly common in some stretches of the Indies, and the process of building roads and railways occasionally brought the Dutch in contact with these animals, even if indigenes had to deal with them on a more sustained basis in rural villages. Killing a tiger was a mark of colonial power over nature, and it was an activity that some eagerly sought out, though occasionally the results of such confrontations did not turn out as humans had planned. More often than not, however, encounters between tigers and humans occurred by chance, not by design, with the outcome depending on the specific context. By the early twentieth century tiger populations were dwindling, as humans increasingly encroached on the animals' natural habitats. There are now almost no wild tigers left in Indonesia.

A Scary Moment

"Toewan! matjan!" [Master! A tiger!]

I was then controller at M . . . E . . . , residence P. and as is usually the case with those poor things, the only European present, so the *first* person over there. Twice a month a small passenger boat came by to drop off and pick up clerks, officers, and lower-ranked soldiers from and to the Upper Lands. However, except for on those few days, during which that happened, there was no *conversation*. I did speak every two or three days to a married inspector from the b.o.w. (Public Services Department) who was working along the river, but those were people who preferred to see anything local over a true European.

When in the mood for cozy, European interaction, I often drove on Saturday afternoons at about 1:30 with my *américain* to the department capital L.,

A tiger shot by Esquire W. Th. Boreel, 1903. Courtesy of Stichting Indisch Thee-en Familie Archief Van Der Hucht c.s.

at twenty-five Sumatra poles distance, where there was a sufficiently (though not too much of a) livable climate of a fraternity for officers and clerks. I spent communal evenings and Sundays there and returned on Monday morning, not always equally fresh, to my post and loneliness.

The road was more or less well-established and maintained so that for someone who knew it well, like me, it was easy to follow on with calm horses, and at pleasant moonlight. Therefore often out of compassion (because of the heat, you see?) for both myself and the horses I only rode after 5 p.m., to still be able to be in time (ca. 9 o' clock) at one of the parties.

In these places where the road went through old woods, it was, especially at certain times during the year, most dangerous because of tigers, mostly those of the Royal kind. We would repeatedly place tiger traps at those points.

Although I knew very well that a tiger was typically too scared to attack a carriage with burning torches lighting the way, I always took the precaution of bringing a Beaumont, fully loaded, and held in the hands of the caretaker next to me. It was a carriage with one couch, and the horses I usually drove myself.

On one of these Saturdays I had been held up until 8 o' clock for various activities. Yet, since it was just past the full moon, I decided to nevertheless undertake the journey, being sure that at arrival in L. around midnight the party would still be in full swing.

At about seven poles from the capital there was a reasonably big stream, where I would cross over for the second and last time; and at a couple of hundred meters from there (in the direction of M. E.) was a small bamboo emergency bridge without supports. That bridge was in a little valley, quite deep (ca. four meters) below the level of the road, while it went through *alang-alang* (tall elephant grass) and very low grass.

It was about 11 o' clock. The moon was high, and for the human eye the terrain as was lit clearly as during a clear day.

Two traps at both sides of the road were testimony to this being a very suspicious tiger place. Therefore, for a traveler the message was "watch carefully"; I myself needed all my attention to direct the horses downward from the steep hill towards the bridge, a bridge that was barely broad enough for my *américaine*.

Halfway on the bridge I heard the caretaker whisper:

"Toewan! Matjan!"

Immediately the man pointed at the top of the upcoming hill.

I was surprised to see there one of the Kings of the Dutch-Indies' wilderness. Crawling across the road, it appeared to walk right into one of the traps, as I had the pleasure to observe this with crystal clarity.

Who is the one who at such critical moments cannot stay calm, and loses control!

Fortunately, the caretaker and I remained calm. The situation appeared hopeless. What to do? As I said, the carriage was in the middle of the bridge, so there was no going back; leaving carriage and horses alone was also difficult, and was very dangerous in itself, since we, before reaching a village, would have to walk for poles along *alang-alang*, possibly getting lost.

No other option than *shooting* remained, which could be successful, since the distance was under sixty meters. Fortunately, the caretaker was a big and a good shooter, the horses were not nervous, and were used to gunfire, since I sometimes shot wild pigeons during the day from the carriage.

I did not dare to speak a word. Perhaps I could not have, even had I tried. The caretaker I gave a silent, though nevertheless very strict, order. He understood my sign, climbed—or rather crouched—carefully, and quickly made his way downward. And, then, while I carefully watched the horses, he fired . . . !

It appeared to be a hit, because the animal stretched entirely and disappeared with a big jump and a nasty scream into the *alang-alang*.

The horses got a little upset but the good animals were soon calmed down.

That all happened in several seconds.

Now the biggest danger was over, but to be sure I had Sirdin shoot six or so times left and right into the *remboe* (jungle) to impress any possibly neighboring fellow tigers.

Then we quickly drove up, where we hurriedly exchanged horses so that with "able speed" we finished the trip.

It appeared that this, by the way very uncommon, incident had not made a small impression on me, because when I some time later entered the fraternity, the effect was so clearly still present in my face that everyone could see it. However, I was not ashamed of that, especially since the bravest among the audience did not appear indifferent to my story after I told them.

In the end I was congratulated, and my happy deliverance was celebrated with the necessary champagne (it was there, in those days, still a really old-fashioned place). The good Sirdin was thanked with a decent tip the next day, and that he had risen not a little in people's regard is needless to say.

The next morning the terrain was searched and the tiger was found dead a short distance from where the incident had taken place.

Translated from Dutch by A. van de Rijt and E. Tagliacozzo

The Endless War in Aceh

Aceh Documentation Center

The Sultanate of Aceh represented the last indigenous polity of any real size to stand in the way of Dutch hegemony in the Indonesian archipelago. Aceh's heyday had been in the sixteenth and seventeenth centuries, when under sultans such as Iskandar Muda (lived 1583–1636) the polity traded with Ottoman Turkey, China, and many other kingdoms along the maritime trade routes. Even in the centuries following these dizzying heights of power and cosmopolitan living, Aceh's influence remained very strong in northern Sumatra, as well as in the eastern Indian Ocean. The slow creep of Dutch power up the length of Sumatra made conflict nearly inevitable, however, and when war came in 1873, much of the archipelago—composed of scores of precariously independent polities—nervously watched the outcome. Amazingly, the first assault by the Dutch was beaten back by fierce Acehnese resistance, though by the following year the Dutch forces had achieved a toehold in Banda Aceh, the capital, and resolute gue-rilla fighting spread to the hills. Traditionally, the end of the Aceh war has been dated to 1903, when the participating parties signed an important treaty, but in reality the conflict continued for several more decades. It was reborn after independence when the Acehnese pursued a similar program of resistance against centralizing regimes in Jakarta, as seen in this hyperpatriotic selection below.

It was Wednesday, March 26, 1873; the 26th day of Muharam 1290 H, in the Is-lamic calendar. The imperial warship, "Citadel van Antwerpen," was anchored off the coast of present-day North Sumatra, between the isle of Sabang and the Sultanate of Aceh on the mainland. From the ship's deck, the colonial Dutch declared war on Aceh, the effect of escalating intrigue and tension between the two nations. From that moment on Aceh, dogged by internal political dissension, would be stricken by disaster and the Dutch would face their greatest opposition since their arrival in the Indonesian Archipelago.

The first step towards the declaration of war by Dutch Commissioner F. N. Nieuwenhuijzen, who was also the Vice-President of the Dutch East Indies Council, was taken with the signing of the "Sumatra Treaty" between the

Dutch and the British in 1871, in which it was stated, among others, that the Dutch were "given the freedom to expand their authority in Sumatra." This annulled any further obligation for the Dutch to respect the rights and sovereignty of Aceh, which up until then had been recognized by both The Netherlands and Great Britain in the "London Treaty" of 1824.

As an independent nation, Aceh had always sought to maintain friendly relations with the countries of Europe and Asia. But, in the middle of the sixteenth century, Aceh found itself in a bitter war with the Portuguese and was put in the position of having to request aid from the Ottoman Empire, the most powerful Islamic nation at that time.

The Sultan of Aceh, 'Ala al-Din Ri'ayat Syah al-Kahar (1537–71), sent his envoy, Husein Efendi, to Istanbul to request assistance from the Sultan of Turkey, Selim II. This request resulted in seventeen warships and two escorts led by Admiral K. Khizir Reis being dispatched to Aceh. Joining the fleet were a number of *ulama* (Muslim scholars), fort construction experts, metal experts, and military instructors.

According to Turkey's former Ambassador to Indonesia, Metin Inegollu, who served in this position from 1986 till 1989, the Turkish naval forces returned home after serving only one year in Aceh. The Portuguese had been driven out successfully. However, two Turkish ships remained in Aceh, in case the Portuguese should return. This experience with the Portuguese resulted in a military academy being established in Aceh, in conjunction with the Turks, named "Askari Baitul Muqaddas." A number of well-known leaders have graduated from this academy since its inception; including, Keumala-hayati, the lady admiral of the Sultan of Aceh.

It is recorded in the annals of international diplomacy that Aceh was the first country to recognize The Netherlands while they were still fighting the Eighty Years War (1568–1648), their struggle to gain independence from Spain, which, in the end was won by the Dutch. This recognition by the Sultan of Aceh was presented by Acehnese Ambassador Abdul Hamid to Dutch Prince Maurits at a battlesite near Utrecht in The Netherlands.

Aceh also had a harmonious bilateral relationship with Queen Elizabeth I of England, who appointed Sir James Lancaster to Aceh as head of the Queen's royal delegation. During the reign of Louis XIII of France, Aceh's Sultan Iskandar Muda fostered friendly relations beneficial to both countries.

Whereas a friendship existed between Aceh and The Netherlands, sustained by the "London Treaty," a special pact was also concluded by the two nations in 1857, whereby both parties reaffirmed to respect and recognize each other's sovereignty. The Netherlands, in this case, was represented by Jan van

Acehnese chiefs in Kutaraja, 1892. Photo no. 4904, courtesy of KITLV, Leiden.

Swieten, the Dutch Governor of North Sumatra, while Aceh was represented by Sultan Alauddin Mansyur Syah. This agreement was ratified by the *Staten Generaal* (Dutch parliament) in The Netherlands.

This was very important from a constitutional point of view, because it was the first agreement ever made by the Dutch with any independent nation within the Archipelago, since they set foot in the region, up until 1945. It should be recognized, therefore, that the declaration of war on Aceh in 1873, made possible by the "Sumatra Treaty," turned the 1857 agreement into nothing more than a broken promise.

Not long after the signing of the "Sumatra Treaty," the Dutch immediately prepared to send their envoys to Aceh to *peacefully* force the issue. However, Aceh, fully expecting such action, sent a delegation to Turkey to ask for assistance, and suggested to the Dutch that their envoys come a little later, in December 1872. Aceh was stalling for time, while it held discussions in Singapore with American and Italian representatives, in the hope of consummating a pact for the protection of Aceh.

Realizing the ramifications of such a pact being concluded, the Dutch took quick action to protect their interests. The East Indies Governor General, James Loudon, immediately sent a fleet to Aceh on hearing that an American fleet led by Admiral Jenkins intended to set sail from Hong Kong to Aceh that March. Anxiety over the possible interference of third party nations resulted in the hastened departure of Nieuwenhuijzen to Aceh, with the task of forcing the Acehnese to recognize the authority of The Netherlands over Sumatra.

On his arrival in Aceh waters, on board the "Citadel van Antwerpen," and escorted by the ships "Siak," "Marnix," and "Coehoorn" on March 22, 1873, Nieuwenhuijzen sent an ultimatum to Tuanku Mahmud Syah, Sultan of Aceh. Since it was certain that the Sultan would never submit to Dutch demands, they proceeded to do what they had already prepared for, namely to officially declare war on Aceh.

This declaration, however, was not immediately followed by military action. The Dutch were waiting to assemble their battle forces, which were already on their way to Aceh.

In facing the fact that war would soon break out, the Acehnese set about mobilizing their forces in the coastal area immediately across the location of the Dutch fleet. These areas were Ulèe Lheuë, Panté Ceureumèn, Kuta Meugat, Kuala Aceh, as well as other strategic sites such as the Mesjid Raya (Grand Mosque), Peunayông, Meuraksa, Lam Pasèh, Lam Jabat, Raja Umong, Pungè, Seutuy, and the area of *Dalam* (The Sultan's Palace).

On Monday, April 6, 1873, shortly after war had been declared, the first Dutch troops landed at Panté Ceureumèn, under the command of Major General J. H. R. Köhler. He was assisted by his deputy, Vice-Commander Colonel E. C. van Daalen, who commanded the Infantry, and with a Chief of Staff, Vice-Chief of Staff, adjutants, battalion leaders, a detachment of army engineers, a medical division, and a topographic unit.

As soon as they reached the shore, the Dutch troops were immediately attacked by Acehnese fighters. Only after several days of fighting and considerable resistance, did the Dutch finally gain control of the Baiturrakhman Grand Mosque in Kutaraja (now known as Banda Aceh) on April 10, 1873. However, persistent attacks from the Acehnese fighters, led by Teuku Imeum Luëng Bata, among others, forced the Dutch to leave the Grand Mosque several days later.

On April 14, 1873, the Dutch troops once again attempted to control the Grand Mosque. During the combat, General Köhler was shot and killed by Acehnese troops. The intentions of the Dutch to seize control over the *Dalam* were thus foiled. Again they were forced to retreat. Casualties recorded were 45 dead (including 8 officers) and 405 (23 of them officers) wounded. Three days after General Köhler's death, the Dutch withdrew to the coast. After obtaining permission from the East Indies government in Batavia on April 23, 1873, the Dutch left Aceh on April 29, 1873.

The first act of aggression by the Dutch was a total failure, although members of this "First Expedition," as the Dutch later called it, were subsequently invited to a dinner in their honour at the palace of the Governor General. But among the Dutch themselves, criticism arose concerning this aggression, to the extent that some officers were summoned by the government to account for their actions and statements.

In the meantime, the Dutch armed forces were preparing for another attack on Aceh, to take revenge on the bitter defeat suffered by General Köhler's troops. While these preparations were underway, Dutch warships blockaded the waters surrounding Aceh in order to prevent the Acehnese from making contact with the outside world.

The Acehnese did not remain idle in this situation. At Pulau Pinang, a "Council of Eight" was formed, consisting of four Acehnese noblemen, two Arabs, and two Kelings of Pulau Pinang (Malay) birth. Their job was to represent Aceh's interest abroad and also to try to smuggle in necessary equipment and supplies by penetrating the enemy's blockade. The Council would also try to make contact with other regions in the Archipelago with the message to oppose the Dutch and thereby create a larger, united front.

In November 1873, the Dutch forces again left Java to sail to Aceh.

The Dutch Second Aggression began on December 9, 1873, with the landing of the Dutch troops on the shores of Lheuë village, near Kuala Gigiëng, Aceh Besar. The Acehnese counter-attack was led by Tuanku Hasyim Bangtamuda, one of the Sultan's younger brothers, who at the time of the First Dutch Aggression happened to be in East Sumatra. He was assisted by Teuku Imeum Luëng Bata and Teuku Nanta Seutia. For eight days they fought at the beachhead, but then retreated to plan and strengthen the defenses surrounding the Baiturrakhman Grand Mosque, Peukan Aceh, Lam Bhue', and *Dalam*.

Although the Acehnese fighters put up a tough battle, the Grand Mosque fell into enemy hands on January 6, 1874, with the losses of many men on both sides. Meanwhile, Panglima Polém Mahmud Arifin had mobilized and trained some three thousand fighters, belonging to Mukim Sagoë xxii, to defend Lam Bhue', the Acehnese stronghold, while the Sultan's Palace was being guarded by a contingent of about nine hundred fighters.

On January 4th, another five hundred fighters arrived from Mukim Sagoë xxii to reinforce the Sultan's Palace. The defense troops were under the command of the Prince of Pidië. The King of Pidië had come to Aceh Besar to set up his headquarters at Luëng Bata with his five hundred–man army. In mid-January, one thousand Acehnese fighters from Peusangan arrived to join forces with these troops. They headquartered in Kuala Cangkôy.

When the Dutch army laid siege to the *Dalam*, an epidemic of cholera had just broken out. The Sultan, Panglima Polém, and Teuku Ba'ét were evacuated to Luëng Bata. In their absence, the Dutch succeeded in taking over the *Dalam* on January 24, 1874. The Dutch hoped to force the Sultan to sign a peace treaty, as they had previously done in Siak (The Siak Treaty), but Sultan Mahmud Syah, who had contracted cholera, died of the disease in Pagar Ayé on January 29. He was buried at Cot Bada near Samahani, Aceh Besar. Although the *Dalam* had fallen to the enemy and their Sultan had died, the fighting spirit of the Acehnese was not lessened.

After having obtained control over the *Dalam*, and with the death of the Sultan, this was a most opportune time for the Dutch to declare on January 31, 1874, that the "kingdom of Aceh has been subjugated and the Dutch government hereby alters the status of the Aceh kingdom, now claiming the territory of Aceh Besar as the *property* of the East Indies government."

Beriberi: Disease among the Troops

Although the Dutch were able to defeat the Sultanate of Aceh, the last polity of any size to resist the afronding (rounding off) of Dutch authority in the archipelago, this victory came at great cost to the European conquerors. By 1874 the war was fought mainly in Aceh's mountainous interior, as the resistance developed into one of the most feared guerrilla forces that Southeast Asia has ever known. Despite their technological superiority, the Dutch paid heavily in terms of manpower to take, and later maintain, their control over the Acehnese population. Armed strikes by the Acehnese caused many casualties among the Dutch forces, but sickness—particularly beriberi and other tropical diseases—also decimated the conquering forces. Thousands of colonial soldiers, as the following chart makes clear, fell victim to this illness, and the Dutch never had as many soldiers in the field as they wished. Europeans died from beriberi, but so did the populations of indigenous colonial soldiery—men from Ambon, Minahasa, and other parts of the archipelago deemed loyal to the Dutch cause. The Dutch even had imported African soldiers fighting for them in their colonial wars—and they died, too, in this graveyard of the tropics.

Casualties from Beriberi in the Aceh War, 1893

MONTH	EUROPEANS	AFRICANS	AMBONESE	NATIVES	TOTAL	EVACUATED	TOTAL
Jan	86	—	17	325	428	417	845
Feb	66	—	19	330	415	482	897
Mar	96	—	33	409	538	593	1,131
Apr	89	—	29	382	500	657	1,157
May	103	1	16	430	550	629	1,179
Jun	93	—	17	390	500	655	1,155
Jul	76	—	22	439	537	633	1,170
Aug	89	—	23	403	515	672	1,187
Sep	111	—	32	357	500	837	1,337
Oct	124	—	16	319	459	522	981
Nov	129	—	25	327	481	558	1,039
Dec	114	—	14	321	449	569	1,018

Source: Koloniaal verslag, 1894: Beri Beri Sickness among the Dutch Troops in Aceh, 1893 (Appendix F), 3.

Protestant Missions in the Indies

Baron van Boetzelaer van Dubbeldam

Protestant missionaries came out with some of the very first Dutch ships to the Indies. Converting indigenes formed an important part of Dutch expansion, even if proselytizing was less pronounced than in the Iberian project of the same era. Protestant evangelizing made steady progress in the Indies, though some landscapes (particularly Minahasa, Ambon, Banda, and certain parts of Sumatra and the interior of Borneo) were considered more fertile ground than others in this respect. Protestant missionary groups spread throughout the Indies and often competed for souls, especially with the Catholic Church, which also eventually established a substantial missionary presence on the islands. Though laws existed declaring Dutch respect for indigenous religions, and particularly for Islam, many Dutchmen—such as the period evangelist Baron van Dubbeldam—did little to hide their conviction that a program of Christianizing the indigenous inhabitants of the archipelago would serve everyone's best interests. Though some Indonesians did eventually convert, the numbers were never as high as these colonial organizations wished. Part of the eventual program of resistance against the Dutch in the early twentieth century drew on a stated desire to work against religious domination by an occupying Christian power, a sentiment that connected many Indonesians across a variety of islands.

When the small Netherlands, in the middle of the Eighty Years' war with mighty Spain, had discovered the sea route to the Indian Archipelago, and great treasures gradually flowed into the country by means of the fleets equipped and sent thence, the war against the Spaniards and Portuguese in those distant regions was conducted with such success that these enemies were speedily driven from the field. An entirely new territory, with millions of inhabitants, was thus brought under the sway of Holland. The fact that this coincided with the prolonged and terrible struggle in which Holland had expended blood and treasure for freedom of faith, and in which Protestantism penetrated deep into the life of the people, proved likewise not to be devoid of great importance for the distant regions themselves. In the first place, it was inconceivable in those days that so many Dutchmen should go to the

Indies and remain there without provision for the practice of their faith. On all fleets which left for the Indies, clergymen went over, or if these were not to be obtained, they were replaced by "sick visitors," a sort of evangelists who did not administer the sacraments, but for the rest often completely took the place of a clergyman. Various pastors and also "sick visitors" remained in the Indies, however, in order to gather their fellow countrymen settling there into Church congregations. Wherever the armies of the East India Company were victorious and a fort of trading office was established, pastors were likewise speedily appointed. In 1615, we already find in the fort of Jakatra, at the place where a few years later Batavia was to rise, a clergyman (Adriaan Jakobszoon Hulsebos), who, amid the long and dangerous siege of the fort, contributed no little to maintain the courage of those who manned it. In the same year, we already find pastors in the Moluccas as well.

It is remarkable in this connection that, immediately after sending out these first clergymen, it was contemplated not only to provide for the religious needs of Dutchmen in these distant regions, but also to convert millions of heathens and Mahomedans for whom the Church felt itself responsible, because by God's guidance they had been placed under Dutch sway. The first inducement to this was that the bold invaders on their arrival found some thousands of Christians among the population, as the fruit of the zealous work of the Roman Catholic missionaries during the Portuguese period. As to the conscience of Holland of those days, to be Roman was worse than to be heathen or Mahomedan; it had to be seen to, in the first place, that the Catholic natives should be converted to Protestants, a change to which they submitted without protest. This motive for undertaking the care of these native Christians, however, must not blind us to this, that it remains a most remarkable fact that in Holland in those days, a warm interest was immediately awakened for the conversion of these new subjects, whilst in other Protestant countries, conscience still remained slumbering for ages with regard to the call upon all Christians to take a living interest in mission work. The very first Governors-General were directed in the instructions given to them to report their yearly accounts of the state of political affairs, trade, war, concerning the propagation of the Christian religion likewise. Moreover, it was specially enjoined upon all clergymen sent out to do their utmost for the conversion of heathens and Mahomedans. The Company promoted this by making special additional allowances to those pastors who could preach in Malay or another native language. In many places, therefore, there speedily arose, in addition to the Dutch service, a service in Malay, and at times in Portuguese also. Some pastors likewise carried out divine services in other native languages.

With great zeal and love, the Churches of the Netherlands undertook the sending out of preachers to the East and West Indies, and indeed gradually to many other parts of the entire world. That the powers of so small a country often fell short of satisfying the great needs will surprise no one.

The greatest difficulty was that the Company had to pay for everything that was done for the religious needs of the Indians in those days; it had the absolute monopoly of all expenditure as likewise of all profit. That the Churches of the Netherlands by private initiative should have been able to do something for preaching the Gospel in the Company's territory was an idea which arose now and again, but which was quite incompatible with the spirit of the time, and above all the Company's desire for domination. The latter suffered absolutely no interference on the part of others in these regions, where it was first and foremost a trading corporation, which had to seek for great profits; therefore it cannot surprise us that mere spiritual needs were somewhat forced into the background.

We must, indeed, acknowledge that the Company expended very considerable sums for the spiritual requirements of its servants and for propagating the Gospel, even though its policy was too often dominated by material aims.

During the Company's time, and at its cost, no less than 254 clergymen were sent to the East Indies, and certainly more than 1,000 "sick visitors." When the Company ended, there were, on a moderate estimate, 70,000 native Christians in the Dutch East Indies.

At this second period, beginning with the restoration of the Dutch government in 1815 after the English interregnum, we must pause a few moments. The East India Company had disappeared never to return. The Indies came under a newly constituted Government, and Church affairs likewise passed into an entirely new phase.

Just as in the Netherlands, the Government in the Dutch East Indies undertook the obligation to meet the costs of the clergymen required to be appointed for the needs of the European congregations. No thought was given, however, to provision for the native congregations, whilst the conduct of the mission work was entirely incompatible with the neutral attitude of the Government towards religion. On the contrary, in the nineteenth century, which may rightly be called the century of missions, as regards the Dutch Indies also, mission work extended and was taken in hand by means of private societies, to which lately a Church Mission was added. In the first place, however, this work aimed at gathering whatever was left of the congregations formed under the rule of the Company. Later on, new missions were opened at a number of places. Success was varied.

Generally the mission bore the greatest fruit among the heathens, where it was still possible to forestall Mahomedanism. The mission to the Mohammedans here, as everywhere else, was found to be an exceedingly laborious field of work. Nevertheless the great German Mission specialist, Professor Warneck, has stated that of all missions to the Mahomedans the Dutch have had the most success.

On the Amboina Islands, where Christianity attained its widest extension during the domination of the Company, the population notwithstanding the long-continued neglect, was still found to have adhered mainly to Christianity. The Dutch Missionary Society found in the most northerly point of Celebes, known under the name of Minahassa, an extremely fertile mission field. Practically the entire population (now consisting of 183,000 souls) came over to Christianity. The Rheinische Missions Gesellschaft [Rhineland Mission Society] (established in Barmen in Prussia) met with a great success in Sumatra, in Batak lands. It now numbers nearly 100,000 converts as a result of its work in the Dutch Indies.

Protestant missions in the Dutch Indies suffer, generally speaking, from the excessive want of unity in their efforts. No less than ten missionary societies were established in Holland. In addition, the Rheinische Missions Gesellschaft, just referred to, does very extensive work. The missionaries of the Salatiga Committee, established in the Netherlands are, indeed, for most part Germans, and are all trained by the Neukirchener Missionsverein [Mission Society of Neukirchen] at Neukirchen in Prussia. Latterly, in addition to the Salvation Army, the following foreign missionary societies have begun work in the Dutch East Indies: The Seventh Day Adventist Church of Iowa, the Seventh Day Adventists of Australia, and the Missionary Society of the Methodist Episcopal Church, which associations for the present number but very few converts. In 1906, the whole of the Protestant missionary societies established the Missionary Consulate at Batavia, as a general representation of the missions, particularly in relation to the Government.

In 1870, the charge of some missionary territories where native Churches had arisen was taken over by the Government, and these Churches were incorporated into the Evangelical State Church. To meet the needs of these, assistant pastors were appointed, who, just like the pastors, have their salaries provided by the Government. These assistant pastors exercise rather a general supervision over a number of congregations; under them are the native leaders, who are at the head of the native congregations, but of whom very few as yet administer the sacraments.

On surveying the present situation (end of 1908), we find in the Dutch East Indies:—The Evangelical Church to which, in the first place, all Protestant

Europeans belong. It now comprises 56,527 members and has forty-one clergymen. Among the European Protestants, there are also in Batavia and Sourabaya small Free Reformed Churches, each having one pastor, whilst at Batavia there is also an English and an Armenian Church, which, however, have no fixed leaders or pastors.

In addition to its European members, the above-named Evangelical Church numbers 281,385 members in its native congregations, for whom twenty-six assistant pastors are appointed.

Besides these Churches we find the work of the Protestant Missionary Associations, with a staff of 192 missionaries (exclusive of the officers of the Salvation Army, of which there are about 30) and 167,856 converts. In the various missions we find 10 training schools for native teachers and preachers, and 829 lower schools with 161,225 pupils; also 6 industrial schools, 2 missionary printing offices, 3 large and a number of smaller mission hospitals, and a number of other institutions.

In general, it can be said, therefore that there are now in the Dutch Indies fully fifty thousand Protestant Europeans and nearly five hundred thousand Protestant natives.

The Oceanography of the Archipelago

G. F. Tydeman

Because the many scattered islands of the Indies comprise the world's largest archipel-
ago, knowledge of the seas was crucial not just for local peoples, who fished and made
a living off of the ocean's riches, but also for the Dutch, who ruled this vast island
kingdom. Oceanography had always formed a part of the Dutch knowledge project
about the Indies; the earliest ships in the late sixteenth and early seventeenth centuries
had taken depth soundings to determine the safest routes to and from selected harbors.
Over the course of the voc period and into the era of direct Dutch administration,
the science of the sea—as shown in this selection by the period hydrographer G. F.
Tydeman—was vigorously championed by colonial administrators and military men
alike. Mapping the sea proved crucial in getting supplies, manpower, and material
from one island to another; it also proved crucial in linking the Indies to the rest of the
world, both through shipping routes and through underwater telegraph cables, which
became important in the second half of the nineteenth century. By the early twentieth
century, oceanography was also being used for extractive purposes in harnessing the
riches of the natural environment, playing a part in the acquisition of numerous sea
products such as pearls, kelp, and underwater oil.

Although observations regarding the nature of the sea had been carried out
by seafarers and coastal inhabitants since time immemorial, oceanography
as a science, which in the broadest meaning aims at systematic research, has
existed for less than half a century. Previous research has been carried out
for the interests of shipping and the fishery, and therefore mainly does not
extend to the surface and knowledge about the depths. Around the middle of
the past century, however, demands of growing world traffic led to research
that extended to greater depths, and to the systematic collecting, processing, and publishing of observations on weather, wind, and currents that have
been included in many logbooks. The telegraph cable came to flit its way
along the surface of the ocean; the American sea officer Brooke invented the
first practical deep-sea sounding in 1854, and a couple of years later, in 1857,

Maury, another American sea officer, published the first sounding chart of the Atlantic Ocean.

Already a couple of decades ago, the same Maury had, through his publication *Wind and Current Charts of the Oceans* (1848), made the first important step out of which modern meteorology and oceanography have been developed.

The discovery that living organisms also exist in the far-reaching depths was due to zoologists. They conducted research in the deep seas while examining oceanographic observations that were necessary for their science. An example was given by Wyville Thomson, who had led the first actual oceanographic voyage with the English warship *Lightning* in 1868, which was thereafter followed by many larger and smaller voyages in all the seas of the world. One of the most well-known voyages, that of the *Challenger* that made a journey around the world from 1872 to 1876, also visited our archipelago in the East Indies. Since then, some other research ships under foreign flags have also carried out oceanographic observations in various parts of our archipelago. Under our own flag the ship H.M. *Siboga*, led by Max Weber, also carried out an abyssal expedition, which lasted for one year (1900–1901) and had exclusively chosen the eastern part of the archipelago as its area of exploration. Processing the extensive results of this expedition, particularly regarding zoological issues, is now by and large completed. By means of soundings carried out by the H.M. *Siboga*, and other existing sources up to 1903, a sounding chart of the archipelago was issued in that year, which is now presentable for general exhibition.

In another chapter of this catalogue one can find the state of knowledge about horizontal projection, that is, the cartography of seas and coasts. Important progress in this area can be ascertained as the result of continuous labor by our surveying vessels and via the contributions of the ships of the *Gouvernements-Marine* [governmental navy]. Yet another chapter shows that due to Van der Stok's immense labor that provides a rather complete survey of vertical water movements in many locations in the archipelago, accurate knowledge of horizontal water movements—the movements of tides and monsoons—is now available.

Until forty years ago, knowledge of the vertical perspective of seas, that is sea depths, extended barely beyond depths that ships were able to anchor. Depths more than 100 fathoms (ca. 180 m) appear on sea charts before 1870 only sporadically. Reliable data on whether depths in the seas of the archipelago could be calculated to hundreds or thousands of fathoms was only present for a couple of locations.

The uncertainty that occurs when a moving ship has to stand still for a moment due to lack of special equipment, preparation, and practice is commonplace. An example to show how unreliable obtained results can be is the case of a sounding that was carried out by one of our war vessels to the west of the Banda archipelago in the Banda Sea. It was assumed that the bottom was reached with a line of four thousand fathoms. Later and very close to that spot, however, H.M. *Siboga* measured a depth of only a little bit more than four thousand meters.

However much important progress was made with the publication of the Siboga chart, many depths of the extensive sea surface of our archipelago were and still are unknown, so that it is impossible to point out the correct course of depth contours. Because survey vessels have to prioritize surveys for nautical purposes, soundings of greater depths will have to wait for cable installers and vessels that are sailing out for scientific research. This does not take away from the fact that since 1903, survey vessels have been equipped with a machine for deep-sea soundings and have acquired welcome data from many locations. These include in the first place H.M. *Bali*, a vessel that has carried out a large number of deep soundings in the Gulf of Tomini, and (from thence) eastward of the Passage of the Moluccas. It is also true as well of a great number of selected locations in the northwestern part of the Banda Sea, northward of the Straits of Manipa, in the Straits of Macassar, the Sea of Flores, and in the Sea of Bali.

These soundings, too, have confirmed the results of earlier discoveries, that almost everywhere in the eastern part of the archipelago, there are greatly variable depths on the sea bottom, and that there are, generally speaking, great depths between short distances along the coast. Moreover, by means of soundings carried out by the *Planet*, among others, it is confirmed that there is a deep rim that is a rather narrow, deep subsidence of the sea bottom, whose contours are parallel to the general course of the coastline. Those soundings presume that there are two similar deep rims to the south of Java, of which the northern most rim counts to a depth of more than three thousand meters and seems to extend eastwards of the Mentawei Basis. The southernmost rim with depths to seven thousand meters is marked on the Siboga chart, and its subsidence is parallel to Sumatra, which has a depth of more than five thousand meters.

In the Pacific Ocean, H.M. *Edi* had carried out soundings of a depth of more than seventy-two hundred meters eastward of the Talauer-islands, which is probably considered as the southernmost part of a deep rim that is parallel to the eastern rim of the Philippines.

There remains, after these contributions in the last couple of years, much to do regarding more detailed knowledge of deeper parts of the archipelago. Broadly speaking, however, one could say that the depth ratios in that area are now rather well known.

Little research has been done regarding the structure of the great depths of the sea bottom. The Siboga expedition and also H.M. *Bali*, among others, had conducted a couple of experiments from the bottom, but the time-consuming research has not been completed yet. The number of sites where small numbers of materials have been acquired from the sea bottom is, compared to this vast sea surface, still small.

Translated from Dutch by Oiyan Liu

VI

The Last Decades of the Indies

During the high colonial period the administration in Batavia pushed farmers on Java to increase their production of export crops such as coffee, sugar, and indigo. Implementing the so-called *cultuurstelsel* (cultivation system, 1830–70), the Dutch made huge profits as they not only levied taxes on agricultural land but also forced farmers to sell their products at fixed prices to the government. Java was drawn into an expanding world economy, its crops competing on the market with those from the West Indies and other places. Revenues, however, flowed only into Dutch coffers, resulting in a credit balance (*batig slot*) for the Netherlands while the population in the colony pauperized. At the same time that the mother country paid off domestic debts and constructed roads, railway lines, and waterways, the infrastructure on Java and the other islands left much to be desired. Highly valued coffee beans might be stored in warehouses in the interior for months while ships lay idle in ports waiting for freight. Hence, to accommodate an efficient way of exporting the products, the government in The Hague reluctantly allowed investment in the Indies to improve the transportation system.

Scientific expeditions to explore Indies' geography, natural environment, and geology principally took place in the second half of the nineteenth century, and the catastrophic eruption of the Krakatoa volcano in 1883 provided scholars research material for years. Pumice, debris, and volcanic ash covered a wide radius, tidal waves were felt as far as Europe, and volcanic dust and gases in the atmosphere wreaked havoc on temperatures around the world. Since that eruption a new volcanic island, Anak Krakatau (Child of Krakatoa), has been pushed up from the ocean floor, and it continues to expand.

A period of laissez faire liberalism in the final decades of the nineteenth century increased private entrepreneurship and intensified the exploitation of agricultural resources and labor. On Sumatra, tobacco and rubber plantations sprung up, attracting a low-paid coolie workforce, and European companies capitalized on these new agro-industries. However, by 1900, Dutch parliamentarians, officials, and journalists expressed concern for the welfare of Indonesians. Out of an awareness that the Netherlands owed the Indies "a debt of honor," a new, so-called ethical policy was implemented. It focused strongly on Western-style education for Indonesian children and aimed at implementing a school system partly in Malay or other vernacular languages, and partly in Dutch. These schools never replaced traditional Muslim teaching, as so-called *pesantrens* continued to train students in reading the Koran and in studying aspects of the Muslim faith. The ethical policy also intended to improve public irrigation and opportunities for financial assistance through community banks and cooperatives. In the face of strikingly low standards of living among the local population, the Indies government announced in 1902 that it would survey "the lesser welfare" on Java and Madura, deliberately eliminating the word *poverty* from its discourse. The inquiry found that not only the indigenous peoples lived in dire circumstances but that many Eurasians, too, lived below the poverty line. As many Eurasians had European status, the latter finding cast a slur on the reputation of the Europeans.

The colonial state expanded in this period. For centuries the Dutch had focused on Java and on the coastal areas of other islands, at first to trade and later to administer. At this time they set out more vigorously to subject the entire archipelago to their control. With the long and disastrous Aceh wars in mind, the Dutch were convinced that they must "pacify" parts of the Outer Islands (*Buitenbezittingen*) not yet under their administration. In some remote regions Christian missionaries had made first contact and paved the way for a colonial presence. This was the case in the mountainous interior of northern Sumatra where the German Rheinische Missions Gesellschaft (Rhineland Mission Society) converted the Batak people to Protestant Christianity. Although the Christian religion had a serious impact on Batak identity, it did not alter everyday life in the village or a sense of Batak origins and rootedness. In central Sulawesi the Dutch Reformed Church had gained access to the Toraja people and successfully proselytized the locals.

On Bali the situation differed quite markedly. Here the *Pax Neerlandica* had to be established by means of military campaigns. For a long time Balinese rulers had felt deeply suspicious toward Europeans, whom they considered mere intruders with no other goal in mind than taking over power and existing commercial networks. By 1900 the northern and western parts of Bali had come under Dutch control, but the rajas of Klungkung, Bangli, Badung, and Tabanan held on to their positions. They remained defiant until the very last moment: when the Dutch encroached on their courts, the rajas resorted to *puputan*, a ritual mass sacrifice in which some Balinese willfully allowed their opponents to kill them, while others committed suicide.

The government schools that introduced Indonesian students to a Dutch curriculum initially only attracted sons from the indigenous nobility. Soon graduates formed an educated class of their own who found employment in the civil service as clerks or lower-rank administrators, as teachers, or in health care as vaccinators or nurses. As a reaction to institutionalized Dutch instruction Ki Hadjar Dewantoro founded Taman Siswa schools in 1922, which offered independent, private education that combined traditional Javanese teaching, including Islam, with modern subjects. Instructors were Indonesians who believed in a nationalist, anticolonial cause. They received a fraction of the salaries paid by the government. Ten years later Batavia responded to these "wild schools" with an ordinance that severely restricted the Taman Siswa mandate.

There is no doubt that colonial officials were wary about emerging nationalist organizations. The Sarekat Islam (Islamic Union) grew out of an initiative that meant to improve the lives of ordinary people and to provide economic support to indigenous entrepreneurs using Islam as a unifying principle. It became a popular association with 360,000 members, in four years increasing to allegedly 2 million. Within a short time Sarekat Islam leaders discussed issues of political representation for Indonesians, as well as self-government. Other associations also formed along geographical, ethnic, or religious lines, and in May 1920 the PKI, the Communist Party of Indonesia (or of the Indies, at first), came into existence. A PKI representative attended the Comintern's Second Congress in Moscow later that same year, and PKI members were present at annual congresses in the years following, despite criticism from the Comintern executive that the party was not truly proletarian. Political unrest and increasingly louder demands to be given a voice led to arrests, imprisonment, and exile. After a rebellion in 1927 the government sent many prominent communists to the remote prison camp of Boven Digul in New Guinea.

While the Dutch kept a close eye on those with explicitly political agendas, youth groups gathered with seemingly innocent fervor. At the first national Youth Congress in 1928 they expressed their commitment to one nation, one people, and one language. In their oath, the *Sumpah Pemuda*, they renamed the Malay language "Indonesian," *bahasa Indonesia*. This became the national language in 1945 when Indonesia proclaimed its independence. The new language inspired creative writers, particularly those who had received a Dutch education, to compose novels, stories, and poetry that addressed topics related to the modern individual who breaks with traditional values and decides for him- or herself what direction his or her life will take. A new magazine, *Pujangga Baru* (*The New Poet*) came out in 1933 under the editorship of Sutan

Takdir Alisjahbana. He and other intellectuals debated modernity, Western-ization, and issues of national identity. While Takdir advocated Western con-cepts of individuality and advancement, his counterparts in the "polemics on culture" emphasized the glorious pasts of the Srivijaya and Majapahit king-doms, which provided them with an indigenous source for creativity and the will to move forward.

Java's Railways

S. A. Reitsma

The introduction of the cultivation system in 1830, in which peasants were to produce export crops for the colonial government, intensified the need for an efficient transportation system, particularly on Java. Buffaloes, but also camels and donkeys supplied by the Ministry of Colonies from the Netherlands in 1840, served to carry freight from the agricultural areas to the major ports. As a result products such as coffee and sugar often piled up in storehouses for months. Clearly the expanding European trade and industry would benefit most from a modernized infrastructure on Java, not the indigenous population, Dutch interests figuring first and foremost. In the four decades following 1840 politicians debated, but could not agree on, whether to construct and operate a railway system through private enterprise or with public money. In 1873 the privately owned Netherlands Indies Railway Company started and completed the operation of two local lines, Batavia–Buitenzorg and Semarang–Central Javanese principalities (Yogyakarta), only after repeated setbacks and financial misfortune.

(Explanatory Notes 1874–1875 II 69. No. 3)

Already for quite some time we have been considering the question of the construction of the railways on Java. Sometimes it was considered the duty of the Government; then again people were of the opinion it should be left to the entrepreneurship of private companies. At times people preferred a railroad system, i.e., an interconnected system of railways, at other times people would rather see local railroad lines.

While two concessions have been released and 261 kilometers of railroads have been established in Central and West Java, people are more and more convinced that railroads are also necessary in other parts of Java to improve administration and military defense and to develop the abundant resources of wealth. This conviction has in recent years intensified more than ever before. Hence the bill that was introduced into Parliament which purported to establish a railway connection paid for by the Crown, along almost the full length of

Construction of a public railway (partially cogway), Sumatra 1890. Photo no. 19381, courtesy of KITLV, Leiden.

Java, from Batavia to Pasuruan. Paid for by the Crown. Not because the Minister in question in principle favored public railways (*Staatsspoorwegen*).[1] On the contrary, he declared explicitly to support in principle the release of concessions. But he saw no possibility of releasing good concessions for the construction of the railways on Java and no sufficient reasons for the Indies to follow a different route than the one in the mother country. The Preliminary Report of Parliament showed that the majority of Members of Parliament who participated in the investigations of the bill in the regions fully recognized the necessity of the railways, but that they were not able to agree with the proposal to construct one main line along the full length of Java. They also objected to the railway construction with the costs thereof carried by the Crown.

This last objection led to an amendment to the bill, which, however, did not satisfy the opponents of publicly funded construction, as is evident from the Final Report of the Committee of Rapporteurs. The bill was therefore withdrawn after a new Minister of Colonies was appointed in June 1872 who sided with the opponents of publicly funded construction.[2] [. . .]

This was the state of affairs when yours truly accepted the administration of the Department of Colonies.[3] He seriously intends to develop the situation further and to advance the railway construction on Java to the best of his abilities. There is no doubt in his mind which route to take. Whatever one thinks in principle about this question, at this point one should expect nothing else from the Minister of Colonies but a proposal for the construction of public railways on Java. Two of his predecessors who wished to see the private sector build the railroads on Java were pressured to abandon that idea and to express themselves in favor of the construction of public railways. If the present Minister were to make the railway construction dependent on the opportunity to release good concessions again, he might be suspected of shelving the issue.

Moreover, yours truly can hardly imagine that today much opposition exists to the construction of the railways by the Crown. Those who are well informed about the advice from the committee that was consulted by the previous Minister will no longer stipulate that releasing concessions is financially in the interest of the Crown. Regarding that advice they will not refer to the modest amount of expenses concerning the construction of the railway line between Semarang and the Central Javanese principalities at the cost of the National Treasury. After all, with the history of concessions for the Netherlands Indies Railway Company in mind no one will consider it desirable to pursue that model further. After the fruitless attempts to design financial conditions of concessions that are acceptable to the Crown as well as to private companies, one can no longer press for a utilization of the private sector to construct the railways on Java, unless there is a clear indication how this can take place with positive results, and unless a formula for good concessions be presented, one which the Government and its advisors have not been able to find so far.

For yours truly there is no doubt in his mind that a satisfactory formula does not exist, because the necessary data for a reliable calculation of the costs for the railway construction on Java are missing. If nevertheless the financial conditions for concessions were based on a cost estimate, an estimate that could hardly be anything else but a shot in the dark, then one would expose oneself, almost knowingly, to a gross miscalculation with its inevitable consequences. If one attempted to provide a total guarantee against damage to the concessionaires, acknowledging the impossibility of reasonable estimates, one would sacrifice all the advantages that were aimed at by utilizing the private sector, because one would take away the incentive for economy's sake.

Translated from Dutch by T. Hellwig

Editors' Notes

1. Minister of Colonies P. P. Van Bosse.
2. Minister of Colonies I. D. Fransen van de Putte.
3. "Yours truly" refers to Minister of Colonies W. Van Goltstein.

The Eruption of Krakatoa

R. A. van Sandick

The Krakatoa volcano is located in the narrow Sunda Strait that separates the islands of Java and Sumatra. Violent eruptions in the fifth and sixth centuries CE are said to have affected the global climate at the time. Its 1883 eruption was one of the most powerful recorded in history. Krakatoa was an island with three volcanic cones: Perboewatan, Danan, and Rakata. In May and June 1883 minor eruptions of steam and ash occurred and seismic activity and earthquakes were registered. During the final explosion on August 27 the walls of Perboewatan and Danan ruptured, and most of the island collapsed into a submarine caldera, leaving only one third of the original, Rakata Island, intact. A tsunami with waves forty meters high washed out the surrounding coastal areas, killing thousands. For months after the eruption ships reported on floating pumice and debris in the Indian Ocean and Java Sea. R. A. van Sandick sailed on board the Loudon *in the Sunda Strait on August 26–27 and here gives an eyewitness account of what happened.*

Krakatoa is an old acquaintance of the steamship "Loudon." When people cruised around after the first eruption in May 1883 in order to see the volcano, the "Loudon" carried passengers to the island for twenty-five guilders. This time Krakatoa provided us with a free show. Even though we were quite a distance from the island, we could see a black, high stack of smoke rise above it which higher up spread out into a cloud. It constantly rained ash. At 7:00 p.m. August 26, we were anchored at the roadstead of Telok Betong in the Bay of Lampong, on the coast of Sumatra.

Suddenly at 6:30 a.m. on August 27 an enormous wave swelled up from the sea and moved with great speed. The "Loudon" steamed ahead so that the wave would hit alongship. One split second . . . and the wave reached us. The ship tumbled down, but the wave passed, and the "Loudon" was saved. Then the wave rolled inland toward Telok Betong. Subsequently three similarly colossal waves followed. With no obstruction in their way they wiped away Telok Betong in front of our eyes. We saw the lighthouse collapse and the

Like Krakatoa, Mount Bromo, eastern Java, is an active volcano in the region. Photo by Dirk Verbeek.

houses disappear. Everything in front of our eyes, the place where a few minutes earlier Telok Betong was located on the beach, turned into ocean.

This overwhelming sight is beyond description. One cannot come to terms with one's perception because of the unexpected and gigantic size of the devastation. Because Telok Betong's post and telegraph office had vanished, it would take a long time before people on Java would hear about the disaster that had hit the town. Captain Lindeman therefore decided to sail back to Anyer [on Java] in order to give an account, and, moreover, because he judged staying at the roadstead was too dangerous. Hence, we sailed back the same way we had come instead of continuing our journey in the direction of Kroë. Everyone on board the "Loudon" was deeply affected by the unforeseen annihilation of Telok Betong. Did all its inhabitants drown? No one could answer that question.

Soon we lost sight of Telok Betong and hoped to leave the Bay of Lampong behind. But the course of events would not be that easy. At 8:00 a.m. daylight began to fade. The twilight increasingly intensified so that at 10:00 a.m. it was pitch-black. Usually, even on a lightless night, one can still distinguish some contours, of white objects for instance. Here, however, a complete absence of light prevailed. The sun rose higher, at noon it reached the zenith, yet no sunrays reached us. This darkness stretched out over a large distance as not the slightest glare in the sky, not the smallest trace of luminescence on the horizon was visible. Everywhere an impenetrable nocturnal veil! Everywhere a sky without stars! And this horrible "night" lasted eighteen hours!

Obviously the "Loudon" had to "hibernate" in the bay during this "arctic" night. Already at 10:00 a.m. we were anchored nearby the small island of Tegal. It was impossible to proceed, not only because of the darkness, but also because the compass showed all sorts of deviations as a result of the increasingly stronger precipitation of ash and pumice.

The dreadfulness of the following moments, dear reader, exceeds anything one can imagine. Language cannot express what we experienced. A dense rain of mud replaced the ash and pumice, and mud soon covered the deck. It penetrated everything and impeded the sailors whose eyes, ears, and noses were clogged up with the awful and foul-smelling substance. Every now and then ash fell from the sky, then again chunks of pumice bombarded the ship. It was hard to breathe as if the atmosphere itself had changed. Some hellish sulfuric acid spread through the air. Some people felt their ears ringing, others had chest pain and felt sleepy. I believe that, had this situation lasted longer, we would all have suffocated.

And this was only the beginning of our misery. More spine-chilling calamities were awaiting us. After a while in the darkness the sea became turbulent. The wind picked up and turned into a wild hurricane. Gigantic waves and sea tremors succeeded each other rapidly. The waves manifested themselves through high seas that suddenly occurred out of nowhere. Some of them hit the "Loudon" athwartships so that she rose up and heeled over badly with the danger that she would career. The ship yawed and everything toppled over, it felt as if we were in the Bay of Biscay during a storm. These high seas were similar to the ones that destroyed Telok Betong in front of our eyes. But no one could see them coming or estimate their size as it remained pitch-black. Our perceptive captain Lindeman, however, never lost his wits. The rescue boats were prepared in case the ship would capsize.

From time to time bright lightning lit up the darkness for a split second. These thunderbolts sometimes hit the mast with a demonic crash and found their way along the lightning rod. On such moments everything was clearly lit and one could see that the rigging, the deck, the crew had turned ash gray because of the rain of mud. One could not help but think of a phantom ship. The fire hoses were ready, as the captain feared the ship might catch fire under the thunderbolts. It is a miracle that it did not happen, and I am still amazed that the "Loudon" managed to survive these high seas. [. . .]

Besides the lightning and thunder we noticed other electric phenomena. We saw fireballs on the ship that moved with great speed and disappeared in the water. On protruding parts of the mast, poles, and yard bluish flames lit up. According to native superstition this St. Elms fire is an omen that the ship will sink. Hence, as soon as a fireball manifested itself, even if it were high up in the rigging, a native sailor would climb up to extinguish it and expel the premonitory messenger.

No one really understood what was actually happening. The annihilation of Telok Betong in front of our eyes, the infernal darkness midday, the electric phenomena, the sea tremors, the rain of mud, the condition of the atmosphere, all of it was too perplexingly eerie to be explained. I do not believe that anyone guessed that Krakatoa, at one point the destination of a picnic for the "Loudon," was behind this all.

Our vigilant Lindeman never ever left his post, as never did the ship's officers under his command. Even though they were almost blinded and numb under the mud, they remained on the deck and only sporadically came into the saloon to reassure us and inform us that the danger had passed. But barely would they have finished speaking, or something uncanny happened that belied their words. They would then rush out of the saloon to their posts—in full peril.

Lindeman was a real sea dog (*zeerot*). He had had, as one says, "his share of experiences." But he, too, had no idea what natural circumstances were happening. "I really believed the world was coming to its end," he said afterwards, when we discussed these horrendous hours again.

Translated from Dutch by T. Hellwig

Colonizing Central Sulawesi

Joost Coté

The larger part of the island of Sulawesi (previously Celebes) remained outside the scope of colonial interest until the 1890s. Because it was considered one of the Outer Islands (Buitenbezittingen), the Dutch felt no need to expand their authority, particularly not over those inhabiting the mountainous inland areas. The To Pamona are a Torajan-speaking people living in the Poso region whose traditional culture and religious beliefs include slash-and-burn farming practices and the concomitant seminomadic lifestyle, elaborate funeral rites and the worship of spirits and ancestors, and headhunting. In 1902 the first assistant resident of Poso was an adherent of the so-called ethical policy. Supposedly concerned with the welfare and economic conditions of the To Pamona, he and colonial administrators set out to "educate" these locals and to "improve" their lives in close collaboration with Dutch Protestant missionaries. The Dutch were convinced of their own cultural and moral superiority and soon traded their humanitarian idealism in for an efficient administration and for financial profit.

Central Sulawesi provides an instructive case study of the implementation of the new colonial policy. Initially "discovered" by Dutch officials in the 1860s, suggestions made at the time for the annexation of the region were turned down in the context of the then current non-expansionist policy. It was brought into formal relations with Batavia in 1888 as part of a flurry of diplomatic activity designed to secure the region against English political and economic intrusion. New style "short contracts" were used in these diplomatic contacts between the Dutch colonial government in Batavia and what for all intents and purposes remained independent states. These contracts formally stated that the native ruler recognized the sovereignty of the Dutch Queen. More importantly, the contracts guaranteed to the colonial government "the distribution of mining and agricultural leases within self-ruled area, together with the payment of moneys to lease holders."

In 1891, a local official reported that "a stream of entrepreneurs" were already in the Tomini Gulf region which was likely to lead to "difficulties" with independent rulers, which in turn might require military action. According to rumors of the time, the inland region of Central Sulawesi was rich in iron ore, coal, and forest products, which remained inaccessible to European entrepreneurs without a significant colonial presence. The same local official argued that such a colonial presence could be funded from an increase in government revenue derived from the taxation of greater economic activity. Significantly, his report argued in terms of the then emerging "ethical" rhetoric, that a colonial presence would bring about "an entirely different situation [. . .] in which agricultural enterprise and mineral exploitation will be possible," which in turn would "develop and raise the welfare of the community." Assumptions about rich mineral deposits as well as large populations (which proved later to be unfounded) continued to inspire interest in the region while it remained essentially an unchartered region and, ironically, long enough for such beliefs to determine colonial policy in the region.

While in the nineties the colonial government was too embroiled in maintaining its prestige in wars against the states of Aceh and Bali, beginnings were made to establish a colonial presence with the appointment in 1894 of the first *controleur* (district officer) in Poso, a trading post on the coast. Poso was to act as a customs office to tax a growing volume of trade between local inhabitants and Chinese merchants. At the same time, the government encouraged and supported the posting of a missionary in the area to undertake "civilizing work" where "the natives" (Alfurs and later Torajans), who had a reputation of being ferocious head hunters, would be "gradually made amenable to a European presence" and at the same time, create a barrier against the growing influence of Islam in the area.

In 1902 the Poso post was upgraded to the level of assistant resident. The initial appointment was A. J. M. Engelenberg, who, as an administrator, had been involved in "the pacification of Lombok [where] all his proposals [. . .] had been accepted by the government." The appointment of such an experienced administrator reflected an official view of the importance of this Outer Island territory in the new colonial regime. Circumstantial evidence suggests that the mission used its close connections with the colonial bureaucracy to obtain a "strong" appointment in its new sphere of operations, which in a climate where there was a growing concern with the expansion of "Islamic fanaticism," was readily accepted. [. . .]

The elements which made up Engelenberg's proposal were drawn from the progressive colonial discourse then being popularized. "Decentralization," "indigenization," and "(re-)education" were the hallmarks of this discourse and were a precise inversion of those arguments which had been used to justify the colonial policy of the nineteenth-century *onthoudingspolitiek* (the policy of non-involvement outside areas of direct control and influence). The state was now seen as having the primary responsibility for creating the conditions of economic development and material progress in general, and rather than limit itself in concentrating limited resources in a few areas, the state ought to mobilize the population to identify with its (humanitarian, "welfarist") policies to provide a broad based development. J. W. T. Cohen-Stuart, member of the Batavian establishment, cleverly rewrote old themes into the new formulation. In supporting the new expansionist policy and the new emphasis on the welfare of the people, he argued for the necessity of an expanded indigenous education to provide the necessary personnel to administer an extended colony. The extension of education in the indigenous community more generally would, he suggested, not only make the task of these native administrators easier, but would help "bind the people to us," with the requirement that villagers establish their own schools, which was seen as a further step in self-responsibility and "decentralization." [. . .]

With the peace and authority established in 1906, a series of edicts, duly translated and communicated by the missionaries, were issued ordering the relocation and unification of villages, abolition of slavery, head-hunting, and witch trials, and the adoption of wet-rice (*sawah*) cultivation. The missionary Albert Kruyt, who acted as adviser to the local administration, provided the initiative with both the policy direction and rationale. Arguing in terms readily comprehendible to the colonial government, Kruyt outlined the conditions of indigenous society which worked against economic progress. The key to the lack of development in the region was its low level of population. This was the result of slavery which discourages child bearing and a child mortality rate of between 22 per cent and 57 per cent due to the "irresponsibility and ignorance" of parents, compounded by features of traditional architecture and family life. Furthermore, traditional agricultural methods promoted the use of temporary dwellings in the fields unsuited to child rearing and the labor intensity of such methods exacerbated the difficulties of child-bearing.

At the same time, long absences of head-hunting expeditions and the collecting of forest products in exchange for decorative articles on the coast affected male stamina and, it was suggested, added to the insecurity of marriage and the reluctance of women to accept the responsibility of having more children. Impotence, as a result of "unbridled sexual activity" and the absence of taboos on pre- and extra-marital relations, further contributed to a net decline in population growth according to this missionary and amateur ethnologist. It was population scarcity that created the oversupply of land which in turn deprived the Pamona people of any stimulus to improve their agricultural methods. Religious practices such as funeral feasts to honor the departed

and the communalistic nature of society prevented the development of indigenous commercial life, because (other than for ceremonial occasions) there was
no impetus for capital accumulation.

The colonial government policies, which were effected on the basis of such
an assessment of traditional society and economy, destroyed the external
manifestations of traditional Pamona culture within a decade. The extinction
of almost the entire formal cultural life of the To Pamona was achieved by
the prohibition of head-hunting, the restriction on ceremonial feasting, and
the introduction of taxation, none of which raised a protest among the Dutch
electorate. Funeral ceremonies, the high point of Pamona cultural life, were
held after the annual harvest of *ladang* (dry field) crops such as maize and rice
cassava. This was the period when the taboo on story telling, poetry recita-
tion, jokes, and riddles was lifted since such activities invoking the magic of
the word could no longer offend the spirits thus ensuring the success of the
harvest. It was at these periods that the rich heritage of the Pamona oral tradition was given full voice. This was when young men and women were initiated into adult society and partners were selected.

The Welfare on Java and Madura

Dutch East Indies Welfare Committee

For centuries the Dutch exploited the natural resources and fertile lands of the Indies. By 1900 a new awareness among colonial practitioners that they owed the peoples of Indonesia a debt of honor (eereschuld), resulted in the so-called ethical policy. Open to multiple interpretations, the policy initially focused on humanitarian concerns. Some Dutch politicians and officials realized they had a moral obligation in the colonies. Cognizant of native poverty, they yet seldom used the term and instead preferred the euphemisms lesser welfare *or* economic situation. *In 1901 Queen Wilhelmina of the Netherlands announced an enquiry into the welfare on the islands of Java and Madura. Its conclusion points not to the colonial system, but to indigenous lifestyles as the originator of native "lesser welfare."*

The personal conditions and circumstances that prevent Natives from prospering are as follows:

1. Foremost a less physically strong body, also the result of less favorable health conditions: lifestyle, early marriage, sexual habits, diet, living conditions—lack of light, fresh air, hygiene—being more exposed to detrimental influences, for example, by walking on bare feet, inadequate care of children, poor medical practices with the result that, according to the health inspector, doctor W. J. Van Gorkom (1914), more Natives fall victim to epidemics (cholera, smallpox, malaria, dysentery, plague) than non-Natives, "both in terms of numbers of infected in relation to the population (morbidity), as numbers of death in relation to those infected (lethality), hence also numbers of deaths in relation to the population (mortality). In regard to endemics (malaria, hookworm disease, tuberculosis, leprosy), too, more Natives than non-Natives are infected. It is impossible to quantify the physical and moral influence of some of these diseases (malaria, hookworm disease) on work capacity, and on lesser welfare, it is immense." No need to explain that long-term illness reduces productivity.

2. The religious convictions and worldviews of the Natives, as far as they lead to fatalism (*takdir, qodrat, iradat*) [fate; power of God; will of

God], and instill indifference for worldly possessions (*ngewulo donyo*), and influence family life and the position of women. Very few observe the *riba* (Muslim interest) prohibitions, or they are artificially put out of order. After all, Arabs were able to make fortunes. Superstition—the member Bosscha drew our attention to this at the meeting—animism, the observation of propitious signs, "auspicious days."

3. Family life, early marriage, polygyny, the quick renunciation of one's wife do not enhance close family ties. Especially the position of women is not sufficiently autonomous and independent, except in those cases where she mostly earns a living. The dependence of a mother, that is her chances of being renounced, has a detrimental influence on her children's upbringing. In cases of children from different mothers or fathers, one often finds discord, leaving aside that envy among the wives in the polygamous household already results in disputes. The distance between father and child is too far apart—probably this is less the case in the lowest social classes—with the result that the father does not disclose to his sons the secrets of his business, he even keeps them out of it altogether, so that they are not capable to continue it after his death. Not to mention that the inheritance often has to be divided among many heirs and this is a bone of contention, more so when the children were born from different liaisons. Moreover, the upbringing of Javanese children leaves a lot to be desired. Parents will spend money for school education only in later years (and among civil servants quite a few make sacrifices for that). Obviously in polygamous marriages there is not much to spend for each child. But more is at stake: deficiency and ignorance on the part of the parents, especially the mother who of course is most involved with the child. These shortcomings are most evident in families with servants. The children get used to being served, to do as they please, and to be spoiled. Generally the Javanese point to these reasons why the Natives are less inclined to subsist successfully.

Translated from Dutch by T. Hellwig

The Balinese *Puputan*

Jhr. H. M. Van Weede

During the nineteenth century the Dutch Indies government made several attempts to extend political influence on the island of Bali and to establish trade relations through diplomatic negotiations. While its missions mostly met with animosity, over the years they scored some success with local leaders. However, irreconcilable conflicts resulted in Dutch military expeditions against the rajas of Badung and Tabanan in 1906 and of Klungkung in 1908. In Badung (Denpasar) and Klungkung Dutch troops were confronted with a ceremonial mass sacrifice, or puputan. *In this ritual the raja, his relatives, and his loyal subordinates advance in procession to face their death either by the firing opponents or by their own lances and krises. The civilian Jhr. H. M. Van Weede accompanied the Dutch expedition as a war correspondent and was able to take photographs of the massacre.*

Because of our march to Sesetan we deceived the raja. He was convinced that we would attempt to invade his residence from the south and had ordered to install all his artillery on that side to prepare for a concentrated defense. When he realized his aberration it was too late to fortify the capital's north and east side. As a matter of fact the sharpened bombardment in the early morning of the 20th September had a major moral impact on his man folk; large numbers of warriors escaped to the northwest, and before we had reached our destination, no one could be found in the inner circle of the *puri* (temple), the *jro* (interior) residences of the nobility, and the area of Den Pasar with its neighborhoods, but the raja himself, his womenfolk, his relatives, his courtiers, and a band of loyal followers. Together with the old and demented king of Pamecutan in whose territory people were panic stricken, the raja united no more than two thousand men in the army. As he was deserted by most of his men and faced the indignity of exile he decided, conform the customary law and his religion, that rather than surrender he would proceed to the *puputan*, that is a general attack with lances in which even women and children participate and all submit to death.

It must have been an impressive spectacle in the front court of the *puri* in the morning of the 20th September when a select crowd assembled in order

The corpse of the raja of Badung after the *puputan*, 1906. Photo no. 10107, courtesy of KITLV, Leiden.

to die in the sight of our ranks. The king and princes with their courtiers in their most magnificent garments had girded on krises whose golden hilts were shaped as Buddha images and were encrusted with precious stones. All were dressed in red or black, and they had combed their hair with care and moistened it with fragrant oil. The women, too, were dressed in their best outfits and jewelry; most of them wore their hair loose and all wore white cloaks. The king had ordered to burn down the *puri* and to destroy all breakables. When he was told at 9:00 a.m. that the enemy had penetrated into Den Pasar from the north, the tragic procession, two hundred and fifty persons in total, started to move. Every man and woman carried a kris or a long lance, children who were strong enough did so too, and infants were carried along. Hence they strode northward along the wide avenue with high trees on both sides, approaching their downfall. The raja went in front, according to tradition carried on the shoulders of one of his courtiers, and in silence they reached the intersection near the Baluan *jro* residences. On they walked until all of a sudden in curve of the road at the Tainsiap residences they could see the dark line of our infantry.

It was the 11th regiment that slowly moved forward from the north. One section, among who was Captain Schutstal van Woudenberg, followed the main road. When the magnificent procession appeared to them, the Balinese were approximately three hundred meters away from them. A small square was located between the two groups.

Immediately they were called a halt and Captain Schutstal commanded the translators with gesticulations and words to tell the approaching group to stop. This directive, however, was without success and in spite of repeated warnings the Balinese now changed their pace to a trot. Incessantly the captain and translators signaled, but in vain, and soon they had to admit that they were facing a crowd who were seeking their death. They allowed them to approach up to one hundred—eighty, seventy feet—but then they changed to a double-quick step with lances and krises raised, the raja still in front. For the safety of our troops it would be irresponsible to linger any longer and we fired the first salvo. A number of victims remained where they were. Among the first ones who fell was the raja and now one of the most horrific scenes took place that one can imagine. While those who were spared continued their attack and the fast firing on our side was necessary out of self defense, we saw how the lightly injured gave those who were seriously wounded the fatal stab. Women opened their chests to be killed or received their final blow between their shoulder blades. And when those who finished off others were hit by our shots, others—men and women—stood up to continue their bloody mission. Suicide too, took place on a large scale, and everyone yearned to die. Some women threw golden coins to our soldiers as a reward for the violent death they desired from them, and they positioned themselves in front of them, pointing to their hearts, as if they wanted to be hit there. If the soldiers did not fire, they stabbed themselves. An old man in particular paced busily over the corpses and stabbed with his kris the injured left and right until he was knocked out. An old woman took over his duty and underwent the same fate, but nothing would stop them, again and again others stood up to continue the extermination. Meanwhile it was important to remain alert because a second group of Balinese approached, commanded by the raja's half brother who was twelve years of age and could hardly carry his own lance. When summoned to halt by the captain and the translators, the boy seemed willing to obey for a split second, when his followers compelled him to continue. A fierce attack followed, and in the firing aimed at his followers, he, too, was slain by a bullet.

With exception of a few who withdrew in houses, and some injured who later recovered, the total crowd of heroes found the death they sought out. The corpses were piled up at the center of the square where the confrontation had taken place. The raja's wives had stabbed themselves with krises while stooped over him, and others, who were wounded, had dragged themselves to him in order to cover him. His body was buried under the corpses and from this mound here and there a gilded spearhead jutted out.

Translated from Dutch by T. Hellwig

The Sarekat Islam Congress, 1916

O. S. Tjokroaminoto

In 1909 the Javanese journalist Tirtoadisurjo founded the Sarekat Dagang Islamiyah (Islamic Trading Association) in Batavia to provide support to Javanese and other Muslim businesses against Chinese competition. Three years later this organization became known as the Sarekat Islam (Islamic Union). It aimed at raising the living standards for its members and expressed not only anti-Chinese but also anti-Christian (read Dutch) sentiments. The Sarekat Islam established regional branches, and its membership grew rapidly. While some Dutch authorities felt apprehensive about the existence of an indigenous mass movement, the governor general A. W. F. Idenburg granted legal recognition to the organization—not to its central head office, however, but individually to its local branches. The Sarekat Islam held its first national congress in Bandung, western Java, in 1916, where O. S. Tjokroaminoto served as the president of the board.

Speech by Mr. Tjokroaminoto

Dear Congress,

It is a great honor that today with God's blessing I may serve as chairman of this impressive meeting, attended by prominent civil servants, respected guests, dear comrades, representatives from various s.i. branches, and other gentlemen and brothers here present. On behalf of the s.i. Congress I welcome you, and I wish you *assalam alaikum* (blessings to you), and I express a thousand times my thanks, gentlemen and brothers. The attendance of our guests convinces me that they all take the fate of our association to heart, while the attendance of our s.i. comrades is evidence of their devotion and commitment to our association.

Gentlemen! How impressive is the name of this Congress: "National Congress"! The word "National" has by no means the intention to express the arrogance of the s.i. members, nor to indicate that its leaders are sharp-witted and open-minded. It merely articulates another aim of s.i., that is, to attempt to ascend to the level of a nation. During this Congress I will address "The

Members of the Sarekat
Islam, probably during a
congress in Blitar, 1914.
Photo no. 8094, courtesy
of KITLV, Leiden.

first endeavors to pursue that the Indies shortly establish self-government,
or at least, that the natives be given the right to have a say in administrative
matters."

Besides taking care of the association's affairs we have worked hard with
the interests of the native subjects in mind. Of the many activities undertaken
I wish to mention at this Congress that our association constantly has assisted
in pointing out the various objections of the people and several regulations
that we consider disadvantageous for the native population to the government. We must cooperate as much as we can to point into the right direction
in order to improve the fate and the circumstances of the natives, to sustain
the welfare of our race and our native soil, the Netherlands Indies.

We are committed to our race and, supported by our Muslim faith, we do
our utmost to unite all of our people, or at least the largest part. We are committed to the land where we were born, and we are committed to the Government that protects us. For that reason we have no qualms to pay attention
to everything that we consider advantageous, and to require whatever we
think will ameliorate *our race, our native soil,* and *our Government.* To achieve

our goals and to simplify our methods to realize our plans it will be necessary to establish a statute that provides us Natives with the right to contribute to all kinds of decrees that are part of our planning today. We can no longer tolerate that laws are created and that ruling takes place *without us*, without any involvement from our side. Even though we are hopeful and filled with yearning, we never dreamed of the arrival of a "Ratu Adil," the Just King according to Javanese tradition, or other unrealistic circumstances that are not to be. Yet we hope sincerely for the establishment of self-government for the Netherlands Indies, or at least the creation of a Colonial Council so that we will be able to participate in administrative policymaking.

Gentlemen, be not alarmed that at this meeting we dare to use the concept "self-government." Obviously we are not reluctant to use this word as a law exists—one which every citizen should read—that also uses "self-government." Respected Congress, be well aware that the Law has created a Regional Council and a Municipal Council, that is, the law of July 23, 1903, concerning the "Decentralization of the Government of the Netherlands Indies." It contains a decree by Her Majesty the Queen in which Her Majesty expresses the need to create the opportunity for Residencies and regions to obtain self-government. Her Majesty's decree declares: "Having taken this into consideration it is advisable to open up the opportunity for regions or parts of regions in the Netherlands Indies to acquire self-government" etc.

Our Queen is without a doubt insightful. Increasingly people in the Netherlands as well as in the Indies are convinced that self-government is a necessity. Increasingly they realize that it is no longer appropriate that Holland controls the Indies as a landlord rules his parcels. It is inappropriate to treat the Indies as a milk cow that only is fed in order to obtain milk. It is unbecoming to consider this country as a place where people travel to make profits, as it is unbefitting that its population, mostly Natives, do not have the right to participate in the administration that determines their fate. . . .

We thank our God who is just and hears our prayers. Our Queen and the Government are discreet. An important change is now taking place: Article III of the Government regulations that prohibits people to gather in political meetings, is defunct (dead), and even though it has not yet been buried (no other article has replaced it), it has not been implemented in the last little while. While this Congress would have been affected by the intent of Article III, we can rejoice that the Government and Administration of Bandung have given us permission to organize this meeting with the condition that we shall not transgress the boundaries of what is appropriate. Therefore, we are hopeful that all of you who will speak at this Congress will take this into consideration, and in case one of you violate these boundaries, I will have the right to cut you short as Chairman of this Congress. But I am hopeful that this will not be necessary, and as long as we remain within the boundaries of what is permitted, this meeting will proceed without disruptions, and we will not be part of the violations of Article III.

Now I will speak about the Colonial Council. As a first step toward obtaining self-government here in the Netherlands Indies, the Colonial Council is of great significance. As a first step, I say. Later, when we will have advanced further, it will, of course, be different. We must be fully aware and understand that administrative matters and state laws are not everyday business and do not come into being overnight. We repeat that a people that can be patient will definitely be able to reach its goals. When a nation wants to move ahead politically or wishes to gain ground, even the slightest bit, in the arena of political struggle, it must make a supreme effort, or use its efforts year after year. Think about this, my people, my dear fellow party members. Therefore we must be grateful that we will soon be granted a Colonial Council: the first step towards self-government. It is not a Colonial Council just for the show, but one that has true meaning.

Translated from Dutch by T. Hellwig

The Youth Oath

Anonymous

For centuries Malay had served as the lingua franca for persons of different ethnic and linguistic backgrounds in the archipelago, as well as for those from foreign lands. By the late nineteenth century the Dutch regarded everyday Malay a low form of the language and termed it "Low Malay" or "Bazaar Malay" as opposed to the "High" Malay used at the courts and for written literature. In early print journalism (1880s) lingua franca Malay constituted the medium of communication across linguistic boundaries. Several youth organizations that moved toward political awakening and nationalist awareness among the Indonesian peoples in the 1900s consciously chose Malay over their own regional languages or Dutch. As the idea of Indonesian unity took shape, the call for a national language became louder. Participants at the 1928 All Indonesia Youth Congress unanimously accepted a resolution that proclaimed the ideal of one country, one nation, and one language. The Malay language was renamed bahasa Indonesia, *Indonesian language. The so-called* Sumpah Pemuda *(Youth Oath) marks explicitly the beginning of a commitment to national unity and freedom.*

The meeting of Indonesian youths that was organized by youth organizations consisting of the nations with the names: Young Java, Young Sumatra, Indonesian Youth, Sekar Rukun, Young Muslims, Young Batak Association, Young Celebes, Batavia Youth Group, and the Association of Indonesian Students;

> opened its session on 27th and 28th October 1928 in Jakarta;
> having heard the speeches and discussions held at the meeting;
> having considered the contents of the speeches and discussions;
> the meeting decided:

Firstly: We the sons and daughters of Indonesia declare that we belong to one motherland, Indonesia.

Secondly: We the sons and daughters of Indonesia declare that we belong to one nation, the Indonesian nation.

Thirdly: We the sons and daughters of Indonesia uphold as the language of unity the Indonesian language.

Having heard these decisions, the meeting expressed the basic conviction on the principles that all nationalist organizations must use;

expressed the conviction that Indonesia's unity would be reinforced by respecting the principles of unity:

determination
history
customary law
education and scouting

and expressed an appreciation for these decisions to be distributed in all newspapers and to be read in front of the meetings of our organizations.

Translated from Indonesian by T. Hellwig

The Adventures of a New Language

Benedict R. O'G. Anderson

Benedict Anderson is one of the most prominent scholars of Indonesian history and politics whose work is widely quoted, also by non-Indonesianists. In his book Imagined Communities *(1983) he examines nationalism and emerging nations and argues that print capitalism and vernacular languages played a pivotal role in the creation of imagined political communities. Nations are, in his view, utopian communities, and in today's world modern communication technology such as television and the Internet sustain nationalist sentiments. In his 1966 article "The Languages of Indonesian Politics," Anderson scrutinizes how various languages in the relatively young nation are interrelated: Dutch, the language of the former colonizer; Javanese, spoken by the nationalist intelligentsia as well as by the largest ethnic group; Arabic, the language of Islam; and "revolutionary-Malay" as shown in the excerpt below. He concludes that "the languages of Indonesian politics are approaching a fusing point," with the rapid fading of Dutch, and Javanese and Indonesian assimilating. "The whole process is obscure, complex and immensely significant," he writes, "for it symbolizes and expresses the conquest of modernity via a new language that at the same time is becoming anchored in traditional conceptions of the world."*

The major public function of Indonesian has lain in its role as national unifier. Though it began to play this part in the 1920s, it was not until the Japanese occupation that it formally became the language of state, to be taught in schools and used in offices as a matter of official policy. During the Revolution of 1945–49 it was the language of resistance to the returning Dutch and the language of hope for the future. The Revolution also accelerated the process of filling Indonesian with the emotionally resonant words that give any language its cultural identity and aura, and that seem to express its speakers' most vital experiences. The key words *Rakyat* (the People), *merdéka* (freedom), *perjuangan* (struggle), *Pergerakan* (the Movement), *kebangsaan* (nationality), *kedaulatan* (sovereignty), *semangat* (dynamic spirit), and, of course, *révolousi:* All stem from the seedtime of the Republic; the time of its deepest awareness of itself as the expression of a hopeful new enterprise and solidarity. Virtually all the emotive words in Indonesian are connected to the struggle and violence of a physical revolution, and most have highly political-heroic connotations. They live and vibrate because they are part of the historical memory of a still surviving generation, and were coined within the most important experience of modern Indonesian life. The contrast with Javanese, where the emotive words, sonorous and onomatopoeic, have grown in depth and resonance over generations, and relate to aesthetic and religious sensibility, is striking.

Aside from the key words born of the Revolution and the struggle that preceded it, Indonesian is a language without extensive historical memories and connotations. It looks to the future; as such, it is par excellence the language of youth and rebellion. For the majority of literary artists too, who resent the oppressiveness of the Dutch and Javanese literary traditions, Indonesian offers an attractive medium of expression. Its very flatness and simplicity allow writers to feel that they can mold it in their own image and according to their own aspirations. Nonetheless, even if for the chosen few Indonesian's lack of givenness creates a sense of liberation, both literary and political, there has always been an underlying cultural risk involved. Especially since the Revolution, the language's lack of cultural resonances, of a solid tradition, has led to unexpected transformations, as we shall see below.

Furthermore, precisely because Indonesian represented a project, an aspiration to unity and equality, a generous wager on the future—in the face of some increasingly intractable social facts—the language has since 1950 gradually developed a "formal" character that has up to now scarcely been commented upon. Contemporary Indonesian has something curiously impersonal and neuter about it, which sets up psychological distances between its speakers. This change is the result, not of any social stratification "built into" the language, but of its democratic-egalitarian character in a society still traditionally status oriented in its deepest thinking. The vitality of Indonesian depending less on its historical antecedents than its symbolic character as an expression of the anticolonial project (at once the unification of the whole former Dutch colonial empire into a harmonious nation, the democratization of the national community, and the growth of a free spirit of fraternity), the postrevolutionary fate of this project has had decisive effects on the language. Forming a new and thin topsoil to the cultures of Indonesia, it has proven only too subject to erosion once the winds began to blow.

It is not so much that the language is continuing to acquire new vocabularies as such (though this indeed is happening) as that the older words have acquired a "satanic" reversed meaning, reflecting the transitions from the hopeful years of the Revolution to the harsher years that followed. The most celebrated example of this reversal has been the fate of the word *bung* (brother). During the Revolution it expressed the real fraternity of the national struggle, and was used freely by all active participants in the struggle. Today, with the exception of a few national figures like Sukarno, Hatta, and Sutomo (and their case *bung* is spelt *Bung*), virtually no one of importance is referred to in this way (outside small nostalgic left-wing cliques). While *Bung* has stayed high and honorific, *bung* has slipped lower and is now generally a peremptory, disdainful means of summoning a pedicab driver, waiter, doorman, or street-side cigarette vendor. Another example is the word *aksi*, which from its popularization by the celebrated early Communist leader Tan Malaka meant action, revolutionary action, and even now crops up in the names of such organizations as KAMI (Kesatuan Aksi Mahasiswa Indonesia—Indonesian Students' Action Union). More often today, however, it is the satanic meaning of *aksi* that is widespread, in the sense of a "show" (pretentious, fake, artificial). Further examples could readily be provided. The point is not that these words are now used cynically. It is that people use *Bung* and *bung*, *Aksi* and *aksi*, quite unselfconsciously, in their disassociated meanings.

This fission within some of the most important emotive words of the Indonesian language reflects both sociological and cultural characteristics of postrevolutionary Indonesia. It indicates the restratification of contemporary Indonesian society and the determination to maintain the aspirations and idealism of Indonesian in a changing social context, by a process of dualization. This situation becomes all the more clear if one remembers that even today, twenty years after the Revolution began, Indonesian is by no means the everyday language of more than a tiny segment of the population. One can say with some confidence that in only two cities in all Indonesia is Indonesian the normal medium of communication outside official channels. The major provincial capitals, Makasar, Padang, Palembang, Bandung, Surabaya, Solo, and Semarang, all speak their own regional languages, be it Makassarese, Minangkabau, Sundanese, or Javanese. Only in Medan and Jakarta is Indonesian the real urban language. Even here, Medanese is really, thanks to close ties to the Malay Peninsula, more Malay than Indonesian, and has much of the character of a provincial dialect.

It is primarily in the metropolitan melting pot of Jakarta that Indonesian has developed and shown its creativity in the post-Revolution years. The energy has come from the immense influx of fortune seekers, especially from Java, but also from all the other islands, into a capital where so much power and wealth is concentrated. Contemporary Indonesian also reflects the peculiar personality of Jakarta, its sense of solidarity vis-à-vis the provinces and the brutal, commercial, power-oriented, and cynical character of its everyday life.

The most distinctive aspect of Jakarta's influence on Indonesian has been borrowings from the so-called *bahasa Jakarta* (Jakartan). Bahasa Jakarta or *bahasa Betawi* has long been in existence, developed over the decades by Balinese, Sundanese, Buginese, Javanese, and Chinese settlers there. It is a rough, lower-class urban speech, totally without "high" moral or status pretensions. It is virtually impossible to be pompous in bahasa Jakarta, so brutally earthy and humorous is its feel. By an unexpected turn of history, however, this lumpen-language has increasingly become the "in" language of the younger Jakarta elite, especially in the later fifties and sixties. Particularly for politicians, newsmen, and students, bahasa Jakarta, in slightly dressed-up form, has become a normal vehicle of social intercourse. Its popularity clearly derives from its intimate, jazzy, cynical character, which forms a satisfying counterpoint to the formal, official Indonesian of public communication. It expresses the danger, excitement, humor, and coarseness of post-Revolution Jakarta as no other language could do. Its acrid onomatopoeia parallels the flavor of *ngoko* in Javanese, while bahasa Indonesia grows more and more into an analogue of *krama*.[1]

Editors' Note

1. *Ngoko* and *krama* are two of the three speech levels in Javanese language. *Ngoko* is the "impolite" level, spoken to those who are younger, lower in social standing, or with whom one is familiar. *Krama* is the "polite" level.

Community of Exiles in Boven Digul

Mas Marco Kartodikromo

The Communist Party of the Indies (later, of Indonesia), established in 1920, was the first communist party in Asia. Socialist and Marxist ideas spread to various parts of the Asian continent and found fertile ground among the colonized subjects who suffered under European imperialism and the dominance of Western capital in the colonies. In 1926 and 1927 Communist Party leaders in western Java and western Sumatra planned an uprising against the Indies colonial government. Their rebellion was crushed and the Dutch retaliated by sending the communists—alongside with other insurgents, those with nationalist or Islamic ideologies—to the isolated prison camp of Boven Digul, up the Digul river in the jungle of New Guinea. Boven Digul was notorious for its harsh living conditions and its death toll. In some cases wives and children joined the prisoners in exile. The writer, journalist, and political commentator Mas Marco Kartodikromo kept a diary during his internment.

October 10, 1931

When we heard that all the Communists in Indonesia were to be exiled to Boven Digul in New Guinea, we thought that surely we could organize our lives according to the Communist ideals that we had been discussing for years in meetings and that we had been writing about in newspapers and books. But we wondered: "Does the Netherlands Indies government exile all Communists and gather them together in that one place of Boven Digul in order to find out about Communist practices that the supporters of the Indonesian Communist Party and the People's Union adhere to?" We did not know the answer because it was unthinkable that the Netherlands Indies or the Dutch government wanted to praise Communist practices to prove their theoretical advantages. We were convinced that the Netherlands in governing Indonesia would definitely always hold on to colonial politics. Therefore we said to ourselves that there would certainly be intelligence spies among the exiled in Boven Digul who would stir up commotion among the Communists in their internment camps, and the turmoil would be published in the newspapers. Then the government could say: "Look at this, Indonesian people! These Communists in Boven Digul cannot organize their own community, and their situation is one of chaos. Therefore, people of Indonesia, obey the legitimate government, the Dutch government."

These were my own thoughts and imaginations when I was still in prison in Solo, Central Java. In June 1927 sixty-four of us were transported to Boven Digul. During the trip we constantly felt the humiliation from the military men who guarded us. On the ship we were treated shockingly, for instance when the ship dropped anchor we all had to be shackled. On June 21, 1927, we arrived in Boven Digul. There were fourteen barracks of thirty meters long and four meters wide with thatched roofs of sago palm and lacquered walls. One barrack served as the hospital, while the others were the residences for the internees. The place looked abysmal, and people's faces were grief-stricken. Most of them were covered with wounds because leeches and other small insects that lived in the jungle around there had bitten them. Ninety percent of the residents had bandages or Band-Aids on their bodies, and every person who did not have malaria was forced to take six quinine pills per week. This, according to the doctor, was to prevent them from malaria infections.

In the barracks every person was given a space of two by two meters to sleep, and two by two meters to eat and store his or her belongings. If someone brought more than one child, he or she would get four by four meters. But when more and more people arrived over time, a family of four was constrained to just two by two meters.

October 12, 1931

The people receive from the government one small mosquito net, one small mat, one small sheet, one blunt cleaver, one axe without a handle, one hoe and one spade, both without a handle. Every two weeks everyone receives a food ration of nine kilos of rice, dried fish, rancid jerked meat, salt, palm sugar, mung beans, and tea. This is the food ration for adults. It all adds up to 6.30 guilders. A person younger than sixteen years receives half the ration of an adult, while someone under the age of six is given one quarter.

At 5:00 a.m. the military wake up the internees, line them up, and accompany them to the forest where they order them to clear the trees for a road and village A. When we arrived in June 1927 the road from the internment camp to village A was as appalling as was the village. The trees that had been felled lay around in disarray. There were twelve houses of four by four meters constructed like Papuan houses. All of this had been accomplished by the first

Mas Marco Kartodikromo and his wife on Java, 1910, before they were exiled to Boven Digul. Photo no. 4451, courtesy of KITLV, Leiden.

to the fourth group of exiled, that is those from Batavia, Bandung, Cirebon, Semarang, Surabaya, etc. These houses were finished by June 1927 when our group of sixty-four people from Solo, fifteen from Sumatra, and seven from Kalimantan left from Java. It was the Military Commander's, Captain Becking's, intention that the residents of the barracks would soon move to the village as the barracks were too crowded. Because the houses had no roofs and we had run out of *nipah* thatch from Ambon, the convicts who joined the military barracks were ordered to collect *gelagah* reed grass from the western bank of the Digul River to be used as thatch. But after some convicts had disappeared, maybe because they fell prey to crocodiles or because they drowned in the river, the internees had to collect the reed grass under military supervision. Those who worked under military supervision received thirty cents in wages. A Lieutenant and his assistant handed the money out every Sunday. The workers were no different from the coolies on Java who would group together to collect their wages. When someone's name was called and he was too slow in stepping forward to the Lieutenant, he did not receive his payment but [. . .] [illegible in original] and was summoned to leave. People suffered enormously.

[. . .]

THE WOMEN IN DIGUL

I read an article on "The Wives in Boven Digul" in "Perca Selatan" nr. 65 of June 11, 1931, page 2, which I was able to borrow. It said that an internee named H. had written a letter to his family on Java. He stated that in 75 percent of the cases the women, who used to be pious and devout on Java, became morally degenerate after their arrival in Digul. To borrow someone's wife was as common as to borrow a book or some pants. For instance, if A's wife moved over to B's house (I should explain to you that one house contained on average five persons), she would return home only after one or two months. (Such events happened because of the coercive circumstances, there were many men and few women.) Suprojo was stabbed because a friend of his from Solo assaulted his wife (Wongso, who now carries out a sentence of five years). The wives who do not go along with such a situation are sent home to their village and have to leave their beloved husbands behind. H. deplored these circumstances. Full stop, reader.

November 25, 1931

Well, I apologize, wise and judicious readers. Yours truly does not intend to display bravery or competence, or only set something straight that he feels is not right. Even though yours truly is a bachelor and not related to the issue, he is convinced that no person could ever be born into this world, had it not been for the mothers who give birth, in spite of the fact that there are fathers too. Thus yours truly here means to defend explicitly the truth about the innocent mothers whose names have been smeared by H. as mentioned.

While H. mentions a number of 75 percent, according to myself it is at the most 8 percent. I dare say so, because I can prove it. I am convinced that H.'s statements are intended to harm the general community because people who do not know the ins and outs of Digul and who do not think about it in any depth, will easily believe them.

The families of the Digul internees who live on Java or Sumatra will of course be displeased and concerned. I reckon that someone like H. belongs at best to the social class of servants. As far as I know, if I am not mistaken, H. has a wife and children, and he is generally known for his felonies when he was in Digul. So it is not unthinkable that this H. person behaved that way.

I indeed must confess that such fornication is ubiquitous, many women are promiscuous, unfaithful to their husbands. But that is everywhere, so not only in Digul. Isn't that true, reader? If H. were truly a gentleman, even though he has already been stigmatized as a spy, he should point out one by one those who commit adultery, and not implicate everyone.

That is why I want to give evidence here so that H. can see with his own eyes. In Digul I can distinguish two groups of women. First, those who before they came to Digul and went home to Java were wives of exiled men (of the political movement), and indeed originally were prostitutes. After they received temporary training from those in the movement, they realized they were on the wrong path and married their trainers. I would say that they were cured from their disease. Then, as soon as they arrived in Digul, their disease struck again. It is not inconceivable. As the Javanese proverb says: the cooking pot is a briny vessel. Even when you wash it ten times a day, it will still smell brackish.

The second group consists of the wives who during the time that their husbands are imprisoned are left to themselves and face many temptations so that they eventually cave in as well. They start to feel good about their immoral behavior. When they arrive in Digul and see their husbands suffering in misery, they feel not so happy, of course. On top of that the womanizers harass them and like to hassle them sexually, even more so the wives of lefties. And the lechers are cast in the same mould! Apart from the fact that those in the movement are used to permissive behavior and they disregard their own morality because many of them are preoccupied with new issues and reflect on their fate—even the bachelors who eat at the expense of those who are married—hence the situation. It happens everywhere, but seldom in Digul.

For example, if a man or a woman is strict in his or her morals like steel, just as steel can corrode, it is not impossible that passion infects these individuals and electric sparks fly to take on fire. As for their morals, the reader can guess for him- or herself what happens if the most pious but hungry cat smells a piece of jerky meat that is placed right next to him.

Such is the situation in Digul, a pocket-sized place that does not match the number of its inhabitants. It is also the case that a situation like that is deliberately set up to cause harm. The hospital is used as a meeting place for men and women. After all, at the hospital men and women work intermixed.

Translated from Indonesian by T. Hellwig

Out of Bounds

Soewarsih Djojopoespito

Soewarsih Djojopoespito, the author of the novel Buiten het Gareel *(Out of Bounds), was born in a small western Javanese town. Because of her father's progressive ideas she and her older sister were allowed to pursue a Dutch education. After her* Meer Uitgebreid Lager Onderwÿs *(Dutch junior high school) graduation she continued her schooling as one of only two Indonesian students at the Teachers' Training College in Surabaya (eastern Java). Following in her sister's footsteps Soewarsih decided against a guaranteed salary at a government school. Instead, she became a teacher at one of the unregulated nationalist schools in Batavia, termed "wild" schools by the Dutch. Here she met her husband Soegondo Djojopoespito. Her largely autobiographical novel relates the struggles of intellectuals committed to nationalist ideals. Soewarsih modeled the protagonist Sulastri and her husband Sudarmo after herself and Soegondo. The couple, both teachers, organizes meetings and discussion groups, and publishes newsletters. They believe in their principles against all odds, meanwhile living in utmost poverty. Soewarsih wrote her novel in Dutch, influenced and encouraged by the Dutch author E. Du Perron. Her own Indonesian translation was not published until 1975.*

On the day the latest newsletters rolled off the presses and were to be distributed, a young man turned up at the school. Sudarmo believed he recognized him as an A.M.S. student,[1] who a year earlier had pleaded passionately in favor of the national cause at the *Indonesia Muda* meeting, but he was not a 100 percent sure, so he asked him straight to his face: "Aren't you Idih from Batavia? I believe I met you before." The visitor confirmed this somewhat shyly and hesitantly, and then identified himself in a soft voice as a candidate native civil servant, assigned at the P.I.D.[2] He had been ordered to collect the newsletters because they contained radical passages. He showed Sudarmo a copy of the organization: the radical remarks were underlined in red. Sudarmo pored over the marked sentences eagerly. Meanwhile Idih said in an apologizing tone: "I am truly sorry, but it is my duty, and I have to follow the orders given to me. Will you please not hold it against me?" He spoke in a sympathetic tone, and his young face affirmed his words. Sudarmo said, affably in spite of himself: "It is your duty, sir. I don't blame you at all. It only disturbs me that this has to take place."

Sudarmo stood up and accompanied Idih to the classrooms where each individual teacher had a pile of newsletters. Idih took them with him and arrived with quite a load in Sulastri's class. Sulastri greeted him brusquely and declared that she had already distributed the papers among the students. Idih looked bashful, stuttered, and announced with great difficulty that he had to gather them all the same. Sulastri asked for the newsletters back, and the children who did not understand what was happening, put them on their desks with startled faces. "You can pick them up yourself," Sulastri said bitterly. Idih went around; Sulastri looked at him in a surly manner and positioned herself directly in front of the door. The visitor bowed in parting, excused himself, said goodbye, and slipped by her on his way out. He met up with Sudarmo, who played his last trump card: "Don't you think it is a ridiculous idea that I could incite the children with my newsletter? These young kids can hardly read, while the older ones just put the paper aside. Moreover, they don't contain any subversive materials. It is self-evident that I compare a government school with a *Perguruan Kebangsaan* school,[3] as well as the fact that the Government comes out on the dark side. One hundred and eighty Dutch-Native elementary schools for a population of 60 million. Tell me honestly, don't you think that is pathetic? Ki Hajar Dewantara established within ten years the same number of schools with no other capital than his enthusiasm and his serious commitment to elevate his people. With regard to the words of that corn-silk, cat's eye person, you, as an Indonesian, cannot say that I am lying. I describe the issues as I see them. Look closely at your superior's hair and eyes. His hair is just like corn silk, and his eyes are exactly those of a cat. Why do the police feel offended and confiscate the newsletters?"

Idih did not reply. He apologized once again and walked with great effort to the awaiting cart, hauling his freight. For the umpteenth time Sudarmo was reminded of the tragedy of colonial relations where brown was unleashed onto brown in order to reinforce white power. At this point Idih still apologized while he executed his duties, but in five years, when he was fully brainwashed by the native administration mentality, he would consider freedom fighters as his enemies, as criminals, who deserved nothing but contempt. A raid on them would mean an opportunity for promotion, and he would feel proud to arrest many of them and crush their activities in the mud.

This event warned Sudarmo that something was brewing. In the afternoon after school was over he rummaged through his closet and took out some boxes. Curtly he ordered: "Sulastri, search for all the letters we sent each other and additional private letters and put them in this basket." When Sulastri looked at him inquisitively: "I want to burn them. Search for them." Sulastri checked through the pile of letters. She disregarded some insignificant ones, the others she placed in the basket. Sudarmo inspected his bookshelves and carried some brochures over to Sulastri. "On to the pyre," he said laughing. Sulastri reread a love letter from before they were married, tried to remember how life was at the time—but Sudarmo's voice interrupted her thoughts abrasively: "Don't be sentimental. Hurry up! Just imagine if our love letters were out on display in the police station!" He jostled in the boxes, threw piles of letters in the basket, and lugged the load outside. The incineration took place under the *buni* tree. With a grief-stricken face Sulastri discarded their old letters one by one in the fire. The flames flared up as if every time they received new fuel. "There goes our love," Sulastri mumbled. "My thoughts for you, my poems." She stared into the destructive flames. Sudarmo placed his hand on her shoulder and consoled her: "Just think how many stamps we spent on them, how much time, and you even your dedication and literary aspirations. It is regrettable, but we have to."

Translated from Dutch by T. Hellwig

Notes

1. *Algemene Middelbare School*, (Dutch) High School.
2. *Politieke Inlichtingen Dienst*, Political Intelligence Service.
3. *Perguruan Kebangsaan* school, Nationalist Education school.

Changes in Indonesian Society

Sutan Takdir Alisjahbana

The 1928 Youth Oath inspired many authors and poets to use the Indonesian language to give voice to social dilemmas and nationalist ambitions. Sutan Takdir Alisjahbana became an extremely influential figure in the prewar cultural world as a poet, novelist, essayist, and editor. He was one of the most articulate and passionate polemicists in debates on culture and nation. Taking for granted an essentialized dichotomy between East and West, Takdir looked to Western civilization as an example of progress, modernity, and individual freedom. He argued that Indonesia lagged far behind in its development compared to other parts in the world because it adhered to outdated traditional values and cultural traits. In terms of education, too, Takdir was convinced that the younger generations would benefit most from Western schooling.

In the *Pujangga Baru* edition of December 1936, I tried to describe the encounter between the old Indonesian society and the modern era. The old society, which is founded on customs, full of the beliefs in magic, oriented toward unity as in communalism, has been shaken to its roots by the onslaught of the West. In fact, it suffers considerable damage; grievances and tears will not be able to help us in any way. We must reflect deeply on what has happened and try to learn as much as we can from it. The victory of the Western world over our country is to a large extent the victory of Western individualism over Indonesian collectivism. Individuality emerged during the Renaissance period in the West, and ever since that time has grown increasingly stronger and resulted in individual creativity and initiative, an individual sense of responsibility, and subsequently in rationalism and pragmatism. Such individualism in the West has given birth to an energy spurred by an extraordinary sense of organization and logic that is unprecedented in history by far, and this is why the West is able to dominate the whole world.

As such, in present-day circumstances Indonesian society is a shambles and disintegrating; what comes to our minds is a society consisting of millions of people who live under subsistence level, with no willpower or dreams, fatalistic, beyond redemption, returning to its point zero. Every attempt to restore all the scattered stones and sticks will eventually end in vain, and it means nothing but self-deception. We must create a new orientation in all areas and lay a new foundation on which we can build anew. This new outlook should replace the old one because it is evident that the old ways of seeing based on customs and magic, as well as on communalism, no longer have any value in this age. In all areas of life and culture we must introduce new criteria and standards lest we will not survive the national struggle in the modern era. We should do away with communalism and its static spirit by moving forward to a more liberated human society that is capable to express individual opinion, to be rational, more pragmatic, and always dynamic. And as a matter of fact, for a while our society has already started moving in this direction. Those who live in cities and experience more exposure to Western influence are more energetic than those living in the countryside are. Intellectuals who enjoy Western education are more individualistic than simple and innocent villagers are.

If I argue now that individual freedom constitutes the only salvation for our society in its survival in the modern age, it does not mean that there is no potential seed of harm in this notion, just as we cannot separate life from death. If man has abandoned all ties with customs, freed from all shackles and control over him, he who always restlessly treads the path of progress, is left with only two options: continue his journey to find freedom so that his thirst for freedom will be drowned in anarchy and individual greed, or return to an orderly life in human society, not as a slave of customs living like vegetables, but as a man with his own will and opinion, who consciously dedicates and mobilizes his efforts to a common interest that accommodates individual interest. Individual freedom has given the West its glorious status and highly civilized culture, but the seed of the destruction of the West is also contained in the individual freedom that turns into anarchy and a war of all against all.

Therefore, viewed from such a perspective, in our effort to revitalize and rebuild our society, we should be able to distinguish the individualism that serves as a motor, a life-giver, and a source of spirit from the individualism that carries the seed of destruction, a phenomenon of decadence.

Freedom in Literature

The transformation to individual freedom currently taking place in our society is certainly reflected in our literature because there is actually no other spiritual mirror of the Indonesian society that is more lucid and reliable than literature. As the avant-garde of our national literature, we can even boast that the individual transformation has already matured. Our men of letters have liberated themselves from the shackles of customs and inherited presumptions in expanding their minds. As for thoughts and senses, verses sung, diction and figures of speech, metaphors and so on, they all have gained autonomy, all are following their own heartbeat. Individuality and authenticity with regards to form and content have long been the guiding slogan of the new Indonesian literature.

This is really a heartening situation to those who understand how to appreciate the arts as an embodiment of spiritual development, as a deep recognition that cannot and should not be compromised with whatsoever or whosoever. And truly, such a slogan of individuality and authenticity has brought about invaluable reforms in the history of Indonesian poetry and prose. Apart from its "dulce in decorum" that flows freely following the sound and rhythm of its own heartbeat, the new Indonesian literature is actually radiant with juvenile rays of life.

Nevertheless, even on this point we have to be cautious. When the individualism process has achieved its objective, the poet arrives at a crossroad: to go forward, to ravish such individualism so that he will be totally uprooted from his society, or to go back to the existing society and become one of the purifiers of the society's spirit. In the excitement of young age, not even once shall we allow our men of letters to follow the path taken by the decadents in the West.

On such a path the spiritual life that we uphold with grace as an invaluable blessing would turn to empty arrogance and megalomania. Thus, those men of letters would fail to realize their utmost privilege and blessings, and all of the past struggles and sacrifices would be in vain. Thus, they would forget their obligations and, in their foolish pride and blindness, they would reject the honor and glory granted to them, that is, to jointly mobilize efforts in order to build the nation towards a happy human society. Thus, they would rather be cold and indifferent spectators than roll up their sleeves to work for the betterment of the nation and the glorification of heart and spirit.

But, no, no, none of us will take that path. If a group takes the direction of decadent individualism, we will always be prepared to reveal it to the public and oppose it. The *Pujangga Baru* artists must produce a strong and unwavering voice, expressing that they want a place worthy of them, side by side with other groups, through their efforts to bring glory to the nation and the country.

Translated from Indonesian by M. Budiman

Me and Toba

P. Pospos

Paian Sihar Naipospos (P. Pospos) was born in 1919 in Tapanuli, the Batak region of northern Sumatra. He attended Dutch elementary school in Balige, south of Lake Toba, before attending a Christian secondary school in a market town. On graduation he moved to Java, where he continued his education and established a career publishing biblical and Christian texts and translations. In his short memoir published in 1950, he reminisces about his childhood years, home village, and high school in Tarutung. He relates his personal story in a conversational style, providing details of everyday life in a remote rural area. He is, however, keenly aware that to his Indonesian readers, mostly to those living on Java, the Batak region appears quaint and distant. Therefore he also recounts his people's origin myths and those of the patriarchal clans (marga) that dominate the kinship system and social structure.

We ate two meals a day, one in the early morning before I left for school, and the other in the evening at about six or seven o'clock. In between those times we children got hungry, of course. Sometimes there was left-over rice from the morning, and we ate that when we got out of school at one in the afternoon. But often there would not be any rice left over, so we were forced to search for edibles from the garden: various sorts of ripe mangoes, *kecapi* and *petai* beans that could be put to use filling up a growling belly.[1] We brought salt from home to put on the sour fruits. Often we were unable to find very many fruits, and children who were still hungry would ask for a few extras from their friends. We had a method for dealing with this: we spat on our fruit so that others would not want any. But some children ate them anyway. We never brought a knife (we were afraid it might get lost), so we took turns biting into ripe mangoes. We also had seed-swallowing competitions; whoever could swallow the big sour *kecapi* seed was the champion. It absolutely never occurred to us that we might get a bellyache. Grownups tried to frighten us by saying that the seeds would sprout in our bellies and come up through our chests and necks and out our mouths, but of course we paid no attention.

Batak market women, 1930. Photo no. 51175, courtesy of KITLV, Leiden.

Because we ate so much fruit, sometimes we really did get bellyaches and that often meant loose bowels. Going to the bathroom in the village was difficult because there were no proper w.c.s.[2] We were forced to look around for a somewhat secluded spot, but even then the dogs and pigs soon came snuffling around. You could only conclude your business by brandishing a cane in your hand. There was no water for washing up and paper was hard to come by, so we used castoff stuff or dry leaves and such to clean our behinds. Often we would rub ourselves against a big housepost, and the posts in the village got to looking sort of yellow. If two children were defecating near each other, they would have to throw something (a rock, a branch, a handful of sand) at each other and say, "On ma holang-holanghu tu ho" (Here's my distance from you). If you did not do this, it was said that the nipples of your mother's breasts would close up.

[. . .]

When evening came we returned home to eat and often would not bathe beforehand. Sometimes I did not bathe for an entire week, but just washed my face in the morning before I went to school. My chest and neck would get all black from the sweat and dirt, but I still had no desire to bathe; my mother would sometimes drag me to the riverbank and give me a bath there, saying, "Anggo nisuan lasiak diandorami manigor do tubu" (Chili pepper seeds would sprout on your chest). That's how dirty I was. I also used to wipe my runny nose on my shirt-sleeve. The snot dried and my sleeve got all stiff, and my nose got red from all the wiping back and forth. As far as I was concerned, handkerchiefs simply did not exist, and even if I had carried one I probably would not have used it. Wasn't it easier just to use my hand?

We had only one water buffalo, which pulled my father's cart. When I was not collecting firewood for my mother I watched over the water buffalo. I was always happy caring for that animal because he always won when matched against another buffalo in a contest. His horns formed a circle with the arc open at the top, which meant he was called a *sitingko*, in our language.[3] Sometimes when Dad was not looking, I paired the animal off against another water buffalo and hugged him happily if he won the contest. We also used our buffalo to pull a plow in the rice paddies. We really loved him. With me, he was always good. He let me sit on his back, or stand on his neck or on top of his head; he let me do anything. When he became old and was no longer so strong we did not have a heart to sell him to be butchered for meat. My Dad arranged for him to be cared for out in a village on a mountain slope and I never saw him again. Later on I heard that my buffalo had fallen into a ravine and died. Apparently he was just too old. [. . .]

Legend has it that the Batak people are the descendants of Si Raja Batak. He was born from his mother, Si Boru Deak Parujar, and was the child of gods. In fact, the child of the highest god, Debata Mula Jadi Nabolon, whose purpose was to create the world. Once the world was created, he lived in Sianjurmulamula.[4] This village also became the residence of Si Raja Batak and was located near the slopes of Mount Pusukbuhit, which is said to be the land of origin of the Batak and Karo peoples. The legend also held that Si Raja Batak had two sons, and from them sprang the Sumba marga and the Lontung marga.[5] These two marga groups later broke apart to become other margas, and even today new margas are still being formed.

The old people in our land knew their family histories in detail, as far back as three or four generations. If someone came to visit, it would have to be ascertained exactly who he or she was (this was called *martarombo*, or investigating the family connections). Often we heard the grownups repeat the saying

The *sanggar* grass is clipped to make a little cage
One's *marga* is asked, so as to know the family connections.

So by asking what the visitor's marga was, who the father was, and who the uncles, grandparents, and so on were, we would know what family relationships we had and in what manner we should serve this guest.[6]

Knowing the family history also meant knowing about one's *dongan sabu-tuha* (literally, womb companions), that is, one's lineage within the marga. Ties within the lineage were still strong, and the members of the same lin-

eage would immediately feel themselves united against outsiders. This sometimes resulted in the desire to put the interests of one's own lineage first and
foremost, before all others. If one's lineage did not get ahead, often a person
would find a way (sometimes a decidedly improper way) to get ahead of another lineage or bring it down.[7] Small margas or lineages often did not have
much room for maneuvering.

In our village our marga was a small one. Even though we were the village
founders or "owners" (in the past, the village took the name of our marga),
after a while we had for the most part gotten crowded out.[8] As a child I did
not feel this too sharply. My only experience was that I had no older brother
within the lineage to complain to or lean on for support if someone was
trying to beat me up. One time the "other side" challenged me to a tugging
match with a kid almost my age, but I was not interested. Then they told my
opponent to flick my ear with his finger. It was customary for us children to
do this as a sign that we were not afraid of someone; it was a kind of insult.
Of course I got angry, and the two of us set to fighting. The others yelled at
us, egging us on. I got so angry I forgot the proper tactics in fights of this sort.
I got flopped on my back on the ground, with my opponent on top of me.
I surrendered, and they shrieked gleefully. I got all red in the face, but how
could I fight that many people all at once? I just remained silent and thought,
So what if he flicked my ear, what good would it do to fly off the handle? After that I realized exactly where I stood. I knew that I was all alone and would
have to rely solely on my own strength. From that time on, I always took care
to avoid fighting; I knew how to carry myself around other children so as to
avoid confrontation. My father called me a "good boy" because I never got
into fights.

Notes

1. A sour fruit, sometimes grown commercially but more often found in home gardens;
the pungent, beanlike fruit of the *petai* tree, eaten raw or cooked.
2. Water closets. In Tapanuli, w.c. is a common term, even today, for toilet.
3. Special sorts of water buffalo all have honorific names in Toba.
4. *Debata Mula Jadi Nabolon* means Great-Creator-God-of-First-Origins, while the place
name *Sianjurmulamula* means Source-Spring-Spot-of-First-Origins. It is located near Pan-
guruan, near Samosir Island.
5. *Marga* can be used to mean a single patrilineal clan, such as the Pospos clan, or an entire
cluster of clans, whose origin point is said to be further back in time nearer to the era of
Si Radja Batak.
6. Sometimes the *martarombo* question-and-answer conversations between new acquaintances are quite stylized and involve sly rhymed jousts and counter-jousts. A pair of

speakers' marriage alliance relationship toward each other's lineage is also of great importance in determining their proper behavior (in *adat* [customary law]) toward each other.

7. Literally, a way that was "not *halal*," which means not pure or permitted according to the tenets of Islam. This conversational turn of phrase has the sense of something "not being kosher," in English language.

8. That is, newcomer marriage alliance partners had eventually swamped the village "owners" in political influence and number of residences there.

VII

From Nationalism to Independence

In early 1942 the Dutch colonial empire in the archipelago came crashing down. On December 8, 1941,[1] four hours after the Japanese attack on Pearl Harbor, the governor general of the Indies declared war with Japan. Japan's subsequent invasion of Southeast Asia proved swift and effective, and Allied troops were unprepared to put a halt to their strategic offensive. On March 8, 1942, the Dutch in Java surrendered. Many Indonesians believed in Japan's promise of a "Greater East Asia Co-prosperity Sphere" and in the propaganda portraying the Japanese as fellow Asians who aimed at establishing an order with more equality in Asia. Indonesians therefore welcomed the new invaders and cheered them on as if they were, indeed, liberators. This enthusiasm soon waned, however, when they came to understand that the Japanese Imperial Army did not prove as altruistic as it had seemed at first. Japan wanted to expand its empire through warfare. This meant that the Japanese not only plundered Indonesia's natural resources of oil, rubber, and agricultural products but also that they recruited laborers, *romusha*, who were sent to Burma and Siam to construct the railroad and to Japan to work in factories and mines. They imposed food (rice) requisitioning, with the result that Indonesians suffered from famine.

The Japanese interned all Europeans in camps except those from fellow Axis powers, Germany and Italy. In the strictly guarded camps living conditions were atrocious. Roll calls occurred three times a day, and internees were regularly mistreated and tortured. Food shortages proved the order of the day, and many died of starvation and disease. Imprisoned women were especially vulnerable as the Japanese had institutionalized brothels they called "comfort stations" in which women were to serve the needs of Japanese troops. While mostly Asian females were forced into sex slavery, European women, too, had to live through this nightmarish experience.

During the occupation of three and a half years the Japanese provided military training to young Indonesians. They organized youth groups and cohorts and disciplined them according to their own strict regulations, hence mobilizing and politicizing a mass movement prepared to fight for Indonesia's independence when the war ended. They also worked closely with Indonesian nationalist leaders, most notably Sukarno and Mohammad Hatta. At the time of the invasion Sukarno lived in exile in Bengkulu, Sumatra. The Japanese returned him to Jakarta, where he immediately played a prominent role in public life, in full cooperation with the military authorities, but ultimately aiming for Indonesia's independence. Sukarno, a persuasive orator, moved many of his compatriots with his speeches. In one address he announced his ideas of the Panca Sila, the five principles for the new republic. Two days after Japan capitulated, on August 17, 1945, Sukarno read the short proclamation of independence, signed by himself and Hatta, in front of a small crowd gathered around his house. This unceremonious declaration at the end of the Second World War marked the beginning of the revolution.

There was no smooth transfer of power after the defeat of Japan. A newly established Central National Committee of Indonesia accepted Sukarno and Hatta as president and vice-president, drafted a constitution, and set out to create some form of governance and a new state. Sutan Sjahrir became the first prime minister and would later take on the role of main negotiator with the former colonizers. Meanwhile, the Dutch failed to understand the radical changes and heightened political agitation that had occurred since 1942. Internees who finally saw an end to their imprisonment met with hostile *merdeka* (independence) fighters in the streets, and women and children retreated back inside the camps where they felt safer than outside. British Allied forces were the first to arrive on Java to accept the Japanese surrender and to secure the evacuation of European prisoners of war. They intended not to involve themselves in Dutch policy to restore the colony, yet they could not avoid being drawn into the conflict, particularly in a fierce battle to take control of Surabaya in November 1945.

The Dutch installed their postwar administration in Batavia, and when troops arrived from the Netherlands, they began to combat the republicans whose leaders had moved their seat of government to Yogyakarta, in central Java. They met with much resistance and guerilla warfare from the youthful Indonesians (*pemuda*) trained by the Japanese. Ordinary men and women (the latter serving predominantly in communal kitchens and as medical assistants) participated in the revolution with a fervor unforeseen by the Dutch. One of their responses was to send Captain Raymond Westerling to Sulawesi and to give him free rein in intimidating and terrorizing the population. They also carried out two so-called police actions in July 1947 and December 1948, respectively. Their attempts to restore colonialism by outmaneuvering the republican cabinet ultimately failed. Under pressure from the United Nations

Security Council and the United States of America they agreed to a round-table conference to discuss the formation of the Republic of the United States of Indonesia (R.U.S.I.).

During the revolution the nationalists mainly desired to prevent the Dutch from seizing power. Yet the republican leadership faced internal Indonesian challenges, too, some of which were to spill over into the postindependence era. In western Java a number of religious figureheads embraced the concept of an independent Islamic state ruled by Muslim law. The ideas of this Darul Islam (House of Islam) movement ran counter to those of Sukarno, each party adhering to widely diverging views about the future of Indonesia. In 1948 an autonomous state, Negara Darul Islam, was founded in western Java. It gained popularity, attracting ambitious Muslims as well as nonreligious adherents, and it explicitly expressed its political stance as antirepublican. In the same year another conflict played itself out in Madiun, eastern Java, when communists rebelled against the republican government. The Madiun incident defied Sukarno's authority, and it tested Indonesia in Cold War politics. It signaled to the Soviet Union and to the United States that communism was an option for this nascent nation. Although troops loyal to Sukarno managed to suppress the uprising in a month, the communist attempt to undermine Sukarno's position proved a major blow to the republican cause, because in the eyes of many Indonesians, the president signified the republic.

Removed from the scene of politics, creative artists and journalists found inspiration in the revolutionary spirit. The Angkatan 1945 (Generation of 1945) was located in Jakarta, where its members regularly met and debated issues of culture and sociopolitical affairs. They published in newborn journals and magazines and served on the editorial boards. Significant ideological differences distinguished the individual authors from one another, and their so-called *Gelanggang* (Arena) Testimonial of Beliefs acknowledged and allowed for a multiplicity of voices, views, and opinions. The poet Chairil Anwar (1922–49) has come to represent this generation like no other. He made history as an unconventional but intense personality "in the making." Chairil is still admired and often quoted because of his innovative use of language and his expressed passion for life.

On December 27, 1949, the transfer of sovereignty to the Republic of the United States of Indonesia was signed in the Netherlands. The R.U.S.I. included the total territory of the former Dutch East Indies except West New Guinea. The fledgling federal republic had to prove to itself and to the outside world that it deserved its independence. Numerous problems remained unresolved and resurfaced sooner or later. In April 1950 the mostly Christian South Moluccas in eastern Indonesia declared themselves independent from Jakarta as they anticipated a move from a federal to a unitary state. Moluccan leaders resisted rule by a Java-dominated regime or absorption into Islamic Java-centrism. When the Indonesian army occupied the Moluccan islands, the leaders of the Republic of South Moluccas (R.M.S.) sought refuge in the Netherlands, where they continued the fight for its independence.

Note

1. It was December 7 on the North American side of the dateline, but December 8 on the Asian side. All subsequent dates in this introduction correspond to the Asian.

Government News

Gunseikanbu (Japanese Military Administration)

Soon after the Dutch surrender of the Indies on March 8, 1942, the Japanese intensified the promotion of their Greater East Asia Co-prosperity Sphere concept, indicating to Indonesians that they had come as brothers and fellow Asians, not as new colonizers. They introduced the Japanese calendar, abolished Dutch as the colony's official language, and erased other Dutch and European influences. Indonesian artists were organized in the Keimin Bunka Shidosho (The Cultural Center for Enlightening the People) that censored their work and directed cultural production toward support for Japanese warfare and its slogans. The Japanese commonly used the Indonesian language in the media and their propaganda campaigns. The following speech was published on August 8, 1942 (the year 2602 of the Koki *imperial calendar, which began in 660 BCE with the legendary Emperor Jinmu) in* Kan Po Berita Pemerintah (The Official Gazette of Government News), *a biweekly published by the military administration from 1942 to 1945.*

Speech for the Java Region, Presented by Colonel Nakayama on 7-7-2602 as a Radio Broadcast

Five years ago the war between Japan and China broke out. Let us remember those past events, because through those events we get a sense of what really happened. The war between Japan and China was in fact meant to liberate the disoriented and hesitant Chinese Chungking government from the clutches and oppression of America and Britain. Hence Japan was forced to go to war with China, even though it felt heavy-hearted to do so as it considers China its own brother. Japan had to wage war with China because of Britain and America's intentions to take over power in the world.

America and Britain assisted China with its goals and objectives so that they grew closer in what they aimed for. Moreover, Chiang Kai-shek, head of the Chinese Chungking government, sided with the Americans and the British. He seemed to forget that his country was in fact part of Asia, and so he followed the wishes and demands of America and Britain, opposing Japan. In the war with Japan Chiang Kai-shek lost 5 million troops, and his country suffered tremendous damage. His was like a Chinese Chungking puppet government, completely at the will of the Americans and the British. Japan has known this from the beginning. When the war between Japan and China started, Britain and America allowed it to happen in the hope that it would weaken Japan. After it had gone on for a while, they thought that it would drain Japan's resources. At that point their intent to establish their power in Asia emerged. They commenced their American-British-Chinese-Dutch alliance, and that is when the Pacific War happened.

If Japan had only wished to wage war against China, it would have accelerated to complete it. But because Japan was aware of America and Britain's destructive actions, it deliberately prolonged and slowed down the war in China to prepare step by step to strengthen its forces to fight Britain and America later on. And in the end it turned out America and Britain had miscalculated the force and power of Japan, because they thought the war against China would weaken us. But what turned out? Japan is a potent country. Britain and America, on the other hand, are impotent, and they have failed in their ideals and intentions so that they now are in a troubled position. During our war against China they were watching from behind the screen, observing the progress. When the screen lifted and opened up, a major war in the Pacific was launched.

And what is the result of the Pacific War? Initially people thought that America and Britain always acted well and followed humanitarianism, but in the Pacific War it turned out that they are corrupt and immoral, plundering the resources of Asian countries to enrich themselves. It is not surprising that everyone around the Pacific and Indian Ocean and in Europe calls for the destruction of their power. Immediately after Japan had declared war on the 8th of December last year, it could rapidly bring down the strongholds in Asia such as Hong Kong, Singapore, and Manila, and in addition Japan was able to conquer the Dutch East Indies, which is rich in natural resources, within a week. Thus, in less than half a year, Japan controlled the Pacific, a fact that shocked the world. It shattered the British and American navy in the Java Sea, the Strait of Malacca, and other seas in the Dutch East Indies.

The Japanese flag waves in a vast area, from the Far East to Burma in the west, from the Aleutian Islands in the north to south of the equator, and not long from now our flag will be raised in Australia and India. Meanwhile America and Britain can only fight a guerilla war and satisfy themselves doing so, because they are not able to wage war in a large area. The American air force once attacked Japan, and it contentedly reported so to the American people. But it did not reflect on its losses, and when one compares American defeats with its attacks on Japan, the latter mean nothing. Until today Britain and America have lost more than thirty divisions, there are two hundred thousand prisoners, eight warships, as well as eight aircraft carriers, have sunk. We do not need to mention their other losses of which there are many.

Japan has lost less than ten thousand troops and only two aircraft carriers, and apart from that, it has not suffered many losses. Moreover, Japan has obtained many of its enemy's war machineries and this has only increased its strength. In the western war in Europe Germany and Italy have gained strength. They conquered the world's largest armada harbor Sebastopol, and from the 1st of July they have started major attacks on Russia.

If we observe the war situation in the South, that is in North Africa, we see that the armies of the Axis countries are moving ahead, while the British troops are withdrawing. No doubt the city of Alexandria and the Suez Canal will soon fall. Certainly this battlefield where the British were victorious for quite some time has witnessed their defeat more recently. Africa is no longer meaningful to the British. Prime Minister [Winston] Churchill's propaganda used to be full of praise on how British strongholds could continue their resistance in North Africa. Now all those words are empty, as the British position in Africa has proven to be weak and insignificant. With all these changes it is now clear that a new world order will be established, particularly in these southern regions. Japan will fortify the fortresses that have not been destroyed in the Great East Asian War. And, respected listeners, in this southern area we have established new laws and rules.

In Japanese we have the following saying: "Zyoosai was otoshi ire yasuku, Kokoro no shiro wa semegatashi," which means, "It is easy to conquer bastions of resistances, but is it hard to conquer people's hearts." Now the people in the South fully understand Japan's true intentions. They assist and support Japan in creating a new world order. This is evidence that their hearts are with the Japanese. In return the Japanese have turned over their navy, army, and air force to the nations of the South and guarantee to defend them. Japan will ward off any attack in the future with all its might.

America and Britain spread propaganda about their strength and power and their good intentions, but the outbreak of the Great East Asian War has demonstrated that this is not the case. They have no strength left! It is truly ludicrous and defective. They propagate that they have bombed Batavia and Surabaya and sunk ten Japanese warships. But what is the reality? We have only heard the sound of birds flying across the sky over Java. It is the same in Asian waters. We have not come across American or British warships; we have not even seen a glimpse of them.

Listeners, it is Japan's intention to destroy the power of Britain and America and to create a new world order in Asia by liberating the Asian nations that inhabit Asia. We do not need to elaborate on this because we all know what it means. Here on Java a new order has already started while the navy, army, and air force are constantly in a state of preparedness and waiting for work that needs to be done! All these facts show us that Japan has almost reached its goals while America and Britain's power is waning. While Japan continues to subjugate Britain and America, Asia will rise and stand up. Japan will work with all its might. Victory will await us! As long as America and Britain still hold positions on the Asian continent, there will be no independence and freedom in Asia.

Clearly it is Japan's responsibility to advance Asia and to make it famous. It is Japan's responsibility to defend the Asian region. Hence, the Asian nations must cooperate to the fullest to assist Japan in its efforts. Let us now await that independence! The bright light shines from the East! Asia will rise and stand up in front of us! Asia's progress will soon be realized! Let us move forward to victory and let us create Asia together!

Translated from Indonesian by T. Hellwig

Fifty Years of Silence

Jan Ruff-O'Herne

Jan O'Herne, one of the 130,000 Allied internees in the Japanese prison camps, spent her childhood years on a sugar plantation in central Java. Of Dutch, French, and In-donesian ancestry, she was nineteen when the Japanese troops invaded. They loaded her, her mother, and her two younger sisters onto a truck and transported them to the Ambarawa internment camp. As harsh as life was for them there, it took a turn for the worse when the Japanese forced Jan to become a sex slave, often euphemisti-cally called a "comfort woman," in a brothel of the Japanese Imperial Army. For some three months Japanese officers raped her and other young women from the camp during their nightly visits. After the war Jan married the Australian Tom Ruff, to whom she disclosed the brutality of her sexual abuse. It took her fifty years of silence, however, before she had the courage to inform her two daughters about her war experiences and to join the Korean comfort women in giving testimony at an international public hearing in Tokyo concerning Japanese war crimes and postwar compensation.

By this time we had been interned in the Japanese p.o.w. camp at Ambarawa for almost two years. It was February 1944, hot and humid, seemingly just another day in our camp. Suddenly there was a great commotion outside. I could hear the sound of Japanese army trucks and the excitement among the guards, signalling that some high ranking military had arrived for inspection, or the giving of new orders and rules.

All single girls, from seventeen years and up, were to line up in the com-pound at once. We were immediately suspicious. There was an uproar among the women, especially the mothers. Nervously, the girls ran towards their mothers and an air of fear rippled throughout our camp. One officer seemed to be in charge. Ten girls were told to step forward; the others could go back to their anxious, waiting mothers. I was one of the ten. I could hear crying and wailing from the women as they tried to pull us back. They were fighting bravely, protesting loudly. There was nothing anybody could do. Our human rights had been taken away, our freedom gone. Oppressed and bullied by the enemy, broken and enslaved helplessly by a brutal force, we were sheep for the slaughter. [. . .]

We were soon to find out what sort of house we had been forced to live in. Nervously, we kept together as we were ushered in by the Japanese officer who seemed to be in charge. He looked sleazy, with a sardonic grin on his face. We mistrusted him immediately and became very suspicious. He took each girl to her own bedroom. As I looked around my room I knew at once that this was a place to be feared, to be avoided. It had a double bed with a "klamboe," or mosquito net, suspended above it. There was a marble-topped table, a mirror and a washbasin with a large matching jug. A towel rack, a wardrobe, and a small table with two chairs completed the furnishings.

Somehow they made us understand that we were in the house for only one purpose. We were here for the sexual pleasure of the Japanese officers. We were here so that the Japanese military could have sex with us. We were to obey at all times and we were not allowed to leave the house, which was, in effect, a brothel. It was to be guarded at all times and trying to escape was useless. We had been enslaved into forced prostitution.

My whole body trembled with fear. My whole life was destroyed at that moment and collapsing under my feet. Not this, surely not this! My thoughts went to my mother and the safety of her embracing arms. I wanted her so much at that moment and in a flash I could see her as the still centre of our loving family; of all that was good and pure and beautiful and safe. The girls all stood there as if they had been struck by lightning. Then we started protesting loudly and with every gesture we could think of. We told them we would never allow this to happen to us, that it was against all human rights; that it was against the Geneva Convention and that we would rather die than allow it. The Japs stood there laughing at us. "We are your captors," they told us. "We can do with you what we like."

Because we were virgins, prices were high on opening night. As soon as it began to get dark, we huddled together in the dining room around the table, terrified. Gerda, who was only eighteen years old, was almost hysterical with fear. I held her close in my arms to comfort her. Never before had I felt such paralysing fear, or felt so helplessly trapped. We sat there waiting, shaking, crying, holding each other close. By now, the fear had completely overpowered my body. Even to this day I shall never forget it, and in a way it has been there with me, all of my life. [. . .]

Hiding crouched up under the table, I saw the boots almost touching me. Then I was dragged out. A large, repulsive, fat, bald-headed Jap stood in front of me, looking down at me, grinning at me. I kicked him on the shin. He just stood there, laughing. He pulled me roughly by the arm. I tried to free myself from his grip but I could not. My fighting, kicking, crying, protesting, made no difference.

"Don't! Don't!" I screamed and then in Indonesian, "Jangan! Jangan!"

He pulled me towards him and dragged me into the bedroom. I was fighting him all the time. Once in the bedroom he closed the door. I ran to a corner of the room, pleading with him in a mixture of English and Indonesian, trying to make him understand that I was here against my will and that he had no right to do this to me. "Jangan! Jangan!" I repeated.

I stooped down and curled myself up in the corner like a hunted animal that could not escape from the hunter's net. "Oh, God, help me now!" I prayed. "Please God, don't let this happen to me." The Jap stood there, looking down at me. He was in total control of the situation. He had paid a lot of money for opening night and he was obviously annoyed and becoming angry. He seemed very tall as I looked at him from my crouched position. Taking his sword out of the scabbard, he pointed it at me, threatening me with it, yelling at me. "I kill, I kill!" he shouted.

At that moment I really wanted to die. Dying was better than giving in to this man and being raped by him. Suddenly I was aware of an enormous strength filling me, a strength such as I had never known before. It was as if Christ himself was taking possession of my whole being, giving me the strength, taking over. I told the Jap that he could kill me, that I was not afraid to die and that I would not give myself to him. "Tidak, tidak—No, no." I repeated it again and again.

He stood right over me now, pointing the sword at my body. I pleaded with him through my gestures, to allow me to say some prayers before I died. With his sword touching my flesh, I fell on my knees to pray. I think at that moment I loved God more than I had ever loved him, or anything, or anyone, ever before.

The Japanese officer was getting impatient now. He threw me on the bed and tore at my clothes, ripping them off. I lay there naked on the bed as he ran his sword slowly up and down, over my body. I could feel the cold steel touching my skin as he moved the sword across my throat and breasts, over my stomach and legs. He played with me as a cat does with a helpless mouse. The game went on for a while and then he started to undress. I realised then that he had no intention of killing me. I would have been no good to him dead. He threw himself on top of me, pinning me down under his heavy body. I tried to fight him off. I kicked him, I scratched him but he was too strong. The tears were streaming down my face as he raped me. It seemed as if he would never stop.

I can find no words to describe this most inhuman and brutal rape. To me, it was worse than dying. My whole body was shaking. I was in a state of shock. I felt cold and numb and I hid my face in the pillow until, eventually I heard him leave. As soon as he had gone, I gathered what was left of my clothing and ran to the bathroom, feeling that if only I could wash everything away from my body, it would be all right. In the bathroom, I found the other girls all crying, all trying to do the same thing. Trying to wash away all the dirt, the shame, the hurt, as if we could wash away all that had happened to us.

Drawings from a Japanese Camp

Mieneke Van Hoogstraten

The Japanese forced Dutch internees to till the land.
Drawing by Mieneke Mees-Van Hoogstraten.

For more than two and a half years Mieneke Van Hoogstraten, her mother, and four younger siblings were interned by the Japanese. She was sixteen years old when her harsh life in the women's camps began, one filled with fear, hunger, and suffering. The Japanese forced the Dutch women and older children to do hard physical labor: they tilled the land under the blazing sun to grow food. Many internees, who were severely malnourished, suffered from tropical diseases such as edema, beriberi, dysentery, and malaria. Diphtheria, a throat and respiratory disease, was rampant too. In 1944 Van Hoogstraten caught this highly contagious disease. She made a sketch of her "diphtheria cell" where she was kept in isolation so as not to infect others. The gate in front reads "No Entry" in Indonesian. The Japanese did not allow the prisoners to have any books, paper, or writing materials, and if they found someone who kept a diary or a sketchbook, they would severely punish her.

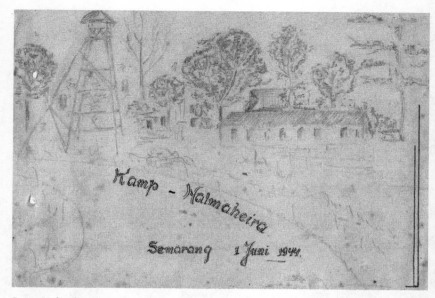

Camp Halmaheira, a Japanese internment camp for women and children near Semarang on Java. Drawing by Mieneke Mees-Van Hoogstraten.

"Diptheria cell" in the Japanese camp. Drawing by Mieneke Mees-Van Hoogstraten.

Exploring Panca Sila

Sukarno

The Japanese were quick to realize that they needed to have local leaders on their side if they were to appeal to the Indonesian masses. Prominent figureheads of the Indonesian Nationalist Party (PNI), founded in 1928, had been arrested and exiled by the Dutch who considered them a threat to the colonial state. Mohammad Hatta and Sutan Sjahrir had been deported to the Boven Digul camp in New Guinea, but were released before the Japanese occupation, while Sukarno lived in exile first on the eastern island of Flores, and subsequently in southern Sumatra. The Japanese returned Sukarno to Java, and together with Hatta he cooperated closely with the Japanese to mobilize the masses. They ultimately aimed to achieve Indonesia's independence. In March 1945 they were among the sixty-four Indonesian members of the Investigating Committee to Prepare Indonesia's Independence established by the Japanese military administration. The following is an excerpt of a speech delivered in June 1945 in which Sukarno proposes the Five Pillars (Panca Sila) as the founding principles of the soon-to-be Indonesian state. To this day the Panca Sila serve as Indonesia's ruling guidelines.

Gentlemen, this is what I am proposing: If we want democracy, it should not be Western democracy, but a democracy that gives life, that is, political-economic democracy that guarantees social welfare! Indonesian people have spoken about it for long. Is this what Ratu Adil is supposed to mean?[1] The notion of Ratu Adil actually refers to social justice. People want welfare. Those who used to be deprived of food and clothing create a new world in which there is justice under the leadership of Ratu Adil.

Therefore, if we really want to understand, to love and to care about Indonesian people, let us adopt this social-justice principle, which is not merely concerned with political equality, gentlemen, but also with equality in the economic sector, which means prosperity for all. Gentlemen, the consultative body that we are about to establish should not just be a politically democratic body but it should be one that works together with the people to uphold two principles: political and social justice.

President Sukarno
speaking to the people,
1951. Photo no. 41407,
courtesy of KITLV,
Leiden.

We will explore these issues further together, gentlemen, in the consultative body. Let me repeat, we will address all of these issues, all of them! Also,
as far as the State Leadership is concerned, frankly, I do not prefer a monarchy.
Why? Because monarchy presupposes hereditariness, it is based on heredity.
I am a Muslim. I am a democrat because I am Muslim, I prefer consensus,
so I request that the Head of State be elected. Does not Islam teach us that
the people should elect all heads of state, be they caliphs or *Amirul mu'minin*
[Commander of the Faithful]?

Each time we need a new head of state, we have an election. Thus, if one
day Ki Bagus Hadikusumo, for instance, is elected Indonesia's Head of State
and then he passes away, Ki Hadikusumo's son does not automatically replace
him. This is why I am not keen on having a monarchy.

Gentlemen, what might the fifth principle be? I have suggested four principles so far:

1. Indonesian nationalism
2. Internationalism or humanity
3. Consensus or democracy
4. Social welfare

The fifth principle should be: to establish an Independent Indonesia based on the belief in one God. The belief in God! Not only do Indonesian people believe in God but each of them also believes in their own God. Christian belief in God is based on the teachings of Jesus the Messiah, Islamic belief in God is based on the teachings of the Prophet Mohammad saw, and Buddhists practice their belief based on their Scriptures. But we all should believe in God. Indonesia should become a state where people can freely practice their religions. Everyone should embrace God in a civilized manner, without any "religious fanaticism." And the State of Indonesia should be a State that believes in God! Let us practice our beliefs, whether we are Muslims or Christians, in a civilized way. What do I mean by a civilized way? It means mutual respect for one another. (*Applause from people in the audience.*)

The Prophet Mohammad, God bless Him and give Him peace, has shown us enough examples of tolerance, how to show respect to other religions. Jesus Christ has also conferred such tolerance. Let us, in this independent Indonesia that we are establishing now, declare: that the fifth principle of our State is the belief in God which is practiced in a civilized manner, the belief in God which upholds noble values, the belief in God which respects one another. My heart will rejoice, gentlemen, if you will accept my proposition that the State of Indonesia is based on the Belief in one God!

It is here, in the spirit of the fifth principle, gentlemen, that all religions of present-day Indonesia will have their rightful place. And our State will also believe in God! Please bear in mind that the third principle, consensus and representation, is the basis of promoting our ideas in a civilized manner by shying away from intolerance!

Gentlemen, the "State Principles" which I propose comprises five principles. Are these *Panca Darma* [Five Duties]? No! The term *Panca Darma* is not really accurate. *Dharma* means duty, whereas what we are talking about is principle. I love symbolism, including numeral symbolism. *Rukun Islam* (The Islamic Duties) also consist of five principles. Each of our hand has five fingers. We have five senses. What else has five items? (*One person in the audience mentions the five Pandawas.*)[2] The Pandawas also consist of five persons. And now the State Principles: nationalism, internationalism, consensus, welfare, and the belief in God also bear the number "five." These are not *Panca Darma*, but I would call them— following the advice given by a colleague of ours who is a linguist—*Panca Sila*.

Sila means principle, and on the ground provided by these five principles we will build the State of Indonesia to be everlasting and eternal. (*Loud applause.*)

Translated from Indonesian by M. Budiman

Editors' Notes

1. *Ratu Adil* is the long awaited messiah in Javanese mythology.
2. The five Pandawas refer to the five sons of Pandu who are involved in the Bharata civil war in the Hindu epic *Mahabharata*.

Memories of a Freedom Fighter

Roswitha Djajadiningrat

On the day Sukarno proclaimed Indonesia's independence, August 17, 1945, the Japanese still controlled most of public and political life while they kept the Europeans and their allies interned in the camps. When the Netherlands tried to restore colonial power with the assistance of the Allied forces, it encountered fierce resistance from Indonesians, many of them trained by the Japanese. Young men and women were willing to sacrifice their lives for their Revolusi. *They received their arms from the retreating Japanese. While the Dutch took control of Jakarta, as Batavia was now called, the republicans made Yogyakarta their headquarters. The revolutionary war of independence lasted more than four years. In July 1947 and December 1948 the Dutch launched two military attacks, euphemistically called police actions, major counterinsurgency operations on de facto republican territory in an attempt to crush their opponents. These tactics backfired as the Netherlands lost the respect of the Americans, the British, and the United Nations Security Council. While the majority of guerilla fighters during the revolution were men, women, too, actively participated on the frontlines. Roswitha Djajadiningrat, Wiet for short, was a woman of noble descent who assisted two doctors, Imam and Ibnu, as a nurse.*

August 6, 1947

I met Dr. Imam. He suggested I join him to South Malang. As he said: "Come and assist me, Wiet. I need young women like yourself. So many men, women, and children are suffering incredibly out there." Spontaneously I said "yes." Why would the very young men of the High School Army leave their homes behind? Why would they be able to devote themselves to their country, calmly and with complete self-abandonment, and I wouldn't? I am sure my sister Net, with whom I am presently staying in Yogyakarta, will not approve. Mom, my brothers and sisters in Jakarta won't either. But no one will stop me. Now I also want to pull my weight (if only some light weight) to achieve the realization of a free and independent Indonesia.

A freedom fighter with a Japanese sword, 1945–49. Photo no. 14045, courtesy of KITLV, Leiden.

Three hours later. For sure, my sister Net is completely crushed because of my plan. From her demeanor I could tell she was very saddened. She didn't say much, only: "What shall I write to Mom if anything happens to you?" I just laughed and said: "I really can't do anything else. You sent your own son Ahmad to the frontline. Why shouldn't I, your sister, go? Maybe I will end up at the same station as Ahmad. I promise I'll keep a close eye on him. Just let me go, it will be all right!"

September 29, 1947

I have to scribble quickly before I go to sleep. It was an exciting night. We escaped by the skin of our teeth. Two minutes later and I was dead or imprisoned by the Dutch. I will relate it from the beginning.

At 7:00 p.m. Dr. Imam said that Roel and I had to come along to Tumpang. He had just received a phone call that some fifty evacuees, women and children from Malang, were on their way. Tumpang is located just behind the demarcation line, so we could take care of them there. Because Ibnu was all by himself in the hospital with five nurses, he asked for our reinforcement. Medical support would definitely be needed. These poor people were chased by the Dutch who put them through hell every day to find out where their husbands and men were. People whose high-priced possessions were robbed such as radios, refrigerators, and cars. They had to leave Malang. When we arrived in Tumpang at 9:00 p.m. we heard an infernal racket of machine guns and mortars. Fortunately the evacuees were already there. Except for a few blisters on some feet no one was ill or injured. Divided over three groups they would be transported by bus to another small town in the republican territory.

After half an hour the first injured individuals entered the hospital. Dr. Ibnu asked for assistance. Iman would operate with Roel and me as surgical nurses. After the third patient a courier ran into the operating room. He almost screamed. "The enemy is only three kilometers away. They are approaching. Maybe our position will not be able to hold much longer." Dr. Imam merely nodded. He wore a surgical mask over his mouth. We were so busy that we had not heard the gunshots, but once we were informed we noticed the blasts much closer than before. Before the fourth patient was placed on the operating table, Imam asked us whether we wanted to stay or preferred to depart with the last group of evacuees who were almost on their way out. We remained with Imam. He looked at me and said: "Aren't you afraid, Wiet, you don't have to stay for me." No, at a moment like this fear is not part of my vocabulary. I always start from the premise: you only die once and it is written down in Our Lord's notebook when your time has come. Whether you are at the front or are lying in bed, you cannot do anything. Fate, *nasib*, as we Orientals call it. I still get goose bumps when I remember this moment.

While we sutured the patient we heard a hissing sound. Imam yelled through his surgical mask: "Quick, under the table!" I forgot everything, the patient, the blood tray in my hand, the entire situation. Silence first . . . then an enormous explosion. The sound of breaking glass. I thought this was my last hour. When I opened my eyes I saw Imam's face. Anxiously he asked: "My dear, are you injured?" "No, I don't think so." "I'll help you." "Why, doc, I'm not hurt." Again a concerned look. I did not understand. Did I maybe lose a leg? With panic-stricken fear I looked at my legs. My skirt was covered in blood, a scarlet puddle on my white apron. I grabbed my legs. They were still there. When I lifted myself up, I saw the kidney-shaped tray. I grimaced with utmost relief: "The blood from the tray spilled over me." A big sigh from Imam: "Thank God, I thought something had happened to your legs." The havoc in the room was incredible. Everything made of glass was shattered. Pieces of glass were everywhere. Our patient was unharmed. With wide-open eyes and his mouth distorted with pain he stared at us. Poor soul! How did he feel when he saw us crawl under the table? He lay there helplessly and could not move one bit. When we had completed the surgery, we went to explore where the mortar had exploded. The missile had reached the ground in front of the house, a couple of meters from our room. Ibnu came running in our direction. "We have to get away, they are crossing the demarcation line. Our men are withdrawing." Our loyal Gurka-truck was ready to transport us. Just on time. Later we heard that two minutes after our departure the first Dutch tank rolled into Tumpang. It was about 1:00 a.m. when we were on our way to Sumberpucung. The Gurka progressed at a snail's pace. We could not speed up because of the patients. They would stay with us and subsequently be transported to Turen. It was a pitch-black night, warm in spite of the fact that all windows of the bus were open. Everyone dozed off, sometimes one of the patients groaned. My thoughts were miles away. Who would ever have guessed that I would sit like this in a bus full of injured soldiers, far from home? Roel had a patient with a fracture of the skull on her lap. She moistened his lips with a wad of wettish cotton wool. Poor guy, I think you won't see the end of the night . . .

Suddenly the brakes of the Gurka crunched. A bunch of shouting people on the middle of the road. Imam asked what was happening. They needed a doctor. Accidentally someone had shot his soldier friend in his abdomen. Imam jumped out and called for me. The victim was bleeding heavily, an open wound at the center of his belly. Imam could only apply a tourniquet and give a shot of morphine against the pain. How could we transport him? It was impossible to add him to the passengers in the Gurka. Fortunately a military truck that happened to pass by brought a solution. I would ride in the truck with the patient's head on my lap. The Gurka would follow.

I felt deeply uncomfortable in the truck with twelve pairs of eyes staring at me. The victim was suffering a lot on the hard bottom of the camion. With a whispering voice he asked whether the injured part of his body could lie on my lap and his head on a knapsack. I fulfilled his request, but in no time my uniform was drenched with his blood. I can still smell the sharp, pungent stench.

In the use of firearms, too, the military command had to provide training. This should not have to happen, this unnecessary loss of human resources and material. When we reached Sumberpucung, my first visit was to the bathroom. The blood stuck to my skin . . .

Now I go to sleep, I only need to get up by 12:00 noon with special permission of Imam.

Translated from Dutch by T. Hellwig

Revolutionary Poetry

Chairil Anwar

In 1945 a young generation (angkatan) of creative writers had reached their twenties. They found inspiration in the newly born republic and the revolutionary spirit that followed the proclamation of independence. The poet Chairil Anwar is best known to represent the group Angkatan 1945. Born in Medan, Sumatra, in 1922, he moved to Jakarta at the age of eighteen. Chairil lived life with great élan, socializing both with intellectuals and prominent figures in the upper social strata and with street people and sex workers on the fringes of society. His passion for life also meant that he was preoccupied with death. He died of typhus in 1949, twenty-six years old. After his death collections of his poems came out in book form. It was then that accusations of plagiarism of Western poetry came to the surface, an issue much debated both by his supporters and by his opponents.

ME

When my time comes
No one's going to cry for me,
And you won't, either

The hell with all those tears!
I'm a wild beast
Driven out of the herd

Bullets may pierce my skin
But I'll keep coming,

Carrying forward my wounds and my pain
Attacking
Attacking
Until suffering disappears

And I won't give a damn

I want to live another thousand years
March 1943

SOME ARE PLUNDERED, SOME ESCAPE

Darkness—a passing wind purifies me
and shakes the room where the one I want is lying
and night squeezes down, trees freeze into columns of stone.

At Karet,[1] at Karet (where I go next) the cold wind moans too.

I'm tidying my room, and my heart, in case you come
and I can set free a new story for you
but, now, it's only my hands that move fiercely.

My body is still, alone—everything I've said, everything I've done
    all icy, stiff.

1949

Note

1. Jakarta's largest cemetery.

Straightening Out Celebes

Raymond Westerling

Diplomatic negotiations took place at the same time that guerilla fighters waged war against a return of their former colonizers. Sjahrir and Hatta emerged as the most important Indonesian mediators because the Dutch refused to enter into discussions with Sukarno, whom they considered a Japanese collaborator. The Linggajati Agreement in November 1946 constituted the signed recognition of a de facto republican sovereignty on Java, Sumatra, and Madura. For other parts of the archipelago the two parties sought a solution in the form of the Republic of the United States of Indonesia. In December the state of East Indonesia came into being. Its territory included the Moluccas, Celebes (or Sulawesi), and Bali. Five months later the state of West Kalimantan was created, and the state of East Sumatra followed in December 1947. The constitution of these states did not automatically lead to peace on the ground. In southern Sulawesi republican youth rebelled against what they believed was Dutch-imposed authority. The Dutch retaliated by appointing Captain Raymond "Turk" Westerling, who headed a detachment of the special troops of the Royal Dutch East Indies Army (KNIL). He was notorious for his relentless use of brutal force and arbitrary terror. An estimated three thousand Indonesians lost their lives within three months. In his memoirs Westerling is completely self-righteous about his actions. They were necessary, in his view, to "pacify the Celebes."

It was my custom at this time to take my meals at the Society Club. It was frequented by an Indonesian who had had extensive business relations with Dutch inhabitants of Makassar before the war, and who was using his acquaintanceships to gather information which permitted the terrorists to carry out successful raids. His work as a spy had cost us dearly. He had been responsible for the creation of several ambushes in which Dutch soldiers had been killed. We had all the proof necessary to have him arrested, tried, and executed. But I thought him one of the persons capable of being saved. He was indisputably a criminal in the eyes of the law, particularly the law of a state of siege (which had been declared for the territory) but I considered him a sincere nationalist, whose convictions were worthy of respect. So, instead

A coup attempt under R. Westerling's command, 1950. Photo no. 43029, courtesy of KITLV, Leiden.

of arresting him, I drew him aside, one day in the Society Club, and told him: "I know everything you have done and everything that you are doing. I am giving you fair warning. Don't let me see you here again." He paled, nodded, and left the Club. I did not see him for a few days. But then I learned that he was still operating as a spy and that he had even dared to disregard my warning and was appearing again at the Society Club and talking with old friends, though he was taking care to go there only in the mornings, when I was not normally there, as I never came before lunch. Therefore I made a point to go to the Society Club in the morning. I found him there, sitting around a table with a few others. I walked up to him. "Do you remember what I told you?" I asked. He nodded, without rising. I drew my revolver and shot him through the head where he sat.

The hullabaloo, which this act caused among the Europeans of Makassar, was terrific. "Murderer" was the politest word they applied to me. I have no doubt that the reader's first reaction also is that I am some sort of monster. But let me put the case before you. My act was not unpremeditated. It was calculated for definite reasons, to produce certain results. I produced them. What was the alternative? A course, which would have shocked no one, which would not have shocked you who are reading these words, was open to me. I could have had him arrested and tried. I am able to state flatly that there would have been no doubt about the result. He would have been executed. Thus, so far as he was concerned, the result would have been no different. Personally, I feel that the way in which he did die was preferable to the other. He was spared some days of anguish during which he would have lived only to contemplate the coming of death. As it was, he died quickly and mercifully. But if he had been tried and then executed, if we had gone through the approved legal forms, themselves certainly cold and inhuman enough, his death would have been accepted as in the normal order of things. It would not have shocked public opinion.

The point is that *I wanted to shock public opinion*. Not European public opinion, which expressed itself so violently against me. But what the Europeans failed to consider at the time was that if this manner of execution was so spectacular that it shocked them, it must also have shocked the Indonesians—and in particular, the employers of the executed spy. If the proof of the pudding is in the eating, the merits of this spectacular execution can be said to have been demonstrated. On the following day there was not a terrorist in Makassar. They had got out like the proverbial rats abandoning a sinking ship. Assaults ceased. There were no more murders, no more rapes. Grenades were no longer thrown at the Society Club, even though its terrace might be thronged with Europeans. It may be that some of those who railed against me so bitterly lived to do so because of the very act they criticized.

The pacification of the Celebes proper was completed in just two months. It began on December 15, 1946, and was ended on February 15, 1947. During that period, I directed eleven operations, in the course of which less than 600 terrorists were killed in the fighting or executed. Of my own 123 men, I lost exactly 3. This, however, was not quite the end of the job. The large island of the Celebes was cleared. But the guerilla fighters who had fled from the Celebes when the peasants joined the struggle against them had not all returned to Java. They had taken refuge in the smaller islands surrounding the Celebes and there, naturally, they had continued their criminal activities. So I took my men to these other islands and spent another month in ridding them of terrorists also and in setting up the same sort of self-defence systems in the villages which had been established in the Celebes proper to guarantee them against a possible return of the Javanese.

Thus ended successfully a mission which had been decided upon in desperation to aid a local government which found itself powerless to cope with internal disorder. When I arrived in Makassar, I found chaos and anarchy there. When I left, early in March 1947, only three months after my arrival, peace and calm had been restored. Communications were operating once more, by land and by sea. The fields about the city, deserted when I had come, were again under cultivation, the green rice-stalks reflected in the water of the paddy fields. The Celebes was its normal self once more. It had been pacified.

The 1948 Madiun Incident

Suar Suroso

During the revolution Sukarno and his governments struggled not only to negotiate with their former colonizers for solutions but also to gain international respect and win the sympathy of those in principle allied with the Netherlands: Britain, the United States, and Australia. When the United Nations became involved in the Indonesia case, India, Australia, and the Soviet Union were quick to support the republican side. But trouble developed in September 1948 with the so-called Madiun Incident, which had significant international implications. One month earlier Musso, an influential leader of the Indonesian Communist Party (PKI), had returned to Indonesia after more than ten years in Moscow. He arrived at a time when many Indonesians felt disillusioned with the revolution. The republican government, which emphasized the irreconcilability of nationalism and communism, viewed Musso's appeal to the masses as a threat. At stake within a larger framework was, of course, Indonesia's primary alignment with either the United States and the West or with the Soviet Union and the eastern bloc at this early stage of the Cold War. When the communists took control of government offices and strategic points in the town of Madiun (eastern Java), Sukarno denounced the coup in a radio speech. In the subsequent violence Musso and other PKI leaders were killed.

In early August 1948 Musso returned to Indonesia. On August 13, 1948, Musso, with Suripno, met with Bung Karno. At that meeting Bung Karno and Musso embraced each other. Bung Karno said, "How come you look so young?" to which Musso replied, "Oh, yes, of course. This is the spirit of Moscow, it is forever young." The conversation went cordially. Bung Karno proudly told Suripno about his friendship with Musso in the past. Among others, he said, "Musso has always been a hotshot. He loved fighting. He was a martial arts expert. He was also fond of music. When he gave speeches, he would roll up his sleeves." He recounted the story of his friendship with Musso at rather great length, and the conversation went on until it reached the topic of Yugoslavia and Tito, who had recently caught the world's attention. Why was Tito slammed by the Cominform? Why was the Yugoslavian Communist Party denounced by the Cominform? Musso tried his best to answer these questions. Bung Karno asked, "Does it mean that the Communist Party there did not play a central role as the avant-garde of the Yugoslavian people's struggle?" On hearing Bung Karno's inquiry, Musso's jaw dropped and he uttered, "How did you know?" Bung Karno responded by saying, "I'm still a disciple of Marx, Pak Tjokroaminoto and Pak Musso after all." To prove his point, he took out the book that he had written, *Sarinah*, and showed the pages in which he cited Lenin, Stalin, and others. Then he gave the book to Musso as a gift, and on the front page he wrote, "To Bung Musso, from the Writer. Yogyakarta 13-8-1948." Before parting Bung Karno asked Musso to help strengthen the country and to carry out the revolution. Musso's answer was brief: "It's my duty. I have come here to bring order!"

On August 20, 1948, Musso gave a speech in Yogyakarta to a large mass gathering that was attended by fifty thousand people. At that time, slander-ous anticommunist campaigns were widespread. However, the huge interest reflected by the sheer number of people attending the gathering showed the increasing influence of the PKI following Musso's return. For the first time Musso delivered a public speech again. He stressed the importance of chang-ing the presidential cabinet with a national front cabinet, as well as the need for the republic to foster international relations with those sympathetic to the republic, particularly the USSR, for the sake of the national revolution. To begin with, Musso called for the ratification of diplomatic relations with the USSR as soon as possible. This would help break up the blockade set up by the Dutch. Musso's endorsement of the ratification of diplomatic relations with the Soviet Union clearly irritated the United States. And Hatta's administra-tion did not approve of it either. [. . .]

Then, on September 8, 1948, Musso and some other comrades went to Madiun. At a mass gathering he delivered a public speech on important is-sues faced by the national revolution at that time. Also, he disclosed the slan-derous, domestic, and foreign propaganda directed against the communists, which discredited them as unpatriotic. Musso explained thoroughly the gen-eral policy of the PKI, which was based on the fundamental interest of the Indonesian people, whose challenge at that point was to unite all the anti-imperialist forces in a single national front if they were to gain victory against any possible aggression by the Dutch. He pointed out that the economic pro-gram of the Indonesian communists adhered consistently to Article 33 of the Constitution of the Republic of Indonesia.[1] To fend off the false accusation launched by the communist's enemy on the antagonism between commu-nism and religion, Musso declared that the communists respected all believ-ers and stood side by side with them in the struggle against the Dutch. He

pointed out that, if the devotees of Islam no longer wanted to live under oppression, it was high time they launched a holy war. Musso fiercely denied the
government's propaganda that he had returned with "some instructions from
Moscow." He further added, "Our politics are founded on the real conditions
and characteristics of our revolution." [. . .]

On September 19, 1948, in Madiun, from 1:00 to 8:00 a.m., the local army
(Brigade 29) disarmed the troops sent by the central government as well as the
mobile brigade, and it was not the first time for such an incident to take place.
On the same day, the Indonesian Labor Party was holding its Congress in
Kediri. In the evening, echoing the voice of Hatta's administration, President
Sukarno announced on a radio broadcast, among others, "yesterday morning
the PKI and Musso staged a coup by seizing power in Madiun and establishing a Soviet government under Musso's leadership." The announcement was
immediately followed by a speech by Sultan Hamengku Buwono IX,[2] urging
that all citizens "take a swift action to crush the rebels." When the shocking
news about the Presidential speech had reached the Congress, the Congress
was adjourned as soon as it had ratified the merging of the Indonesian Labor
Party into the PKI.

Translated from Indonesian by M. Budiman

Editors' Notes

1. Article 33 stipulates that the state controls the economy.
2. Sultan Hamengku Buwono IX of Yogyakarta strongly supported the republicans during
the *Revolusi*.

The South Moluccan Case

Department of Public Information

of the Republic of South Moluccas

The Republic of the United States of Indonesia faced a variety of problems with its federal states, and in the end it lasted only until August 17, 1950. Strong resistance against a push from Jakarta to replace the federation by a unitary state came from the South Moluccas, part of East Indonesia. This state, established in December 1946, consisted of thirteen regions, and for the most part the Dutch soon took control again over its economy, political affairs, and military. Even though there were transfers of administrative power to the East Indonesian government in certain areas of public life, the latter was in reality a lame duck at the mercy of Dutch corporations and decision making. The South Moluccan islands, most prominently Ambon, were home to many Christians and pro-Netherlands members of the Royal Netherlands Indies Army. In April 1950 Chris Soumokil proclaimed an independent Republic of South Moluccas (R.M.S.). He was later sentenced to death and executed. When republican troops coerced the South Moluccas into the unitary state, the R.M.S. leaders fled to the Netherlands and continued to fight for the state's cause through a government in exile.

Many years have passed since the United Nations in January 1946 first occupied themselves with the Indonesian question. A lull came with the conclusion of the *Round Table Conference Agreements* on November 2, 1949; but it was not long before new unrest arose. It is the purpose of this publication to reveal the fundamental causes of this flaring up of the Indonesian question, and to show how necessary it is that the United Nations direct their activities towards removing these causes.

The Republic of the South Moluccas has a special right to appeal to the United Nations to this end. It derives this right directly from the agreements of the Round Table Conference, for the implementation of which the United Nations bear the responsibility; they have for this purpose a special organ, the United Nations Commission for Indonesia. The case of the Republic of the South Moluccas is a part of the Indonesian question. Moreover, the *South Moluccan case* and the *New Guinea question* are inseparably bound up together. Both problems are a consequence of the abdication of the sovereignty by the Netherlands, which was the fruit of the agreements which had been brought about with such difficulty and under pressure of the U.N., and which are decisive in determining *which authority is entitled to claim this sovereignty at the present moment.* The parties which concluded these agreements on November 2, 1949, were: the Netherlands, the Republik Indonesia, and the Federal Consultative Assembly (F.C.A.).

There was, therefore, in addition to the Netherlands and the Republik Indonesia, a *third party*, and *this third party has just as much claim to the protection of the United Nations as the other two parties.* This protection is the only key to the ultimate solution of the Indonesian question. It is based upon the fundamental aim of the United Nations, which is to put an end to every colonial domination on the sole basis that the interests of the inhabitants are paramount (art. 73 of the U.N. Charter), and to found the relations between the nations, including the emancipated Peoples, "on respect for the principle of equal rights and self-determination of peoples" (art. 1, par. 2 of the U.N. Charter). Neither the New Guinea question nor any other part of the Indonesian question can ever be finally solved but with the help of this key alone. The Government of the Republic of the South Moluccas noted with wholehearted approval that this was emphasized by Dr. [Victor Andres] Belaunde, the representative of Peru, when the New Guinea question was discussed at the meeting of the First Committee on November 26, 1954. Claiming the rights of the "third party" for itself and its territory, the Republic of the South Moluccas publishes this review of the "South Moluccan case" to vindicate its rights and to show the necessity of *setting the U.N. machinery in motion* in order to find a just and fair solution for the Indonesian question, on which the interests of the people of the South Moluccas depend no less than those of the people of West New Guinea.

In the Second World War Indonesia had already been transformed by the Japanese, and, while the Javanese leaders were collaborating with them, the Peoples in the East of the Indonesian archipelago were foremost in proving their loyalty to the allied cause by heavy sacrifices. In the territory of Ceram (the main island of the South Moluccas) and of West New Guinea the Japanese never got any farther than the occupation of a few places along the coast. During the last days of the Japanese occupation the Japanese marshal [Hisaichi] Terauchi on August 7, 1945, proclaimed an independent unitary state for the whole of Indonesia, including the South Moluccas and New Guinea. On August 8, 1945, the Japanese charged Mr. Sukarno with putting

Mrs. Soumokil, widow of Chris Soumokil, arrives in Amsterdam, 1966. Behind her stands J. A. Manusama, who served as president in exile of the Republic of the South Moluccas in the Netherlands (1966–93). Photo no. 919_3949002, courtesy of Nationaal Archief, the Netherlands.

the proclamation into effect. On August 15, 1945, came the capitulation of Japan, and on August 17, 1945, the Republik Indonesia was proclaimed on Java; whereby the foundations were laid for the Indonesian question, which has ever since 1946 kept the United Nations busy. These historical facts succeeded each other so closely that it is impossible for the United Nations not to see the causality, which must be perceived in order to be able to understand that the Indonesian unitary state has not proved to be acceptable to all the Peoples of the Archipelago.

Neither the Japanese proclamation of the unitary state nor that of Mr. Sukarno were in any way put into effect in the territories outside Java and Sumatra, nor were they in fact of any importance before the liberation by the Allies, who in those territories brought about a swift and complete liquidation of the influence of the Japanese. On July 14 and 15, 1946, the British handed over to the Dutch the control over *Borneo,* the *Great East* (*East Indonesia*), and the islands of *Bangka* and *Billiton.* Representative bodies of the various territories were soon given the opportunity to decide for themselves the constitutional form for their territories. Among the first to receive this opportunity were the South Moluccas (August 20, 1946), which were geographically comprised in the territory of the Great East (East Indonesia). On December 23, 1946, the *representatives of the territories in East Indonesia*, which differed strongly from one another in culture, origin, development, religion, etc., made an *agreement to unite into one single state*, which would contain 10 million inhabitants, and would, in the proposed Indonesian Commonwealth, collaborate with the Republik Indonesia, Borneo, and, possibly, other states as an independent unit on a basis of free self-determination and absolute equality. No representative of New Guinea was a party to this agreement; the reason for this was probably that there was as yet no organisation nor a sufficient maturity for representatives to be appointed by the people. But under the Netherlands Government New Guinea belonged to the Residency of the Moluccas.

The representative body for the South Moluccas, the *Council of the South Moluccas*, ratified the agreement of December 23, 1946, but only conditionally; by Decree of March 11, 1947, they qualified their ratification by a condition subsequent in case of East Indonesia being unwilling or unable to protect the interests of the South Moluccas. In this form the adhesion of the South Moluccas, with the unilateral right of denunciation, was expressly accepted by the then Prime Minister of East Indonesia, as appears from public announcements. That the Council of the South Moluccas remained free to revise their legal position in relation to the Indonesian Commonwealth has been shown by subsequent developments to be of the utmost importance.

East Indonesia developed favourably and vigorously and succeeded in checking corruptive influences from within and without. President [Tjokorda Gde Raka] Sukawati was appointed as Head of the State and on August 14, 1947 (through the intermediation of Belgium) he, together with Sultan Hamid of Borneo, offered to acquaint the Security Council with the facts of the Indonesian question. On May 11, 1947, West Borneo also became an independent state, under Sultan Hamid II as Head of State.

The Governments of East Indonesia and West Borneo had to face and overcome many difficulties in the years in which the Republik Indonesia and the Netherlands were fighting out their differences in conferences and by force of arms, while the United Nations intermediated and later as arbitrators took part in the settlement of the dispute. In order to define and protect their position with respect to the conflict, the above-named Indonesian States constituted themselves as a *Third Party*, under the name of the *Federal Consultative Assembly* (F.C.A.), for the joint conduct of negotiations with the Netherlands and the Republik Indonesia. This decision to act together is known by the name of the *Bandung Resolution of July 15, 1948*. [. . .]

Immediately after the Dutch had transferred their authority in pursuance of the Charter of Transfer of Sovereignty, law and justice in Indonesia were disorganised by the most appalling corruption. In March 1950 Sultan Hamid, the Head of State of West Borneo and Chairman of the Federal Consultative Assembly, described it in a letter to H.M. the Queen of the Netherlands in her capacity of Head of the Netherlands-Indonesian Union. The contents of this letter came to the knowledge of the rulers of the R.I. [Republik Indonesia], and the result was the immediate arrest of Sultan Hamid on April 4, 1950, shortly afterwards followed by a mock trial and a lengthy term of imprisonment. The following may be quoted from this letter:

"All over Indonesia the same symptoms of dissolution and decay are to be seen. At the moment only the States of East Sumatra, East Indonesia and West Borneo and the district of Riouw form a favourable exception, but even there the subversive powers are active, and it is doubtful whether the Government in those states will continue to be able to hold the helm. For the leaders of the people, exposed to continual pressure and terrorisation, are beginning to weaken and are tending to yield and give way against their principles and better judgment. . . . *In its efforts to extend its territories by abolishing component states the Republic of Indonesia (Djocja) employs all the illegal methods described above, while the provisions of the Constitution are trampled under foot.*"

[. . .]

The description of the consequences of the breach of Indonesian peace and order must be preceded by an account of some historical facts. On April 17, 1950, the invasion of troops with which East Indonesia was assaulted landed to the south of Makassar. When their positions had been consolidated, mass arrests and executions followed and many victims are still languishing in prison. The administration was in a state of chaos, the Government had resigned, and Parliament was unwilling or unable to take any action, save for a small pro-Javanese opposition, which had collaborated with the agents of the R.I. before. President Sukawati was deprived of his liberty and transported to Jakarta. Other federalist authorities had fled. *Among them was the Attorney-General of East Indonesia, previously Minister of Justice, Dr. Chr. Soumokil,* who had fought against the reign of terror to the last. Dr. Soumokil retreated to the South Moluccas, the country of his birth. As a result of military operation East Indonesia was as it were decapitated. There was no longer any authority capable of taking a stand against the invasion. Thus the western part of East Indonesia was easily occupied. But in the eastern part of East Indonesia the situation developed on far different lines as a result of the self-confidence and

energy of the South Moluccan Council and the people of the South Moluccas. So there came to be a line of demarcation, which the R.I. in August 1950
turned into a military front.

On both sides of the line the military invasion of East Indonesia was soon
followed by a consolidation of the positions. After having amply consulted
the population the *South Moluccan Council on April 25, 1950, proclaimed an independent republic for the territory of the South Moluccas.* The legal validity of this
decision can bear the closest scrutiny by the United Nations. It is based on the
legal principles set out above. The Republic of the South Moluccas was recognized by a resolution of the Netherlands Branch of the International Law
Association and by various judgments of Courts, which have been added as
appendices to this memorandum for reference.

On the other side of the line of demarcation the R.I. dissolved the Federal
Government and invested itself with the supreme power in the area under its
control. As far as the R.I. did so in its own territory it only realised its own
right of self-determination, just as the South Moluccas had done. But it was
not possible nor permissible for the R.I. to interfere with the right of self-
determination of the other component states, which had been specifically
defined and reserved. By its seizure of power over all the great territory of Indonesia the R.I. cancelled and tore to shreds both the inter-Indonesian agreements of July 22, 1949, August 2, 1949, and October 29, 1949, and the Round
Table Conference agreements.

VIII

The Old Order, the New Order—Political Climate

The Republic of the United States of Indonesia lasted less than a year. The federal state proved too much of a Dutch construct, the result of negotiations with the former colonizer, to be viable. Hence, on August 17, 1950, five years after Sukarno proclaimed independence, Indonesia became a unitary state under one (albeit provisional) constitution with Jakarta as its capital. Its leaders faced the enormous task of building a nation and a social order that was fair and just. Many Indonesians lived in poverty, had received little or no formal education, and remained politically uninformed. The economy was in shambles and relied largely on agriculture and the rural areas. Of all the islands only Java had sizable urbanized areas and boasted a reasonably developed infrastructure.

In April 1955 Sukarno gained international prestige when he hosted the Asian-African Conference in Bandung, attended by twenty-nine countries from the two continents. This gathering formed part of a larger movement of national liberation with strong anticolonial and anti-imperialist overtones. None of the Western colonial powers participated. China, on the other hand, played an important role and used the occasion to strengthen its relations with those present. The delegates at the conference expressed their intention not to become involved in Cold War politics. The Bandung meeting laid the groundwork for the Non-alignment Movement, founded in 1961.

Within Indonesia a liberal democracy gradually fell into place with a parliament (People's Representative Council) and a multiparty system as governing structures. By the time the first free elections took place in September 1955, four coalition cabinets had come and gone and the fifth had just been installed. Considering the low levels of education and the high percentage of illiteracy it seems remarkable that 91.5 percent of registered voters used their franchise. Indonesians were proud and keen to cast their ballots and to participate actively in determining the future of their country. Parliamentary democracy, however, was only granted a short life: it ended when President

Sukarno declared martial law in March 1957. Voters would have to wait until 1999 for the next truly free democratic election.

During the 1950s groups with different ideologies clashed with each other and with the central government. Earlier elements of resistance resurfaced. Throughout the decade the Communist Party of Indonesia (PKI) grew considerably in size and influence. It had ties both with the Soviet Union and with China. Students and scholars left for the USSR, eastern bloc countries, and mainland China to pursue further education. The PKI and Sukarno needed one another to remain in power, so they supported each other. In West Sumatra and in Sulawesi rebel governments, strongly opposed to the president and the PKI, inaugurated themselves. The United States and other anticommunist countries, such as neighboring Malaya, backed them. Darul Islam forces were agitating against Jakarta from West Java, Aceh, and South Sulawesi. In a joint statement these three regions expressed their goal to establish an Islamic state, explicitly undermining Jakarta's authority. While the economy deteriorated and inflation rates skyrocketed, Sukarno walked a tightrope between diverging ideologies to keep Indonesia's unity. His solution to what were considered serious threats to the nation was a "guided democracy." It granted him, the president, ultimate authority. From then on power was concentrated in Jakarta, and Indonesia turned extremely Java-centric.

Sukarno faced many challenges: the Communist Party gained support at a time when the capitalist world internationally watched communist activities closely, the position of the army strengthened, and the economy needed a major boost. The nationalization of Dutch enterprises and businesses as a result of the unresolved New Guinea question meant a radical shift, and not only for economic purposes. Army officers filled the vacuum left after many Dutch citizens were expelled; they took over the management of businesses. It led to large-scale corruption and "a consolidation of political, military, administrative and economic power in army hands."[1] Meanwhile, through U.S. intervention, an agreement was reached on West New Guinea (also called Irian). The Dutch transferred authority to the United Nations Temporary Executive Authority (UNTEA) in October 1962. Through the so-called Act of Free Choice to be held soon afterward, the local population, mostly Papuan, would be able to determine its future, that is, decide whether to become an independent state or to join Indonesia. While UNTEA transferred Irian to Indonesia in May 1963, the Act of Free Choice did not take place until 1969. By then Irianese witnessed a significant Indonesian military presence on their territory. Only a selected group of Papuan leaders were allowed to cast ballots, and they were pressured to vote in favor of integration with Indonesia. Resistance to incorporation has continued to exist until the present.

In these same years Sukarno and the army launched the so-called *Konfrontasi* (confrontation) policy against Malaysia. Jakarta could not forgive its neighbor for having supported the 1950s rebellions in West Sumatra and Sulawesi. At this time the status of the formerly British colonies on Borneo Island—Sabah, Sarawak, and Brunei—was at stake. The question was whether and in what form they would join Malaysia. As these states bordered Indonesia's Kalimantan province, Sukarno took a strong anti-Malaysian stance. This turned the United States against Indonesia, while the Soviet Union and China praised the confrontation policy. At this time the PKI developed closer ties with China because of the latter's strong opposition to Malaysia. *Konfrontasi* resulted in a number of armed conflicts along the border on Borneo.

Sukarno's twenty-year presidency came to an end after a failed coup attempt during the night of September 30, 1965. Six army officers were kidnapped and murdered, and troops involved in the coup took over the presidential palace, radio station, and communication systems in Jakarta. The next day General Suharto took control of the situation and crushed the insurrection. While some facts remain unclear about the instigators behind the events, Suharto immediately blamed the communists. In the confusion following the putsch, student demonstrations spilled into the streets, leaving individuals bewildered and overwhelmed. The chaos unleashed an anarchic violence against communists, left-wing sympathizers, and their family members. According to estimates up to 500,000 people were killed and 250,000 individuals detained as political prisoners. During the thirty-two years in which Suharto held power the Communist Party was banned and liquidated. Relatives of communists continued to be regarded guilty by association and therefore suffered demonization. Memories of the mass killings and the bloodshed that brought Suharto to power were to be erased through collective government-encouraged amnesia.

The period 1966–98 is known as Suharto's New Order, during which Indonesia embarked on a distinctly novel course politically and economically. Through an authoritarian, militaristic regime Suharto pushed for socioeconomic changes, foreign investment, and industrial growth and productivity. The armed forces played a major role in the economy: their *dwifungsi*, dual (military and civil) function, was not to be questioned, resulting in uncontrolled corruption and cronyism. Politically Suharto strengthened the concept of functional groups, that is, societal groups such as workers, farmers, religious leaders, but also women and youth, who were represented in assemblies. General elections were held every five years, but they only masqueraded as democracy, for the political Golkar party's (short for Golongan Karya, Functional Groups) victory was secured beforehand. Suharto forged ahead with economic development, but he did so at a price. Nepotism was rampant, and only a small minority, mostly friends and relatives of the president, benefited from monopolies and concessions. Many believe Suharto created a climate of corruption, but only after he stepped down was he accused of embezzling money. The family fortune he shared with his six children was estimated at $15 to $35 billion in overseas bank accounts, corporate assets, real estate, and artworks. Even though the lives of average Indonesians improved with better living conditions, schooling, and health care, and an educated urban class with significant purchasing power came into existence, the majority of the population did not have the opportunity to develop their full potential. A large percentage worked in appalling circumstances without labor or even basic human rights.

The ruthless 1975 annexation of East Timor would haunt Suharto to the end. A year earlier Portugal had abandoned this colony that had afterward declared itself independent. Indonesia's army invaded the eastern part of Timor, claiming it would steer a communist course as an independent nation. The United States, Australia, and other parts of the Western world tacitly approved of Jakarta's aggression, still fearing a communist domino effect in the region. In the following decades these nations remained silent and watched passively as Indonesia usurped East Timor and responded to its guerilla resistance with brutality and genocide.

Note

1. M. C. Ricklefs, *A History of Modern Indonesia, c.1300 to the Present* (London: Macmillan, 1981), 249.

The 1955 Elections

Herbert Feith

In 1955, for the first time Indonesians had the opportunity to vote in a nation-wide parliamentary election. In September they cast their ballots for 257 members of the People's Representative Council. The ten years since the proclamation of independence had seen a range of cabinets and prime ministers, with a variety of coalitions formed and dissolved. Adhering to a multiparty democracy Indonesians had to choose from a total of twenty-nine political parties and individuals, twenty-eight of which obtained seats in the parliament using a system of proportional representation. The outcome of the elections—with as the four largest parties the ideologically divergent Indonesian Nationalist Party, the Consultative Council of Indonesian Moslems, the Ulama Association, and the Indonesian Communist Party—did not result in a strong democratically chosen majority. The Australian political scientist Herb Feith observed the elections from close by and reported on ordinary citizens' excitement at participating in the first and, for a long time to come, freest election.

No account or assessment of the parliamentary election is complete without a discussion of the very remarkable level of voters' participation, and the atmosphere which characterized balloting.

In the last few days before September 29th the atmosphere was one of tense anticipation. Election Committees were completing their organizational preparations in a rush of last-minute activity. The itinerant officials of the Information Ministry, at the climax of years of elections publicity work in the villages, were giving their last instructions on voting procedure. The parties were still campaigning intensively, and continued to do so by house-to-house canvassing even after the government ban on electioneering (of a public kind).[1] From cities, towns, and villages in every part of the country hundreds of thousands of people were travelling home to the places where they were registered.

Alarmist rumors about the elections had been abroad in village communities in many parts of the archipelago for some months. In some areas these were inchoate; in others there were detailed stories of forthcoming submarine landings, of white men about to descend from mountains, and of impending attacks from yellow-clad ghost armies. Invulnerability dealers were reported from several parts of Java to be selling special election potions, many storekeepers hoarded goods, and in a few isolated places there was a rush to the pawnshop. The poisoning scare which spread through almost all of Java immediately before and immediately after the parliamentary elections is to be seen as an expression of the same abnormal socio-psychological conditions.[2]

Such rumors as were abroad in the last few days before the elections were scarcely checked by the government's frequent radio appeals for calm. The movements of troops to be seen in cities and towns and on every major road in the few days before September 29th served only to heighten fears that awesome and calamitous happenings might occur on that day. In many parts of the country an unproclaimed curfew was observed for two or three nights before election day. Accounts from every part of the archipelago tell of the spontaneous closing down of all shop and market trade in town and village areas alike after midday on September 28th. In some areas the quiet was described as comparable to that after an air raid.

On election day itself a striking atmosphere prevailed. Voters arrived at their polling stations early. By seven in the morning large numbers were gathered at every center, and everyone had arrived by eight. The number of those assembled occasioned a great deal of surprise. Whole families had come, with the old, the sick, and the very young. Women in an advanced stage of pregnancy came, and in a number of cases had their babies at the polling station. In very many cases villagers were there who had long been away from the village. And all were in good clothes. Almost everywhere solemnity prevailed and at many places tension. An unnatural uncanny quietness, broken only by whispering, has been reported from a large number of polling stations. But in many of these there was a remarkable release from tension as soon as polling had got under way. The first voters were confused, and ashamed to be so. Some pierced a symbol on the candidate list on the wall of their cubicle instead of on the ballot paper; others could not fold the paper properly. But then most frequently they were corrected by the spectators, with the children joining in lustily. After some time everyone understood the procedure. It continued to have awesome quasi-religious significance, but, like a religious rite repeated a number of times, it ceased to inspire disquiet. At the same time everything was peaceful. Except in insecure areas there were no soldiers or policemen to be seen at the polls. Nothing remained to sustain the earlier vague fears. The widespread feeling that something very bad would happen on this day was gradually disappearing.

Thus a new atmosphere came to prevail at very many polling stations, an atmosphere like that of a national celebration, serious but no longer tense. There, too, order characterized the proceedings but the dominant reaction of the voters was one of relief, pride, and satisfaction. Many villagers, as well as townsmen, were jubilant after casting their vote, proud to have been able to participate in this important ceremonial activity.

In some areas the tension continued. There was little relief from it at that small but significant minority of polling stations where voters were afraid lest they should be punished for having voted as they had done or were thought to have. Three cases were reported in the press of villagers who suffered sudden mental derangement on voting day, and one of these in a fit of *amok* killed three fellow-villagers. In some areas an unusual quiet hovered over the countryside even in the afternoon and evening of September 29th; those who were not at their polling stations were mostly indoors. Indeed, even when fear no longer prevailed, the element of the solemn and uncanny remained as a chief characteristic of the election day atmosphere.

87.65 percent of registered voters cast a valid vote; approximately 91.54 percent voted.[3] Another 2.5 percent or so would have died in the twelve to seventeen months since registration.[4] Thus only about 6 percent of the registered voters failed to use the franchise. This 6 percent included many from areas directly threatened by rebel groups. It included some of the very old and the very ill. It included some who could not travel to where they were registered and were ignorant of the procedure for absentee voting. It included a very small group of city dwellers unaffected by the social pressure for elections. And finally it included small groups in several parts of the country who had conscientious objections to voting.[5] Whatever the composition of the group, it was tiny. It was smaller than that of those who failed to use their rights in elections of village heads in almost any area of the country.

It was not concern about the political issues at stake which brought such very large numbers to the polls. Was it then simply fear? Fear undoubtedly played an important part. Villagers in many areas believed that voting was compulsory and that those not voting would be punished severely. Even where no rumors of this kind circulated voters were afraid of the wrath of their *lurah* [village head] and other village councilors if they did not go to the polls. Again they were afraid of the anger of the party leaders who had canvassed for their votes.

But probably more important than specific fears of this kind was the powerful general sense of community obligation which villagers felt. To distinguish this sharply from fear is impossible. Community obligations are sanctioned by fear, if only fear of isolation and social and moral censure. However there is an important sense in which village voters discharged their obligations voluntarily and comprehendingly.

Notes

1. This ban, which affected public meetings, demonstrations, and marches, operated for September 28th and 29th in all parts of the country. It operated from September 25th in all West Java and Greater Jakarta, in South Sulawesi, Aceh, and the *kabupaten* [regency] of Hulusungai in South Kalimantan. In the West Java *kabupaten* of Ciamis, Tasikmalaya, and Garut and the Central Java *kabupaten* of Cilacap it took effect as from September 22nd.

2. This scare led to beatings up of foodsellers in many parts of the island and was even discussed at some length in cabinet. The Eyckmann bacteriological institute of the Central Public Hospital in Jakarta received more than six hundred samples of supposedly poisoned food within a period of four days, but it found that none of this was actually poisoned. Nor was there evidence elsewhere that there was any foundation in the rumor. Charges were levelled against several parties for instigating the poisoning and, later, for spreading the false rumors, but the evidence suggests that the tensions of the social situation were the primary cause of the scare.

3. This figure assumes that the valid vote was 95.75 percent of the total vote. Figures for invalid voting are available to the writer for only eleven of the fifteen electoral districts, but it is a reasonable estimate that between 4 percent and 4.5 percent of all votes cast were no [sic] valid.

4. The mortality rate is currently estimated at twenty per one thousand, but no information is available on mortality by age groups. The figure of 2.5 percent is based on the assumption that the death rate among voters was no higher than amongst those too young to vote.

5. Among the latter were some members of the small Javanese anarcho-communalist sect of the *Samins*, some members of organizations with their origin in the pre-war West Sumatran Moslem Communist Party (*Partai Komunis Indonesia locaal Islamij*), a section of the Batak regionalist sect *Si Radja Batak*, and the followers of the individual religious teachers in several other parts of the country. A large part of the membership of the groups which took this stand initially were later won over to participation in the elections by government information officers. Some of those most strongly opposed refused to be registered and so had no opportunity to vote.

Joint Proclamation Text

Abdul Qahhar Mudzakkar

Abdul Qahhar Mudzakkar from Sulawesi fought as a commander against the Dutch during the revolution. Thereafter, however, he defied Sukarno's republic and joined the Darul Islam (House of Islam) movement that aimed for an Islamic State of Indonesia. Founded in West Java by S. M. Kartosoewirjo, Darul Islam also found adherents in Aceh under the leadership of Daud Beureu-eh and in South Sulawesi under Mudzakkar. In 1961, the three leaders presented the following declaration. Their concept of a "Unitary State of Indonesia" was only granted a short life as Kartosoewirjo was executed in 1962 and Mudzakkar was shot dead in 1965. Darul Islam constituted only one of many rebellious movements against the central government that were prevalent in the newly independent state throughout the 1950s and the first half of the 1960s. While Darul Islam specifically sought to establish an Islamic state, some non-Muslim officers and politicians from North Sumatra and North Sulawesi also signed the declaration, representing non-Javanese, nationalist elements disillusioned with the growing domination of the Java-based central government. The proclamation text was endorsed by two rebel movements, the Islamic State of Indonesia and the Revolutionary Republic of Indonesia, which were initially hostile to each other but subsequently united due to a common objective.

In the name of Allah the Benevolent and Merciful

We, the Government of the Islamic State of Indonesia as the 1st Party, and the Leadership of the Council of Struggle of the Revolutionary Government of the Republic of Indonesia as the 2nd Party, on behalf of religious leaders, ethnic groups, and all the people of Indonesia who are undergoing an inhuman onslaught and oppression by the cruel Sukarno Administration, having experienced various kinds of hardship and anarchy in the life of Indonesia's statehood under the Sukarno Administration that does not reflect truth and justice in upholding the harmonious and democratic values of social life, based on the geographical morphology of Indonesia which consists of thousands of islands, and dozens of Indonesian ethnic groups, inspired by a common will and conviction in promoting the unity of Indonesia, hereby annul the Sukarno Administration and we proclaim the establishment of a Democratic State of Indonesia called "The Unitary Republic of Indonesia."

The Unitary State of the Republic of Indonesia upholds the Rule of Law based on:

> 1. Islamic teachings and belief in God for all the ethnic groups of Indonesia, based on their own religious sharia.
>
> 2. Social justice along the line of Islamic teachings and other religious teachings embraced by ethnic groups of Indonesia, based on their own religious sharia.
>
> 3. True democracy along the line of Islamic teachings and other religious teachings embraced by ethnic groups of Indonesia, based on their own religious sharia.

Herewith, the two parties also declare that there is no other legitimate government in the Indonesian territory except the *Unitary Republic of Indonesia*.

Muslim Tarich calendar   1381 H

Date   1961 CE

ON BEHALF OF THE PEOPLE OF INDONESIA

1st Party, Government—Islamic State of Indonesia	2nd Party, Government—Revolutionary Republic of Indonesia
1. S. M. Kartosoewirjo	1. Sjafruddin Prawiranegara
2. Muhammad Daud Beureu–EH	2. Muhammad Natsir
3. Abdul Qahhar Mudzakkar	3. Burhanuddin Harahap
	4. Sumitro Djojohadikusumo
	5. Zulkifli Lubis
	6. M. Simbolon
	7. J. F. Warouw
	8. Ahmad Husain
	9. V. Sumual

The above-proposed joint proclamation text is, more or less of course, subject to amendments and inappropriate wording in the sentences can be deleted.

In my opinion two of our leadership figures, S. M. Kartosoewirjo and Sjafruddin Prawiranegara, can sufficiently represent the joint proclamation.

But if we all want to express the democratic spirit of the proclamation, which can reach out to and satisfy the conscience of all groups and ethnicities throughout the Indonesian Archipelago, considering the presence of the twelve Revolutionary Warriors in the proclamation text, I believe that their names and personal qualities are in no way "obscure" to all of the Indonesian people and therefore "acceptable" to represent the people of Indonesia. *Insya Allah*, God willing!

The Joint Proclamation does not mean that we act immaturely by merely denying the responsibility of our past actions, that is, the proclamation of the establishment of the Islamic State of Indonesia made by S. M. Kartosoewirjo on August 7, 1949 / 12 Sjawal 1368 H, followed by a proclamation made by Abdul Qahhar Mudzakkar in Sulawesi in 1953, and the proclamation made by Tengku Muhammad Daud Beureu–EH in Aceh in 1953, as well as the proclamation of the Revolutionary Government of the Republic of Indonesia on February 15, 1958.

In the Joint Proclamation we declare our rejection and annulment of the Sukarno Regime which has arbitrarily and coercively violated and oppressed its fellow countrymen, creating infinite chaos and rebellions, and which incapacitates Indonesia under the Sukarno administration to benefit from and contribute to the world's community, if the current states and governments in the world fail to critically see the chaotic and corrupt practices of the government of the Republic Indonesia under Sukarno, and if these states and governments do not want or wish to recognize the Unitary Republic of Indonesia with all its truth.

So is my hope as stated in the joint proclamation. *Insya Allah*, God willing.

Translated from Indonesian by M. Budiman

I Am a Papua

Zacharias Sawor

West New Guinea, also called West Irian or West Papua, had remained under Dutch colonial administration following the independence of the former Dutch East Indies. But the indigenous Papuan people wished for the self-determination the Dutch had promised. The elected New Guinea Council started the process of decolonization preparing for independence. Under pressure from the United States the Netherlands transferred power over West New Guinea to the United Nations in 1962, which then handed over the territory to Indonesia in 1963. One condition of the New York agreement was that all Papuans would be able to vote in the so-called Act of Free Choice to decide whether they wanted to remain part of Indonesia or to become independent. In the eyes of those in the central government in Jakarta, however, Papuans were illiterate, backward, and tribal, and thus incapable to participate in a plebiscite. After "consultation" with handpicked Papuan leaders who were to speak and decide for their people, Jakarta made Irian Indonesia's twenty-sixth province in 1969.

The Netherlands transferred the responsibility for the administration of West New Guinea to the United Nations on October 1, 1962, for an interim government. After 134 years Dutch rule over New Guinea came to an end. At the same time an iron curtain fell over the western part of this large island. For Papuans the change of administration meant entering a period of gloomy years. Years in which the population would see its freedom melt away and would experience firsthand the oppression of the occupying forces. For the Indonesian people the year 1962 signified the liberation of New Guinea. At least, that was their interpretation. While the Indonesians were shouting "Merdeka" (Freedom), the Papuans saw their freedom evaporate. In practice the word "Merdeka" entailed for the Papuans: numerous arrests, armed threats, martial law, termination of employment, robbery/depredation by Indonesians, internment, and secret liquidations. A lot has happened in this area since the iron curtain came down. I will highlight some events, from the transfer to UNTEA [United Nations Temporary Executive Authority] to the total oppression by Indonesia. [. . .]

A Papua widow who has applied clay to her body with a Caucasian woman, date unknown. Photo no. 142_0473001, courtesy of Nationaal Archief, the Netherlands.

The hasty departure of a large number of Dutch civil servants caused chaos, as could have been foreseen. In spite of some advantageous guarantees granted by the Netherlands' government to its personnel in case it was willing to serve under UNTEA, it became immediately clear that most government employees intended to leave as soon as possible. A variety of factors played a role in this, mostly of psychological nature. Particularly the transfer of administration to Indonesia was a decisive factor. Besides the disappointment over the attitude of the Netherlands the exodus was caused by the arrogant, impertinent behavior of members of the Indonesian army (the so-called green berets) who looked down on the local population. The Indonesian troops behaved like "the victors"; they considered the Dutch as defeated and the Papuans as collaborators of the Dutch. They commonly snubbed the Dutch and sometimes molested them.

The rapid withdrawal brought disorder to the administration, as I already mentioned. While the Dutch implemented "Papuanization," that is, appointments of Papuans in positions of distinction, and aimed at employment of Papuans in various functions, and hence impossibly could count on a rapid transfer of power, this process was completely disrupted. As far as Papuans held positions, many did so unprepared or insufficiently prepared. All in all one can conclude that the Papuans did what they could and took their duties seriously.

The language was also a critical impediment for a smooth state of affairs. Dutch was, after all, the language of the administration. The older Papuans often just spoke Malay. The UNTEA officials, on the other hand, spoke English. The Indonesians, at least the younger generation, used merely Indonesian. Only some of the older people could handle the administration because of their knowledge of Dutch. And with all of this one should be aware that the present-day Indonesian language differs distinctly from the Malay language as spoken in eastern Indonesia. [. . .]

It has never become clear whether the U.N. Secretary-General judged it desirable to maintain Indonesian troops in the area. These troops were never withdrawn, so either they must have received the approval from the Secretary-General, or they must have decided in favor of a unilateral, forced deployment without approval. The fact is that they remained in the area and that the presence of Indonesian troops was disastrous for the local population.

The Indonesian troops, dropped by airplanes in Fak-Fak, Teminabuan, Kaimana, and Merauke during the first half of 1962, were larger in numbers than the Pakistani contingent.[1] Their imposed presence served merely in a psychological way toward the population, even though that was not necessary. They supposedly would maintain law and order. Alas, it was them who violated and disturbed law and order in various places in western New Guinea. In the towns of Hollandia, Manokwari, Sorong, Merauke, and Biak they provided pro-Indonesian Papuan groups with firearms to kill their fellow countrymen and -women, the nationalistic Papuans. In December 1962 the boarding schools of the Teacher's College, the College for Administrative Studies, the Agricultural College, and the Christian schools in Kota Raja, Hollandia, were one after the other targets of nightly attacks by Indonesian soldiers with assistance of pro-Indonesian groups. The reason was that the students were preparing for the December 1, 1962, demonstration in favor of the plebiscite. The half-sleeping, half-awake students got into a panic. They were beaten until they bled and transported to the military camp in Ifaar where they were crammed into a cell that was partially submerged with water for twenty-four hours. All men of Ifaar were arrested and tortured in the same way. They were forced to drink their own urine. Characteristic of this inhuman, in this case Indonesian, behavior is that people were assaulted before it was proven that the accusation was justified and the accused deserved such a treatment. The arrests mostly took place during nighttime. It often occurred that the next morning tens to hundreds of arrested were taken to hospital for treatment accompanied by the police or military. White clothing was drenched in blood, turned into rags. When the blood coagulated, these rags stuck to the body. Hundreds of pedestrians, who saw this spectacle, cried, out of anger too, because of the abuse and the suffering their fierce, young fighters who struggled for the Papuan case had to endure. It was striking that this did not diminish people's courage and that many young Papuans were not intimidated by the brutal conduct of the Indonesians. They became the regular "customers" of the prison cells. Yet again we ask the Dutch people: would the Papuans, having lived through all this, have to choose for their tyrants, the enemies of their personal and national freedom, for the sake of the Netherlands?

Translated from Dutch by T. Hellwig

Editors' Note

1. Pakistani troops were part of the UNTEA administration.

A Soldier Statesman

Julius Pour

Before L. B. ("Benny") Moerdani entered the reserve-officer training in 1951, he had fought in the guerilla war against the Dutch during the revolution. In his military career he served as an intelligence officer and an army commander, and in his civilian life he was a minister in the Suharto government. In 1964, during Sukarno's Konfrontasi politics directed at Malaysia, the army supported the president in undermining its neighbor's unity and political stability. Tunku Abdul Rahman served as Malaysia's prime minister at the time. On the island of Borneo Indonesia's Kalimantan province bordered the Malay states of Sarawak and Sabah, making the site prone to cross-border conflicts. Moerdani was deployed in Kalimantan where unbeknownst to him his British enemies almost shot him, aiming to kill him. Julius Pour, a senior journalist with the leading national newspaper Kompas, relates this incident in his biography of the "soldier statesman."

When the Brunei revolt occurred,[1] Tunku Abdul Rahman directly accused the Indonesian Government of being one of the prime forces behind the revolt. He totally overlooked the fact that when the coup took place Azahari [Sheik Ahmad Azahari, leader of the People's Party of Brunei] was in Manila, not in Jakarta. In Manila, Azahari was holding secret meetings with the Philippines Vice President Emanuel Pelaez. This baseless accusation President Sukarno took as a personal attack. Adding salt to this wound was the fact that Sukarno could never forget that when Indonesia was seriously troubled by the PRRI/PERMESTA [Revolutionary Government of the Republic of Indonesia/Universal People's Struggle] rebellion in the mid-fifties, many of the rebels sought refuge in Malaya. It was from Malaya that the Indonesian dissidents had been able to organise, with complete freedom, the opposition to overthrow the Indonesian Government.

Conflict was inevitable. Previously, the Indonesian Government had only given its blessing to border crossing guerillas, but after this the Indonesian Armed Forces were seen, actively and openly, to be supporting the North Kalimantan people's struggle. The confrontation against Malaysia could not be stopped. On May 3, 1964, in front of a huge, seething crowd in Jakarta, President Sukarno declared the order [*sic*] the People's Dual Command—DWIKORA—which was designed firstly to heighten the revolutionary defenses of Indonesia and secondly to assist the people's revolutionary forces in Malaya, Singapore, Sarawak, and Sabah to crush—or *ganyang*—Malaysia.

On September 17, 1964, Malaysia severed diplomatic relations with both Indonesia and the Philippines. Later that day demonstrations broke out in Kuala Lumpur and the Indonesian Embassy was partly damaged by stones thrown by the mob. During the demonstration, the Indonesian national crest, the *Garuda*, was taken from the front wall of the Embassy and ceremoniously presented by the mob to Tunku Abdul Rahman. The Indonesian version has it that on receiving the *Garuda* crest, the Tunku threw it on to the ground and stomped on it. However, the Malaysian version claims that the Tunku made a brief speech thanking the mob for their spontaneous concern and politely accepted the *Garuda* crest, which he returned right away to the demonstrators.

In the unruly political climate of Jakarta, aimed mainly against the British, Benny was called to the office of the Army Commander, Lt. Gen. Ahmad Yani, where he was briefed about increasing the military effort of *Konfrontasi*, as Confrontation became popularly known. Yani mentioned that both cross-border operations by Indonesians and British infiltration efforts were likely to increase.

The North Kalimantan border extends for over fifteen hundred kilometres. This unclearly marked line, cutting across mountain ranges and jungled swamps, had to be constantly guarded if enemy infiltration was to be prevented. This was an impossible task at a time when Indonesian military resources were extremely limited. In this briefing, the impression Yani gave Benny was that he was very worried that if the enemy infiltration continued it would make the security situation almost impossible to control if the conflict with the British broke out into a full scale war. As a first step Yani ordered Benny to Kalimantan to try to stem the British infiltration from the north.

When undertaking one particular infiltration operation in North Kalimantan, Benny almost met his death. This is briefly recorded in SAS [Special Air Service] records, which Benny learnt about only during his official visit to the United Kingdom in 1976 where he met the two men who nearly shot him. The incident occurred on a small river in East Kalimantan. A flotilla of native canoes carrying a group of guerillas were heading upstream, unaware that a SAS ambush had been set. Benny, who was sitting in the lead canoe, came into the SAS gun sights. The weapon was raised ready to be aimed, but was not fired because the whole flotilla passed in front of the SAS without opening fire. "You were really patrolling there at that time?" asked Benny to the two

British soldiers. "Why didn't you pull the trigger?" Nudging his colleague, one replied straightaway: "He told me to wait for the Queen Elizabeth, Sir!" (The Queen Elizabeth was the name of the largest British passenger liner.) His colleague's intention was that they should hold fire until the expected large boat at the back of the flotilla came into range. Obviously, there was not a large boat at the end and thus Benny escaped being fired upon. After hearing this story, Benny responded: "If you had pulled the trigger, you know, you would've caused the highest ranking casualty on our side."

Editors' Note

1. The revolt in the Sultanate of Brunei, a British protectorate on the island of Borneo, took place on December 8, 1962. The military wing of the People's Party of Brunei seized power while the Party's leader, Sheik Ahmad Azahari, was away on a visit to the Philippines.

The Mass Killings of 1965–66

Robert Cribb

The bloodbath that followed the September 30/October 1, 1965, coup attempt marks one of the darkest pages of Indonesian history. The Palace Guard responsible for the coup attempt killed six army generals and one adjutant who allegedly plotted against President Sukarno. They immediately proclaimed a so-called Revolutionary Council. Within a day, however, Major General Suharto took control, and his troops crushed the rebels. Suharto was quick to blame the Communist Party for the coup. Members of the party, left-wing supporters, and those suspected of leftist sympathies became victims of unrestrained violence and of killing squads. The subsequent massacres, lasting some six months, eliminated the Communist Party and leftist political power. Although the exact number of victims remains unknown, estimates of people who lost their lives range from 150,000 to 500,000. The army used mass organizations such as Ansor, the militant youth arm of the Muslim party Nahdatul Ulama, to carry out the killings.

East Java

The following document is a rare Indonesian report on the killings in East Java in 1965–1966. The origin of the document itself is obscure. It deals with the period from December 1965 to January 1966 but was apparently compiled in the 1970s. There is no clue to the identity of the author—for obvious reasons—but there is no evidence that he or she was a witness to any of the killings. The document, which came into the hands of the British campaigning organization Tapol in the mid 1970s may in fact have been compiled from information collected amongst Indonesian exiles in Europe;[1] the document is a collection of specific reports on a number of distinct incidents rather than a narrative of one person's experience. Part of the report was published in Tapol's *Bulletin*, but the sharpness of the individual accounts makes the report worth reproducing here. [. . .] Detailed accounts of individual killings are themselves uncommon, and accounts by Indonesians are even more so. [. . .]

Although parts of this report make particularly unpleasant reading, the document opens a rare window to the massacres.

ANONYMOUS

Lawang, Malang regency

Members and sympathizers of the PKI who were murdered had their hands tied. Then an *Ansor* gang, accompanied and protected by an army unit, ZIPUR V (Combat Engineers) took them to the killing places, the village of Sentong and the Botanic Gardens of Purwodadi. Holes had already been prepared in these places. The victims were taken one by one up to the holes; nooses were put around their necks and then tightened until the victims collapsed. Then they were beaten with iron rods and other hard implements. After the victims had died, their heads were cut off. Dozens of people were killed like this [in] Sentong and about a thousand in the Botanic Gardens. Banana trees were planted over the graves.

Singosari, Malang regency

A young boy, member of the IPI (Union of Students of Indonesia) and son of Pak Tjokrodihardjo, who was a member of the local PKI committee in Singosari subdistrict, was arrested by Ansor. He was then tied to a jeep and dragged behind it until he was dead. Both his parents committed suicide. Urip Kalsum, a woman who was *lurah* [village head] of Dengkol in Singosari, was a member of the PKI. Before being killed, she was ordered to take all her clothes off. Her body and her honor were then subjected to fire. She was then tied up, taken to the village of Sentong in Lawang, where a noose was put around her neck and she was hacked to death.

Nglegok, Blitar regency

Japik, a leading figure in the local branch of Gerwani and a member of the PGRI Non Vaksentral was killed along with her husband Djumadi, also a member of the PGRI Non Vaksentral.[2] They had been married only thirty-five days. She was raped many times and her body was then slit open from her breasts to her vulva. This was done by an Ansor gang. Nursamsu, also a member of the PGRI Non Vaksentral, was dismembered and the pieces of his body were hung in the homes of his friends. Sutjipto, a former *lurah* [village head] of Nglegok and member of the PKI was castrated and then killed. This was also done by an Ansor gang.

Pare, Kediri regency

Suranto, headmaster of the High School in Pare and one of the leaders of the Pare branch of Partindo and a member of the DPRD Kediri district, lived in the village of Pulorejo, Pare.[3] On October 8, 1965, at about 5:00 p.m. he went by bicycle to meet his wife, nine months pregnant, who had been at an *arisan* (rotating credit and social club). On the way home, they were stopped and taken prisoner by an Ansor gang. They were beaten until they fell unconscious and were then killed. The man's head was cut off and his wife's stomach was cut open, the baby taken out and cut to pieces. The two bodies were thrown down a ravine to the east of the market in Pare. For a week afterwards, their five children who were all small (the oldest was eleven) had no-one to help them because the neighbors were warned by Ansor members that anyone helping them would be at risk.

Bali

BY SOE HOK GIE

The situation in Bali remained unchanged until a month after the coup. Suteja was still Governor, and even went twice to Jakarta (on October 8 and 17). In front of Sabur, Sumarno, Subamya, Chaerul Saleh, and Syafiudin himself, he was asked if he was PKI.[4] He replied that the accusation was only slander. Bung Karno convinced Suteja that he should continue to hold his position.

The situation in Bali was now becoming tense. People who had previously been silenced by Bung Karno now began to speak out. News of the killings in Central and East Java began to spread in Bali. In Jakarta Bung Karno still held the highest position of state, but Pak Harto was beginning to take control. At the beginning of November, still no arrests had been made. While Puger (PKI) was busy with his guests from KIAPMA,[5] Kompyang and Kandel went to Jakarta several times to assess the situation. Now people began to get impatient and ask why no action was being taken against PKI dignitaries. The people were waiting to see what the Armed Forces would do to solve the situation. But it seemed that the military leaders in Bali, especially Syafiudin, wanted to see how things developed, and to see who was going to win the power struggle going on in Jakarta, Sukarno or Suharto, the Nasakom or the Pancasila group.[6] Syafiudin, with reptilian cunning, saw which way the wind was blowing, and perhaps he realised that history wanted the Pancasila group to win. Eventually, sooner or later, the time would come when Bung Karno would be pushed aside.

Survival is a very strong motive for action. To succeed, one has to cover one's tracks and leave no traces. Killing is the easiest and safest way to do this, because dead people do not speak. For the Nasakom clique which was in power in Bali at that time, mass killing was the way to show the outside world, especially Jakarta, that they were strongly anti-PKI and strongly pro-Pancasila. [Dewa Made] Wedagama,[7] a PNI figure, incited the people to violence by saying that God approved of the killing of PKI people, and that the law would not condemn people for it. Wijana,[8] another figure close to Bung Karno, told the people that taking property belonging to the PKI did not break the law. Thus the leaders who had been the strongest supporters of Nasakom were now the strongest and most active PKI haters.

Vigilante groups began roaming around dressed in black and armed with swords, knives, cudgels, and even firearms. Houses of people accused of being PKI were burnt as part of the warming up for much crueler actions. Then the killings began everywhere. For the next three months, Bali became a nightmare of killing. If there is anyone amongst my readers who has a Balinese friend, ask him if he has a friend who became a victim of this bloodbath. He will certainly answer affirmatively, because that was the reality of the situation in Bali. There is no-one living in Bali now who does not have a neighbor who was killed and left unburied by the black devils with red berets who roamed about at that time.

By the most conservative estimate, at least eighty thousand people were killed, including young and old, men and women. The burning of houses and the amount of property either destroyed by fire or lost in robberies cannot be estimated. Rape of women accused of being members of Gerwani occurred everywhere, the example being set by local party leaders. The most monstrous example was Widagda, a PNI leader from Negara, and a younger brother of Wedastra Suyasa, a leading Balinese PNI figure who was a member of the DPRGR at the national level.[9] He raped tens of women who had been accused without basis [of being PKI]. Three of them brought a case to court last March and in a decision given in June 1967 Widagda was sentenced to three years in jail in Negara. [. . .]

The killings which occurred in Bali were not *sportariffet* but something which was just left to go on.[10] If the government or officials had really wanted to stop them, then the killings need not have occurred. But government officials did absolutely nothing. In fact, they even initiated the killings in some areas. We can understand the reason for this from the above analysis. The killings in Bali were supported and allowed to go on unchecked by officials who were affiliated with the PKI. By supporting the killings they could wash their hands of any involvement with the PKI.

Notes

1. *Tapol* is an abbreviation of *Tahanan Politik*, Political Prisoner.

2. *Gerwani,* an abbreviation of *Gerakan Wanita Indonesia,* is the Indonesian Women's Movement that had ties with the Communist Party. *PGRI Non Vaksentral,* an abbreviation of *Persatuan Guru Republik Indonesia,* is a Teachers' Union.

3. *Partindo,* an abbreviation of *Partai Indonesia,* is a political party. *DPRD* stands for *Dewan Perwakilan Rakyat Daerah,* the Regional House of Representatives.

4. Brigadier-General Mohammad Sabur was commander of the palace guard; Major-General Sumarno Sosroatmojo was governor of Jakarta; I Gusti Gde Subamya was chairperson of the national Gotong Royong People's Representative Council (DPRGR); Chaerul Saleh was second deputy prime minister.

5. KIAPMA, *Konferensi Internasional Anti-Pangkalan Militer Asing,* is the International Conference against Foreign Military Bases, held mid-October 1965.

6. Nasakom (*nasionalisme, agama* [religion], and *komunisme*) was the formula employed by Sukarno to reconcile and unite the major conflicting groups in Indonesian politics.

7. Dewa Made Wedagama was third chairperson of the PNI-affiliated National Students' Movement of Indonesia.

8. A leader of the Balinese resistance to the Dutch in the 1940s, Wijana was a major figure on the left wing of the PNI.

9. DPRGR, *Dewan Perwakilan Rakyat Gotong Royong,* stands for the "Mutual Assistance" House of Representatives.

10. It is not clear what Soe Hok Gie meant by this term.

Suharto, My Thoughts, Words, Deeds

Suharto

Two weeks after the 1965 coup attempt, Major General Suharto was promoted to the army chief of staff. With President Sukarno's waning political power Suharto maneuvered to seize emergency governing powers. The presidential letter of March 11, 1966, that gave him supreme authority to restore peace and order is known in its abbreviated form of Supersemar, referring to the indigenous Javanese deity Semar who appears in the wayang as Arjuna's servant-clown. As Indonesia's second president from 1967 to 1998, Suharto was often compared to a fourteenth-century Javanese king in the way he used spiritual strength to project an aura of omnipotence. Although a devout Muslim, Suharto was also a true believer in Javanese mysticism, meditation, and contemplation to gain and maintain personal and political power. He would seek religious advice from occult leaders and traditional seers. Because Suharto managed to solidify his power over the years, a personality cult began to take root. Suharto was rumored to be of aristocratic descent as Indonesians could not believe that someone of his stature could be anything less. Yet Suharto wanted to set the record straight about his humble family background in a central Javanese village. In this selection he presents himself as an honest man with high moral standards, which appears ironic in the face of the corruption charges leveled against him and his children after 1998.

It never occurred to me that one day I would have to clarify my family descent, but it so happened that in October 1974 someone fabricated a story about me in a magazine. I told Dipo to counter the story by denying it in other magazines and newspapers in Jakarta.[1] A day later I summoned reporters to my office at Bina Graha.[2] I wanted to explain personally about my real family tree. I told both local and foreign reporters that in no way had I descended from the nobility, and with some elderly people, living witnesses who knew for certain of my actual family background, convinced them of the truth.

I said I was the son of Bapak Kertosudiro,[3] who was known as Kertorejo, an irrigation officer who did not even own one handful of land. I told them honestly that in my childhood I had to endure such suffering which perhaps others could not imagine. [. . .] The story goes like this: After I was born,

President Suharto's family. From left to right: Sigit, Bambang, Suharto, Tommy, Ibu Tien Suharto, Mamiek, Titik, Tutut. O. G. Roeder, *The Smiling General* (Jakarta: Gunung Agung, 1969).

I didn't stay long with my mother. I was hardly forty days old when they took me to live with Mbah Kromodiryo,[4] because my mother was ill and could not breastfeed me. In Mbah Kromo's home Mbah Amat Iris often cared for me. Mbah Kromo helped me when I first stood up and began to walk. He often took me with him to work.

When my grandmother was called away as a midwife and could not take me with her, I would accompany my grandfather to the paddy fields. Sometimes he carried me on his back while working the land, and when I grew up, let me ride the plough. It was great fun, moments that I will always treasure, when I would sit on the plough and spur the buffalo on, steering them left or right. I would leap into the paddy field, playing in the water, getting covered in mud. When I became tired, I was told to wait at the ditch by the roadside. My days in the fields with Mbah Kromo also gave me the chance to catch eels, which were turned into a dish that I continue to like very much to this day.

When I turned four, and hadn't even begun to wear trousers yet, my mother, Ibu Sukirah,[5] took me back to stay with her and my stepfather, Pak Atmopawiro. I remember when my sister Sukyem died soon after she was born. A year later a healthy brother, Sucipto, was born, and other brothers and sisters followed.

One day I was playing with my cousin, Darsono, in front of the house of Mbah Buyut Notosudiro, my mother's grandfather.[6] Great-grandmother had just made a shirt and asked me to try it on, and I felt so happy. Suddenly, though, she took a closer look at me and exclaimed, "Oh, you're Harto. Get your cousin, Darsono." Mbah Buyut told me to let Darsono try on the shirt and then told him it was his; it wasn't meant for me. I was devastated. My heart cried, "Mbah Buyut loves Darsono more than me." In fact, he was the son of a well-to-do family, my aunt's boy. His parents were much better off than mine. So why did my great-grandmother give the shirt to a boy who already had enough? I felt humiliated, hurt, very forlorn, and sad. I wondered why life was like this? I thought, we were both her great-grandchildren. Why were we treated differently? Darsono already had enough shirts. I didn't. Why did great-grandmother make one for him and not for me?

Fate decided that I had to move from one school to another. I began at a school in the village of Puluhan in Godean. Then I had to switch to a school at Pedes because my mother and stepfather had moved again to south Kemusuk. My father then decided to take me to Wuryantoro where he left me with my aunt, his only younger sister. I remember well what my father said to my uncle and aunt when he left me with them: "I leave Suharto with you. Please take care of him. I am afraid of what will become of him if he stays in Kemusuk. Therefore, I will be most grateful if my son can receive the education and upbringing that he deserves."

And so it was there that I was sent to school and received a better education than when I was in Kemusuk. I studied each subject diligently, especially math, which I liked so much and excelled in that I won special praise from the teacher. I also underwent serious religious training, because my uncle and his family were firmly steeped in the spiritual way of life.

However, hardly a year had gone by living with the Prawirowiharjo family when my stepfather and his brother along with his brother-in-law all came to see me to tell me that mother was longing for me. They promised they would let me return after *Lebaran*, the end of the fasting month of Ramadhan, when school would resume. But that promise was broken. I had to stay much longer at Kemusuk and went to school in the village of Tiwir. It was a year later when my uncle and aunt arrived to take me back to Wuryantoro to continue my education there.

Pak Prawiro's tireless work and creativity as an agricultural officer inspired me. I became more energetic and even won a contest in growing crops, coming in ahead of his sons in the categories of onions and garlic, which were rated the best. In the evenings, I learned to read the Koran at the *langgar*, a small house of worship. Often I stayed there all night reading with my friends.

The hardships of life that I had experienced, the family traditions, which strictly followed the teachings of our ancestors, my education at the Junior High School, as well as religious teachings all helped to shape my character. In addition I also received spiritual training from my foster father, such as fasting every Monday and Thursday and sleeping on the verandah of the house. I followed all his advice consistently and faithfully. But there was one suggestion I didn't take up—sleeping on a *pawuhan*, a burnt-rubbish dump. So that was the time when my character was formed and I was taught the family philosophy of life. I learned about religion and the Javanese way of life. There were three "don'ts": "Don't be easily surprised, don't be overwhelmed by anything, and don't overestimate your own position." These became the guiding principles of life which gave me strength to face problems which otherwise might have shaken me.

I always remember the teachings of our ancestors: respect for God, teacher, government, and parents. Even though I am the President, I have not changed in this way in the least. I always live up to these principles and advice, because I believe in their truth.

Editors' Notes

1. Dipo is G. Dwipayana, Suharto's biographer.
2. Bina Graha is the office of the President.
3. *Bapak*, or *Pak*, literally means "father." It is also used to address a male who is considered one's senior.
4. *Mbah* is the Javanese word for grandfather or grandmother.
5. *Ibu* literally means "mother." It is also used to address a female who is considered one's senior.
6. *Mbah Buyut* is Javanese for great-grandfather or great-grandmother.

Student Demonstrations

R. Slamet Iman Santoso

In the turmoil of political change and social unrest of 1965 students took to the streets in large numbers to demonstrate against the Sukarno government and against communist activities. They showed that they could rally the crowds to make their voices heard. At the time R. Slamet Iman Santoso was a professor and prominent public intellectual at the Faculty of Psychology at the University of Indonesia. Below he relates his personal experiences, his ignorance, and his nonpolitical stance. His account speaks volumes about the chaotic circumstances and the potential for misinterpretations of the situation on different sides.

By the end of 1965 the most dangerous phase of the political upheaval had ended. Nevertheless, rampant social disorders were still pervasive, and a strong popular movement demanding change rose up, later known as TRITURA (Three Demands of the People). Several student organizations were formed in conjunction with the movement, such as KAMI (Unity of Indonesian Student Action), KAPPI (Indonesian Student Youth Action Group), while faculty members established KASI (Indonesian Scholar Action Group). As for myself, I did not have any interest in politics, so I did not join any of these groups. I would just do my daily job while at the same time trying not to let the political turmoil disrupt my overall work.

In the context of TRITURA there were rumors that the Minister of Education was abducted and detained at the Faculty of Medicine for interrogation by students. It can possibly be compared with "hazing." I was most worried that the Faculty of Medicine was used as KAMI's headquarters. For this reason Air Force personnel heavily guarded the complex, but even such a precautionary step seemed to be a half-hearted one. The street in front of the Salemba campus was heavily barricaded, but the short cut that connects the campus with the general hospital was left totally unguarded. It was all just a ploy. And when Mrs. Ahmad Yani came with food supplies for KAMI members, she did not have any trouble getting through the barricade.[1] The security postings lasted three days, thereafter no guard was to be found anywhere. It was a free for all!

One day the Minister of Higher Education summoned all the KAMI members to a meeting at the Faculty of Psychology. Since at the initial stage of its establishment KAMI had received support from the minister, naturally they all showed up. I attended the meeting as well. Unexpectedly the minister ordered that KAMI stop all the demonstrations and return to class. If they did not obey the order, everybody would face the consequences. The meeting was adjourned with the minister declaring, "I have just received this order from President Sukarno!" Of course, the meeting immediately turned into pandemonium. Fortunately, in such circumstances I could still do something to prevent matters from getting worse by helping the minister get out of the angry crowd of KAMI members into his car and back to his department office.

A few days after the incident, the students' and people's movements became even more widespread. Protestors halted all cars that happened to pass on the streets and punctured their tires. Strangely enough, they did not disturb my car. In fact, I was given free gasoline many times. Up to now, I am still baffled by this fact. I can only assume that it was my good fortune.

In early 1966 the popular movement grew bigger. One morning, it was before 7:30 a.m., I arrived at the Salemba campus and found the grounds totally deserted. Salemba Street, on the other hand, was jam-packed with people: commoners, youths, and students. The crowds crisscrossed in different directions back and forth. I had no idea what was going on and was curious, so I went with the flow of the huge masses, asking questions to anyone who wanted to answer. I gradually found out that they rallied in order to assert their popular demands: (1) cut down the prices of basic life necessities, (2) dissolve the cabinet of one hundred ministers, and (3) abolish the PKI (Indonesian Communist Party). These demands became known as TRITURA.

Similar rallies also took place in other parts of the capital city, such as Harmoni, CSW (Kebayoran Baru), Tanjung Priok, and Tangerang. Among those whom I ran across in the crowd was Abdul Gafur.[2] When I asked around who organized the mass rally, how it was organized, and what the next goals would be, no one could provide me with the answers. As none of my questions was answered, all along the way I tried to explain to the huge crowd that their actions would only lead to temporary results. A popular action that relied on nothing else but zest and ardor would eventually disappoint those who had built up high expectations. I tried to cool down the atmosphere by warning them that this was only a temporary surge of emotion with no certain, clear objectives. Suddenly, when I got to Matraman Street, I was arrested by two police officers and brought back to the Salemba campus. As we entered the Rector's office (at that time the Rector was in Germany as part of an Indonesian official delegation), I learned that three government officials had been waiting for me since 7:30 a.m. They were Jakarta's Vice-Governor, Jakarta's Police Chief, and Jakarta's Garrison Commander. They required information about the student rallies taking place on Salemba Street: who masterminded them and who were the leaders.

Based on the limited information obtained from the masses before I got arrested, I told them that similar rallies were happening in various parts of the capital and not only in front of the Salemba campus. Subsequently they made several phone calls, which confirmed the information I had given them. What is ridiculous, stupid, and funny at the same time was that, while I was talking to the three officials, the two police officers who had arrested me contacted the Police Headquarters and the Palace to report that "Professor Slamet Iman Santoso is the intellectual actor behind of the rally and he was already arrested in Matraman area!" As a result, all this time I was officially stigmatized as a stupid, old troublemaker!

In the afternoon as I drove home, no one stopped my car at all, and all along the way home the masses shouted "Long live, Mr. Slamet!" Again, I felt amused, annoyed, foolish, and baffled mixed into one because personally I thought that I was never involved in anything and completely ignorant of what happened.

Translated from Indonesian by M. Budiman

Editors' Notes

1. She is the widow of General Ahmad Yani, who was assassinated on September 30, 1965.
2. Abdul Gafur later became Minister of Youth and Sports.

Cartoons *Sjahrir*
as Chair of KAMI

Sebagai aktivis Sjahrir pernah menjadi Ketua KAMI FE UI, kemudian menjadi ketua bidang kemahasiswaan KAMI Jakarta Raya. Sesudah itu dia menjadi salah seorang ketua KAMI Pusat sebagai wakil dari Sekretariat Bersama Organisasi Mahasiswa Lokal (Somal). Sjahrir terus-menerus menjalani kegiatan KAMI sampai dengan tahun 1969.

– 42 –

Cartoon of Sjahrir as president of the KAMI student organization. *Sjahrir* (Jakarta: Perhimpunan Indonesia Baru, 2004).

"As an activist, Sjahrir was elected the president of KAMI FE UI *(Faculty of Economics, University of Indonesia), then the vice-president for* KAMI *Student Affairs of Greater Jakarta. Later he served in the leadership of* KAMI's *Central Chapter in his capacity as representative of the Joint Secretariat of Local Student Organizations (Somal). Sjahrir was active in* KAMI *until 1969."*

Pada 1969 di dalam tubuh KAMI timbul perbedaan pandangan tentang kelanjutan kesatuan aksi itu yang akhirnya membuat KAMI praktis tidak efektif lagi. Pada tahun itu Somal bersama Persatuan Mahasiswa Katolik Republik Indonesia (PMKRI) menarik diri dari KAMI, dengan alasan tidak ada lagi issue yang dapat mempertemukan semua organisasi mahasiswa yang tergabung dalam kesatuan aksi itu.
- 46 -

Somal: "I'm out … It's no longer fun!!" PMKRI: "Me, too!!" *Sjahrir* (Jakarta: Perhimpunan Indonesia Baru, 2004).

"In 1969 KAMI experienced internal frictions regarding the organization's future, and in practice KAMI was losing its effectiveness. That year, Somal and the Association of Indonesian Catholic Students (PMKRI) withdrew from KAMI as a result of the lack of a common platform uniting all student organizations encompassed by KAMI at that time."

Our Struggle against Indonesian Aggression

Republica Democratica de Timor Leste

On December 7, 1975, Indonesian armed forces invaded East Timor. The former Portuguese colony was subsequently annexed as Indonesia's twenty-seventh province. From April 1974 onward, when Portugal witnessed a change in regime, the two most significant nationalist parties that came to the fore were the Timorese Democratic Union (UTD) and the left-wing Revolutionary Front for an Independent East Timor (FRETILIN). The latter enjoyed greater popular support and pushed more strongly for decolonization. On December 6, 1975, Suharto received the American president Gerald Ford and the secretary of state Henry Kissinger in Jakarta. During their meeting the latter two assured the Indonesian president that they would not press him on East Timor. They condoned the integration of East Timor into Indonesia and basically gave the green light for a military occupation. As a result, FRETILIN launched a guerilla war that would last until independence in 2002.

Statement delivered to the Fourth Committee of the United Nations General Assembly by the Delegation of FRETILIN and the Government of the Democratic Republic of East Timor

Abílio da Conceição Abrantes de Araújo, Member of the Central Committee of FRETILIN and Minister of State for Economic and Social Affairs (Head)

Olimpio Maria Alves Gomes Miranda Branco, FRETILIN's Representative

New York, 1978

"While a single Indonesian soldier exists on the soil of the Democratic Republic of East Timor, irrigated with the blood of heroes, we will continue to shout: 'Down with Indonesian colonial expansionism!'" (East Timor 20/5/78)

Nicolau Lobato, President of FRETILIN, President of D.R.E.T.

It is clear that not only the Indonesian arguments but mainly, its expansionist and militarist repressive practice, succeeds in showing the inconsistency and weakness of the Indonesian government both in the international arena and in East Timor.

Mr. Chairman, Distinguished Delegates,

The people of East Timor, under the leadership of their sole legitimate representative, the Central Committee of FRETILIN, greeted with enthusiasm the three General Assembly and two Security Council resolutions. These United Nations resolutions, calling for the total and complete withdrawal of Indonesian forces from East Timor and rejecting the claim that East Timor has been integrated in the Republic of Indonesia, constitute, no doubt, major victories for the people of East Timor as well as for all peoples, countries, and nations represented here.

These resolutions are also a victory of this organization since they reflect the correctness of its members in the understanding of the justness of East Timorese people's struggle. But, overall, these resolutions are a shameful defeat for the government of Indonesia in spite of its gigantic efforts to prove that black is white and bullets are bread.

Nevertheless, Mr. Chairman, Distinguished Delegates, what have we witnessed? We have witnessed a persistent refusal on the part of the government of Indonesia to comply with the relevant United Nations resolutions. We have witnessed an arrogant defiance directed at the international community by the government of Indonesia. We have witnessed all this and as if that wasn't enough, we are witnessing a brazen arrogance on the part of the government of Indonesia which carries on its annexacionist policy, and here, in the United Nations tries to present the East Timor question as a "fait accompli." This Indonesian action can only be seen as an attempt against the United Nations organization and an insult to all peoples, countries, and nations represented here.

Mr. Chairman, Distinguished Delegates, we consider the armed struggle against Indonesian expansionism as the determining and decisive factor in our global struggle. The people of East Timor have chosen the road of armed resistance in order to safeguard the sovereignty and the territorial integrity of their independent state, and to safeguard their national identity, forged in the course of their centuries-old struggle against Portuguese colonialism. Further, we are certain that the armed struggle now being waged on our soil is a guarantee that the people of East Timor are offering all those—peoples, countries, and nations—who in the course of these three years stayed on their side.

It is a guarantee because by not laying down our weapons but by fighting until the final victory, we also support all those, who, now, defend the cause of our people, who don't betray the principles enshrined in the United Nations Charter and don't trade away the fundamental principles of international relations and of the rights of the peoples. Therefore, it is with great pleasure that we inform this distinguished committee that the East Timorese National Liberation Armed Forces control at this point in time some 85 percent of the territory and that 90 percent of our people live in the liberated areas. However, this positive balance registered in the beginning of the fourth year of wide people's resistance against the Indonesian occupying forces cannot conceal a bitter and difficult reality.

Indeed the people of East Timor have undergone enormous sacrifices in the defense of their just cause of liberation. The government of Indonesia has resorted to all military capacity to exterminate the people of East Timor. The resort to massive war machinery ranging from heavy land and naval artillery to air force to effect bombing raids against defenseless peoples and the use of chemical weapons to destroy crops, is a clear evidence of the aggressiveness and of a primitive disrespect of the most fundamental human rights.

It is clear that in present circumstances facing the government of Indonesia, namely its external debt over 12 billion dollars, the war would have ended with consequent victory of the people of East Timor. This has not happened yet because some United Nations member states have echoed Indonesian claims over East Timor and have stepped up their arms sales and military assistance to the military government of Indonesia.

Mr. Chairman, Distinguished Delegates, the Central Committee of FRETILIN and the government of the Democratic Republic of East Timor basing itself on the fundamental rules of international relations among states do not comment on policies of other states. We feel compelled to speak out only when from a sovereign act effected by two states disastrous consequences are created and affect our people and threaten regional and international peace.

We are talking about the sale of weaponry by some countries, particularly the U.S.A., to the Republic of Indonesia. It is widely known that the government of Indonesia made large use of American weapons in its war of aggression against East Timor. The situation becomes more serious when one knows that while Indonesia could not win the war in East Timor with the weaponry available to her in the initial period following the invasion, the U.S.A. government delivered to Indonesia a squadron of sixteen OV-10 Bronco, a counter-insurgency plane largely used in Vietnam. More recently the U.S.A. authorized the sale of twelve F5-E Bombers to Jakarta. Last but not least, Mr. Walter Mondale promised the sale of another squadron of A4 Bombers to Gen. Suharto following his visit to Indonesia.

Last August, we reported to the special committee on the situation with regard to the implementation of the declaration on the granting of independence to colonial countries and peoples, that in addition to quantities of American arms, there was direct American involvement in the Indonesian aggression. Americans have been acting as military advisors to the Indonesian army in East Timor, and run two training camps. One at Laklubar and one at Aileu, where they train Indonesian soldiers. They also have been flying Bronco aircraft and repairing damaged planes. In August, an American was shot by FALINTIL [Forças Armadas da Libertação Nacíonal de Timor-Leste] forces while he was on maneuvers with the Indonesian troops. But an Indonesian helicopter quickly recovered his body to prevent our forces from identifying him.

Social Issues and Cultural Debates

The political directions taken by Sukarno and Suharto, respectively, had an acute impact on society and culture. The revolutionary spirit of the Generation of 1945 and its members' claims as heirs of a world culture faded away with the untimely death of Chairil Anwar and the completion of a sovereign Indonesian nation-state. Reflections on universality and human dignity led to skepticism and a sense of the artist's necessary honesty and loneliness. The aesthetics of socialist realism and accompanying communist ideas of how art should function in society and serve commoners and the working classes also appeared in Indonesia. In 1950 the Institute of People's Culture (Lembaga Kebudajaan Rakjat, or Lekra) was founded as an organization for Marxist intellectuals, writers, and artists. Their publications appeared in the cultural magazine *Zaman Baru* (*New Era*) and the cultural supplement of the newspaper *Bintang Timur* (*Eastern Star*). One of the prominent Lekra spokespeople was the prolific writer Pramoedya Ananta Toer.

While the nation was trying to find its political bearings during the first decade of independence, the search for a national identity through cultural and intellectual expressions intensified. It did not take long before different ideologies clashed, sometimes violently. With the increased political weight of the Communist Party that received support from Sukarno, Lekra's position in the cultural world became more influential. Socialist realism and the artistic mandate of returning to the countryside to empathize with farmers, villagers, and proletarians were strongly promoted. By the early 1960s those who opposed Lekra directives as too restrictive and oppressive began to speak out. Twenty intellectuals and artists signed and published the "Cultural Manifesto" ("Manifes Kebudajaan" or "Manikebu") in which they advocated freedom of expression, diversity of cultural production, and aesthetic creativity. This manifesto was declared illegal by presidential decree and the so-called Manikebuists were silenced.

The shift in political power in 1965 meant sweeping cultural changes. As a result of Suharto's condemnation of the communists as masterminds behind the coup and of the mass arrests and executions that followed, Lekra was eliminated, its members killed or detained as political prisoners. Like many others Pramoedya was arrested in 1965. After four years of imprisonment on Java he was exiled to Buru Island in the Moluccas. He and his fellow prisoners, mostly intellectuals, suffered tremendously. They were stripped of their human dignity and found themselves completely at the mercy of their military commanders. The last detainees left Buru in 1980, but many of them were placed under house arrest. Pramoedya's books remained banned until Suharto's fall from power.

Suharto's regime was military in nature, authoritarian and repressive. Neighboring countries went down a similar route: in the Philippines Ferdinand Marcos (1966–86) declared martial law in 1969 to remain in power, and Singapore's prime minister Lee Kuan Yew (1959–90) ruled with an iron fist, silencing anyone who opposed his People's Action Party. In the immediate aftermath of Indonesia's coup the Chinese, overseas as well as local, saw themselves targeted for their supposed affiliation with communism. Chinese families, some of them Chinese Indonesian (*peranakan*), who had settled in the archipelago for generations, were all of a sudden set apart and discriminated against. Schools were closed to Chinese children and restrictions were placed on Chinese language, religions, and customs. The New Order's commitment to economic growth meant an interest in utilizing domestic Chinese capital. A *cukong* system became common practice in which "a skilful Chinese businessman closely cooperates as a middleman with those [Indonesians] in power, especially the military."[1] In such alliances Chinese entrepreneurs emerged as less vulnerable, and their Indonesian partners would benefit economically.

As Suharto's grip on the country continued and the political dominance of his Golkar party was guaranteed, an increasingly oppressive discourse of national unity and conformity took over everyday life. Civil servants, their wives, and children from elementary school up to university students were indoctrinated with special courses on Panca Sila ideology that now had come to mean the security of the nation-state and was directly identified with the president and the armed forces. A well-established bureaucracy and the omnipresent military enforced stability; the police locked up or eliminated dissidents, silencing protest. Suharto was a devout Muslim, yet he suppressed Islamic fundamentalism that might challenge his New Order regime. State censorship was a given for creative writers, journalists, and television and radio programmers. On campuses students and scholars had to comply with limitations on freedom of speech and on critical thinking.

As the president took on the role of the ultimate father figure, paternalism, patriarchal standards, and the family principle formed the underlying guidelines for the state and for social organization. An official gender ideology was formulated through the Five Duties of Women (Panca Dharma Wanita, 1974). These principles defined women in their primary roles of loyal and supportive wives, nurturing mothers, and caretakers of the household. Even today for most Indonesians, women's ultimate destination is to be married and produce future generations. Parents have not fulfilled their obligations as long as their daughters remain unmarried. With double sexual standards firmly in place, men (fathers, husbands) will guard female virginity and sexuality while they themselves are allowed polygamous and promiscuous relationships. Young divorcees or widows are often shunned, as they are sexually experienced but no longer under male supervision. Female sex workers can be found at all social levels, but the most destitute live in impoverished conditions with few opportunities to change their future.

Ironically, in contradiction to the official Panca Dharma Wanita policy, women in rural areas entered the labor force in droves in the 1970s and 1980s due to industrial growth and the development of a modern manufacturing sector. Companies attracted young, single females with little or no education. They often worked on a production line in a tedious routine with minimum wages. Women were considered docile employees, easy to exploit and to discipline if necessary. They generally remained unaware of labor laws and their rights, but even if they knew their rights, state politics protected management and capitalist gains and condoned corrupt practices. With trade unions suppressed, no organization existed that could protect workers, individually or collectively.

By the mid-1990s Suharto had ruled the country for three decades. Much had changed since 1965: Indonesia was more prosperous, living standards had improved, and an urban class that could afford consumer goods and both domestic and international travel had emerged. On the surface political life was calm and society unperturbed. Yet clearly discontent and suppressed criticism bubbled underneath a layer of outward complacency. When the widely read magazine *TEMPO* published a disparaging article on a government purchase of used German warships, the government responded by banning it together with two other weeklies. The public was outraged at this blatant act of censorship and demonstrated its support for the silenced journalists. Others expressed their condemnation through creative writing and theatre performances. In April 1998 Ayu Utami, a young female novelist, made her debut with her book *Saman*. The novel critiques New Order practices of intimidation and oppression. One month later Suharto was forced to resign.

Note

1. O. G. Roeder, quoted in Leo Suryadinata, *Pribumi Indonesians, the Chinese Minority, and China* (Singapore: Heinemann Asia, 1992), 140.

Cultural Workers Must Lead the Way

Amya Iradat

In 1950 a small group of mostly Marxist artists, critics, and intellectuals founded the Institute of People's Culture (Lembaga Kebudajaan Rakjat, or Lekra). Linked to the Communist Party Lekra strongly reacted against the concept of so-called universal humanism that Chairil Anwar and his Angkatan 1945 adhered to. While committed to creating a national culture based on various regional art forms, Lekra adhered to socialist realism and anti-imperialism. Two important slogans were "Moving Down" (among the people) and "Politics Is the Commander," both indicating the organization's political commitment to ordinary people, farmers, and proletarians. In their creative work Lekra artists displayed a combination of realism and revolutionary romanticism, although the idea of marrying these two concepts apparently never became a strict command. Amya Iradat, whose identity is unknown—it may be a pseudonym—published in the leftist daily newspaper Bintang Timur *(Eastern Star, 1958–65), which became one of Lekra's mouthpieces with its weekly page on cultural affairs.*

Bintang Timur, *August 25, 1961*

Someone with a big heart must be able to transcend the period in which he lives and work harder for the sake of common interests. Only then a genial human being will be born, as a result of struggle and unrelenting hard work. Without sacrifice there is no gain. Therefore, only through enormous efforts can we pick the fruits of our labor. Let us not only make demands but also prove through our deeds that we deserve respect. As cultural workers we must be steadfast. As individuals who have a long-term vision, we must know the path we will tread. We cannot be like those who toil without knowing what they are doing, like a wobbling cart that has lost a wheel.

Under the banner of art for the People we move forward together. And upon our shoulders rest victory or downfall, as well as the success or failure of this conviction that we hold high. A true idealist must show loyalty and responsibility. To realize our dream of uniting ourselves under the same roof and within the same house, that is, art for the People, we cannot just sit idly and daydream indefinitely. Without courage and solid planning we will miss all the golden opportunities to crush the enemies of the People and national revolution. Thus, proletarian cultural workers must possess a mentality that is psychologically conditioned to be revolutionary. Without revolutionary ideas, we will not be able to aspire to achievements that boost the People's fighting spirit.

Everyone must be reminded that art for the People is not merely talking about the people, but also struggling for them and mobilizing their revolutionary potential. There are some who view workers and farmers as "weak" beings. Shame on them! Workers and farmers are, in fact, looked down upon as part of the proletariat by the clique of elites who enslaves them, as well as by other antiproletariat cliques. Thus, we must never allow artwork by them to claim itself as art for the People. In the implementation of Ampera, Manipol and Indonesian Socialism we must condemn such ruthlessness.[1] Isn't it true that only the working class, consisting of workers and farmers, is hardened in the storm of revolution and struggle against poverty and starvation? Cultural workers must not be afraid to face criticism or the turmoil of struggle. If possible, we must examine all truths thoroughly. To implement the struggle of art at the level of science we must do away with blind dogmatism.

As of recently many venomous predators have wanted to trap us, such as those who preach that art for the People is antireligion, anti-God, and so on. But to them, let me ask this question: Isn't the struggle to improve people's conditions in line with God's will upon his servants? Why trash the relationship between art and society with nonsensical theories? If, for instance, you cannot write for the people, or suffer from writer's block, take a break while trying to be more perseverant in your study.

A proletarian art worker must not only struggle for his own sake or for a particular time period, but for the sake of common basic rights that are timeless and ever-lasting. We support the People and are backed up by the People. Along the same lines we must exchange ideas more frequently, making use of our studies and training to be more familiar with people's problems and keep up with the progress of revolution so that we will find solutions. Only by being well versed in the basics of mass struggle can we debunk unscientific arguments of the cliques of chameleons and monkeys who do not take side with the glorious struggle of the People.

And what we must keep in mind is that we must not let ourselves be pitted against each other, but we must be able to make the leap forward as a shepherd and leader of the workers' and farmers' movement and national revolution. As such, by mobilizing the full potential of our people, our artists will be able to follow the example provided by cultural workers in socialist countries who strive to accomplish the proletarian revolution and bring about a just and prosperous society. This will be another blow struck by the geniuses to the cliques full of bourgeois anachronism and banditism of enemies of the People.

Translated from Indonesian by M. Budiman

Editors' Note

1. Ampera (*Amanat Penderitaan Rakyat*, or Message of the People's Sufferings) and *Manipol (Manifes Politik*, Political Manifesto) were policy directives announced by President Sukarno.

The 1963 Cultural Manifesto

The increasing influence of the Institute of People's Culture (Lekra) and its Marxist views on the role of the arts provoked a counterreaction among other writers, artists, and intellectuals who felt that their creativity and freedom of artistic expression were curbed and ideologically restricted. They refused to subscribe exclusively to l'art engagé, art that engaged with its audience to guide the masses, and they objected to being stigmatized as capitalist bourgeoisie or universal humanists for whom the revolution had failed. The different convictions were irreconcilable and the opposing groups clashed head-on after the publication of the "Cultural Manifesto" in 1963, which strongly opposed the straitjacket of a leftist-dominated cultural life. A number of signatories of this manifesto had to face the political consequences: they were silenced, their journals or magazines were banned, and H. B. Jassin in particular was forced to discontinue his position as a university lecturer.

- We, Indonesian artists and intellectuals, hereby proclaim a Cultural Manifesto, which affirms our position, aspiration and politics regarding the National Culture.
- For us, culture is a struggle to improve human's living conditions. We do not prioritize one cultural sector over another. Each sector struggles together with another for the sake of culture based on each respective uniqueness.
- In carrying out the National Culture we strive to be creative based on our truest commitment to the struggle to defend and foster our dignity as the Indonesian nation among the community of nations.
- PANCASILA is our cultural philosophy.

Jakarta, August 17, 1963

Drs. H. B. Jassin
Trisno Sumardjo
Wiratmo Soekito

Zaini
Bokor Hutasuhut
Goenawan Mohamad
A. Bastari Asnin
Bur Rasuanto
Soe Hok Djin
D. S. Moeljanto
Ras Siregar
Hartojo Andangdjaja
Sjahwil
Djufri Tanissan
Binsar Sitompul
Drs. Taufik A. G. Ismail
Gerson Poyk
M. Saribi Afn.
Poernawan Tjondronagoro
Dra. Boen S. Oemarjati

Translated from Indonesian by M. Budiman

The Chinese Minority in Indonesia

Leo Suryadinata

The issue of the Chinese minority and of the so-called peranakan (persons of Chinese Indonesian descent or locally born Chinese) is immensely complex and multifaceted. In the postindependence period the position of the Chinese in Indonesia shifted from one of marginalization, both social and political, during the Sukarno years to one of frequent stigmatization under Suharto's presidency. Historically, Chinese and peranakan played an active role in business, trade, and entrepreneurship, and many of them have been economically successful. A movement in 1956 aiming to protect and promote pribumi (indigenous Indonesian) enterprises and economic initiatives discriminated explicitly against the Chinese. The latter group has also been largely excluded from political office. In times of crisis the Chinese were, and still are, often targeted as a visible minority. Government-imposed assimilation policies forced the Chinese to revisit their identity, loyalties, customs, and religious beliefs. Leo Suryadinata, a scholar of Chinese-Indonesian descent based in Singapore, is an expert on this topic, on which he has authored numerous publications.

Indonesian educational policies have an "assimilationist" flavour. The reduction of the use of the Chinese language was a major objective. In April 1958, [A. H.] Nasution as the Commander-in-Chief of the Army issued a decree declaring that all newspapers published with other than Latin and Arabic letters would be forced to close. However, these newspapers would be allowed to operate again if they published in the Indonesian language. Following the announcement of the decree, a spokesman of the Army noted that the ban was aimed at "restricting the use of a language with which the Indonesian people are not familiar." The regulation, however, was later modified. A few Chinese newspapers were permitted to publish on the grounds that there was still a need for such newspapers in order to inform the Chinese about government policies, regulations, and other matters. But these newspapers were soon banned again. Only in 1963 when Sino-Indonesian relations were cordial, did Chinese language newspapers reappear, but this time they were

A Chinese family in a garden in Surabaya, 1900. Photo no. 6601, courtesy of KITLV, Leiden.

all owned by Indonesian nationals who were affiliated with existing political organizations. [. . .]

Use of the Chinese language in public was discouraged. For instance, the Pontianak local authorities held an "Indonesian Language Week" and urged the Indonesian citizens of Chinese extraction to abandon their use of Chinese. Not only was the Chinese language considered "harmful," but even Chinese religion and customs were regarded as undesirable. In December 1967, a Presidential Instruction was issued. It stated that

> Chinese religion, beliefs, and customs [in Indonesia] originated in their ancestral land and their various manifestations may generate unnatural influence on the psychology, mentality, and morality of Indonesian citizens and therefore impede natural propensity [for assimilation].

It was therefore instructed that Chinese religions could only be observed in the family circle. Religious and customary celebrations, if held in public, should not be conspicuous. This would be regulated by the Ministry of Religion upon the recommendation of the Attorney-General. [. . .]

The first difficulty arose from the Chinese communities themselves. Peranakan Chinese, in general, no longer speak Chinese and their culture has been heavily influenced by Western ideas and the Indonesian environment. Many of them are Protestants and Catholics. "Chinese culture" is quite alien to most of the peranakan Chinese, especially to the younger generation who have been required by law to go to Indonesian schools since 1957. Their way of thinking, therefore, is more Indonesian than Chinese.

In China, the Chinese are patrilineal; however, the peranakan kinship system is somewhat different. G. W. Skinner maintained that "no stigma whatsoever was attached to matri-locality. In Madura and West Java, the wedding was held and marriage consummated in the home of the bride's parents." It is also true that the daughter holds more esteem than the son in the peranakan family. In a society where the power of an elder son is not absolute, Confucian principles are not likely to prevail.

The clearest manifestation of the assimilationist principle in the cultural field was the name-changing regulation issued in December 1966. Before this, there was already a law (u.u. no.4/1961) which allowed Indonesian citizens of foreign descent to change their names to Indonesian (sounding) names. The applicant was required to obtain recommendation letters from governors or local *Bupati* (regents) and local police chiefs. Nonetheless, the law was not widely publicized and the government was not active in promoting this regulation.

In December 1966, however, the Suharto government simplified the procedure to encourage name-changing among Indonesian citizens of foreign descent (read: Chinese). The government was active in promoting name-changing and the regulation was also widely publicized. The regulation stated that the Indonesian government intended to accelerate the assimilation of Indonesian citizens of foreign descent into the "Indonesian nation"; changing non-Indonesian names into Indonesian ones was perceived as one way to speed up the assimilation process. Therefore, the government believed that Indonesian citizens who wanted to change their Chinese names to indigenous names should be given as many opportunities as possible.

According to the regulation, citizen Chinese who intended to change their names could simply submit their applications to local authorities (usually governors, *Bupatis*, or mayors) to be registered. A low fee would be charged for registration. These applications would be passed on to the Department of Justice. If no objection was raised by the local community in three months, the new name would become legal. This regulation would be effective from

January 1967 to March 1968. It was later postponed for one more year because citizen Chinese who changed their names were fewer than expected. In August 1969, the Department of Justice announced that only 232,882 persons had changed their names. Reasons for name-changing were varied. Some changed their names for practical reasons. They believed that it would make life in Indonesia easier (e.g., to get licenses, to get places in the schools or colleges, to be accepted by indigenous Indonesians). Some liked to identify with the "Indonesian nation." They genuinely believed that the solution of the "Chinese problem" was through complete assimilation. Others did not think that the Indonesian nation should be defined in terms of an indigenous Indonesian nation. They were proud of their ethnic origin and wanted to remain ethnic Chinese.

The Young Divorcee

Nh. Dini

Pressure on women to marry and have children remains powerful in Indonesia even now. Parents consider themselves a failure if their daughter has not found a proper spouse by the time she has reached her mid-twenties. A single woman of that age or older is considered an "old maid," an object of pity or ridicule. Parents and extended family members often make arrangements to avoid the embarrassment of an unwed daughter. Once married, women are to remain faithful to their husbands and to stick to their marriage. People treat a janda, a widow or a divorced woman, with circumspection, especially when she is young, as she is no longer tied to a husband yet has tasted the sexual pleasures of married life. Double sexual standards have long allowed men privileges and liberties denied to women. This holds particularly true in the case of Muslim men, as they can be polygamous, whereas women do not have that option. Even though sex and gender politics have evolved since independence sixty years ago, double standards that favor men are still firmly in place. The short story by Nh. Dini (born 1936), one of Indonesia's prolific women writers, depicts the fate of a young village woman.

Of the five children Warsiah had the best results at school, and her parents were proud of her. She was accepted at the Teacher's Training College. With the permission of her father she left the village and stayed for three years in a boarding house to attend classes. In fact, it wasn't too far away. There was a good bus connection between the two places. She could also take a train, for a cheaper fare even. But Warsiah would visit her family by bus during the holidays. She would get off on the side of the main road, close to her village.

During those three years Warsiah received a government scholarship with the stipulation that she be employed at a public school. Her father, who was moving on in age, suggested that his beloved daughter request to be placed in their village after she graduated. In her heart Warsiah aspired to see more of the city, to get to know other parts of the country. But she was not the type of woman to oppose her parents' wishes. She could understand that her family wanted to show her off. She became the village's first teacher since the revolution. A real educator in the family! How lofty! A woman who taught at the school in her family's village.

Three years had gone by, and Warsiah's father had been feeling concerned for quite a while. Since his admired daughter had returned home, she had devoted herself to her duty to provide a good education for the future generation. From year to year her father had hoped that a man would propose to her. One or two times a male colleague would come to visit. But they were just friends. He had noticed that his daughter was only interested in talking about school issues. The two of them had even accompanied students from the highest grade on a field trip to Borobudur. But nothing more had developed. He asked around, talking to neighbors who had eligible sons, and heard about a young man who was enrolled at the Technical University in West Java. This fellow had never been home since he left for college, but the two fathers often met at the coffee stand on the main road. They would talk about new sowing seed or other rice-growing issues. Warsiah's father could not find an opportunity to marry his daughter off to this university student until the time came that a new water reservoir was being constructed at the edge of the village. His heart pounded as if he himself was going to get married, when he saw the young man for first time after many years. He was happy, yet insecure. Eventually, in conversations with the chap's father, full of jokes and innuendo, the two men agreed to hire the shrewd Mak Sum, a middle-aged woman who prearranged marital but also extramarital relations. The matter did not take much time. Warsiah was an attractive daughter-in-law. Mak Sum planned a first meeting between the two. They knew each other from their childhood years. Many years had passed, and from children they had grown into young adults, each in his and her own environment.

Warsiah was happy. Then her father informed her the parents on both sides were preparing their marriage. The harvest time was approaching. The paddy fields would yield enough for the expenses as long as no plague of rats or pestilence happened. "This will be the last wedding we'll organize," he said. "The last and the biggest, because you're a teacher and your future husband will be an engineer."

Warsiah's initial admiration for the young man had developed into love and affection. When they were together in private, she trembled hoping for some intimacy. A stroke of his hand, an arm around her shoulders. But it never occurred. One time, at the movies, and another time in a pedicab in the rain, the young man had suddenly pulled her face toward him and kissed her the French way. His long and hot tongue had almost choked her and made her

A poster in an antipolygamy campaign. Courtesy of Koalisi Perempuan Indonesia untuk Demokrasi dan Keadilan.

throw up. He treated her roughly; she was shocked. But she did not dare to resist. She allowed him to embrace and touch her. But with her hand she nervously tried to find something to hold on to. This, too, was what happened when they ended up in a shelter on her father's paddy field. As the young man was passionately kissing her, Warsiah had not noticed that he had moved up her dress and that his hand freely caressed the curve between her thighs. She almost screamed when like an electric shock she felt his hand enter her sensitive parts. But her voice was smothered in her throat, gagged by her lover's mouth.

Warsiah knew nothing about sex education or sexuality. At the College no one mentioned anything about relations between men and women. But in the boarding house the women usually did exchange ideas and told each other what they had heard. The moment when Warsiah noticed for the first time that blood trickled down from a secret part of her body, she had sobbingly run to her mother. Her mother had calmed her and informed her that this was normal when girls matured. Her sisters and female relatives started to make jokes and friendly insinuations. They held a ritual meal to celebrate that she had entered the stage of adulthood. That day she had received various special presents.

The wedding took place with much splendor. There were all kinds of performances. Both families had exhausted the complete harvest of that year, and they had mortgaged next year's harvest as well. It did not matter if they had to pay off their debts in the years to come. Most important was that their fellow villagers would not easily forget such a grand wedding celebration.

Six months passed by. The completion date for the water reservoir was approaching. The new husband was about to finish his practical and to return to the city to continue his studies. After consultation with the families they agreed that he would go back by himself. Warsiah would wait for him in the village, living with her in-laws. Once a month she would send him some extra travel money—he still was a student after all—so that he could come and visit her.

Time progressed slowly. For Warsiah every day meant waiting for a letter or some news. One month, two, three months. All went well as planned. But in the fourth month she tragically miscarried after a two-month pregnancy. From the hospital she went straight to her parents' home. It was as if from that moment onward she felt something had changed in her relationship with her husband. Another month went by without him visiting. In subsequent letters he wrote how busy he was with exams and other matters. Warsiah read the news about classes that took up all of his time without suspicion. At one point the families conferred again and proposed that Warsiah could possibly request a transfer to West Java. Strangely enough, it was her husband who strongly objected. He constantly emphasized her career and how attached she was to her village. He added he would not be able to focus on his studies if Warsiah lived with him.

Another month went by. During Lebaran her husband was in a faraway place.[1] Other months followed during which he remained absent. His letters arrived less and less frequently. When Warsiah lost her patience and decided not to write him anymore, her parents and in-laws interfered. "Such a university study isn't all that easy. You have to be patient. You must write him about how you're doing," one said. "Maybe he is not well. The poor boy, he is so far from home," said the other. Then Warsiah would give in again.

But at one point, her father-in-law decided to leave for West Java to meet with his son. As a proper daughter-in-law, Warsiah saw him off at the station. But she was not very hopeful. Her intuition told her that it was all over, that something had happened that she had sensed from the very beginning. Ten days later her father-in-law returned. In the evening he visited Warsiah's family accompanied by his wife. His face looked grim. It seemed the lines in his brow were deeper, the rings under his eyes had darkened. Speaking falteringly he related that his son's address was not the place where he lived. For days he had been searching for his son. In the end he had found him. Warsiah's husband turned out to be married to a West Javanese woman and to have a child with her. This was what her mother-in-law had feared all the time. Her motherly instinct had sensed it correctly. While her husband disclosed what he had found out, she sat silently, sobbing in a corner not daring to look her daughter-in-law in the eye. Warsiah also was speechless. Finally her father-in-law said that he and his wife felt completely embarrassed toward Warsiah, as well as toward everyone in the village, because their son's marriage to her had turned out to be his second. He did not come up with a solution. Then the two fathers started to debate and negotiate. They considered the Muslim law. The women remained silent. Warsiah listened to their discussion without uttering a word. Something hard and heavy pressed on her chest. But no tears welled up in her eyes.

"If Warsiah is willing to be his second wife, her husband will come home and stay here for a few days. His school is about to have a break," her father-in-law spoke. Warsiah did not immediately reply. Her father turned to her. Warsiah looked at her mother and said: "For months we haven't been living together. Also for months I have been providing for myself with my own salary. So, if I request a divorce, the Muslim law should grant it to me and my family." "Warsiah!" her father shouted. And her father-in-law declared, "It is better if you wait a few days. I understand this is not such a pleasant experience for you." Was being a second wife "not such a pleasant experience"? As gently as possible Warsiah repeated her wish. Her own mother and father did not say a word. But when the visit was over, they took turns trying to convince her to accept being a second wife. This way she would not lose face and not be subjected to slander and ridicule. But Warsiah did not change her mind. From when they had started dating, they had not belonged together.

She was only twenty-five, but she mostly socialized with older relatives. During excursions or meetings Warsiah had the opportunity to make new friends. For a short while she would feel happy to interact freely with her peers, without ulterior motives, even though her past would catch up with her. Young men preferred to hang out with women who did not use "Mrs." in front of their name. They were also very impressed by her degrees and diplomas. But Warsiah always faithfully used "Mrs." on all her official letters and papers, and that was exactly what scared young men away.

Every time the same scene repeated itself. Warsiah's optimism diminished. Wasn't there one man in this vast country who would treat her as a young woman, who would date her for who she was, to watch a movie or eat in a restaurant? Because of tragedy or misfortune—it depended how you viewed it—Warsiah had been married and lost her virginity. She was no longer a virgin because of a man! She remained hopeful. Every time there was a party or special occasion she dressed up and took much care of her appearance. Female charm made women attractive, she could count on that.

Translated from Indonesian by T. Hellwig

Editors' Note

1. Lebaran is the celebration at the end of the fasting month of Ramadan; it is the most important holiday in the Muslim calendar, during which families traditionally gather.

Tracing the Twilight of Jakarta

Yuyu A. N. Krisna

In 1979 Yuyu A. N. Krisna, a female reporter with a prominent newspaper, researched the sex trade in the nation's capital and surrounding areas. She visited and interviewed sex workers in different parts of the greater Jakarta area and published the results of her investigation in a small book titled Tracing the Twilight of Jakarta. *It relates the dire circumstances in which the women live, the widening gap between haves and have-nots, and the relations between the brothel owners and their employees. Even though some women find opportunities to develop professional skills, most of them cannot break away to escape poverty's constraints.*

Boker, Cijantung—It was a rather quiet afternoon.[1] The red-light district of Cijantung, which is very much alive at night, saw only two red Citroens 1220 GS, a white Cortina sedan, and the car that I drove that afternoon. The district is not directly visible from the main street that connects Jakarta and Bogor. There are some small kiosks across the street, which sell food, cigarettes, and household items. That afternoon all those kiosks were closed. We parked our car under a waru tree near a cigarette stall. Three parking boys came over and opened the car door for me. The parking lot of the complex is not very big and is surrounded by houses and entertainment bars.

Some women wearing housecoats were sitting in a house. But out of nowhere, from the right corner of where my car was parked, a woman in a low-cut pink blouse appeared. Her hair was loose, as if she had just washed it. She used a minimum of makeup and held a *kretek* clove cigarette between her fingers. She drew my attention and so I approached her.

"Looking for somebody, Ma'am?" she greeted me in a familiar manner.
I smiled at her but did not answer her question. I conversely asked her:
"Are you the owner of this house?"
"No. My madam lives behind this house. I'm not the owner. I'm just one of her workers!" she said.

"What's your name?"

"Yuli. Yuliana. Please come by at my place."

Both of us walked past the patios of several houses. The house where Yuli lives is partly made of bricks, and the walls are densely covered with moss. The pathway in front of the house is muddy and full of stagnant water. Apparently it had rained the night before. Then Yuli took me to sit in one of the foam rubber chairs covered by red plastic. They were tattered at places where the foam rubber burst out. Twenty chairs were arranged along the walls as if there were going to be a party. Only a dilapidated glass window separated the anteroom from a small bar on the left. The wooden pane was old and ridden with termites. There were three bedrooms near the anteroom. On the left next to the bar there were another four bedrooms.

The conditions of these seven rooms seemed to be poorer than those in Kramat Tunggak. In Kramat Tunggak, each bed had a pink bedsheet with bathroom en suite, as well as some other furniture. The only facility provided by the rooms in Boker Cijantung was a third-rate bed covered with a filthy bedsheet. There were two equally shabby pillows, two chairs, and a mirror hanging on the wall. A plastic pail and bottle containing water sat in one of the corners of the room. The stench was awful! It was so stuffy and humid that I could not tell what other nasty smells emanated from this room.

Such conditions were not only typical of the house where Yuli lived but they were also common in the other three houses.

Yuli's madam, Mak Asi, and her husband, Najab, started this business fifteen years ago. It is a family business. That afternoon, Imang, twenty-two, a handsome man, the son of Mak Asi from her previous husband, met us. A high school graduate he knew the metropolis situation very well. Imang accompanied me and Yuli and responded to my questions cordially.

"How much do your girls have to hand over to you?"

"Rp.1,500 for each customer!"[2]

"And what do they get in return?"

"Just a room in the conditions that you have seen. The room can only be used when there's a customer. All my girls live somewhere else. In addition to the room they receive a vaccination every Thursday morning. I have to spend Rp.10,500 every week for vaccinations. It doesn't matter how many of them get vaccinated at a time. Altogether there are twenty girls working here. But sometimes only ten of them show up for vaccination. Still, I have to pay Rp.10,500 to the health officer from the East Jakarta District Health Office."

"Are you married?"

"Yes, I am. I have two kids. We don't live in this complex. Only my mother and stepfather live here."

"Does your wife know that you work here?"

"Of course she does, Ma'am. This is our livelihood."

"Is it your own house or do you rent it?"

"It's our own house. My mother's."

"I heard the houses here are for rent."

"It's true. The one over there across the street belongs to an important person. A high-ranking official. His son is now in charge of it. Most of the houses here are for rent. Only we and two others have their own houses. We've been in business here for a long time!"

Yuli was quiet the whole time, patiently listening to my conversation with her boss, Imang.

"Yuli, have you worked here for long?"

"Yes, Ma'am. I've given birth to nine babies here."

"What? Nine? Are you married?"

"No."

"Whose babies are they?"

"Well, they could be anybody's. I don't know who the fathers of those nine kids are. There's just too many of them!" Yuli said, laughing.

I was rather moved. This girl seemed so happy telling me her life story, which I thought was quite bleak. But for her it was not a big deal. Yuli told her life story matter-of-factly. "I'm originally from *Betawi*, Ma'am.[3] My children live with their grandmother in Tangerang. Some were adopted by people."

I plunged into my own thoughts again. Life is really too hard to understand. On the one hand, people yearn to have children to make their happiness complete. I can testify from my own experience how difficult childbearing is. During the first three months of my pregnancy I suffered from extreme pain. Not to mention the delivery process, which most of the time ends up on the operation table. A caesarian operation. I envied her and at the same time felt sad for her. Imagine, Yuli gave birth to nine children and then she gave them away to other people!

"How many customers can you serve per night?"

"Well, it's tough nowadays, Ma'am. We're here from noon to 5:00 p.m. And then from 7:00 to 11:00 p.m. Before *Kenop* (aha, so she also had some knowledge about Kenop 15),[4] I could serve three to five customers from afternoon to nighttime. But now we're even lucky if we can get

one customer from afternoon till night. Sometimes there's no customer
at all!"

"What's the rate here?"

"It's all the same, Ma'am, Rp.5,000. The room charge is Rp.1,500 per day. So
I roughly collect Rp.3,500 for each service."

"Who are these customers?"

"Well, they come from different walks of life, Ma'am. There are even some
foreigners. As you might notice, there are fancy cars as well. They're
not the drivers. They're the car owners who just want to kill some time
here. Right in the middle of an afternoon like this! Can you believe it,
Ma'am?"

As we were having our conversation, a little girl in a white-and-green
school uniform came in with a pile of books and folders. She wore white
socks and shoes. She looked pretty cute. But my first impression that she was
just a common schoolgirl was suddenly gone as I saw her lips painted bright
red. Her nails were as red as her lips. Like Yuli, the little girl was a smoker.

"Ma'am, this is Sri Nurhaeni. She just got back from a dressmaking course.
Here you can take various vocational courses which are administered by the
East Jakarta District Social Welfare Office," Yuli introduced Sri to me.

"Yul, Yul, now I know how to cut fabric, you know!" Sri told Yuli about her
progress in the dressmaking course. Yuli smiled. Then Sri went inside and did
not reappear. It seemed she had some business to do. A customer!

Translated from Indonesian by M. Budiman

Editors' Notes

1. Cijantung is located in the eastern part of Jakarta.

2. Less than U.S. $2.50 at the currency rate in 1979.

3. *Betawi* stands for Batavia, the colonial name for Jakarta. *Betawi* people have their roots in
this city and are not otherwise ethnically defined (as Javanese, Sundanese, etc.).

4. *Kenop* or *Kenop 15* is the abbreviation of *Kebijaksanaan November* (15th November Policy),
which refers to an economic policy issued by the government on November 15, 1979, that
devalued the Rupiah as much as almost half of its initial rate against the U.S. Dollar prior
to the policy.

The Mute's Soliloquy

Pramoedya Ananta Toer

The prolific novelist and essayist Pramoedya Ananta Toer was a political prisoner (tapol) under three different regimes. First, the Dutch imprisoned him in 1947. Under Sukarno he ended up in jail in 1960–61 after the publication of a book on the Chinese. Yet his longest period of incarceration began in October 1965 when he was accused of communist sympathies and labeled a "B" category tapol, that is a prisoner who was suspected of being involved in the coup but whose case would take time to build. Pramoedya was a Lekra member and one of the fiercest opponents of those who signed the "Cultural Manifesto" ("Manifes Kebudayaan"). In 1969 he was exiled to a penal colony on Buru Island in the Moluccas with thousands of fellow prisoners who were forced to do hard physical labor under incredibly poor living conditions. Initially Pramoedya was not allowed to read or write, and no reading materials, paper, or pens were available. As he had done research on nationalist awakening in the early 1900s, he created a fictional story based on the life of a journalist and shared it orally with his camp mates. When the head of the National Security Command gave him permission to write in 1973, he typed up four novels, later published as "The Buru Quartet." He also scribbled down fragmentary notes about his experiences on Buru that appeared as a memoir after his release in 1979.

My daughter Rita,

I received your letter of July 1977. It's really too bad that you weren't able to go to Surabaya. I lived there once, for quite some time, but the last time I visited the city was in 1964 when I was on a tour of Java. I can't say I like Surabaya very much. For me, it's a bit like Medan—I just don't feel comfortable there.

You said that you're not interested in seeing Borobudur and Prambanan? Why not? A visit to those two ancient temples would provide a good lesson for you on what your ancestors were able to do. There's nothing to see in Surabaya, it's just hurly-burly, but at Borobudur you can study reliefs that depict the lives of your ancestors in the eighth century: their houses, ships, clothing, tools, and customs. The temple presents a display of their wealth of knowledge, including at least one foreign language: Sanskrit. You'd be amazed that your ancestors of twelve centuries ago could build such magnificent structures. Each stone is laid with precise reckoning, just so, according to plan.

If you get red marks in your report card, that's normal. You shouldn't worry too much. There are times when a person just can't seem to get excited about something, a school subject for instance, but at other times—when she discovers how useful the subject might be to her life—she gets all fired up. When I was in primary school, I hated to study and it wasn't until my mother, your grandmother, died, that I came to the realization that I had an obligation to fulfill my mother's wishes; I wouldn't fail in achieving the dreams she had for me. So, I began to study and began to like doing so. I studied any and every subject, most of them without a teacher, the English language included. Because at that time there weren't many lesson books in Indonesian, like it or not I had to study foreign languages in order to increase my knowledge.

Three languages were taught when I was in primary school: Javanese, Dutch, and Malay. At my school we studied formal Javanese for half a year, in the fourth grade, and Malay for half a year, in the fifth grade. The language of instruction from grades one to three was Javanese, while from grades four to seven it was Dutch. The students had to know those three languages, both written and spoken. By the time I was in seventh grade, I had a fair knowledge of Dutch and this greatly helped me in my studies. My father had his own library, including an extensive selection of Dutch books and publishers both in Java and in the Netherlands would send him complimentary copies of their publications.

For an Indonesian speaker Dutch is a far more difficult language to learn than English. Except for its use of adverbs English seems to share more grammatical similarities with Indonesian than Dutch. Even if you use Indonesian grammar in stringing together an English sentence you can usually be understood. The most difficult thing about English is its idioms and pronunciation. I, too, experienced many difficulties, but mainly because I had to study on my own. Maybe your teacher isn't very good at his job. [. . .]

You asked me about trapping animals. I've never been one for that. The one time I went along on a deer hunt, a huge wild boar caught sight of us, forcing me to scramble up a tree. Matyani, a friend of mine from Cengkareng, hunts crocodiles. He takes a dagger, jumps into the river or swamp, and then overpowers them. He contends that crocodiles are near-powerless in water and argues that they're very dangerous on land where they can attack with both their snout and their tails. Monkeys? There are no monkeys here. Monkeys aren't native to the Moluccan Islands. And the number of deer here is dwindling. I suspect they're not native to the region either, that they were brought in by settlers along with cattle and buffalo.

Why would you want a gift of maleleuca oil? Isn't it easy to come by in Jakarta? Visitors to Buru usually take back birds as gifts. Every day the swamp and the forest are filled with a choir of birds' voices, a virtual canon of song. There are numerous kinds of cockatoos: red ones, green ones, and red-and-green ones. There are both large ones and small ones as well. A friend of mine has a pet bulbul, which is about the ugliest bird you can imagine but it can speak. My friend feeds his bulbul palm sap, and now the thing is huge, a giant among its race. Even though it's not kept in a cage, it always comes home to drink. Of course, the only place it's going to get palm sap is from its master's hand. I wouldn't suggest that you try eating civet cat, not if there's something better to eat. But here we don't always have a choice of what to eat. When food was really scarce some of the men ate raw baby mice. One man I know eats live *cicak* lizards and another one live *walang sangit*, that smelly kind of locust. Have you heard of *oret*? *Oret* are a kind of worm that lives in the bark of *kapok* trees. They're fat, cream-colored worms about the size of a thumb. When there's no other source of protein around, we dine on them too. But you throw away the head first so that only the fatty part of the body remains. When pounding sago in the marsh you find an especially large amount of worms in the rotting wood. Don't stop pounding! Just pulverize them along with the sago and cook them up, too. But some of the men like to eat them raw.

A man I know who was suffering from tuberculosis got better by eating fetal mice every day. There are an abundance of mice and rats here, in all shapes and sizes. The fields of elephant grass are a haven for them and what with our fields located nearby, they've become very fat. But now that we have chickens, ducks, and geese to eat, we're not eating them anymore. We've cut down on dogs and cats too. I recall another time when food was hard to come by. A group of men were out in the forest sawing wood. When taking a break near the river, they saw what looked to be a piece of meat floating downstream. They caught it, roasted it, and when they thought it was done, began to eat it, but still there was blood inside. Surprised, they took a better look at the thing and do you know what they discovered they were eating? A baby's placenta! One of the locals must have thrown it in the river. All of the men threw up immediately, right then and there, and started to curse and swear. But that's how it is, Rita, when you're trying to stay alive and healthy.

There's almost no fruit to be found in the jungle here, and what there is, is almost inedible. There are candlenuts but the variety here have very thick shells. But did you know that you can break a shell open with the midrib of a banana leaf? It's strange but true: you place the candlenut on the top of a banana leaf cone, strike it with the midrib and—lo and behold!—the shell breaks right open. Once we found a *keluak* tree but didn't know at the time that you can't simply cook the raw fruit. It wasn't until later that we learned you first have to boil it and bury in mud or soil for about three weeks. Sometimes we'll come across wild nutmeg. The trees are very tall with roots that rise about one yard from the ground, making the tree look like a person who's tiptoeing through the mud and not wanting to get spattered. All in all, conditions are better now than they used to be, but the men are getting older and starting to lose their strength. There's no reduction of the work load, though!

Thank you for reminding me to be careful when taking a bath in the river. Once, one of my friends fell in and disappeared for a long time before coming up and finding a handhold on the edge of the raft. It was five in the morning. I grabbed his hand and pulled him up. The water was up over the riverbank at the time, and was a thick yellow color. Right now, the Wai Apo river is very far down, so low that in some places you can even wade across. Stumps of trees and clumps of bamboo that were torn from the banks by flood waters are now visible. When the water is this low, you can't take a boat very far up river, especially not a fifteen-ton boat. All the boats have to dock much farther down river.

The soil here is new and loose and the topsoil so thin that it's not at all stable. Even a drainage channel of less than one yard deep and one yard wide can cause extensive landslides and erosion. Four years ago, about one hundred yards from where I'm working now, we dug a canal six feet wide and six feet deep. That canal is now a river bed thirty feet wide and almost thirty feet deep. In 1971 a crew of us excavated a canal measuring six feet wide, two feet deep, and two miles long. In the process we had to remove a hill, the layers of soil in which were different kinds of colors—gray, blue, yellow, red, and pink. That is why we christened the canal "Bantalawarna," which means "colored layers." We discovered that the soil, when mixed with a little starch, could be used as paint and, in the end, our barracks came to be all sorts of different colors. But anyway, that canal is now a river, a real river. The soil's instability makes irrigation a very expensive and never-ending task.

I remember when we dug that canal and what hard work it was. Because the work site was so far away we had set off from camp by five-thirty in the morning and often worked until eight o'clock at night. The canal cut through jungles, fields of the local settlers, bamboo groves, and forests. In the fields of elephant grass we were scorched by the sun. In the jungle we wrestled with trees, prying them up by their roots. But worst by far were clumps of rattan:

thorns is all they are—long, thin, razor-sharp thorns that pierce your skin and break off inside. If you find yourself standing under a rattan vine, before you know it, your skin starts to itch and become red and inflamed. Just brushing up against one makes your skin start to swell. And the mosquitoes! Don't even ask! In the jungle, Rita, they are incredible. That canal I just told you about is no longer usable because it, too, has turned into a river.

We once had to "dig" the craziest ditch imaginable, one that traversed a stretch of low land and marsh. For that one we didn't have to dig so much as to build mounds for the canal on both its sides. As you can imagine, working in the swamp made it very difficult for us to find enough earth to build those mounds. In the end, we were forced to ferry it in by raft from quite far away. We used poles to pull and drive the rafts forward. That idiotic canal turned out to be more than one mile in length and then, when we let water through it, it couldn't be used anyway. The water proved to be more powerful than our ability to cope with it using our primitive tools, working methods, and knowledge about the primitive area in which we were living.

It's between seasons right now and the sky is a constant gray. Out at sea, the easterly winds churn up tall waves and make it impossible for small boats to call into Namlea. That's why I have no onionskin paper on which to write. For the past three months there hasn't been any lightning but when it does come, it comes down hard. Several men have been killed by lightning. One man was in the storehouse when lightning struck the building. He was knocked to the ground, unconscious, with blood coming out of his ears. He didn't die but he did lose his hearing. [. . .]

That's enough for now, Rita. In your next letter tell me a story about something interesting that you've experienced, or maybe about a dream that you've had, or about your lessons, or your teachers. Write clearly. You don't have a boyfriend, do you? You're too young for that but remember, when you do start going out, you must ask permission from your mother and father first. We don't want you sneaking around. Be open with us always.

Hugs and kisses for my Rita.

Marsinah Accuses

Ratna Sarumpaet

The New Order regime suppressed labor activism for the sake of national stability. Many factory workers—women, men, and sometimes children—had no union representation or national labor standards to prevent abuse. In May 1993 a wild strike broke out among workers of a factory in East Java who demanded supplemental payment for food and transportation. Some five hundred employees participated. Marsinah, a twenty-four-year-old, was one of the spokeswomen who tried to negotiate with the management. She disappeared on May 4 after a demonstration; her mutilated body, obviously tortured, was found four days later. It is widely believed she was murdered by the military, but the perpetrators were never brought to justice. The playwright and political activist Ratna Sarumpaet composed a monologue in which the spirit of Marsinah speaks out.

The voices of the past die away, but Marsinah looks even more distressed and angry. She drops to the floor wearily. She speaks, as if to herself.

I see so many blood-stained hands . . .
I see how greed can be perpetuated,
How capitalists can keep raking in profits,
Managers and those in power continue to laugh
and chat over every drop of my sweat.
But if a lowly worker like me dares
open her mouth to demand a pay raise?
She'll be killed.
And now, see how they're using my death for humanity's sake;
For upholding justice;
For improving the lot of workers.
[. . .]
Improving the lot of workers . . .
How can the death of a lowly worker
like me possibly cause workers to be treated

humanely in a sick society?
The pounding voices of the past begin again,
startling Marsinah. But she is not afraid.
I'm not afraid. I'm not afraid. *(to her companions)*
I'm not afraid. *(to the voices)*
I can justify it . . .
My life, where I was thrown around,
forever haunted by fear, can justify it.
My painful death; my shattered bones;
My blood spilt on the ground, wetting your heel . . .
Can justify all of it.
What sort of society did you expect I'd call it?
I scratched out a living for a mouthful of rice there,
always stumbling, hounded by your bullying and threats.
I was tortured there . . .
I was raped there, brutally murdered . . .
You killed me.
You tore from me the right to live . . .
What sort of society did you think I'd call it?
What sort of society?
[. . .]
I remember clearly how fear took hold of me
when rough arms suddenly grabbed me from behind
bound my eyes, tightly,
then pushed me into a car, which sped off
to who knows where . . .
There was no sound . . .
I don't know how far I was taken . . .
But I remember clearly that when the car stopped,
I was pushed out roughly
I was dragged, carelessly . . .
I don't remember how far I was dragged along like that.
I only remember how my body shook,
in the grip of a terrible fear.
Then I heard a door being opened right in front of me.
I don't know whether my head hit the wall
or whether I was hit on the brow with a club
I only know I fell headlong on the floor . . .
When I tried to move, feet in heavy boots
quickly restrained me, standing on

my shins, my belly, my chest, my arms . . .
I was abused with streams of filthy words
during every torture that followed.
I don't know how many times my body was lifted up,
then smashed down, hard.
Lifted up again, then smashed down again . . .
Onto the floor . . .
Onto the corner of a table . . .
Onto a chair . . .
Until at last I was truly helpless . . .
Such brutality knows no satisfaction . . .
I could no longer even move my fingertips
when they began to wildly grope
my whole body.
Marsinah is again choked up with emotion,
and stumbles over her words.
God! Stop this . . .
I cried to myself . . .
I fought to break free. I kept struggling . . .
I screamed with all my strength,
even though I knew my voice would not be heard.
My voice fought against the gag stuffed in my mouth.
My mouth and jaw felt torn.
I kept struggling . . .
Struggling . . .
Until at last I'd used up everything . . .
My voice . . . My energy . . . Everything
I let them devour me until they were sated.
I let my bones be shattered.
And . . .
And something, big, sharp, hard . . .
I can't even imagine what it was . . .
be thrust into me, breaking my pubic bone.
Marsinah throws herself down.
She moves, half crawling.
God, why? Why me?
I really wanted to cry, but I couldn't.
I was too broken to shed even one tear.
Blood . . .
I saw blood everywhere.

The blood was black and dirty . . .
Really dirty . . .
It covered my belly . . .
Covered my inner thighs.
It was spattered on the floor,
all over the door, on the table legs . . .
Everywhere . . .
Those were the last moments
I was able to feel something.
Something too painful.
Something so terrifying . . .
So brutal . . .
God, no one deserves to suffer like that.

Why Was TEMPO Banned?

Team of TEMPO Journalists

TEMPO *news weekly was founded in 1971, five years after Suharto had taken over the presidency. As an independent magazine it succeeded throughout most of the 1970s and 1980s in balancing conscientious reporting and integrity with conforming to the limitations on freedom of speech that the New Order imposed on news media and publications. In 1982, however, the Department of Information for a few weeks froze its publication license. With Goenawan Mohamad and Fikri Jufri at the helm of its editorial board* TEMPO *came to symbolize freedom of expression even though its journalists and editors continuously lived with the sword of censorship hanging over their heads. When the magazine was banned—for good, it seemed—in June 1994, it caused an outrage among its readers. The publication went "underground" on the Internet until 1998, when the end of the New Order rang in a new era that allowed its rebirth in print.*

There was no thunderstorm. Nor were there any riots. No buildings were on fire or being bombed. The Commander-in-Chief of the Indonesian Armed Forces, General Feisal Tanjung, never tired of asserting that national stability was at its peak. Therefore, it really came as a shock that, out of the blue, the Director General of the Press and Graphics, H. Subrata—on behalf of the Minister of Information, Harmoko—announced the banning of TEMPO, DETIK and *Editor*, by the Ministry of Information on June 21, 1994.

While looking somewhat tense, the senior official who used to be an anchor for *Echo Sepekan* on national television read the ministerial decree in a firm voice without hesitation. But it did not last long. When reporters asked about the banning of the three leading magazines, Subrata, who is usually very articulate, spoke haltingly and failed to provide satisfactory answers.

Subrata was just doing his job. As he himself revealed to TEMPO's Vice Director, Haryoko Trisnadi, on the announcement of the banning of TEMPO, "I only tried to do my job by conveying the decision to you. . . ."

It remains unclear why a director general instead of the Minister of Information himself signed the decree. Some explained that the Minister of Information, Harmoko, did not want to "dirty" his hands. After all, he comes from a media background, and cutting short the life of some print media would not be good for his future image—as he realized that he would not hold his ministerial post forever. Some others speculated that Harmoko was reluctant to be held responsible for this particular ban, since it was not his decision at all. He, too, was only doing his job.

Whatever the explanation might be, the three magazines had been killed. In the TEMPO office the news was firstly received from *Antara* News Agency at around 3:00 p.m. On that fateful Tuesday of June 21, all of TEMPO's journalists had just wrapped up their meeting, and they had just begun to distribute assignments for the following week's cover story—planned to focus on Indonesia's monetary situation. All columnists and editors, who usually arrived late in the afternoon to collect their free copy of the most current edition, were immediately summoned by phone and pager to come to the office at once. The situation was chaotic. Telephone calls from reporters who were still at home never ceased to pour in. Shock. Disbelief. Apprehension. Irritation. Anger. All mixed into one.

Perhaps it was because he had a hunch of upcoming trouble that Goenawan Mohamad, Senior Editor and former Editor-in-Chief of TEMPO, was on his way to the Soekarno-Hatta airport that afternoon. According to one source Goenawan (more popularly known as GM) wanted to visit his hometown in Batang, Pekalongan, to pay homage to his parents' graves. As soon as he received the news from his secretary, GM called off that important personal trip. He returned to TEMPO's headquarters at Kuningan, South Jakarta. [. . .]

Suddenly some crew of the RCTI television channel appeared on the seventh floor. They interviewed FJ [Fikri Jufri] who bluntly stated that the government had violated the Press Law by revoking TEMPO's license. Mulya Lubis also spoke "harshly."[1] He said that it was a "gross" violation of the law. And somehow those harsh statements made by FJ and Mulya managed to provide some consolation to TEMPO's staff. Every now and then one could hear cheers, along with two fingers raised signifying "victory," and some even raised their fists with no particular target. "Don't you dare not relay it in full," said some fellow journalists to the RCTI crew. Alas, the RCTI, like other broadcasting media, was too scared to air the interviews with FJ and Mulya—which apparently were not meant for public consumption but rather for RCTI's documentation purposes. AN television, which arrived later, was a little "better." It aired the banning in a more representative manner on its midnight news program.

Sjahrir, a TEMPO columnist, Marsillam Simanjuntak, a political observer, and the lawyer Adnan Buyung Nasution also showed up on the seventh floor. Buyung made his speech like a raging tiger in front of some fifty TEMPO staff members. "What the hell does this government have in mind? Is this a republic based on the rule of law or a monarchy? I just can't understand why they did it. I will see Minister Harmoko tomorrow for clarification. I will lead a demonstration to the Ministry of Information," Buyung shouted. And the next day witnessed the first demonstration protesting the 1994 banning of TEMPO.

Goenawan Mohamad arrived at Kuningan during Buyung's fiery speech. As soon as Buyung left TEMPO's office, GM gathered all of TEMPO's staff on the seventh floor. Standing in front of them GM reminded them that a publication ban was a risk that he had always had to anticipate ever since he began his pioneering career at TEMPO. GM admitted that the news came to him as no surprise. For critical media such as TEMPO a ban is just a matter of time. "We don't want to be heroes, but we cannot prostitute ourselves," he said. "Therefore," he continued, "If you want to be angry, be angry with those who banned you, because they have mistreated you badly." But GM also promised that the firm would do its best to take care of its employees. GM's speech managed to bring some peace to the confused minds of the staff that evening.

What is the real reason for the banning of the three media? It is not really clear. In the Ministerial Decree No. 123/1994 issued by the Minister of Information regarding the banning of TEMPO, there is no explanation whatsoever of which news items in particular led to the banning of the weekly magazine that boasts a circulation of two hundred thousand copies. The last written warning that TEMPO had received was dated February 1, 1994, regarding the book *Primadosa* by Wimanjaya Liotohe.[2] Ever since that time TEMPO had never written about *Primadosa* anymore. DETIK was targeted because it was considered inconsistent with its mission as a crime magazine, whereas *Editor* was penalized for administrative problems related to editorial affairs that could easily have been addressed differently.

It is likely that, based on the information and inside sources in the government, the banning of TEMPO had much to do with the heavy-handed speech by President Suharto at Teluk Ratai, Lampung, on June 9, 1994, during the inauguration of a naval base construction. It seemed that the issue surrounding the purchase of thirty-nine warships from East Germany triggered the TEMPO ban.

The purchase of thirty-nine former East German warships by the Minister of Research and Technology, B. J. Habibie, was indeed reported in the "Economics and Business" rubric on June 4, 1994, and then again in the cover story of the edition of June 11, 1994. The two reports revealed the conflict taking place between the Minister of Research and the Minister of Finance in terms of how much funding was to be spent. Minister Habibie initially wanted

US$1.1 billion, and then reduced the amount to US$760 million. Subsequently, however, he postponed the installation of various types of equipment on the ships and cut down other expenses as well, so that the total purchasing cost incurred on the state budget did not exceed US$480 million.

The secondhand ships were sold at a very low price, indeed. The total armada—consisting of sixteen Parchim-class corvettes, fourteen Frosch-class, and nine Condor-class Landing Ship Tanks—cost only US$12 million or about 24 billion rupiahs. The thirty-nine ships had just recently been deactivated from military service and disarmed. A source in the Board of Technological Research and Implementation (BPPT) disclosed that to disarm the thirty-nine ships, the Indonesian government had to spend up to US$4 million. It meant that Indonesia would have to renovate the ships and reinstall the weaponry. Thus the price of the thirty-nine warships, including their renovation and shipping to Indonesia—some of them even had to be tugged due to their inability to sail by themselves—soared from US$12 million to US$345 million, or in other words an increase of 2,875 percent!

The increase of cost did not stop there. For instance, the same source in the BPPT further mentioned that the cost of repowering the main engines would amount to US$63 million. How come? It turned out that the engines of six of the Parchim-class corvettes had to be replaced. Thus entirely new engines made in Britain replaced the Russian-made engines. Furthermore, there were some other costs related to the repair work by PT PAL, a ship-building company led by Habibie, which amounted to US$63 million—or almost thrice as much as the principle price of the ships. Thus the total cost that the state had to bear was US$320 million. This is how the interministerial conflict began.

What TEMPO did is based on the journalistic principle of covering both sides. It means that not only did TEMPO have to give space to Minister Habibie's opinion but it also must provide an equal space for the Ministry of Finance to voice its opinion. Inevitably the Minister of Research and Technology, who is expected to purchase sophisticated equipment, will always be arguing with the Minister of Finance, who is supposed to be "thrifty," because both try to do their jobs. Moreover, the budget used for buying the ships came from the taxpayers' money, and people must be informed about how it is spent.

When President Suharto delivered his off-the-cuff speech at Teluk Ratai, which was aired on the same day in the evening by national television, almost all TEMPO's staff gathered in front of a twenty-nine-inch television located in the Reportage Coordinating Room on the seventh floor. President Suharto—who had just celebrated his seventy-third birthday the day before—explained that the purchase of the ships was his personal initiative and it was he who assigned Minister Habibie to do a feasibility study. The German Chancellor,

Helmut Kohl, was mentioned as one of those who had played an instrumental role in making the negotiations happen.

Thus, the President pointed out, assigning Habibie to the job did not mean that he distrusted the Department of Defense. As a matter of fact, Chancellor Kohl himself wanted the negotiations to be kept secret because "many countries were interested in the ships." This is why the President was upset with the press which he accused to "know only a little but they are fond of writing news items following their own opinions, as they like to capitalize on things that have not yet been clarified. It all amounts to making the situation worse, pitting us against each other, and eventually spreading mutual suspicion." Therefore, he went on, "like it or not, if such a situation continues, it will lead to political and national instability. . . . If warning alone is not enough, then we have to take action, because they have threatened to disrupt the development process which we uphold together. . . ."

Translated from Indonesian by M. Budiman

Notes

1. Mulya Lubis is a prominent human rights lawyer.
2. The title *Primadosa* is a wordplay on primadonna and translates as "prime sins." The book reveals the "sins" (*dosa*) and corruption of the Suharto family and was therefore banned.

Saman

Ayu Utami

In 1998 Ayu Utami made a stunning debut as a novelist when her manuscript Saman *won the annual Literary Award of the Jakarta Arts Council. The book was launched one week before Suharto's fall from power in May and has come to signify not only a sociopolitical critique of his regime but also women's sexual liberation. The protagonist Wisanggeni ("Wis") is a young Roman Catholic priest who challenges the authorities in cahoots with corporate power. A palm oil company threatens to force the Lubukrantau villagers to turn their rubber plantation into one of palm trees. Initially Wis is concerned only about the fate of a mentally disabled woman, Upi, but before he knows it, he stands side by side with her brother Anson, her mother Mrs. Argani, and others to defend the villagers' rights. After having escaped unlawful imprisonment Wis changes his name to Saman and gives up his vows. With the assistance of three women—Yasmin, Laila, and Cok—he manages to be smuggled out of the country to New York where he works for Human Rights Watch.*

The Bishop had granted Wis his request to work on the plantation. But one week in each month he returned to Perabumulih to help Father Westenberg, to whom he felt he owed a debt of gratitude. On one occasion he stayed for a fortnight because the old man was ill with fever. Upon his return to Lubukrantau Mrs. Argani greeted him with some shocking news. Two men had broken into Upi's little house and raped her, leaving bite marks on her chest. Upi was now twenty-one. Wis swallowed and bit his lip so hard it almost bled. "How is she?" he asked, rushing to her house before her mother had even finished telling him the story. He felt powerless to do anything, especially since she may well have enjoyed the experience. He had never known what to do about her sexual urges.

"Upi's okay," replied Anson, falling into step beside him. And when he got to the cage there she was, laughing with delight at seeing him again. "What if she's pregnant?" Wis said sharply to Anson. "I don't know. If she has a baby my wife will look after it. But Upi's never gotten pregnant before." Anson had been married for three years. He was always curious about why Wis, seven years his senior, had never married, and Wis had never felt inclined to explain. Anson glanced at his sister for a moment then looked at Wis as if he had something to tell him. "There's something more serious," he said. Wis turned around, a frown deeply etched in his forehead. Tensely he listened to what the man had to say. Anson was convinced that the rape was part of a campaign of terror by a mob who wanted to take over their land. They did it deliberately in order to intimidate us into handing over the plantation. Then he took Wis to the dam to look at the windmill that they'd built as a mini electricity generator for their smokehouse. In the last three years it had produced five thousand watts of power, enough to enable the village (which now consisted of about eighty houses and a prayer house) to be brightened by electric lights and radios. The electricity itself was a source of wonder for the villagers. But now the windmill had been toppled over.

Wis stared at the destruction in front of him, incredulous that anyone could do such a thing. "Let me check out the damage. You go home!" he said to Anson, his voice trembling. "Go home! Sort out that fertilizer I brought with me. There's urea and KCI." When Anson didn't move immediately, Wis became very abrupt. He wanted to be alone. The moment Anson had gone, he went inside the windmill, into which he had invested so much time and energy. The turbine had been smashed; it looked as if someone had taken to it with an axe. In order to repair it he would have to buy a new generator. He took a deep breath and pressed his forehead against the damp wall. Something seemed to be caught in the base of his throat. He let a tear or two fall, then gave way to his grief, weeping silently.

He recalled a visit by some men the previous year. Their faces flashed into his mind, the faces of wild boars: greedy, cruel, spiky-haired. There had been four of them, dressed in safari suits, and they had come into the smokehouse when he and Anson were sorting out sheets of rubber. "Who are you?" Wis asked. "Officials." "From where?" "Just officials. It doesn't matter where from," one of them replied. "What do you want?" "We need to see a Mr . . ." he looked at his notes for a moment, "Argani." "That's me. Anson bin Argani." Anson stepped forward without taking the cigarette out of his mouth. His scarred face gave him a swaggering sort of appearance, especially since he'd recently taken to covering his blind left eye with a black patch. The men stepped back a little.

They only spoke briefly. "We're here to carry out instructions from the Governor." One of them held up a piece of paper with government letterhead on it, but he didn't give it to Anson. "According to the Governor's decree of 1989, the Sei Kumbang transmigration area is to be turned into a palm oil plantation. The successful tendering company has been appointed, it's Anugerah Lahan Makmur." He paused for a moment, looked around the processing plant, glanced out the window, and turned to Anson again. "We notice that this village is the only one that hasn't yet signed the agreement with the company."

Wis interrupted. "You should know that we have never agreed to replace our rubber trees with oil palms. And this plantation is not the property of the company." But the man replied more vehemently, "Our business is with Mr. Argani. Not with you!" Anson immediately chimed in, repeating what Wis had said in an equally irate manner. "We heard that the company was losing money here and that they had handed over the plantation to a new company that wanted to turn it into a palm oil plantation. But not all the rubber crops in Sei Kumbang have been a failure. Ours has been profitable and we have always paid off our installments on time. We've already started tapping the new trees that we planted. This village is prospering. If the company wants to turn the failed rubber plantations into palm oil plantations, let them. But don't let them touch our trees. The farmers are the ones who are supposed to benefit from transmigration, aren't they?"

"You can raise all those matters with the company officials. We're just here to convey the orders of the Governor." Then the four men left, leaving an ultimatum: the people of Lubukrantau must sign the agreement and cut down their rubber trees. The company would distribute the palm oil seeds and the villagers would have to plant them. If they hadn't complied within a month the bulldozers would be sent in to raze the trees.

[. . .] [After some thugs have burnt down the village and taken Wis as prisoner] Wis felt as if he'd died. And he was distraught because God obviously didn't exist. Christ had clearly not saved him, because he was here in the valley of death, a long silent oppressive corridor, and he was falling, falling at terrifying speed into a bottomless well. Every bone in his body hurt. He could hardly move his hands even though they were no longer handcuffed; they'd been forced into such an awkward position for so long. When his eyes became accustomed to the light he saw that he was in a room of about four meters by four meters. There was a door and two high air vents, but it was dark outside. The color of night. And he was wearing nothing but a pair of underpants which he didn't even think was his. When he checked he saw that they were a pair of light blue women's pants, edged with lace. So he knew that he had been the object of torture and ridicule by these people. There was a piece of bread and a glass of water by his side. He consumed them both because he was very hungry. He knew that he would be here for the long haul and that nobody would be able to help him because this was an illegal kidnapping. None of the newspapers would find out about this because he was the only Lubukrantau villager who had any contact with the outside world. The church might look for him but they wouldn't know where to start. Father Westenberg had no access to the villagers. Wis himself had no idea who had kidnapped him and where he was being imprisoned. This obviously wasn't a real jail. Then he remembered Upi and began to weep. This time he allowed himself to succumb to his tears.

At that point the death of the girl seemed to change everything: he was no longer afraid about what might happen to him, because he felt there was nothing left that was worth defending. Nevertheless the torture to which he was subsequently subjected caused his body to tremble. He felt a shiver of fear each time he was led to the interrogation room and told to sit down, or was left standing, while he tried to guess what sort of tactics they would use this time. He could never see for himself because he was always blindfolded. Sometimes they put lit cigarettes to his skin, sometimes they put his fingers in a clamp, sometimes they whipped him, sometimes they put an electrical charge through his neck, sometimes they just kicked and punched him. No one tactic was preferable to the others. He had never before endured such pain. [. . .]

[From Wis's diary after his escape:]

19 APRIL

Yasmin came back to my hideout this morning in the company of a stylishly-dressed Malay woman. Like Yasmin and Laila, this woman was a former pupil of mine at Tarakanita High School. Three school kids—now all grown-up! It suddenly dawned on me that I'm nearly thirty-seven. I can't really picture them as kids, except for Laila—I got to know her through the letters she often sent me. And now Yasmin is organizing everything for my departure from Indonesia. Yasmin decided that this woman, Cok, should be the one to accompany me out of Medan. I was dubious at first because I hardly know her. But Yasmin obviously had utmost faith in her friend. The two of them took very seriously their job of disguising me. First they attached a false moustache, then shaved my hair and plucked my eyebrows to give them a new shape. They made me look as much as possible like the photo on an ID belonging to one of the workers at Cok's hotel in Pekanbaru. Yasmin had organized everything in her usual efficient manner.

My heart was in my throat as we backed the car, a Honda Accord, out of the garage. I sat in the rear, playing the role of an unassuming houseboy. None of the policemen we passed took any notice of me. Their eyes were only for the two sexy women in the front seat. Tonight we're staying at the luxurious Lake Toba International Hotel. Tomorrow we'll leave in a different car. To make it harder to keep track of us, they said. (Successful deception is costly. I don't know what a person without money or rich friends would do.)

22 APRIL

Cok's not back yet. We've only had one phone call from her. What can be keeping her? For a second night, Yasmin and I sat around talking. The day after tomorrow I will have to depart (wish me luck). If everything goes according to plan, I'll stay in the U.S. for a year or two. If not, I'll be here, languishing in jail anywhere from three to thirteen years, depending on what legal clause the authorities invoke—subversive or criminal. When this possibility dawned on her, Yasmin started to cry. I held her in my arms to comfort her. She wept inconsolably, like a child, and I held her tighter. Then, rather incomprehensibly, I became the child and buried myself between her exposed breasts, like a hungry baby. We pressed close together. I was trembling. It was over before it started. I had no time to fathom what was happening. But Yasmin seemed to have no qualms—she led me to the bedroom. I don't know how I did it. When it was over, I felt so ashamed. But I was also overcome by relief and fell into a deep sleep. In the middle of the night I was woken up because something was biting me near my armpit. I saw her fingers masturbating. She climbed on top of me after she finished. I knew that I don't know how to satisfy her.

23 APRIL

I woke up feeling bewildered. Since leaving the parish, I hadn't given much thought to relinquishing my vows. And now here I am, covered in love-bites. I really don't understand how Yasmin could be attracted to a scrawny, unkempt body like mine. She's so beautiful. All day long she marked my body with bites. I'm like a caged mongoose, covered in dark spots. She's sapped me of all my strength.

24 APRIL

Cok finally showed up, apologetic, to take us to the airport. She deliberately avoided looking at my neck. I was so embarrassed; I kept my head bowed the whole time. I didn't want to leave, and Yasmin cried again. But the plane had arrived.

X

Into the Twenty-First Century

The Asian financial crisis of 1997 hit Indonesia particularly hard and eventually led to Suharto's downfall. The economy was not as robust as the New Order regime had claimed. In half a year the rupiah depreciated almost 80 percent against the U.S. dollar, prices of food and basic supplies shot up, and many Indonesians could no longer afford their daily necessities. Layoffs worsened the situation for ordinary citizens, pushing families further into poverty. While the International Monetary Fund (IMF) negotiated with the government on reforms and assistance, riots broke out in major cities. Students held street demonstrations demanding for Suharto to step down. They were joined by other protesters, among them women activists who had grouped together as the Voices of Concerned Mothers (Suara Ibu Peduli). They complained that they could not buy milk for their babies and children, using the New Order's ideal of motherhood to challenge their leaders. When four students were shot dead, the frenzy and looting intensified to reach its lowest point in May 1998, when violence turned against Chinese residents and their properties, and Chinese women were systematically abused and raped. On May 21, 1998, Suharto resigned, handing over the presidency to his vice-president B. J. Habibie.

In his short term as president, until October 1999, Habibie managed to achieve some remarkable successes. He announced an era of *Reformasi* (Reform), indicating that the New Order was over. He lifted restrictions on freedom of speech and allowed for the formation of political parties, labor, and other organizations. Habibie scheduled parliamentary elections for June 1999, the first free elections since 1955. The most unexpected decision he made was to allow the East Timorese to vote on their independence. As an outcome of the referendum, held in August 1999 under the United Nations' supervision, East Timor declared itself a sovereign nation-state in May 2002.

The political changes since 1998 have been monumental. While only two presidents ruled the country in fifty-three years, the presidency moved between four individuals in six years. Of the forty-eight political parties taking

part in the 1999 general elections, the Indonesian Democratic Party of Struggle (PDI-P) won most of the ballots. However, its leader, Sukarno's daughter Megawati Sukarnoputri, was not appointed Indonesia's next president:
neither leaders of Islamic parties nor liberal intellectuals were willing to accept a female president. Megawati agreed to serve as vice-president under the
presidency of Abdurrahman Wahid. Among those opposed to Megawati was
Amien Rais, the leader of the Muslim National Mandate Party and an outspoken critic of Suharto in the 1990s. He was appointed chairman of the People's
Consultative Assembly (MPR). When Wahid was forced to resign because of
allegations of corruption, Megawati took over the top position after all and
held it for three years. In the first ever direct presidential elections of 2004
Susilo Bambang Yudhoyono (commonly known as SBY) of the Democratic
Party (PD) defeated her.

Reformasi opened the door to dramatic social changes: not only were the
media cleared from state scrutiny but at various levels of education students
were allowed to voice critical comments and women no longer had to follow
strict gender patterns that forced them into becoming housewives and mothers. As the concepts of the family principle and of strong patriarchal authority
crumbled, not only women experienced a sense of liberation, socially and
sexually; heteronormativity also eroded. Gays, lesbians, bisexuals, queers, and
transpeople could more easily come out and celebrate their gender identities
and sexualities. Even though taboos still exist and the average Indonesian adheres to heterosexuality, gay and lesbian magazines and organizations have
sprung up, injecting new ideas into society and advocating acceptance. Because of long existing taboos concerning homosexuality, information and
awareness about HIV/AIDS remains limited among the population at large.
The epidemic is more associated with sex workers and drug users than with
the queer community. In 2005 an estimated 170,000 people were infected with
HIV.

The New Order's strong emphasis on economic development combined
with corruption, cronyism, and military involvement in businesses pushed
concerns regarding the environment and preservation to a second tier. Indonesia's biodiversity is immense, but its natural resources have been plundered
and its ecosystems have deteriorated. Illegal logging and the wholesale de-
forestation of tropical rain forests have caused erosion, while overfishing and
the pollution of the coastal waters have done irreversible damage. In recent
years slash-and-burn practices as well as out-of-control forest fires created
a haze that seriously affected the air quality in neighboring countries. On a
more positive note we see that the establishment of national parks has helped
protect specific areas and their flora and fauna. One such park was founded

in 1980 on Komodo Island, the habitat of the Komodo dragon. This prehistorical species related to monitor lizards is found exclusively in Indonesia and
now has its natural habitat protected as a UNESCO World Heritage site.

While Indonesia was cautiously taking first steps to recover from the economic crisis and to restore balance after the major shift in the political and
social climate, conflicts between Muslims and Christians in the Moluccas escalated into violent clashes and ongoing fighting in early 1999. On Ambon
Island some two hundred people lost their lives, and many were displaced
fleeing from their homes and neighborhoods that were destroyed in the hos-
tilities. This outburst of violence signaled that tensions between the different
religious groups had been smoldering for quite some time and that they were
hard to contain once released. Religion and Islam became a focal point of
attention after the September 11, 2001, terrorist attacks on the World Trade
Center in New York. Suddenly Indonesia came to be known as the world's nation with the largest Muslim population. Islam in the archipelago has always
been of the moderate kind, and on Java, where the majority of Indonesians
reside, the Muslim faith has habitually been mixed with pre-Muslim practices
and beliefs. Suharto was one such Javanese Muslim, observing the core aspects of Islam but also following Javanese mysticism and occultism. As president he kept any form of Islamic fundamentalism at bay.

It was impossible for Indonesia not to be affected by the events of 9/11. In
October 2002 two powerful bombs exploded at a beach resort on Bali, targeting primarily Western tourists. Two hundred and two people lost their lives
in the blast, and many were injured. The radical Islamic organization Jemaah
Islamiyah, known for its ties to al-Qaeda, was immediately held responsible
for the bombing. Its leader Abu Bakar Ba'ashir denied involvement, yet he
was later found guilty of conspiracy and sentenced. Two others, Iman Samu-
dra and Amrozi bin Haji Nurhasyim, were sentenced to death for carrying
out the Bali bombing.

While radical Islamist groups made their presence felt through acts of
terror on Bali and in Jakarta, Aceh on the northern tip of Sumatra, one of
the oldest and most prominent Muslim regions in Indonesia (as indicated in
its name "the Verandah of Mecca"), continued its struggle for independence
from Indonesia. The Free Aceh Movement (GAM), founded in 1976, claimed
that Aceh should never have been incorporated into the Indonesian republic.
For decades GAM employed guerilla tactics against the Indonesian military,
at times negotiating with Jakarta to find a diplomatic solution. Everything
changed, however, when Aceh was hit by a devastating tsunami following an
earthquake on December 26, 2004. The movement laid down its weapons and
eventually signed a peace agreement with the central government in August

2005. The epicenter of the 9.15 earthquake on the Richter scale was located in the Indian Ocean off Sumatra's west coast. While the tsunami affected the shores around the Indian Ocean—particularly those of Sri Lanka, India, and Thailand—the death toll was the highest in Indonesia, with over 167,000 estimated killed, 37,000 people missing, and infinite numbers of displaced. Reconstruction is slow, and it will take many years of planning and financial assistance to rebuild Aceh's infrastructure.

The September 11, 2001, attacks in New York drastically changed global perceptions of Islam, raising a new awareness and sensitivity around issues of the religion. In 2005 a Danish newspaper published cartoons depicting the Prophet Mohammed in a derogatory way. When the drawings started to circulate, it sparked furor among Muslims all over the world. On different continents they protested and demonstrated against the publication of the images, declaring that at stake was not freedom of speech, as those who released the cartoons claimed, but a lack of respect. While angry Indonesian Muslims, too, took to the streets and made their way to the Danish embassy, the president, SBY, urged his citizens to remain calm and reasonable. International changes have also affected domestic politics. Traditional Muslims proposed an "Anti-pornography and Porno-Action Bill" (RUU-APP) aiming at the implementation of sharia law in Indonesia, particularly regarding sexuality and women. The bill has faced much opposition, not only from feminist activists but also from parts of Indonesia such as Bali, Manado (northern Sulawesi), and West Papua that have non-Muslim majority populations.

Jakarta, February 14, 2039

Seno Gumira Ajidarma

The 1997 economic crisis hit certain parts of Asia hard, and it particularly affected Korea, Thailand, and Indonesia. In Indonesia's case it resulted in a serious dissatisfaction with the government because the latter failed to overcome the devaluation of the rupiah and to assist average citizens with financial hardships such as increased prices of fuel and of daily necessities. Students protested in the streets and were joined by other groups to demonstrate against the economic and political state of affairs. Riots and violence escalated in looting sprees and the arson of often Chinese-owned businesses. On May 13 and 14 Indonesian Chinese women were targeted for brutal rapes in Jakarta, in some cases gang rapes and mutilations. In his short story "Jakarta, February 14, 2039," the author Seno Gumira Ajidarma depicts from three different perspectives a day in Jakarta exactly forty years and nine months after the mass rapes took place: from that of a forty-year-old woman conceived as result of rape, from that of a rape victim, which is the selection presented here, and from that of a rapist. Seno's story was also published in a cartoon version.

Jakarta, February 14, 2039, 11:00 p.m.

"WHERE ARE YOU MY CHILD?"
Today is the birthday of my child. If she is still alive, her age would be forty. Where are you, my child? Where are you? I've never known for sure if I should regret or how I should feel for having given you up back then. I placed you in a basket and I set that basket in front of a door. After that I left the country and tried to forget everything. I hope the letter I placed in the basket was enough to make the person who read it understand my situation and after that, be willing to care for you. It's true I felt a great relief after giving birth to you, because the whole time I was pregnant, I felt like I was carrying the child of the devil. I felt cursed with misfortune. Without having experienced it oneself, no one could ever understand how it feels to be a woman who has been raped. Raped by a gang of men, not because you're beautiful or attractive, but rather out of the deepest hatred because we were different and not wanted here,

hated because we're different, not even animals have ever been hated the way people hated us. For forty years I've tried to forget the whole incident but for the same forty years that curse has always hounded me. Memories, why do we humans have memories? I might even forget some things but I can never erase the fact that I was once raped in that way, beaten down, dishonored, abused. I hate the fact that I was ever born and I hate the fact that you were ever born. It's clear I gave birth to a child of the devil. A child of the rapists, who knows which one. How long ago did it happen? I was raped on the 14th of May, 1998, at ten at night, in a building with words of abuse written on the wall. Flames raged around me and I could hear the screams of women being raped all around me. Nine months later, on exactly the 14th of February, 1999, you were born. For nine months I felt there was a horned serpent in my belly. I didn't agree to carry you. I didn't agree. I didn't accept it. I wasn't willing. In fact I never even looked at you. I heard your crying, but my heart was so full of resentment that all motherly feelings within me were completely deadened. I never even glanced at you in that basket, as though I was carrying an object of no importance. After that, I went far away, far away to foreign lands. I went to the ends of the Earth never reached by humanity. I went to a vast uninhabited plain, dove to caves beneath the sea which not even fish entered, climbed the snow-capped peaks of mountains, and built a house in a hidden valley. Still, none of that could make me forget you, my child. Where are you, where are you, where are you? I know you're not to blame, but that's how I feel now, I don't know whether to regret or how I should feel. Maybe I would always torture and whip you if you lived with me, because you would surely always remind me of that incident. You're probably happier never knowing who you really are. And I don't even know who your father is, which one, from among so many rabid dogs the devil sent to me, your father was. My child, my child, my child, you're forty years old now. Is there some way we could be brought together? I'm sixty years old now. I'm old, but very healthy, even though my heart is suffering. For forty years I've struggled against that pain. I could never have imagined that an incident like that would strike me. I'm so very sad, my child. I'm so very sad. But I have to block that out, because I won't allow myself to feel the suffering which they brought upon me. Rabid dogs. No, even a rabid dog is more honorable than a rapist. How could all this have happened? Why did all of this have to happen? So that I hate you and now, long for you? My child, my child, my child, and I don't know if you are male or female. Forgive me, my child, forgive me, forgive me. I've tried all kinds of ways to forget the entire incident and you. I married, had children, and divorced. I wanted to forget. But as it turns out, one who forgets still can't forget her deepest pain. I want to accept this pain, regard it as sheer bad luck, but it turns out that's impossible, because all of this is no accident. I'm the victim of hatred. I'm the victim of a crime. This fact is so painful that I can't ever forget it. Today is your fortieth birthday, my child. I'm learning to accept this curse in its entirety, even though I continue to deny it, but I hope you'll never know who you really are, my child, that's the only thing that can bring me happiness.

Jakarta 2039,

Forty Years after May 13–14, 1998

Seno Gumira Ajidarma and Zacky

That is how, my camera,
From that 80-year-old woman
I found out that
I am not who I thought I was.

It turns out
that I am the
child of a rapist.

My mother was gang-raped in the mass riots in Jakarta On May 13–14, 1998.

Cartoon version of the events that happened forty years and nine months after the May 1998 rapes and violence in Jakarta. Seno Gumira Ajidarma, *Tahun 2039: 40 tahun 9 bulan setelah 13–14 Mei 1998* (Yogyakarta: Galang, 2001).

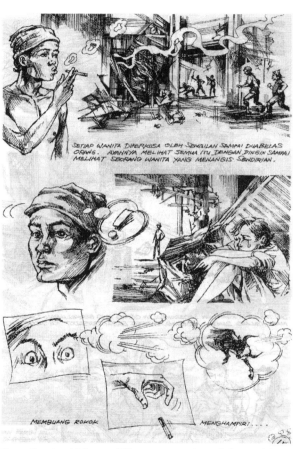

Each woman was raped by nine to twelve men. Her father saw it all with indifference until his eyes caught sight of a woman crying by herself.

He threw away his cigarette Approached her . . .

Seno Gumira Ajidarma, *Tahun 2039: 40 tahun 9 bulan setelah 13–14 Mei 1998* (Yogyakarta: Galang, 2001).

And dragged
the woman into
a corner . . .

*Translated from
Indonesian by
T. Hellwig*

Seno Gumira Ajidarma, *Tahun 2039: 40 tahun 9 bulan setelah
13–14 Mei 1998* (Yogyakarta: Galang, 2001).

If PAN Wins the Election

Amien Rais

Amien Rais is a university professor turned outspoken Muslim politician who holds a doctoral degree in political science from the University of Chicago. He was known as a Muslim activist and led the Islamic social organization Muhammadiyah from its main office in Yogyakarta. He also headed the Association of Muslim Intellectuals (ICMI, Ikatan Cendekiawan Muslim se-Indonesia) for two years. In early 1998 he became one of Suharto's fiercest political opponents when he joined student demonstrations calling for the president to resign. He subsequently cofounded the National Mandate Party (PAN, Partai Amanat Nasional) and was appointed speaker of the People's Consultative Assembly (MPR, Majelis Permusyawaratan Rakyat) from 1999 to 2004. He ran as a candidate in the first direct presidential elections of 2004. Since his defeat he has returned to his position as a professor of political science at Gadjah Mada University in Yogyakarta.

In solitude, I often feel that I seem to be taking another solitary journey into the *Reformasi*, just as I did in 1993. Many of my friends who were expected to help keep the *Reformasi* on the right track, have demonstrated a blatant compromising attitude instead. And one of the culminating points is the attempt to restore Suharto's place in the national political arena for all kinds of reasons. In addition, there is a move made by Abdurrachman Wahid,[1] which I was able to foresee before. Then, there are other groups that have apparently amassed a great deal of funding through money politics. These in turn have helped strengthen the status quo that may lead to the return of Suharto.

Before addressing the question of whether I am traumatized by Suharto's regime, I would like to express the kind of feeling and thought that I had after watching a documentary film titled *The Fall of Mr. Suharto* about two weeks ago. The film was produced by a foreign television station and lasted for forty-five minutes. I was moved when watching this film because at that time all students were united and had only one goal in mind: to bring down Suharto, who was considered a major stumbling block for the *Reformasi*.

I was also moved to see my role represented almost in its entirety. At that time, I fearlessly led demonstrations and gave speeches to various large audiences. This includes my presence at the Parliament Building on May 18, 1998,[2] to push for Suharto's immediate resignation from the presidency. Perhaps, ever since that time, I have been considered the catalyst of the *Reformasi*.

It is worth mentioning that since 1993 I have raised important issues on the national leadership succession, although at that time I felt isolated in the political swamp of the New Order, which was ruled by a management of fear and the abuse of the politics of fear by Suharto's regime. However, I always remained optimistic. Deep in my heart, there was a conviction that Suharto would eventually fall down.

Now, Suharto has stepped down, but the pyramid of power that we inherited from him remains intact. Only the tip of the pyramid has gone. It is safe to say that the transitional administration of [B. J.] Habibie is not altogether different,[3] even though, credit goes to where credit is due, there have been some changes taking place, such as freedom of the press and freedom of expression for people to stage protests. Other than that, everything else remains the same. The bastions of kkn (corruption, collusion, and nepotism) remain formidable. They are never dismantled. Then, bureaucratic machineries are still operating in the old way. The leadership of the Armed Forces (abri) is still very loyal to its former supreme commander. And so is the Attorney General. Golongan Karya (Golkar) is still as arrogant as usual.[4] And what is more dangerous, I'm afraid, is that money politics is beginning to spread like mushrooms.

In the documentary film that I mentioned, there is also an interview with Abdurrachman Wahid. It turns out that on the night of May 20th, Tutut (Siti Hardijanti Rukmana) called Abdurrachman Wahid to reveal Suharto's intention to step down.[5] Therefore, until the last days of Suharto's regime, there had been a cordial relationship between Cendana and Abdurrachman Wahid.[6] However, I do not mean to launch any sharp criticism, for in this *Reformasi* era everybody has the right to express their opinion. Even if that means dedicating oneself to Suharto again.

Truly, it makes me sad nowadays to see that Suharto is still very much in power and can play his mind-boggling game. And Abdurrachman Wahid's statement confirms my fear further. Abdurrachman Wahid stated that all of the riots taking place after Suharto had stepped down were related to Suharto's supporters. And what is even more shocking, Abdurrachman Wahid admitted that the idea of having the four-party meeting (Suharto, Habibie, Wiranto,[7] and Abdurrachman Wahid) was originated from Suharto instead of Abdurrachman Wahid.

At the moment, the *Reformasi* forces seem to be in danger of being over-whelmed by the status quo that justifies all means, especially money politics. This is my greatest worry with regards to the future of the *Reformasi*. Never-theless, I am still optimistic. I mean, the reformists will eventually come out the winner despite their disadvantageous situation in this worrying stage.

As students were overly enthusiastic to arrange a meeting between myself, Megawati,[8] Gus Dur,[9] as well as Sultan Hamengku Buwono,[10] I adopted it as my political standpoint. However, in the process, the Ciganjur Declaration seems to have been pushed to the past and undermined by Abdurrachman Wahid's maneuver.[11] The Ciganjur Declaration is in contradiction with the latest bargaining talks between Gus Dur and Habibie, Wiranto, and Suharto himself.

If we look back to May 19, 1998, Gus Dur asked students to stop their action. On the contrary, on the same day I planned to bring a million people to the National Monument to push Suharto to step down.[12] And on May 20th I sub-sumed to the students' demand to reject Suharto's offer to be part of a reform team. And so did some other figures such as Adnan Buyung Nasution and Emil Salim.[13] My standpoint was exactly the opposite of that of Gus Dur. In my opinion, that's alright. People can see for themselves what has happened, and the whole documentation of the event can be reviewed. I am happy being part of a history in the making.

Nowadays, of course I watch my step more carefully. Thank God, I am not easily defeated nor do I succumb to pessimism, let alone losing hope. I will certainly be fighting back. At that time, I firmly demanded that Su-harto should step down, and I was also against Abdurrachman Wahid's wish to bring Suharto back to the political stage. There is no ill feeling or hatred in me. God willing, my mind is still clear, rational, and forward-looking. That is how I deal with Gus Dur's game. And I consider Suharto responsible for the widespread KKN system that has sucked the blood of our nation.

Translated from Indonesian by M. Budiman

Editors' Notes

1. Leader of the Nahdatul Ulama, the largest Muslim group in Indonesia.
2. Students and other demonstrators occupied the parliament building at that time.
3. Habibie is Suharto's former vice-president who later became his successor.
4. The ruling party during Suharto's era.
5. Tutut is Suharto's oldest daughter.
6. Cendana is the name of the street on which Suharto's family resided.

7. The commander in chief of the armed forces during Suharto's and Habibie's administrations.

8. Then leader of the opposition party, the Indonesian Democratic Party of Struggle (PDI-P).

9. Abdurrachman Wahid's popular nickname.

10. The Sultan of Yogyakarta.

11. The declaration was the outcome of a meeting that took place at Ciganjur, Abdurrachman Wahid's base.

12. The National Monument was a strategic choice of location as it lies across the street from the presidential palace.

13. The first is a prominent human rights lawyer, the second the former minister of environment in Suharto's administration.

Gays and Lesbians in Indonesia

Dédé Oetomo

During the New Order period state-imposed sex and gender ideologies defined women and men, their roles and behaviors, according to strictly heteronormative regulations. Young adults, particularly women, were often unable to escape the social and familial pressure to marry and reproduce, and would therefore succumb to their parents' and relatives' wishes to enter matrimony. Sexuality was, and to a large extent is, a difficult subject to speak about openly, but non-heterosexual relationships and identities, be they gay, lesbian, bisexual, or transsexual/transgender, were, and are, even more taboo and socially unacceptable. Society has always been most tolerant toward (male-to-female) transvestites, known as banci. Since 1998 the Reformasi has opened the door to more gay and lesbian liberation, activism, and visibility and to non-heterosexual identity politics. This does not mean, however, that gays, lesbians, trans or queer persons have achieved equal rights, or even general respect and acceptance of society at large. Dédé Oetomo is the founder of the first gay activist organization, Lambda Indonesia (1982), later reorganized as GAYa INDONESIA. He has worked tirelessly to raise awareness about HIV/AIDS.

As is the case in other parts of the Third World, gays and lesbians in Indonesia are largely influenced by Western gay/lesbian lifestyles in terms of looking for entertainment and dates in bars, pubs, discos, and parks. In big cities, at least on Java, one finds unofficial brothels with male sex workers. A lot of such free-lance workers are also located in areas where gays temporarily gather. Some lesbians visit areas of female sex workers. Both lesbians and gays meet their same-sex partners in normal places such as at home, school, in the workplace, places of worship, and so on. Generally there are many gay men in the glamorous worlds of fashion and makeup, singing, and the performing arts.

People strongly believe that what we see of gay life is only the tip of the iceberg. That is, there are many more homosexuals in our society who do not always know of each other. Closeted homosexuals tend to live a less glamorous, more invisible life. This is especially the case with lesbians. Their status as women in Indonesian society does not give them the same social mobility as men, and they deal with their sexuality in much more concealed and abstruse ways.

Contact and "crossing" to a transvestite identity is common among those in the middle and lower classes. Gay men sometimes dress as transvestites, even for quite extended periods or when they travel to other cities. On the reverse, a small part of transvestites pass as gay men on certain occasions. The boundary between gays and transvestites is a sociological one based on the awareness of gays and transvestites themselves. The general public tends to be more familiar with transvestites (whom they know as *banci* or *bencong*) than with gays, but this is changing because of media coverage.[1]

The traditional forms of transvestitism that used to run parallel with homosexual behavior in many of the Indonesian cultures are disappearing, and a new social category has emerged, that is the transvestites who since the 1960s form a social movement in the larger cities on Java. In fact, gay as a social category has similarly surfaced. So, contrasting with the traditional social groupings of *gemblak*, *bissu*, and so on,[2] that would not have a sexual connotation, in today's society new social categories with explicit sexual connotations have transpired, namely, transvestites, gays (and also lesbians). Overall, the general public is not aware of gays and lesbians in their midst. Their knowledge of homosexuality is still very basic, not to say almost nonexistent. [. . .]

Thomas, twenty-nine years old, is an employee in a furniture-producing company. He comes from a decent and devout village family (even though when his mother was young, she once was involved with another woman). He moved to the city with his brother-in-law, Mas Pono, who works as a driver for a pharmaceutical company. Yusuf, the manager of the furniture company, is a gay male who had a sexual relationship with one of Thomas's cousins before. He immediately felt attracted to Thomas, who was nineteen at the time. He invited Thomas to live with him. Clearly Yusuf's appearance and behavior appealed to Thomas ("I like adult males who are chubby and fatherly," were the comments of this masculine-looking man with lots of body hair), so he agreed. They were together for almost a year.

Since then Thomas has shifted from one relationship to another, all with men who look and behave like Yusuf. But at some point Thomas was also involved with women. Sometimes, for instance, his boss invited him to the red-light district, and he enjoyed that too. (When he was in junior high school, he once had a quickie with a girlfriend in the changing rooms.) He dated women a number of times, and he would always have sex with them.

To his family he has come out as a gay man. In spite of initial resistance his family accepted it eventually, so that he now can enjoy being gay and live his daily life without significant constraints. In his neighborhood people know he is gay, but because he is a good citizen, everyone treats him well. Most parents, while knowing their son is gay, still want to find him a bride to have grandchildren who will take care of them in the future. So, half forced and half intentionally, Thomas dated Ratih, a student at a private university, who was his parents' choice. At the same time he continued his sexual contacts with men. Even though Ratih was jealous on occasion, their relationship carried on. While Thomas did not really want to marry, he did so because of social pressure. He dated Ratih for a very short time and married her without love.

During the first months the well-built man with Middle Eastern features fulfilled his conjugal duties. But because of his gay orientation, he became tired of his wife and turned to his true appetite, gay men. Every Saturday night he gathered with his gay friends in the Calfor area of Surabaya Plaza, just to chat or to pick up a date. The relationship with his wife could not be sustained, and in five months the marriage was over.

Translated from Indonesian by T. Hellwig

Editors' Notes

1. *Banci* and *bencong* are slang words for a male-to-female transvestites.
2. *Gemblak* is a Javanese term for a pederast, while *bissu* is Buginese for a (traditional) transvestite priest.

The Violence in Ambon

Human Rights Watch

Less than one year into the Reformasi, *intense religious riots raged through Ambon and the other Moluccan islands. For centuries Christians and Muslims had lived side by side in this eastern part of the archipelago, most of the time peacefully. What could have been an insignificant incident of harassment ignited a conflict in Ambon that took on major proportions. Houses, churches, and mosques were burnt down or damaged, some two hundred people died in the violence, and more than twenty thousand were displaced. Each party accused the other of provocation and of instigating the fighting and destruction. Both Christians and Muslims made allegations that the police and military deployed to restore security were biased in favor of the other. Even though the situation calmed, tensions have remained, and violence occurred again in 2004.*

On January 19, 1999, as Muslims around the world were celebrating the end of the fasting month, a fight broke out on the island of Ambon, in Maluku (Moluccas) province, between a Christian public transport driver and a Muslim youth. Such fights were commonplace, but this one escalated into a virtual war between Christians and Muslims that is continuing as this report goes to press. Much of the central part of the city of Ambon, the capital of Maluku province, and many neighborhoods (*kampung*) in other parts of Ambon island and the neighboring islands of Ceram, Saparua, Manipa, Haruku, and Sanana have been burned to the ground. Some thirty thousand people have been displaced by the conflict, although the figure is constantly changing.

The death toll by early March was well over 160 and rising rapidly as army reinforcements, brought in to restore order, began firing on rioters armed with sharp weapons and homemade bombs. The head of the Christian documentation center in Ambon told Human Rights Watch by telephone on March 10 that eighty-three Christians had been killed between January and March 9, 1999, twenty-three of them at the hands of the military. Nur Wenno, head of the Muslim relief efforts at Ambon's largest mosque, said there were no precise figures on the Muslim death toll, but it was over one hundred.

Questions as to who was accountable for the violence in Ambon and sur-rounding islands focus on three issues: Who started it? Why did it escalate so fast? What, if anything, could the government have done to halt it? And what should the government be doing now?

Outside Ambon, as reflected in the country's major news weeklies and statements of political opposition leaders, the near-universal belief is that the violence in Ambon is one of a number of outbreaks of unrest around the country deliberately instigated by people loyal to former President Suharto, his family, a group of disgruntled army officers, or all of the above. The out-breaks in question include the shooting of four students and subsequent ri-oting in Jakarta in May 1998 that preceded Suharto's resignation; killings in Banyuwangi, East Java, in the latter half of 1998; clashes in Semanggi, Jakarta, on November 13 between students and members of a pro-government civil-ian militia set up by the army; communal violence in Ketapang, Jakarta, on November 22; communal violence in Kupang, West Timor, on November 30; and communal clashes in Sambas, West Kalimantan, in January and February 1999. Unsuccessful efforts to spark unrest around the end of the Muslim fast-ing month were also reported in the cities of Manado, North Sulawesi, and Malang, East Java.

However the conflict started, the violence took on a life of its own. Each outbreak or clash increased the polarization between the two communities and the feeling of fear among the general populace. Even while we were still there, whenever anyone saw smoke there was an instant reaction of panic that a new attack was on the way until the smoke could be traced to a trash fire or some other innocuous source. Any sudden noise had the same effect.

There is a widely held perception that the conflict in Ambon is one be-tween Muslim migrants and indigenous Christians, but as the following nar-rative will show, it is not that simple. The presence of migrants, especially from Sulawesi, unquestionably heightened communal tensions, but there was friction between Ambonese Christians and Muslims going back to the colo-nial period, and much of the current fighting has involved (and been directed at) Ambonese Muslims as well as Bugis and Butonese.

January 19: The Beginning

Even for the most thoroughly covered and analyzed incident in Ambon, the fight on January 19 that ignited it all, there are two very different accounts. One, circulated by the legal team representing Christian detainees, portrays a Christian Ambonese public transport driver, Jacob Leuhery, otherwise known as Yopy, as the victim of harassment by two Bugis Muslims, Usman and Salim.

A second version, circulated by the fact-finding team of the Moluccan branch of a Muslim political party, the Justice Party, portrays the Bugis as the victims of intimidation by Yopy. When interviewed by Human Rights Watch, Yopy reiterated the first version. On February 15, however, he was arrested and detained on charges of assaulting the Bugis.

The first version states that around 2:30 p.m. on January 19, Yopy, a Christian from Aboru village near Batu Merah, was just starting his shift as a driver of a public transport van at the Batu Merah Terminal. Two youths approached him, and one of them demanded Rp.500. That youth, named Salim, was arrested in Bone on February 3, and was returned to Ambon for questioning several days later. Yopy refused to hand over any cash, saying he didn't have any because he was just starting his shift. He then went on to the Mardika terminal. After about half an hour, he returned to Batu Merah, without passengers. The youths were still there, and the one came up to him again and demanded money. He replied he didn't have any because he didn't have any passengers. He told the youths to stop their demands. One of them took out a traditional knife (*pisau badik*) and held the point to Yopy's neck, but Yopy was able to push him away with the door of the van and drove off to Mardika, in the hopes that the two would leave. But when he came back, still without passengers, the youths were still there. Salim reached in his pocket to pull out his knife. Yopy ran to his home, near the terminal, got his own knife, and ran back, chasing this would-be attacker into the market of Batu Merah village. The youth got away, and Yopy eventually went home.

The Muslim version, which apparently has been accepted by the police, says that Yopy was the driver of a van that was owned by a Bugis resident of Batu Merah. His conductor was also a Muslim from Batu Merah Bawah. Yopy had used the van for a charter or private rental, and the conductor, acting on behalf of the owner, asked Yopy for the money he had received. Yopy refused and threatened the conductor. Several Christian passengers then joined Yopy in assaulting the conductor, who ran to Batu Merah Bawah to get reinforcements from his friends. The two groups clashed, and religious and racial tensions erupted into violence.

The Christian account states that less than fifteen minutes after Yopy got home, he saw hundreds of Muslim youths from Batu Merah coming to attack the largely Christian residents of Batu Merah Dalam, the area near Yopy's house. They went back and mounted a second attack, this time with an even larger group: six hundred to seven hundred people, according to a church report. They then went back and returned a third time.

Human Rights Watch interviewed "Amir" (not his real name), one of the few Muslim residents of Batu Merah Dalam. He said that at about 3:30 p.m., when stone-throwing started on January 19, he did not pay much attention, because fights between the Muslim and Christian neighborhoods were so common.

But then, around 4:00 p.m., a Muslim crowd came back and attacked. They came across the bridge into the village in large numbers, Amir couldn't see how many. He came out of the house to look carrying a Quran, so people would know he was a Muslim. Amir said that he had lived in Batu Merah all his life, but he did not recognize the men leading the mob—all he knows is that they weren't from Batu Merah. Some five or so people at the front were wearing a white cloth on their arms. Amir called the military police, but they said they had already told the regular police. They themselves didn't have many men. There were about ten intelligence people in civilian clothes around at the time. One of them fired his pistol in the air, but it did not do any good; the crowd kept advancing.

The attackers stopped at the auto repair garage below his house and apparently found oily rags there that they set on fire. Then they used their long knives to toss the burning rags into houses, the windows of which had already been broken. Amir's house was burned to the ground, like every other house in the neighborhood. People were also shouting that the mosque in Bawah Merah [sic] had been burned, although it had not been touched. Eventually the riot police (known as Brimob, for mobile police brigade) came, but only after everything was already destroyed.

From Batu Merah, the crowd went on to Mardika, a market area in the center of town. There the first homes to be burned were those of Silas Noya, Empi Tuhumena, Boy Huliselan, while a fourth building used as a auto repair shop was also torched. Another house was burned, and six others were slightly damaged. [. . .]

From January 19, when violence first erupted, until February 14, when security forces intervened in the clash on Haruku island, the military were roundly criticized for failing to prevent the attacks on villagers of both faiths. The official National Human Rights Commission in Indonesia (Komnas) said the military was slow to respond, and the first accusations of security force bias that emerged were based on their inaction, not action. By mid-February, both sides were accusing the military of actively helping one side or the other to attack or of shooting at only one party involved in the clash.

But accounts of the fighting in Batu Merah and other areas of the city of Ambon on January 19–20 suggest that the army and police were both understaffed and wholly unprepared for the violence. The fact that violence broke out during Lebaran meant that many soldiers were on leave. In addition, on January 14, many soldiers from Ambon had been sent as reinforcements to help in quelling an outbreak of violence in nearby Dobo, meaning the city's core territorial force had been reduced.

While both Muslim and Christian communities alleged that military inaction favored the other side, it would have been difficult to allege communal bias in those first weeks. Muslims got little help when their neighborhoods were being torched during the first two days of the conflict. Christians cited military inaction as leading to the destruction of the village of Benteng Karang on January 20 and subsequent violence the same day in the village of Nania. Muslims tried to call for help when they were being attacked in Kamiri, Hative Besar, on January 20, but no one answered the telephone at the three military posts they called. When people approached individual commanders directly, as in Passo, the response was either that the various posts were short of personnel or that they did not have orders to intervene. The latter is no excuse when lives are in jeopardy. [. . .]

The conflict by early March had enormous social and political consequences. It had left close to two hundred dead, although both sides agree that it is difficult to produce exact figures. The government did not release separate figures for Christian and Muslim deaths, but it is clear both suffered immense losses in terms of deaths, injuries, and destruction of property, including homes, businesses, and places of worship. In addition, tens of thousands of people had been displaced and were in need of assistance. The divisions between the two communities had become so deep that local politicians were suggesting complete separation of Muslims and Christians as a solution to the conflict, but one that everyone realized was impossible.

Politically, the conflict had polarized Christians and Muslims in other parts of Indonesia, but particularly among the political elite of Jakarta, in a way that could have serious repercussions for the forthcoming June elections.

The Bali Bombing

Interview with Imam Samudera

In the evening of October 12, 2002, two powerful bombs exploded at Paddy's Bar and the Sari Club in the tourist district of Kuta, Bali. The death toll amounted to 164 foreigners, mostly Australians, and 38 Indonesians. Many more were injured, and the material damage was immense. These events left everyone on the otherwise tranquil Hindu island in shock, local inhabitants and visitors alike. The police accused the militant Islamist group Jemaah Islamiyah (JI) of carrying out the terrorist attacks. One of its leaders, Abu Bakar Ba'ashir, spent only about two years in prison, while another leader, Hambali (alias of Riduan Isamuddin), with allegedly close al-Qaeda connections, was arrested in Thailand and is currently held in American custody. Three JI members were sentenced to death, and one to life imprisonment. Most notorious for his media performance was Amrozi bin Haji Nurhasyim who was defiant throughout the court hearings, smiling and giving himself the thumbs up when his death sentence was read out loud. Imam Samudera, too, showed no remorse, as can be seen in the following interview. On November 9, 2008 at 00:15 a.m., Imam Samudera, Amrozi, and Mukhlas were executed by firing squad.

The convicted bomber in the first Bali bomb blast on October 12, 2002, Imam Samudera alias Abdul Azis, is now facing the death penalty. He and his family declined to ask for clemency from the President, although the Attorney General as the prosecutor has offered him the opportunity several times, as part of an offender's rights. Not only Samudera, but also his entire family such as his wife Zakiyah and his mother, Embay Badriyah, turned down the offer.

Abdul Azis, born in Lopang Gede, Serang, Banten on January 14, 1970, is of the opinion that the request for clemency to the President is in contradiction with his fundamental belief that underlies his mission in the first Bali bombing. Imam Samudera's family, communicating through their lawyers, the Muslim's Advocacy Team (TPM), prefers a judicial review by the supreme court regarding the death-penalty ruling made by Denpasar District Court on September 10, 2003.

It was by no means easy to meet with Imam Samudera for an interview. Therefore, Bantenlink.com sent Lulu Jamaludin, Imam Samudera's younger brother, to see Imam Samudera, together with the Muslim's Advocacy Team, on various occasions, including a visit to Nusakambangan Prison, where the death row inmate is held. Based on a previously prepared list of questions, the interviews took place during a family gathering attended by Samudera's lawyers.

Why not ask for clemency?

I beg you all to understand that this is my jihad. Asking for clemency would mean asking for pardon from a human being because a president is only a human being. In the jihad context, pardon can only be granted by Allah, praise be to God and He is sublime, and not by a human being. To Allah alone must mankind beg for forgiveness. He is the One who owns jannah (heaven). He is All Merciful, He is Most Affectionate.

Can you elaborate it further?

In the jihad related to Bali bomb blast all was carried out based on conviction, and such conviction has its accountability, its underlying laws are open to validity tests. It would be indecent for a person on a jihad mission to ask for clemency to the President in order to get a lighter punishment. My knowledge of jihad is not a shallow one, but it has been perfected since I was twelve to thirteen years old. Asking for clemency would amount to regretting the act. To regret it would mean to regret my belief. A betrayal of the belief itself, a betrayal of Islam. *Naudzubillahi min dzalik.*[1] To ask for clemency would mean to admit that the law of unbelievers is legitimate; to admit that there is truth outside Islam is a negation of the syahadat.[2]

So?

On the contrary, the President and all the cronies of the law—from cabinet ministers, state dignitaries, judges, prosecutors, police to all of those who uphold the Dutch law, especially those who help the U.S. and its allies— must ask for pardon from Allah. It is compulsory for them to do so, as well as to ask for forgiveness to all the mujahidins.[3]

If the U.S. was the target, why a bomb blast in Bali?

This is not a simple matter to explain. Based on the intention or the target, it is clear that the Bali bomb blast was a jihad fi sabilillah,[4] because its primary target was nations of oppressors such as the U.S. and its allies. They gathered in Bali, so it was not the place that became the target. It becomes even more obvious with the massacre of Muslims in Afghanistan during the Ramadan in 2001, which almost entire mankind all over the world could witness. These nations of oppressors massacred innocent babies. Unbelievers have to be attacked, wherever they are (*Imam recites At-Taubah verse 36*),[5] including Bali.

Are you sure you will go to heaven?

(Imam Samudera only smiles, his eyes flash sharply. He mumbles something, as if chanting a dzikir.[6] Then he recites At-Taubah verse 111, which goes: Verily Allah has bought from the believers their selves and properties by granting heaven to them. They fought in the way of Allah, then they killed or got killed. This (has become a promise) truly given by Allah as stated in the Torah, Bible, and al-Quran. And who is more faithful to his word (other than) Allah? Therefore be content with the transactions that you have undertaken, and that is the true victory.)

What about the death penalty?

In the police interrogation report of Imam Samudera, which I had a chance to read, the act fulfills the requirement of chapter fifteen and is considered an extraordinary crime. I understand, what I and my friends committed is punishable by death according to chapter fifteen of the antiterrorism law. I am neither trembling nor afraid. I told the investigators to change the phrase extraordinary crime. Because what I did is not a crime, based on al-Quran and the Sunnah,[7] it is called jihad fi sabilillah.

What was their reaction?

As I told you, there is no time for remorse. Cherish it; cherish it because I and my friends have done a transaction in accordance with the word of Allah. The transaction is either to kill or to be killed, either instantly or through a process that I and my friends have undergone. And that is a huge victory.

So death is nothing to be afraid of?

Death is just an episode that all human beings have to go through, and then they will live an eternal life. The Muslims undergo suffering, pain, and sorrow, and so do the unbelievers. The difference is that the Muslims will receive the blessings of Allah, while the unbelievers will not.

Do you have any remorse about what happened in Bali?

Till death come for me, up till now I have never regretted the Bali bomb jihad and the other jihad bombings. Neither will I ask for clemency to the unbeliever's law or the neo-Ilyasiq.[8]

Are you ready for your death penalty?

May Allah grant me strength on this path of Islam, till the angel of death comes for me. I will hold onto Islam tightly in my heart and negate all of the thaghut laws,[9] I will hold the reigns of Allah tightly. No remorse, no clemency. I only surrender myself to the law of Allah. Be my witness that we are Muslims.

Any other message, Mr. Teacher?

(Imam Samudera hands in some notes, saying that they were written for a book about Imam Samudera, which was eventually banned. The notes contain among others a plea to stop addressing Imam Samudera as Ustadz [religious teacher] if he ceases to uphold the spirit of jihad, beg for forgiveness from the pirates of Allah's law. Imam also asks that we cry for him if he were to become too friendly with the enemies of Allah, for the sake of a spoon of rice that will soon be stale and a handful of sugar that is not more precious than a fly.)

Translated from Indonesian by M. Budiman

Editors' Notes

1. Naudzubillahi min dzalik is an expression in Islam used for asking God's protection from committing an act that is contrary to Islamic teachings.
2. Syahadat is the basic tenet of Islam that recognizes Allah as the true and only God and Muhammad as the Prophet of God.
3. Mujahidins refer to the soldiers of God.
4. Jihad fi sabilillah means fighting in the path of God.
5. At-Taubah is a chapter in The Qur'an, which means "Repentance."
6. Dzikir means "recollection" of the name of God, for example through chanting praise to Allah and the Prophet Muhammad.
7. Sunnah means Islamic laws other than The Qur'an which are not binding.
8. Ilyasiq loosely means the legal system allegedly installed under Chinggis Khan.
9. Thaghut means oppressor or oppression.

Megawati Sukarnoputri

Fabiola Desy Unidjaja

In 1993 Megawati Sukarnoputri, the daughter of Indonesia's first president Sukarno, became the leader of the Indonesian Democratic Party (PDI). Suharto considered her popularity a serious threat to his power and forced her removal from the party. Megawati subsequently founded her own party, the Indonesian Democratic Party of Struggle (PDI-P), taking most of the PDI members with her. In 1999, after the parliamentary elections, her party came out the strongest, but it did not receive a majority of the votes. While she could have claimed the presidency, many Muslim political leaders objected to having a woman as president. As a result, Megawati agreed to be vice-president to Abdurrahman Wahid, the leader of the National Awakening Party (PKB), which proclaims not to have any specific affiliation, but its members are mostly Muslim. When the president was impeached in July 2001, Megawati became Indonesia's fifth president. She lost her position after the first-ever-held presidential elections of September 2004.

The Jakarta Post, October 2004

Psychologists would have a field day with Megawati. Under pressure she is full of grace, motherly even; yet, that pride can also make her stubborn as a mule. Like a five-year-old in a toy store—who believes he is invincible—she breaks all the rules. And, while others may bear the cost, Megawati shows no remorse. Her argument is strong—in that she sticks to it—but it falters in terms of logic. Her past is marked by triumphs and tragedies that would turn a lesser man or woman into an emotional basket case. Her complicated personal life story saw her brought up in the Palace, demoted to second-class citizenship, and rise as the great hope of democracy, before being rejected in the [2004 presidential] election. All this—including two marriages and an annulment—occurred within a span of fifty-seven years.

Accompanying her father, founding President Sukarno, Megawati, as a teenager, traveled the globe and was hugged by kings and presidents. She was never absent from state receptions, at which Sukarno encouraged her to dance before dignitaries. But at nineteen years of age her charmed life suddenly came to an end when her father was removed from office in 1966. Banished from the palace grounds, the Sukarno children were reduced to begging to see their ailing father, who remained under house arrest. She lost her father in 1971, and her first husband, the late Captain Surindro Supjarso, in 1970. From that marriage she has two sons, Mohammad Rizky Pratama and Pramudya Prananda. Her second marriage was to the Egyptian diplomat Hasan Gamal Ahmad Hasan, but only lasted a few months as the Sukarno family were against it. In 1973 she married Taufik [Kiemas] and was blessed with her only daughter, Puan Maharani.

Her political career, which began with the Indonesian Democratic Party (PDI) in 1987, was not a smooth journey either. She was not spared the restrictions of Suharto's regime. As her popularity increased and she was perceived to be a threat, there were times when she was told to disembark from a commercial plane via the cargo exit, rather than the front door. During these crazy days, Taufik was solid in his support, but in her glory days, this outgoing and explosive personality became her worst enemy. Many considered that Megawati was the victim of her marriage. Bad judgments, erroneous political moves, and money-oriented policies were driven by Taufik in the public's eyes. Although Taufik's image may be accurate, it cannot be denied that Megawati's fragility was in her inability to challenge him—even when his actions threatened her administration, party, and credibility. However, despite the talk that surrounds her, not many are fortunate enough to see her Midas touch—a rare gift that is not bestowed on many. Megawati smiles from the heart. Her gestures of compassion stun, so that the more time you spend with her—Megawati the person, not the president—the more she grows on you, even if you differ in opinion. The sincerity of the president's daughter is second to none. If she comes to trust you, and is comfortable in your presence, her jokes and light stories may take you by surprise. Her belief in the pluralistic nature of Indonesia has been a sanctuary for all, especially minorities in the world's most populous Muslim nation. "There is no such thing as indigenous or non-indigenous; anyone born here is an Indonesian, and those who have clear citizenship are Indonesians," she often said.

Saving the Komodo Dragons

Indira Permanasari

Environmental preservation has emerged as one of Indonesia's major challenges in the past few decades. Increased industrialization, urbanization, and traffic have resulted in air and water pollution, and tropical forests are disappearing rapidly to make room for agricultural lands. Smog caused by slash-and-burn fires in Kalimantan and Sumatra has affected the air quality to dangerous levels in recent years, not only locally but also in neighboring Singapore and Malaysia. Overfishing and water pollution has led to a depletion of ocean resources. The creation of national parks has helped protect the environment in specific areas. One of those parks, located on Komodo Island and Rinca Island, has been successful in preserving the habitat of the Komodo dragon, a monstrous-looking prehistoric lizard. Surrounded by several other small islands, Komodo Island and Rinca Island lie between Sumbawa and Flores. This is the only place in the world where the species, known locally as ora, *finds a home. Tourists visit the park, but they are warned about the animal's ferocious nature: these monitor lizards can swallow a whole goat, and they have attacked locals. One European visitor who wandered off from a group has disappeared without a trace.*

Last mid-June a motorboat anchoring off Komodo Island, West Manggarai, East Nusa Tenggara, had a rather unusual load on its deck. Normally, boats of this kind are loaded with tourists who sometimes stay overnight on board to seize the early-morning opportunity to take pictures of the Komodo dragon. However, this particular boat was fully loaded, among other things, with large metal plates with holes on their surfaces, which turned out to be some sort of knock-down traps, several laptop computers, and, last but not least, five live goats. "We need the goats as bait in our next research on Rinca Island," said M. Jeri Imansyah, a member of the research staff at the Center for Conservation and Research of Endangered Species of the Zoological Society of San Diego. Sitting at the bow with stretched legs were the other members of the research team and some observers from Metrozoo Florida, U.S.A., who looked dead tired. They had just finished three weeks of fieldwork for their research on the population of the Komodo dragon on Komodo Island.

A Komodo dragon, Rinca Island. Photo by Agus Hidayat. Photo no. 20030317, courtesy of TEMPO.

Throughout the four-hour journey from Loh Liang to Labuan Bajo, the passengers were mercilessly shaken by the waves of the Batu Tiga waters, known to have claimed many lives, and for a while they were entertained by a group of dolphins and an eagle hovering over the water surface. All the time there was, of course, the never-ending bleating of the poor goats.

The islands west of Flores Island serve as a source of attraction not only for a good number of tourists but also for researchers. The Komodo National Park was declared a world natural heritage site in 1991 and a Man and Biosphere Reserve by the UNESCO, and it indeed boasts a vast amount of biodiversity that makes it earn its reputation as a center of the world's biodiversity. Bob Mese, Project Leader of the Nature Conservancy, who is active in water preservation at the Komodo National Park, revealed that the waters around the park serve as a habitat for around 1,000 species of fish. Other inhabitants of the area are 260 species of coral, 70 species of anemone, 2 species of turtles, and 9 species of seaweed. One also finds here the smallest type of seahorse with a length of just two centimeters and giant stingrays, which provide an astonishing spectacle for many tourists. The sea also serves as a migratory route for five types of whales, ten types of dolphins, and for manatees. Some winged inhabitants of the area are, for example, little yellow-crested cockatoos, kingfishers, *Philemon Buceroides neglectus* (a type of rare dusky honeyeater), and wattled brush turkeys. Another precious treasure the islands have in store is the population of Komodo dragons (*Varanus Komodoensis*), the primary inhabitants of the park. These lizards are believed to be creatures from the Jurassic age. The western part of Komodo Island was formed during the Jurassic era about 130 million years ago. The eastern part, as well as Rinca Island and Padar Island, were formed around 49 million years ago. Komodo dragons as prehistoric lizards managed to survive due to the absence of bigger predators in the area.

The research team from the Center for Conservation and Research of Endangered Species has been conducting research on these prehistoric animals for the past four years. They set up metal traps using goat meat as bait. Once the dragon walks into a trap, its legs are tied and its mouth taped. The dragon is then weighed and a marker or a GPS is attached to monitor its future movements.

Prehistoric Animal

Catching these prehistoric lizards requires great care. It only takes one bite for Komodo dragons to kill their prey, which will eventually die of a bacterial infection caused by the dragon's saliva. In addition to the two big islands, Komodo Island and Rinca Island, some Komodo dragons can also be found on smaller islands such as Gili Motang and Nusa Kode. These two islands have a land surface of less than 11 square kilometers, while Komodo Island and Rinca Island measure more than 230 square kilometers.

What is interesting, according to the research team, is that the size of the dragons living on the minor islands is much smaller than those found on the bigger islands. "About ten years ago the biggest sized Komodo dragon on Gili Motang reached thirty-four kilograms. But now it only reaches twenty-four kilograms. In contrast, those living on Komodo Island can reach eighty kilograms and can be three meters long," said Tim Jessop, the team leader.

The significant contrast in the size of the Komodo dragons is determined, among others, by the density of the population of their primary prey, that is, deer. The most sizeable Komodo dragons on the two minor islands equal the size of the most dwarfish dragons living in the park, as the density of the deer population on those islands is three to four times lower than that in the national park. Also, there is no other prey available such as buffalo and wild boar. Komodo dragons grow to be most voluminous on the big islands where the populations of deer, wild boars, and buffaloes are most dense.

The availability of a bigger primary prey determines the size of the dragons. However, this availability is inseparably linked to shortages of food and water on that island, especially since there is neither interisland migration nor an increase in the deer population. To estimate the index of the deer population and other varieties of big prey, the team had to follow their tracks for days and count their droppings.

Another research staff member, M. Jeri Imansyah, further added that the lack of such natural resources had brought about a substantial risk of extinction on the smaller islands compared to the bigger ones. The Komodo population on Padar Island, for instance, has been extinct since the 1990s. "We have made some recommendations to the Komodo National Park concerning the conservation of the dragons on the minor islands. To conserve Komodo dragons on islands such as Gili Motang, additional water sources or deer population could be worked out, but it must be done with great care and based on a thorough consideration of its impact since it will affect the habitat," he emphasized.

The chances of survival for the dragons on the islands such as Komodo Island and Rinca Island are much better. For some time the rapid increase of the human population on Komodo Island caused the park administrator worry. In the 1980s there was even a plan to relocate the people to another island, but it never materialized. As an illustration, in 1928 there were only 30 people living on Komodo Island. However, in 1999 the population of the island reached 1,169 people, and in 2004 there were 1,235 people.

Fortunately, so far the dragons and the local people still manage to live in peaceful coexistence. There have been stories passed down from generation to generation about a human being and a Komodo dragon, or *ora*, as twin brothers, and so they are not supposed to disturb each other. H. Abidin, the village chief of Komodo Island, told a story of how in the distant past a group of primitive people with huge ears inhabited the island. A patriarch named Empo Najo was their leader. "Whenever there was a woman in the village who was about to deliver a baby, the *empo* (chief) would split the woman's womb, resulting in the death of the woman, but the fetus would survive. One day, Empo Najo's daughter-in-law gave birth to a baby and her stomach was split. From her womb came out a twin, *ora* the Komodo and a human baby." People coming from Sumba would later settle on that island as well.

Existing Threat

Nevertheless, there are many more threats to the whole area of the national park. Rusman, Deputy Head of the Komodo National Park, explained that forest fires happen nearly every year. In 2004 alone there were two incidents of forest fires. These have the potential to burn down all the grass that serves as the primary food for deer, which are Komodo dragons' main prey. The waters surrounding the park are also threatened by the presence of ring trawlers and the use of fishing bombs, which can bring destruction to coral reefs despite their far less frequent use. It is suspected that the culprits come from other places outside the park area. The Komodo National Park Administrators, supported by three speedboats owned by the Nature Conservancy, have intensified patrols. Zoning for fishing has also been established.

But the area is quite vast, comprising 173,300 hectares, consisting of 40,728 hectares of land and 132,572 hectares of water. As a result, monitoring becomes a tricky business. Occasionally, the illegal fishermen would play a hide-and-seek game with the park rangers. People's awareness—both within and outside the Komodo National Park—as far as the conservation of this protection center of the world's biodiversity is concerned, eventually plays a determining role in preserving the site.

Translated from Indonesian by M. Budiman

Post-Tsunami Aceh

Scott Baldauf

On December 26, 2004, a massive earthquake in the Indian Ocean that measured 9.15 on the Richter scale caused a colossal tsunami that swept away the surrounding coastal regions. Aceh in northern Sumatra was one of the hardest-hit areas. This province had been living under martial law for eighteen months because the central government wanted to curb the activities of the Free Aceh Movement rebels who waged a guerilla war for independence. Since May 2003 Aceh had been closed to international organizations and journalists. The tsunami left 170,000 people killed or missing and destroyed 80 percent of Aceh's infrastructure. Aid was slow to reach the province partly because of the existing tense relations with the central government. A Reconstruction and Rehabilitation Agency was created to recover the area and to provide houses and schools for the tsunami survivors. Scott Baldauf, staff reporter for the Christian Science Monitor, below reports on the gender disparity in decision-making processes and suggests it takes a woman to rebuild a village. In August 2005 the Free Aceh Movement and the government in Jakarta signed a peace agreement, which gave Aceh special territory status with the guarantee of more autonomy than a province.

Deyah Mapplam, Indonesia—After the December 26 tsunami wave receded, Deyah Mapplam became a village of men. Of 4,500 people, just 270 survived, and only one-third were women. And it is that gender imbalance, as much as the loss of homes and livelihoods, that remains a concern here. For local men like Mohammad Nur, the solution is simple: to get remarried. But female survivors and Mr. Nur's new wife, Hadijah, say it is more complex than that. Women need to be involved in the planning process to rebuild Deyah Map-plam—or else the town may not be fit for habitation.

Hadijah, a twenty-something who recently came to Deyah Mapplam to marry a local farmer here, says one needs look no further than the temporary barracks where she and the village survivors now live. Clearly, they were not designed by a woman. "The main thing is that the toilet is too far from our rooms, so if you have to go to toilet at midnight, it is too dark to go" and still

A mosque in Krueng Raya, Nanggroe Aceh Darussalam, after the 2004 tsunami. Photo by Arie Basuki. Photo no. 20041231, courtesy of *TEMPO*.

feel safe, says Hadijah. "And there is no privacy inside the houses," she adds, noting that she and her new husband would like to have a baby.

Six months after the tsunami the disproportionate toll on women is still being felt. According to some reports, the survivor ratio of males to females averages almost three to one. The imbalance has made it more difficult for women to have a voice in the planning and reconstruction of their communities—especially in a Muslim country where men tend to make major decisions. But women's activists and many Acehnese female survivors say that women's involvement is crucial to creating livable communities. "Basic community planning decisions affect most of the aspects of family life," says Nicola Rounce, a project coordinator at UNIFEM, the UN's agency for women's development. "It affects the right to food, the right to sanitation, the right to have guardianship of children, and even access to marketplaces. We used to say [to Acehnese officials] that you're leaving out 50 percent of the population in the decision-making process," she says, but today's gender balance has made that situation even worse. "If only we could say [it was 50 percent] now," she says wryly.

The gender imbalance in Indonesia's Aceh Province is a phenomenon found in most of the dozen or so countries affected by the tsunami of December 26, 2004. Reasons for the disproportionate death toll range from the fact that women are less likely than men to know how to swim to the fact that women were more likely to be carrying babies or holding elderly relatives when the flood hit. Traditional long dresses also made it difficult for women to flee. But if the giant wave hit women hardest, cultural norms in a traditional province like Aceh are doing little to ease matters.

In a report issued by Flower Aceh, a nongovernmental organization based in Singapore, Suraiya Kamaruzzaman wrote: "Coordinators in charge of relief work are not gender sensitive. They think giving cooking utensils and washing detergent equals meeting women's needs." Last month, close to four hundred women from Aceh's twenty-one districts gathered to discuss women's participation in the recovery and reconstruction process. The All-Acehnese Women's Congress submitted recommendations to the Indonesian government's Aceh Reconstruction Agency. The No. 1 recommendation: the re-establishment of *balai inong*, or "women's houses."

UNIFEM officials say that before the tsunami struck, every village in Aceh had a *balai inong* where women could meet to network and work together on projects. Congressional participants said that rebuilding these women's houses in villages would be an effective way to ensure that women's concerns were being heard, while also providing a safe space for women to grieve, share experiences, and develop skills to sustain their livelihoods. At Camp Pidie, on the western coast of Banda Aceh, some parents of teenage girls are so concerned about their daughters' safety that they are marrying them off at age sixteen, according to Ms. Kamaruzzaman. At least then, the parents reasoned, the girls will have husbands to "protect them."

Down the coast from Deyah Mapplam, Mohammad Daud Agam cradles his three-year-old granddaughter, Alfiatun, in the town's coffee shop. The girl and Mr. Agam's son are the only family he has left, and the elderly fish-seller admits he is having a hard time adjusting to life without women. "All the women in my family died, so now I have to do all the cooking," he says, adding that his own experience is unusual in the village. The hills in his village of Pulot are close enough and low enough to climb, a fact that contributed to a relatively low death toll, and higher survival rates for women. Now Mr. Agam just hopes that he and his family can survive his cooking. "This is a new experience for me," he smiles. "I just cook and we eat, and maybe I'm getting a little better."

In Meunasah Mesjid—where only 159 of the 1,110 residents survived, and only 45 of those were women—Hajji Rusli, a local businessman, says that most of the widowers who can afford to marry are doing so, although men who have no surviving children are focusing on getting jobs and building up their savings to build their homes later. "It's really, really difficult to live without women," says Hajji Rusli, sitting at a coffee shop. "But, personally, I don't want to remarry. I want to remember my wife, how she behaved, how she thought about things. She was a business partner; she managed my rice factory. I just want to remember her a long time."

Amiruddin Sulaiman—a farmer who lives in the Deyah Mapplam barracks—also misses his former wife and family, but says he can no longer afford to mourn. Last month, he married a nineteen-year-old girl named Linawati, and he plans to start a new family soon. His new wife does not attend planning meetings, Sulaiman says, but she does have lots of ideas of how the new village should be built. "She says if we have a new house, she wants a bathing room and toilet inside the house. Of course, women need a place to sit together and they should have a say in how to make the new village," he says.

The Danish Cartoon Controversy

Susilo Bambang Yudhoyono

A Danish newspaper published controversial cartoons depicting the Prophet Moham-mad in September 2005. While at first the issue remained an affair discussed only within Denmark, Danish imams took the matter to the Middle East to seek support in their condemnation of what they considered blasphemous drawings and commen-tary. Newspapers in other countries reprinted the cartoons, claiming their right to freedom of expression. This ignited large-scale demonstrations in the Muslim world, including Indonesia, and in some cases embassies of countries where the cartoon had been reprinted were set on fire. Among the tumultuous worldwide debates on whether this was a matter of self-censorship or of freedom of speech, Susilo Bambang Yud-hoyono, the president of the most populous Muslim nation, reasoned for calm and for cooler heads to prevail.

International Herald Tribune

FRIDAY, FEBRUARY 10, 2006

Jakarta. The distasteful cartoons of the Prophet Muhammad, first published in Denmark in September 2005 and subsequently reproduced in other me-dia, continue to spark a chain of reactions ranging from peaceful protest to violence in many Muslim communities. The international community must work together to put out this fire. A good start would be to stop justifying the cartoons as "freedom of the press," which only hardens the Muslim commu-nity's response. Another vital step would be to discontinue their reproduc-tion, which only prolongs the outrage.

To non-Muslims, the image of the Prophet Muhammad may only be of casual interest. But to Muslim communities worldwide, it is of enormous spiritual importance. For the last fourteen centuries, Muslims have adhered to a strict code that prohibits any visual portrait of the Prophet. When this code was violated and their Prophet mocked for the purpose of humor, Muslims felt a direct assault on their faith.

Reprinting the cartoons in order to make a point about free speech is an act of senseless brinkmanship. It is also a disservice to democracy. It sends a conflicting message to the Muslim community: that in a democracy, it is permissible to offend Islam. This message damages efforts to prove that democracy and Islam go together. The average Muslim who prays five times a day needs to be convinced that the democracy he is embracing, and is expected to defend, also protects and respects Islam's sacred symbols. Otherwise, democracy will not be of much interest to him. The cartoon crisis serves as a reminder that all hell may break loose in a world of intolerance and ignorance. The global community needs to cultivate democracies of freedom and tolerance—not democracies of freedom versus tolerance. It is tolerance that protects freedom, harnesses diversity, strengthens peace, and delivers progress.

Since the September 11 terror attacks, many in the Western world have shown increasing interest in the Islamic world. Yet this interest has not been accompanied by a greater knowledge and understanding of Islam. In December last year, the summit of the Organization of the Islamic Conference in Mecca lamented "the feelings of stigmatization and concern over the growing phenomenon of Islamophobia around the world as a form of racism and discrimination." The West and Islam need not collide in a clash of civilizations. Many Islamic communities comfortably embrace some Western habits. Correspondingly, Islam has become the fastest-growing religion in some Western nations, including the United States. The Western and Islamic worlds can conscientiously work together to nurture a global culture of respect and tolerance.

The international community must not come out of the cartoon crisis broken and divided. We need to build more bridges between religions, civilizations, and cultures. Government leaders, religious figures and ordinary citizens can go beyond supporting religious freedom—they can express solidarity with those who are defending the integrity of their faith. We also need to intensify interfaith dialogue so that we may further tear down the walls of misunderstanding and mistrust—an undertaking that Indonesia has actively promoted.

Muslims around the world also have responsibilities. No one—certainly not Muslims—will be better off if the current crisis descends into open conflict and more bloodshed. The best way for Muslims to fight intolerance and ignorance toward Islam is by tirelessly reaching out to non-Muslims and projecting Islam as a peaceful religion. We also need to be forgiving to those who have sincerely apologized for offending Islam. Indeed, at this difficult moment, Muslims might emulate the Prophet Muhammad's well-known qualities in dealing with adversity: composure, sound judgment, magnanimity, and benevolence.

The Politics of Bare Flesh

Desi Anwar

The controversial Anti-pornography and Porno-Action bill, originally proposed in 1999, was reviewed by the Indonesian parliament again in early 2006. While it has always been difficult how to define what constitutes pornography, "porno-action" is an even more contentious concept. Apparently, kissing in public, sensual dancing, erotic artwork, and certain kinds of clothing (for women) fall under the category of porno-action. From the moment the bill came up for debate again, groups have rallied and voiced their opinions both in favor of and against it. Although Indonesia is the world's most populous Muslim country, most Indonesian Muslims are moderate and tolerant in their views. In conservative Islamic circles, however, there is widespread support for the restrictions on pornography and porno-action. Many women, on the other hand, believe that the bill violates women's rights as it forbids, among other things, women going out alone at night to constrain prostitution. Artists oppose the proposed bill, as it will curb their freedom to express themselves, whereas opposition in West Papua and on Bali is based on the way in which it clashes with indigenous cultural practices and the tourist industry. Desi Anwar is a Jakarta-based television and print journalist. On October 30, 2008 the Indonesian parliament ratified the so-called Anti-pornography bill. In protest two political parties, the Indonesian Democratic Party of Struggle (PDI-P) and Prosperous Peace Party (PDS), refused to vote.

March 18, 2006

Bali—The Balinese are calling it the third Bali bomb, threatening to frighten even more foreign tourists away from their beaches. A proposed bill on pornography currently under deliberation by Indonesia's parliament could be the coup de grace for the island's tourism industry—already in the death throes after a second bomb attack that targeted tourists (in October 2005) and recent fears over the uncontrolled spread of the bird-flu virus, according to Tjokorda Oka Sukawati, head of Bali's Hotel and Restaurant Association. Hotels, restaurants, and souvenir shops are slashing prices to compete

Mass rally to protest the Anti-pornography and Porno-Action bill (RUU-APP) in Jakarta, 2006. Photo by Gunawan Wicaksono. Photo no. 20060503, courtesy of TEMPO.

for the continually dwindling number of tourists. Many vendors are closing down and contemplating going back to till the land, says Tjokorda. The proposed pornography ban—which would make kissing and baring flesh in public punishable by possible jail terms and fines reaching into the millions of rupiah—threatens to drive sunbathers to neighboring countries' beaches at a time when Bali's tourism industry is already deep in the doldrums.

Economics aside, the proposed anti-pornography law and its oddly named companion the "anti-pornoaction" bill vie to push modern, moderate Indonesia in the direction of the many repressive regimes seen in the Middle East. The bill is generating a wave of popular resistance from women who see the bill as a further violation of their already limited rights. More broadly, the proposed legislation threatens the harmony of a predominantly Muslim nation that has historically celebrated its unity in diversity. The bill also threatens to undermine Indonesia's hard-won democracy and new laws aimed at protecting freedom of expression.

The porn law threatens to criminalize various actions that by their very nature are subject to interpretation and would necessarily result in arbitrary enforcement. For example, showing one's buttocks in public can get you two to six years in jail, though for some reason showing your genitals or breasts is less of an offense, earning you only one to five years in the clink. For masturbating in public, you can get two to ten years behind bars, which incidentally is an offense viewed only slightly less seriously than pedophilia, a crime that carries three to ten years in jail. That is on par with moving one's body erotically in public, which to some legislative minds might incite sexual arousal and other moral depravities.

Why Indonesia's legislators are expending their valuable time to deliberate the proposed legislation, particularly considering that the laws on the books regulating public decency, domestic violence, and other sexual offenses are still in need of better enforcement, is mind-boggling. Syafriansyah, a legislator with the Muslim PPP (United Development Party), has said the country's morality is in decline and hence the people need to be controlled to make sure that the nation doesn't go collectively to hell. The unnerving subtext is that prominent members of certain Muslim parties are trying to use the proposed legislation as a beachhead for pushing forward their broader political agenda of implementing Sharia law nationwide.

Aceh, whose special autonomy status allows it to impose its own brand of sharia law, which includes the use of public lashings, publicly parading alleged prostitutes, and casting judgment on women's attire, is the model these legislators aspire to. In several urban areas, such as the regency of Tangerang on the outskirts of Jakarta, some local governments have taken advantage of their new regional autonomy to arbitrarily force women to wear headscarves and stay home at night or risk being charged with soliciting. Increasingly these Muslim politicians are obsessed with issues of morality rather than delivering on their electoral promises of cleaning up corruption and creating a more just and equitable society—the issues that got them elected in the first place. Now that questions of morality have entered the national agenda in the shape of an anti-pornography bill, it looks as if the central government also is keen to impose these narrow sectarian values on the entire nation—which could stoke ethnic, religious, and cultural tensions across the archipelago.

From Papua, where normal clothing consists of penis sheaths and grass skirts, to Bali, where the baring of the flesh is an integral part of its cultural traditions reflected in dances, paintings, sculptures, and even religious worship, to Java, where female traditional costumes such as the *kebaya* are designed to enhance a woman's curves rather than hide them, Indonesia is a testimony to a pluralist society that celebrates its beauty and art in all its different manifestations.

To force a restrictive style of clothing, where women cannot show their hair, arms, and legs or move about in a manner that might provoke lust in men, not only violates Indonesia's basic laws and cultural character, but threatens to undermine the greater regional autonomy and grass roots democracy-promoting policies the government is meant to be implementing. The secessionists in Papua see this as another form of central government arrogance and another reason to opt out of the republic. Banners protesting the anti-pornography bill in Bali are already calling for the Hindu island's independence. At the same time, other non-Muslim Indonesians are wondering how they fit into all of this discussion.

The Asian financial crisis hit Indonesia particularly hard, and many people are looking to the government to find ways to improve the economy and up the national standard of living. Many wonder why parliamentarians instead are dedicating so much time and national resources to a cause that appears to be a distinct move away from pluralistic democracy and toward the authoritarianism seen in many Middle Eastern countries. In practicality, it would be difficult to impose this kind of law short of assigning moral police across this archipelago of more than 17,000 islands and 215 million people. Most of the local arts and entertainment would have to be banned as nearly all of the traditional dances figure sensual movements and bare shoulders of some sort, not to mention hiding away paintings, sculptures, and all kinds of traditional art works that pertain to fertility and physical beauty. Women would conceivably be forced to stay at home, as they fear being mistaken for a prostitute or arrested for showing too much flesh. The bill's hugely adverse impact would be as much social as it would be economic.

Supporters of the bill, who often decry the country's trend toward liberalization as kowtowing to the degenerate West, might be wondering why they have encountered so much popular resistance. Past efforts to turn Indonesia into an Islamic state have been launched and failed. As a full-fledged representative democracy, parties that campaigned on fundamentalist platforms performed poorly during the last round of presidential and parliamentary elections. And if those that were elected prioritize anti-pornography legislation over improving the overall national good, they could find themselves out of jobs after the next polls.

Suggestions for Further Reading

Broad Histories

Brown, Colin. *A Short History of Indonesia: The Unlikely Nation?* New York: Allen and Unwin, 2003.

Cribb, Robert. *Historical Atlas of Indonesia.* Honolulu: University of Hawai'i Press, 2000.

Friend, Theodore. *Indonesian Destinies.* Cambridge: Belknap, 2003.

Ricklefs, M. C. *A History of Modern Indonesia Since c. 1200.* 3rd ed. Stanford, Calif.: Stanford University Press, 2001.

Taylor, Jean Gelman. *Indonesian Histories.* New Haven: Yale University Press, 2003.

Vickers, Adrian. *A History of Modern Indonesia.* Cambridge: Cambridge University Press, 2005.

I. Early Histories

Bellwood, Peter. *Prehistory of the Indo-Malaysian Archipelago.* Rev. ed. Honolulu: University of Hawai'i Press, 1997.

Coedès, Georges, and Louis-Charles Damai. *Sriwijaya: History, Religion, and Language of an Early Malay Polity; Collected Studies.* Kuala Lumpur: MBRAS, 1992.

Higham, Charles. *The Bronze Age of Southeast Asia.* New York: Cambridge University Press, 1996.

Miksic, John, and Endang Sri Hardiati Soekatno, eds. *The Legacy of Majapahit.* Singapore: National Heritage Board, 1995.

Munoz, Paul Michel. *Early Kingdoms of the Indonesian Archipelago and the Malay Peninsula.* Singapore: Éditions Didier Millet, 2006.

II. Early Modern Histories

Andaya, Leonard. *The Heritage of Arung Palakka: A History of South Sulawesi in the Seventeenth Century.* The Hague: Martinus Nijhoff, 1981.

———. *The World of Maluku: Eastern Indonesia in the Early Modern Period.* Honolulu: University of Hawai'i Press, 1993.

Barnard, Tim. *Multiple Centers of Authority: Society and Environment in Siak and Eastern Sumatra, 1674–1827.* Leiden: KITLV Press, 2003.

Gaastra, Femme S. *The Dutch East India Company: Expansion and Decline.* Zutphen, Netherlands: Walburg Pers, 2003.

Jacobs, Els M. *In Pursuit of Pepper and Tea: The Story of the Dutch East India Company*. Amsterdam: Netherlands Maritime Museum, 1991.

Lombard, Denys. *Le sultanat d'Atjeh au temps d'Iskandar Muda, 1607–1636*. Paris: École Française d'Extrème-Orient, 1967.

Reid, Anthony. *Southeast Asia in the Age of Commerce, 1450–1680. Volume One: The Lands below the Winds*. New Haven: Yale University Press, 1988.

————. *Southeast Asia in the Age of Commerce, 1450–1680. Volume Two: Expansion and Crisis*. New Haven: Yale University Press, 1993.

Ricklefs, M. C. *Jogjakarta under Sultan Mangkubumi, 1749–1792: A History of the Division of Java*. London: Oxford University Press, 1974.

Sutherland, Heather, and Gerrit Knaap. *Monsoon Traders: Ships, Skippers, and Commodities in Eighteenth-Century Makassar*. Leiden: KITLV Press, 2004.

Watson Andaya, Barbara. *To Live as Brothers: Southeast Sumatra in the Seventeenth and Eighteenth Centuries*. Honolulu: University of Hawai'i Press, 1993.

III. Cultures in Collision

Blussé, Leonard. *Strange Company: Chinese Settlers, Mestizo Women, and the Dutch in VOC Batavia*. Dordrecht, Netherlands: Foris, 1986.

Boomgaard, Peter, Freek Colombijn, and David Henley, eds. *Paper Landscapes: Explorations in the Environmental History of Indonesia*. Leiden: KITLV Press, 1997.

Braginsky, Vladimir. *The Heritage of Traditional Malay Literature*. Leiden: KITLV Press, 2004.

Elson, R. E. *Village Java under the Cultivation System, 1830–1870*. Sydney: Allen and Unwin, 1994.

Geertz, Clifford. *Agricultural Involution: The Processes of Ecological Change in Indonesia*. Berkeley: University of California Press, 1963.

Taylor, Jean Gelman. *The Social World of Batavia: Europeans and Eurasians in Dutch Asia*. Madison: University of Wisconsin Press, 1983.

IV. Through Travelers' Eyes

Nieuwenhuys, Rob. *Mirror of the Indies: A History of Dutch Colonial Literature*. Amherst: University of Massachusetts Press, 1982.

Reid, Anthony, ed. *Witnesses to Sumatra: A Travellers' Anthology*. Kuala Lumpur: Oxford University Press, 1995.

Resink, G. J. "The Eastern Archipelago under Joseph Conrad's Western Eyes." In *Indonesia's History between the Myths*, 1–11. The Hague: W. van Hoeve, 1968.

Rush, James R., ed. *Java: A Travellers' Anthology*. Kuala Lumpur: Oxford University Press, 1996.

Savage, Victor. *Western Impressions of Nature and Landscape in Southeast Asia*. Singapore: Singapore University Press, 1984.

Sherry, Norman. *Conrad's Eastern World*. Cambridge: Cambridge University Press, 1966.

Warren, James Francis. "Joseph Conrad's Fiction as Southeast Asian History." In *At the Edge of Southeast Asian History: Essays*, 8–22. Quezon City: New Day Publishers, 1987.

V. High Colonial Indies

Cribb, Robert, ed. *The Late Colonial State in Indonesia: Political and Economic Foundations of the Netherlands Indies, 1880–1942.* Leiden: KITLV Press, 1994.

Laffan, Michael. *Islamic Nationhood and Colonial Indonesia: The Umma below the Winds.* New York: Routledge, 2003.

Locher-Scholten, Elsbeth. "Dutch Imperialism in the Indonesian Archipelago and the Imperialism Debate." *Journal of Southeast Asian Studies* 25, no. 1 (1994): 91–111.

Mrázek, Rudolf. *Engineers of Happy Land: Technology and Nationalism in a Colony.* Princeton: Princeton University Press, 2002.

Rush, James R. *Opium to Java: Revenue Farming and Chinese Enterprise in Colonial Indonesia, 1860–1910.* Ithaca: Cornell University Press, 1990.

Shiraishi, Takashi. *An Age in Motion: Popular Radicalism in Java, 1912–1926.* Ithaca: Cornell University Press, 1990.

Stoler, Ann Laura. *Capitalism and Confrontation in Sumatra's Plantation Belt, 1870–1979.* New Haven: Yale University Press, 1985.

VI. The Last Decades of the Indies

Gouda, Frances. *Dutch Culture Overseas: Colonial Practice in the Netherlands Indies, 1900–1942.* Amsterdam: Amsterdam University Press, 1995.

Locher-Scholten, Elsbeth. *Women and the Colonial State: Essays on Gender and Modernity in the Netherlands Indies, 1900–1942.* Amsterdam: Amsterdam University Press, 2000.

McVey, Ruth. *Taman Siswa and the Indonesian National Awakening.* Ithaca: Cornell University Press, 1967.

Niel, Robert Van. *The Emergence of the Modern Indonesian Elite.* Dordrecht, Netherlands: Foris, 1984.

Siegel, James T. *Fetish, Recognition, Revolution.* Princeton: Princeton University Press, 1997.

Teeuw, A. *Modern Indonesian Literature.* 2 vols. 2nd ed. The Hague: Martinus Nijhoff, 1979.

VII. From Nationalism to Independence

Benda, Harry J. *The Crescent and the Rising Sun: Indonesian Islam under the Japanese Occupation, 1942–1945.* The Hague: W. van Hoeve, 1958.

Cribb, Robert. *Gangsters and Revolutionaries: The Jakarta People's Militia and the Indonesian Revolution, 1945–1949.* Honolulu: University of Hawai'i Press, 1991.

Frederick, William H. *Visions and Heat: The Making of the Indonesian Revolution.* Athens: Ohio University Press, 1989.

Jong, L. de. *The Collapse of a Colonial Society: The Dutch in Indonesia during the Second World War.* Trans. Jennifer Kilian, Cornelia Kist, and John Rudge. Leiden: KITLV Press, 2002.

Kahin, Audrey R. *Regional Dynamics of the Indonesian Revolution: Unity from Diversity.* Honolulu: University of Hawai'i Press, 1985.

Kahin, George McTurnan. *Nationalism and Revolution in Indonesia*. Ithaca: Cornell University Press, 1959.

Raben, Remco, ed. *Representing the Japanese Occupation of Indonesia: Personal Testimonies and Public Images in Indonesia, Japan, and the Netherlands*. Amsterdam: Netherlands Institute for War Documentation, 1999.

Reid, Anthony. *The Blood of the People: Revolution and the End of Traditional Rule in North Sumatra*. Kuala Lumpur: Oxford University Press, 1979.

Shiraishi, Saya, and Takashi Shiraishi, eds. *The Japanese in Colonial Southeast Asia*. Ithaca: Southeast Asia Program, Cornell University, 1993.

VIII. The Old Order, the New Order—Political Climate

Anderson, Benedict R. O'G. *Language and Power: Exploring Political Cultures in Indonesia*. Ithaca: Cornell University Press, 1990.

Anderson, Benedict R. O'G. and Ruth McVey. *A Preliminary Analysis of the October 1, 1965 Coup in Indonesia*. Ithaca: Cornell University Southeast Asia Program, 1971.

Budiman, Arief, ed. *State and Civil Society in Indonesia*. Clayton, Vic.: Centre of Southeast Asian Studies, Monash University, 1990.

Dijk, C. van. *Rebellion under the Banner of Islam: The Darul Islam in Indonesia*. The Hague: Martinus Nijhoff, 1981.

Hill, Hal, ed. *Indonesia's New Order: The Dynamics of Socio-economic Transformation*. St. Leonards, N.S.W.: Allen and Unwin, 1994.

Mortimer, Rex. *Indonesian Communism under Sukarno: Ideology and Politics, 1959–1965*. Ithaca: Cornell University Press, 1974.

Roosa, John. *Pretext for Mass Murder: The September 30th Movement and Suharto's Coup D'État in Indonesia*. Madison: University of Wisconsin Press, 2006.

Shiraishi, Takashi, ed. *Approaching Suharto's Indonesia from the Margins*. Ithaca: Southeast Asia Program, Cornell University, 1994.

IX. Social Issues and Cultural Debates

Foulcher, Keith, and Tony Day, eds. *Clearing a Space: Postcolonial Readings of Modern Indonesian Literature*. Leiden: KITLV Press, 2002.

Matheson Hooker, Virginia, ed. *Culture and Society in New Order Indonesia*. Kuala Lumpur: Oxford University Press, 1993.

Purdey, Jemma. *Anti-Chinese Violence in Indonesia, 1969–1999*. Leiden: KITLV Press, 2005.

Robinson, Geoffrey. *The Dark Side of Paradise: Political Violence in Bali*. Ithaca: Cornell University Press, 1995.

Schiller, Jim, and Barbara Martin-Schiller, eds. *Imagining Indonesia: Cultural Politics and Political Culture*. Athens: Ohio University Center for International Studies, 1997.

Sears, Laurie J., ed. *Fantasizing the Feminine in Indonesia*. Durham, N.C.: Duke University Press, 1996.

Sidel, John. *Riots, Pogroms, Jihad: Religious Violence in Indonesia*. Ithaca: Cornell University Press, 2006.

Suryadinata, Leo. *Pribumi Indonesians, the Chinese Minority, and China*. 3rd ed. Singapore: Heinemann Asia, 1992.

X. Into the Twenty-First Century

Abuza, Zachary, *Political Islam and Violence in Indonesia*. New York: Routledge, 2006.

Bouchier, David, and Vedi R. Hadiz, eds. *Indonesian Politics and Society: A Reader*. London: Routledge Curzon, 2003.

Eliraz, Giora. *Islam in Indonesia: Modernism, Radicalism, and the Middle East Dimension*. Brighton: Sussex Academic Press, 2004.

Heryanto, Ariel, and Sumit K. Mandal, eds. *Challenging Authoritarianism in Southeast Asia: Comparing Indonesia and Malaysia*. New York: Routledge Curzon, 2003.

Lim, Merlyna. *Islamic Radicalism and Anti-Americanism in Indonesia: The Role of the Internet*. Washington: East-West Center, 2005.

Oey-Gardiner, Mayling, and Carla Bianpoen, eds. *Indonesian Women: The Journey Continues*. Canberra: Australian National University, Research School of Pacific and Asian Studies, 2000.

Robison, Richard, and Vedi R. Hadiz. *Reorganizing Power in Indonesia: The Politics of Oligarchy in an Age of Markets*. London: Routledge Curzon, 2004.

Sen, Krishna, and David T. Hill. *Media, Culture, and Politics in Indonesia*. Melbourne: Oxford University Press, 2000.

Steele, Janet. *Wars Within: The Story of "Tempo," an Independent Magazine in Soeharto's Indonesia*. Jakarta: Equinox, 2005.

Suryakusuma, Julia. *Sex, Power, and Nation: An Anthology of Writings, 1979–2003*. Jakarta: Metafor Publishing, 2004.

Vatikiotis, Michael. *The Rise and Fall of the New Order*. London: Routledge, 1998.

Acknowledgment of Copyrights

I. Early Histories

Expansion of Indo-Aryan Culture during Pallava Rule, by Ch. Chhabra (Delhi: Munshi Ram Manohar Lal, 1965), 85, 86, 90.

"India and the Malay Archipelago: A Study in Cultural Interaction," by Upendra Thakur, in *India's Cultural Relations with South-East Asia*, ed. Manjushree Rao et al. (Delhi: Sharada, 1996), 43–54.

"On the Conditions and Scope of the Development of Archaeology in Indonesia," by R. P. Soejono, in *Prehistoric Indonesia: A Reader*, ed. Pieter van de Velde (Dordrecht: Foris, 1984), 16–20.

Corpus of the Inscriptions of Java, by Himansu Bhusan Sarkar (Calcutta: K. H. Mukhopadhyay, 1971), 1:15–24.

Sriwijaya: History, Religion, and Language of an Early Malay Polity, by George Coedès and Louis-Charles Damai (Kuala Lumpur: Royal Asiatic Society, Malaysian Branch #20, 1992), 95–102. © 1992 by Malaysian Branch of the Royal Asiatic Society. Used by permission.

The Malay Peninsula: Crossroads of the Maritime Silk Road (100 BC–1300 AD), by Michel Jacq-Hergoualc'h (Leiden: Brill, 2002), 233–40. Used by permission.

Arab Navigation in the Indian Ocean before the Coming of the Portuguese, by G. R. Tibbetts (London: Royal Asiatic Society of Great Britain, 1971), 489–503. © 1971 by Royal Asiatic Society of Great Britain. Used by permission.

Former Points of View: Postcards and Literary Passages from Pre-independence Indonesia, by Stephen Grant (Jakarta: Lontar Foundation, 1995), 158. © 1995 by Lontar Foundation, used by permission of John McGlynn (director).

Deśawarnana (Nāgarakrtāgama), by Mpu Prapañca, trans. Stuart Robson (Leiden: KITLV, 1995), 71–73. © 1995 by KITLV. Used by permission.

II. Early Modern Histories

Ibn Battuta: Travels in Asia and Africa, 1325-1354, trans. H. A. R. Gibb (London: Routledge, 1929), 273–76. Used by permission.

III. Cultures in Collision

Max Havelaar; or, The Coffee Auctions of the Dutch Trading Company, by Multatuli [Eduard Douwes Dekker] (Leiden: Sijthoff, 1967), 211–16. © 1967 by Uitgeverij Sijthoff. Used by permission.

The Malay Archipelago, by Alfred Russel Wallace (London: Macmillan, 1869), 90–93.

Two Letters on Arabs in the Netherlands East Indies, 1876 (#121, 20 March 1876, Dutch Consul, Penang to Koo Chan Kay, Managing Owner of the British Steamer *Batara Bayu Sree*, and the latter's reply, 24 March 1876). Source: Arsip Nasional Republik Indonesia.

Letters of a Javanese Princess, by Raden Adjeng Kartini, trans. Agnes Louise Symmers, ed. Hildred Geertz (Lanham, Md.: University Press of America, 1985), 31–35. © 1985 by University Press of America. Used by permission.

"Cheah Sin Ng, Lim Shit, Chew Ah Nyee, Hang Ship Ug, Leong Ship Sam, and Lew Ship Yit," in "Paper Laid before the Legislative Commission, Friday 23 Feb. 1877; Report by Mr. Pickering on Kidnapping Sinkehs," in *Straits Settlements Legislative Council Proceedings* (1877): 4.

IV. Through Travelers' Eyes

A Voyage to and from the Island of Borneo, in the East Indies, by Daniel Beekman (1718; London: Dawsons of Pall Mall Reprint, 1973).

A Voyage to New Guinea and the Moluccas, 1774-1776, by Thomas Forrest (Kuala Lumpur: Oxford University Press, 1969), 95–98.

"The Vicissitudes of Maritime Trade: Letters from the Ocean Hang Merchant, Li Kunhe, to the Dutch Authorities in Batavia, 1803-1809," by Leonard Blussé, in *Sojourners and Settlers: Histories of Southeast Asia and the Chinese*, ed. Anthony Reid (Honolulu: University of Hawai'i Press, 2001), 154–63. © 2001 by University of Hawai'i Press. Used by permission.

The Eastern Seas, by George Earl (London: Hallen, 1837), 36–42.

"Koloniale geographie," by C. M. Kan, *Indische gids* (1889) 1:419–20.

Drie maal dwars door Sumatra, by H. H. van Kol (Rotterdam: W. L. Brusse, 1914), 181–85.

"Zoology," by L. F. de Beaufort, from *Science in the Netherlands East Indies*, ed. L. M. R. Rutten (Amsterdam: Koninklijke Akademie van Wetenschappen, n.d.). Royal Netherlands Academy of Arts and Science. Used by permission.

"Indië en de bedevaart naar Mekka," by Johan Eisenberger (PhD diss., Leiden University, 1928), 204.

V. High Colonial Indies

"Chinese Traders in the Villages," in *Chinese Economic Activity in Netherlands India: Selected Translations from the Dutch*, ed. M. R. Fernando and David Bulbeck ([Published jointly] Singapore: ISEAS, 1992; Canberra: RSPAS [ANU], 1992), 21–25. Reproduced here with the kind permission of the publishers, Institute of Southeast Asian Studies, Singapore, and Research School of Pacific and Asian Studies, Australian National University.

"Zou de opium wel zooveel kwaad doen?" by J. Groneman, *Indische Gids* (1882) 2:461–69.

"Uit de Padangsche bovenlanden, uit het dagboek van een jong ambtenaar bij het binnenlandsch bestuur," anonymous, *Tijdschrift voor Nederlandsch-Indie* (1884) I:380–85.

"Soemba en de Soembaneezen," by J. J. van Alphen, *Tijdschrift voor Nederlandsch-Indië* (1884) I:205–8.

Ambtelijke adviezen van C. Snouck Hurgronje, ed. E. Gobee and C. Adriaanse (The Hague: Martinus Nijhoff, 1957), 828–31.

"Het huwelijk in de Minahassa," anonymous, from *Tijdschrift voor Nederlandsch-Indië* (1894) I: 357–65.

"Een benard oogenblik," anonymous, from *Tijdschrift voor het Binnenlandsch Bestuur* (1895) 1-6: 421–25.

Perang kolonial belanda di Aceh (Banda Aceh: Pusat Dokumentasi dan Informasi Aceh, 1990), 54–79.

Koloniaal verslag, 1894: Beri Beri Sickness among the Dutch Troops in Aceh, 1893 (Appendix F), 3.

"Dutch Protestant Church and Missions," by Baron van Boetzelaer van Dubbeldam, in *Twentieth Century Impressions of Netherlands India*, ed. Arnold Wright (London: Lloyd's Greater Britain Publishing, 1909), 236–37.

"De oceanographie van den Oost-Indischen archipel," by G. F. Tydeman, in *Koloniaal aardrijkskundige tentoonstelling* (Amsterdam: Stedelijk Museum, 1913), 57–65. © 1945 by Stedelijk Museum. Used by permission.

VI. The Last Decades of the Indies

De verkeersbedrijven van den staat: Spoorwegen, post-, telegraaf- en telefoondienst, havenwezen, by S. A. Reitsma (Weltevreden: G. Kolff, 1924), 67–69, 78, 82–83.

In het rijk van Vulcaan: De uitbarsting van Krakatau en hare gevolgen, by R. A. van Sandick (Zutphen: W. J. Thieme, 1891), 59–67.

"Colonising Central Sulawesi: The Ethical Policy and Imperialist Expansion, 1890–1910," by Joost Coté, *Itinerario, Bulletin of the Leyden Centre for the History of European Expansion* 20, no. 3 (1996): 87–108. © 1996 by Joost Coté. Used by permission.

Onderzoek naar de mindere welvaart der inlandsche bevolking op Java en Madoera (Batavia: Landsdrukkerij, 1906), 79–81.

Indische Reisherinneringen, by H. M. van Weede, Jhr (Haarlem: H. D. Tjeenk Willink, 1908), 462–64.

Sarekat-Islam Congres (1e Nationaal Congres) 17-24 Juni 1916 te Bandoeng, Speech Delivered by O. S. Tjokroaminoto (Batavia: Landsdrukkerij, 1916), 2–3, 13–15.

"Sumpah Pemuda (Oath at the Youth Congress)," October 28, 1928, in *Sumber Terpilih Sejarah Sastra Indonesia Abad XX,* ed. E. Ulrich Kratz (Jakarta: Kepustakaan Populer Gramedia, Yayasan Adikarya ikapi dan Ford Foundation, 2000), 1–2. © 2000 by Kepustakaan Populer Gramedia. Used by permission of E. Ulrich Kratz.

"The Language of Indonesian Politics," by Benedict R. O'G. Anderson, *Indonesia* 1 (1966): 105–7. © 1966 by Southeast Asia Program Publications, Cornell University. Used by permission.

Pergaulan orang buangan di Boven Digoel, by Mas Marco Kartodikromo (Jakarta: Kepustakaan Populer Gramedia, 2002), 1–6, 137–141. © 2000 by Kepustakaan Populer Gramedia. Used by permission of Koesalah Soebagyo Toer.

Buiten het gareel, by Soewarsih Djojopoespito (Utrecht: W. de Haan NV, 1940), 96–98.

Perjuangan Tanggung Jawab dalam Kesusasteraan, by S. Takdir Alisjahbana (Jakarta: Dunia Pustaka Jaya, 1977), 58–61. © 1977 by Dunia Pustaka Jaya.

Telling Lives, Telling History: Autobiography and Imagination in Modern Indonesia, by Susan Rodgers (Berkeley: University of California Press, 1995), 87, 89, 101–3. © 1995 by The Regents of the University of California. Used by permission.

VII. From Nationalism to Independence

Kan Po: Berita Pemerintah (biweekly official gazette of military administration on Java), 1942–45.

Fifty Years of Silence, by Jan Ruff-O'Herne (Sydney: Tom Thompson, 1994), 64–86. © 1994 by Jan Ruff-O'Herne. Used by permission of Carol Ruff.

Bung Karno Menggali Pancasila (Kumpulan Pidato), ed. Wawan Tunggul Alam SH. (Jakarta: Gramedia Pustaka Utama, 2001), 26–30. © 2001 by Gramedia Pustaka Utama. Used by permission.

Herinneringen van een vrijheidsstrijdster, by Roswitha Tanis Djajadiningrat (Den Haag: Nijhoff, 1974), 1, 6, 40–43. © 1974 by Martinus Nijhoff, reprinted by permission of Pia Alisjahbana.

"Aku" and "Jang Terampas dan Jang Luput," by Chairil Anwar, in *The Complete Poetry and Prose of Chairil Anwar*, ed. and trans. Burton Raffel (Albany: State University of New York Press, 1970), 19, 147. Used by permission.

VIII. The Old Order, the New Order—Political Climate

IX. Social Issues and Cultural Debates

The Cultural Manifesto, in *Sumber Terpilih Sejarah Sastra Indonesia Abad XX*, ed. E. Ulrich Kratz (Jakarta: Kepustakaan Populer Gramedia, Yayasan Adikarya IKAPI dan The Ford Foundation, 2000), 500–501. © 2000 by Kepustakaan Populer Gramedia, reprinted by permission of E. Ulrich Kratz.

Pribumi Indonesians, the Chinese Minority, and China, by Leo Suryadinata, 3rd ed. (Singapore: Heinemann Asia, 1992), 159–64. © 1978 by Leo Suryadinata.

"Janda Muda," by Nh. Dini, in *Segi dan Garis* (Jakarta: Pustaka Jaya, 1983), 66–86. © 1983 by Pustaka Jaya. Used by permission of Nh. Dini.

Menyusuri Remang-remang Jakarta, by Yuyun A. N. Krisna (Jakarta: Sinar Harapan, 1979), 89–94. © 1979 by Yuyun A. N. Krisna.

The Mute's Soliloquy, by Pramoedya Ananta Toer, trans. Willem Samuels (New York: Hyperion, 1999), 283–91. © 1999 by Pramoedya Ananta Toer and Willem Samuels. Used by permission.

"Marsinah Accuses," by Ratna Sarumpaet, *Inside Indonesia* 55, July–September 1998, n.p. © 1998 by Ratna Sarumpaet and *Inside Indonesia*. Used by permission of Ratna Sarumpaet.

"Mengapa Tempo Dibredel?" by Tim Wartawan Tempo, in *Buku Putih Tempo: Pembredelan itu* (Jakarta: Alumni Majalah Tempo, 1994), 96, 97, 98–99, 101–3. © 1994 by Alumni Majalah Tempo. Reprinted by permission.

Saman, by Ayu Utami, trans. Pamela Allen (Jakarta: Equinox Publishing Jakarta, 2005), 85–88, 98–100, 162–64. © 2005 by Ayu Utami. Used by permission.

X. Into the Twenty-First Century

"Jakarta, 14 February 2039," by Seno Gumira Ajidarma, in *Jakarta at a Certain Point in Time: Fiction, Essays, and a Play from the Post-Suharto Era in Indonesia*, trans. Michael H. Bodden (Victoria: Centre for Asia-Pacific Initiatives, University of Victoria, 2002), 38–47. © 2002 by the Centre for Asia-Pacific Initiatives, University of Victoria. Used by permission.

Amien Rais Menjawab Isu-isu Politis Seputar Kiprah Kontroversialnya, ed. Imron Nasri (Bandung: Mizan Pustaka, 1999), 251–54. © 1999 by Mizan. Used by permission.

Memberi Suara Pada Yang Bisu, by Dede Oetomo (Yogyakarta: Galang, 2001), 41–45, 85–86. © 2001 by Dede Oetomo and Galang. Used by permission.

Indonesia: The Violence in Ambon, from Human Rights Watch New York. Asia, Vol. 11, No.1 (C). 1999, excerpts (New York: Human Rights Watch/Asia, 1999). © 1999 by Human Rights Watch. Used by permission.

"Wawancara Dengan Terpidana Mati Bom Bali I. Kematian Hanya Sepenggal Episode Untuk Hidup Kekal Di Akhirat," no. 52 (2006), www.bantenlink.com. © 2006 by Bantenlink. Reprinted by permission.

Index

468   *Index*

Darul Islam, 293, 330, 337–39
Darwin, Charles, 133, 185
Dawlasa, 68–69
Dayak, 4, 153
de Greve, engineer, 207, 210
de Houtman, Cornelis, 80, 87
"decentralization," 257–58
Demak, 89, 141
Denpasar, 262–63; District Court, 429
Department of Justice, 376–77
deTIK, 397, 399
Dewan Perwakilan Rakyat Daerah (DPRD), 348, 351
Dewan Perwakilan Rakyat Gotong Royong (DPRGR), 350–51
Dewantoro, Ki Hadjar, 247, 281
Deyah Mapplam, 440, 442–43
Diamond Dragon, 73. *See also* Swan Liong
Dieng, 14, 29
Dipanagara, Pangeran, 121, 123–24
Dipo. *See* Dwipayana
Djambi. *See* Jambi
Doerian Gedang, 207, 210
Dory, 163–64
duiten, 197–98
Dutch Crown, 249–51
Dutch East Indies, 1, 92, 165, 193, 293, 296, 315; archaeological research service of, 30–31; Christians in, 238–40; Council of, 228; end of, 9; government of, 31–32, 129–32, 144, 172, 178, 182, 202, 205, 207, 231, 238–39, 262; kings of, 226; tigers of, 224; welfare, 260
Dutch East India Company, 32, 64, 95, 167–69, 236–40. *See also* United East India Company; Vereenigde Oost-Indische Compagnie
Dutch East Indies Council, vice president of. *See* Nieuwenhuijzen
Dutch Government, 214, 233, 238, 245, 249–51, 267, 275–76
Dutchmen, 63, 88–89, 95, 121–22, 124, 184, 193, 211, 218, 236–37
Dutch New Guinea, 187, 189. *See also* West New Guinea; West Papua

Dutch Parliament, 199, 230, 249; members of, 245, 250, 326; preliminary report of, 250
Dutch Queen. *See* Wilhelmina
Dwipayana, G., 352, 355
dzikir, 431–32

East Asia, 21, 33
East India Company. *See* Dutch East India Company
East Indonesia, 315, 322, 324–27
East Timor: as colony of Portugal, 332, 361; Democratic Republic of, 361; East Timorese and, 362, 407; Indonesian aggression of, 332, 361–64, 407; National Liberation Armed Forces, 363; Timorese Democratic Union (UDT), 361
Editor, 397, 399
"Eighty Years War," 229, 236
England, 88, 130
English, 202; Church, 240; houses, 89; language, 11, 75, 290, 342, 389; merchant, 174; islands, 8; interregnum, 238; political and economic intrusion, 256; ruler of Java, 113; ships, 156, 242; trade station, 97; traveler, 173
Englishmen, 8, 63, 65, 174–75
Equator, 2, 134, 296
Eurasia, 64, 246
Europe, 11, 64, 80, 113, 131, 141, 159, 194, 229, 245; customs in, 219; expedition from, 127; Indonesian exiles in, 347; Industrial Revolution in, 184; war in, 296–97
European: authors, 50; colonialism, 4, 234, 257; educations, 141; forms of plants, 135; hegemony in Indonesia, 137, 151, 194; impact on Indonesia, 63–65, 295; imperialism, 275; markets, 76; missionaries, 7, 238–40; notions of superiority, 150; prisoners of war, 9, 292, 309; Protestants, 240
Evangelical State Church, 239–40

Faculty of Psychology, 356–57
Fa Hsien, 48, 64

TINEKE HELLWIG is an associate professor of
Asian studies at the University of British Columbia.
ERIC TAGLIACOZZO is an associate professor
of history at Cornell University.

Library of Congress Cataloging-in-Publication Data
The Indonesia reader : history, culture, politics /
edited by Tineke Hellwig and Eric Tagliacozzo.
p. cm. — (The world readers)
Includes bibliographical references and index.
ISBN 978-0-8223-4403-2 (cloth : alk. paper)
ISBN 978-0-8223-4424-7 (pbk. : alk. paper)
1. Indonesia—History. 2. Indonesia—Civilization.
3. Indonesia—Social conditions. 4. Indonesia—
Politics and government. I. Hellwig, Tineke.
II. Tagliacozzo, Eric.
DS634.I53 2009
959.8—dc22   2008041803

Made in the USA
Lexington, KY
15 June 2017